Julie Jie Wen
University of Western Sydney, Australia

Clement A Tisdell
University of Queensland, Australia

TOURISM AND CHINA'S DEVELOPMENT

Policies, Regional Economic Growth and Ecotourism

World Scientific
Singapore • New Jersey • London • Hong Kong

Published by

World Scientific Publishing Co. Pte. Ltd.
P O Box 128, Farrer Road, Singapore 912805
USA office: Suite 1B, 1060 Main Street, River Edge, NJ 07661
UK office: 57 Shelton Street, Covent Garden, London WC2H 9HE

British Library Cataloguing-in-Publication Data
A catalogue record for this book is available from the British Library.

TOURISM AND CHINA'S DEVELOPMENT
Policies, Regional Economic Growth and Ecotourism

ISBN 981-02-4433-9 (pbk)

Printed in Singapore.

To Our Mothers

Contents

List of Figures

List of Tables

Preface

We first began jointly researching on tourism in China in 1989. At that time, Julie Wen was a graduate student and Clem Tisdell was a visiting professor at Nankai University in Tianjin, China, lecturing on tourism economics. His visit had been arranged by Professor Mao Yushi, a former student of Nankai High School, classmate and friend of Chou-en-Lai, and at that time a professor at the Chinese Academy of Social Sciences (CASS). Without this visit, it is unlikely that this book would have been written. We are grateful to Mao Yushi.

From 1989 onwards, we wrote several joint articles on tourism in China. In the 1990s, Julie Wen came from lecturing in management at Zhongshan University in Guangzhou, to study for a Ph.D. in Economics at The University of Queensland. Clem Tisdell was appointed the principal supervisor of her thesis and Joseph Chai the co-supervisor. While this book draws heavily on the material in this thesis, extensive rewriting and updating has been undertaken and considerable new material has been introduced. The result is a "fresh" manuscript based on the earlier foundation.

When we first began our research into tourism in China little did we know that China would, before the end of the 20th century, become one of the world's top ten nations as a destination for international tourists. This is a particularly remarkable achievement because China is the only developing country to make it to the top ten — most developing nations do not even approach the top ten. China's performance in developing tourism is all the more remarkable because in 1978 its tourism industry was insignificant by world standards.

Apart from considering the overall expansion of tourism in China and its implication for China's economic development, this study pays particular attention to the regional distribution of tourism in China and the potential of tourism to act as a regional economic growth-pole. In addition, ecotourism in China's interior, the sustainability of China's tourism development and environmental problems faced by the tourism industry are given consideration. Throughout this book, we endeavour to relate our findings for China to general theories and principles both of economic development and of the growth and nature of tourism.

Most books rely on the support and assistance of others for their production. This one is no exception. First we have benefited from some support with resources from The University of Queensland and The University of Western Sydney, Hawkesbury. Furthermore, the Australian Centre for International Agricultural Research (ACIAR) provided some financial assistance for our research in Yunnan from ACIAR Research Project 40. We are thankful for this support.

We are especially indebted to the following people who supplied useful data or made valuable suggestions on our draft materials: T.A. Balasingam (Temasek Polytechnic, Singapore), Derrin Davis, (Southern Cross University, Australia), John Gowdy (Rensselaer Polytechnic Institute, NY, USA) Colin Mackerras (Griffith University, Australia), Luo Mingyi (Yunnan University, Kunming) and Yan Min (National Tourism Administration of China, Beijing) and at The University of Queensland, Brisbane, Mohammad Alauddin, Joseph Chai, Sukhan Jackson, Rod Jensen, Kartik Roy and Guy West.

Special thanks also to Gopal Regmi and Alistair Robson for providing timely research assistance, and to Alison Mohr and Genevieve Larsen for completing the word-processing of the final typescript for this book. Naturally we absolve all of the above from responsibility for any shortcomings of this book.

We are indebted to David Sharp for commissioning this book and to Karen Quek at World Scientific Publishing for copyediting/managing the typescript for production of the book. Thanks once again to all the above and to others whom we may have accidentally overlooked.

Julie Wen   Clem Tisdell
Richmond, NSW.   Corinda, Qld.

Chapter 1

Tourism, Economic Growth and Sustainable Development

1.1 Introduction

This book focuses mainly on the expansion of tourism (primarily international tourism) in China since 1978 when China decided to embark on its economic reform program and "open up to the outside world". In doing so, it pays particular attention to the regional distribution of China's tourism development and possible consequences of this for China's regional economic growth. Special attention is given to the potential of tourism to contribute to the economic development of China's interior. The inland province of Yunnan is selected as a case study, and in view of the importance of ecotourism in inland China, considerable consideration is given to the role of ecotourism in economic development.

One might, however, ask why a book on tourism and the development of China. First, it is clear that the development of tourism in China, especially international tourism, is a relatively sensitive barometer of the progress of China's reforms since 1978. It indicates the extent to which China has opened up to the outside world, reduced controls on the movement of people in China and is permitting social interaction between travellers and locals. Furthermore, it can reflect changes in the state ownership and management of industry and liberalisation state administration of industry. In short, the extent to which a nation has adopted liberal policies can often be gauged from a study of its tourism industry.

Secondly, development of China's tourism industry mirrors altering official views in China about the type of industrial policies needed to maintain China's economic growth. In the Maoist period, the expansion of heavy

1

industries was seen as the key for economic growth. Both light industry and service industries were relatively deprived of resources for expansion, and the service industries (which includes tourism) were castigated in particular, as being "unproductive". During the reform period, however, this view was subject to growing criticism as China increasingly adopted economic pragmatism as its guide under the leadership of Deng Xiaoping. Supply-driven industrial development was increasingly replaced by demand-driven (market-led) development, even though by the end of the 20th century China still had not fully completed its economic transition to a market economy (cf. Kornai, 1999) and at the beginning of the 21st century, still needed to make further major decisions about the future of its state-owned industrial enterprises (Duncan and Huang, 1998). Nevertheless, by the beginning of the 21st century considerable economic liberalisation had occurred in China and personal freedom had expanded greatly compared to the Maoist period.

A third reason for giving attention to China's tourism industry is that it is one of China's largest industries. It accounts for more than five percent of China's GDP and its contribution to China's GDP has been rising rapidly. According to the estimates of the China National Tourism Administration (1999: 11), in 1998, 1.83 million Chinese were directly employed in tourism and about nine million indirectly, that is over ten million in total. By any standards, China's tourism industry is a large one.

A fourth reason for giving particular attention to China's tourism industry is that China is a major tourism destination on a world scale, it has become a major "international tourism player". Since beginning its economic reforms, China has progressed from being an insignificant world international tourism destination in terms of visitor numbers and receipts to being one of the top ten nations in terms of international tourist arrivals and receipts. Furthermore, it has been moving upwards in the top ten. The World Tourism Organisation (WTO) estimated that in 1999 China (Hong Kong, Macau and Taiwan excluded) ranked fifth in the world in terms of the number of international tourist arrivals and seventh in terms of international tourist receipts (see Tables 1.1 and 1.2). Note that WTO estimates include tourists from Taiwan but not from Hong Kong and Macau.

Table 1.1 World's top ten tourist destinations in 1999 (preliminary results).

Rank	Country	International tourist arrivals (000)	
1999		1998	1999
1	France	70,000	71,400
2	Spain	47,749	51,958
3	United States	46,395	46,983
4	Italy	34,829	35,839
5	**CHINA**	**25,073**	**27,047**
6	United Kingdom	25,745	25,740
7	Mexico	19,810	20,216
8	Canada	18,837	19,556
9	Poland	18,780	17,940
10	Austria	17,352	17,630

Source: World Tourism Organisation (WTO, 2000).

Table 1.2 World's top ten tourism earners in 1999 (preliminary results).

Rank	Country	International tourism receipts (US$ million)		
1999		1998	1999[a]	
1	United States	71,250	73,000	
2	Spain	29,737	25,179	(9)
3	France	29,931	24,657	(9)
4	Italy	29,809	31,000	
5	United Kingdom	20,978	20,972	
6	Germany	16,429	9,570	(7)
7	**CHINA**	**12,602**	**14,099**	
8	Austria	11,184	11,259	
9	Canada	9,393	10,282	
10	Mexico	7,897	7,850	

[a]Estimations for the full year, except when a number of months is put between brackets.
Source: World Tourism Organisation (WTO, 2000).

From Tables 1.1 and 1.2, it can be seen that no developing country ranks ahead of China in relative importance in terms of inbound international tourism. Furthermore, it is the only Asia-Pacific country which is amongst the top ten. This suggests that the extraordinarily successful international tourism experience of China might be profitably studied by other developing countries. In particular, given India's lack-lustre performance in relation to the development of international tourism (Roy and Tisdell, 1998), India might gain by considering the type of tourism policies adopted by China.

A study of the expansion of China's tourism industry is also worthwhile because it raises questions (especially important questions in the Chinese context) about the ability of tourism to assist in regional development and promote decentralisation of the economy, as well as issues about the role which ecotourism can play in regional development, and difficulties involved in ensuring the sustainable development of tourism.

1.2 China and the Global Development of Tourism

Several authors claim that tourism is the world's largest industry. But it is a composite industry, the size of which cannot be measured with a high degree of precision. The problem is further compounded by the fact that many governments do not collect or report statistics on the size of the industry in any detail. Nevertheless, taking into account the composite nature of the industry, it does seem in all probability that tourism is the world's largest industry in terms of its contribution to the gross value of production. It is also an industry which has grown at a very rapid rate since the end of World War II.

The rapid expansion of tourism in the second half of the 20th century has its roots in rising global incomes, increasing leisure time, a rising world population and a greater level of well-educated persons globally, as well as a fall in real transport costs, reduced travel time and a globalising world economy. International tourism has in fact been expanding at a faster rate than world trade. Before the Asian financial crisis occurred in 1997, international tourist arrivals and receipts worldwide were expanding at a rate in excess of five percent per annum. This was down (although still positive) in 1997 and 1998 but some recovery in growth rate was already evident in 1999. About 660 million international tourist arrivals were recorded in 1999 and in 1998 international tourism receipts were estimated to have reached about US$442 billion (WTO, 2000). When one considers that global combined size of domestic tourism markets significantly exceeds that for international tourism industry, the gigantic size of the tourism industry becomes even more apparent.

However, for several decades in the second half of the 20th century, China stifled its domestic tourism industry and was virtually a non-participant in the development of the international tourist industry. The reason for the low development status given to the domestic tourism industry in the period 1949–1977 was that it was considered to be unproductive. During this period, international tourism in China was largely limited to politically inspired and motivated visits (Uysal *et al.*, 1986) with most visitors arriving from other communist countries. However, after political relationships between the former Soviet Union and China deteriorated and Soviet aid for China ceased in 1960, the number of international visitors to China amounted to little more than a trickle. Hence, for about three decades China denied itself an international tourism industry. Only after 1978, did Chinese tourism industry begin to grow rapidly. By 1987, the Chinese Communist Party had accepted international (inbound) tourism as a key industry for China's further economic development (Zhao Ziyang, 1987). At the same time, negative attitudes were increasingly replaced by positive sentiments in favour of the expansion of China's domestic tourism industry which in recent years has been expanding at a rapid rate. Given that China has gone from an insignificant position in international tourism to being one of the most highly ranked countries, the rate of growth of its international tourism industry has in most years since 1978 been substantially in excess of world tourism growth. While the rate of this growth now shows signs of falling, there is still scope for continued growth in inbound tourism to China as Asia recovers from its financial crisis and Asian incomes and employment start to rise again.

1.3   Tourism Development as a Response to Economic Growth

Clearly China eventually decided that tourism development could make a positive contribution to its economic growth and the welfare of its people. In practice, tourism development is both a response to economic growth and a contributor to economic development. Each of these relationships will now be considered in turn and related to China's situation.

Despite some possible negative impacts of economic growth on the development of tourism, overall a strong positive association exists between indicators of economic growth, level of development and tourism. But negative consequences are also possible. The possibility that economic and tourism development may prove to be unsustainable will be considered later in this chapter.

Economic development can foster the expansion of a country's tourism industry in several ways:

1. Rising domestic per capita incomes may stimulate the demand for tourism, including domestic tourism.
2. Rising levels of per capita income overseas, especially in countries nearby a nation, are likely to increase inbound tourism in the nation.
3. Rising incomes are usually associated with rising levels of education and greater investment in human capital and these tend to increase tourism demand.
4. In a nation experiencing economic development, its infrastructure and available supply of tourist services and facilities usually expands. This supply-side change is favourable to tourism development.
5. As a nation develops, reduced risks of disease and higher levels of education and management seem likely. These are favourable to expansion of tourism.

Liu (1998) provides global statistical evidence supporting most of these above hypotheses.

Figure 1.1 indicates a schematic manner from development factors which could have a positive impact on the expansion of the tourism industry in a country. This figure takes into account both domestic and inbound tourism.

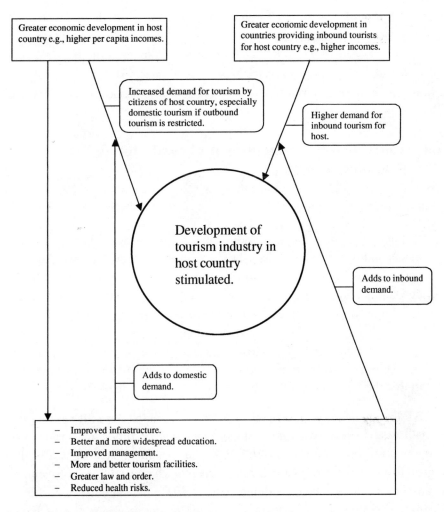

Fig. 1.1 Some possible influences of economic development on the expansion of tourism in a country.

Economic growth in China has definitely stimulated the development of its tourism industry in recent decades, and China's tourism industry has benefited from world economic growth, and particularly substantial economic growth in East Asia. Consequently tourism development in China since

1978 has mainly been a response to economic growth, as well as a consequence of more liberal economic policies being pursued by China after 1978, policies which in turn helped to generate China's continuing economic growth. But we should also examine the other side of the coin, namely the extent which tourism development is a contributor to economic development.

1.4   Tourism Development as a Contributor to Economic Growth

According to Liu (1998: 27):

"Although tourism has been advocated by numerous scholars, governments and international organisations as a path to development, for most countries, it is only one option among a wide range of alternatives of development thus 'not all states have equal interests in tourism' (Williams and Shaw, 1991: 267). Indeed, tourism development itself is a policy choice. It has been discouraged in some countries, prioritised in some others, and encouraged in most countries. The management of tourism in a country also bears a clear mark of its economic development level in that the latter affects the objectives, patterns and features of industry."

As already mentioned, official views in China about the ability of tourism growth to contribute to its development changed from negative prior to its economic reforms to positive after 1978. For example, Zhao Ziyang (1987) argued that expansion of international tourism in China could add substantially to China's foreign exchange earnings which in turn play an important role in financing the import of new technologies and modern equipment for China's development.

Nevertheless, it is easy to overestimate the contribution made by inbound tourism to the foreign exchange position of a country (cf. Tisdell, 1991, Chapter 11). Leakages of funds in order to import commodities for international tourists or pay profits or dividends to overseas investors in the domestic tourist industry should be taken into account. Nevertheless, the larger and more diversified an economy, the lower is likely to be the relative level of these leakages (Liu, 1998: 30). But it has been argued by some writers (e.g., Britton, 1982) that foreign leakages may be so high in small economies that tourism expansion makes little or no contribution to their development. This could also be so for some large developing countries which lack a diversified and sophisticated economy. However, it seems likely even after foreign leakages are taken into account that China enjoys a substantial foreign exchange surplus on its inbound tourism. Its economy is relatively diversified. One further reason why China currently has a large surplus in its overall international tourism account because its outbound tourism is subject to restrictions, for example, slow issue of passports, restrictions which are slowly being relaxed or reduced.

Apart from those who warn that receipts from inbound tourism provide a deceptive indication of foreign exchange gains from tourism development, others argue that foreign inbound tourism is likely to create or reinforce economic dependency relationships between developed and developing countries, and that this may in fact reduce the opportunities of the latter for development (Britton, 1982; Brohman, 1996). Developing countries and regions can also pay too high a cost to encourage tourism development (Liu, 1998: 33; Bosselman, 1978; Bryden, 1973). Despite this view, there is no obvious evidence that China has experienced "de-development" of its economy due to its opening up to tourism and generally to the outside world. Indeed, the evidence points in the opposite direction. Nevertheless, there are obvious dangers for China as a result of its involvement in the economic globalisation process.

Note that industries with a large external economic leakage can have a very positive local economic impact. Even after considerable external leakage, the net contribution of the local economy may remain high. This may be the case for tourism development in some areas. In addition, few growth opportunities may exist in a locality, and the growth alternatives to tourism expansion may have an even weaker local economic impact. Obviously, a great deal of care is needed in assessing whether tourism development is likely to be a suitable economic growth option for a region.

In many regions in developing countries, including in China, employment opportunities are limited and surplus labour exists. It is estimated that a very large pool of surplus labour exists in China in agriculture (Tisdell, 1993, Chapter 7) and even in manufacturing (Tisdell and Chai, 1998). The expansion of service industries, including tourism, could in many cases provide opportunities for at least some of this labour to be more productively employed.

A further way in which travel and tourism may stimulate economic development is through the exchange of ideas which are valuable for the advancement of economic and social activity. Tourism and travel can be an important means for exchange of information. On the other hand, some writers (de Kadt, 1979; Lea, 1988) warn of the possibility of negative socio-cultural impacts from tourism, especially international tourism. It is necessary therefore to judge this aspect of tourism development by weighing up its positive and possible negative consequences.

In some regions, the provision of economic infrastructure needed for the development of a tourism industry (such as roads, airports and improved transport and communication generally) enhances the economics of production other local industries. Spin-off or complementary economic benefits for other industries may arise from the development of a tourist industry in a locality. In addition, backward and forward linkages from tourism provide possible economic benefits for the growth of other interdependent industries.

Differences of opinion exist about whether the tourism industry is a labour-intensive or a capital-intensive industry. Much seems to depend on the type of tourism promoted. On balance, however, the modern tourism industry seems to be capital-intensive (Diamond, 1977; Sinclair, 1991); although contrary views can be found in the literature. Because most developing countries experience capital-scarcity (and have a labour surplus), doubts have been raised about the wisdom of them relying on the tourism industry as a contributor to their economic growth, unless the capital for the industry is supplied from abroad. But it by no means follows from this that tourism development is inappropriate as an economic means for development in China or in other less developed countries (LDCs). If the return to the nation on the capital invested is high enough, the development of tourism can be appropriate even if the capital-labour ratio of tourism is high and local capital is used.

Although there are obviously many positive ways in which expansion of the tourism industry can contribute to economic development, this does not mean that it will do so in every place and in every circumstance. Furthermore, one should not leap to the conclusion that because tourism development may have some negative consequences, it is inappropriate to pursue it as a possible contributor to economic development.

1.5 Expansion of Tourism and the Achievement of Sustainable Development

As one might expect from the above discussion, the possibilities for achieving sustainable tourism and sustainable development are often interdependent. For instance, in some circumstances failure to achieve sustainable tourism development will result, at least locally, in inability to maintain economic development, as for example could occur when tourism is a key local industry. Given that economic development has the type of positive impacts on tourism expansion outlined above, inability to sustain economic development is likely to be damaging to the tourism industry as well.

Unless efficiently managed, development of a tourism industry can destroy future tourism if it erodes the tourism assets and attractions which tourists seek. This is a particular risk for nature-based tourism, for culturally-based tourism and tourism relying on artefacts and objects which may be worn-down or damaged by tourists. Nevertheless, even though negative environmental and cultural impacts occur as a result of tourism, it does not follow that tourism should be prevented. The benefits from tourism must be weighed against its costs. In theory, tourism ought to be allowed to expand from an economic point of view up to the point where the extra benefits obtained equal the extra costs of the abovementioned nature. Decision-makers should be aware of the existence of such costs and make sure that desired levels or degrees of sustainability of tourism are not forgone.

In other words, the user costs, in economic parlance, (that is the future costs) of tourist expansion should be taken fully into account. And the social and external costs and benefits of tourism expansion should be fully accounted for.

Note that those who favour sustainable tourism should specify which tourism attributes or characteristics ought to be sustained. Is it tourist numbers or tourist revenue or some other attribute which ought to be maintained? Movements in these indicators can sometimes be in conflict (Tisdell and Wen, 1997a). Furthermore, while the achievement of ecological sustainability may be complementary to sustainable tourism in some circumstances, in other cases, these objectives can lead to conflict (Tisdell and Wen, 1997b). In addition, and to emphasise further the last point, land-uses which maximise the *total* economic evaluation (TEV) of an area and include tourism as one possible land-use may compromise ecological sustainability (Tisdell and Wen, 1997b).

Neither the sustainability of development (cf. Tisdell, 1999) nor the sustainability of tourism are absolute virtues. However, it can be chastening to realise that neither development nor tourism may be sustained. Furthermore, it is important to bear in mind that today's decisions can be expected to influence the degree of sustainability of development and of tourism in the future. Therefore, this emphasises that user costs (the future economic costs of current decisions) should be fully taken into account in development policies. This is especially important in China where much tourism depends on nature, culture and cultural objects.

1.6   The Nature and Scope of this Study

This book deals mostly with the development of tourism in China since 1978 and important impacts of this on its development. Naturally this book cannot deal in depth with all aspects of the expansion of tourism in China and all the implications of these for China's development. Nevertheless, it deals with many development issues which have not been considered in depth for China before. The next chapter reviews changing tourism and policies in China, changes in tourism administration since 1978 and using statistical data outlines broad trends in tourism development in China. The discussion next focuses on regional economic inequality in China and regional inequality in tourism development in China, a major focus of this book. This book examines regional economic inequality in China, regional and spatial disparity in the distribution of tourism in China and how this distribution has changed in recent times. Inequality in the spatial distribution of tourism is compared with that for income and economic variables, and the extent to which China's tourism development has modified or exacerbated this inequality is discussed.

The inland region of China is an economically disadvantaged region compared to its coastal region. To what extent has tourism expansion in China reduced the economic disadvantage of the inland compared with the coast? If it has not reduced this economic disparity, has the expansion of tourism in China and in its interior, nevertheless, helped to stimulate economic development in its interior? These issues are addressed, particularly in Chapter 5.

Because nature-based tourism (loosely ecotourism) combined with ethnically-based cultural tourism (eco-cultural tourism) is an important form of tourism in inland China, Chapters 6 and 7 pay particular attention to ecotourism; its nature, its sustainability, its evaluation and various problems related to it.

China's inland province of Yunnan has outstanding resources for eco-cultural tourism and much of its tourism expansion utilises these resources. It is China's major inland province for tourism. A case study of Yunnan is therefore completed to identify difficulties which Yunnan has experienced in developing ecotourism and to identify its policies for tourism development. Furthermore, the spatial spread and impacts of tourism within this province are considered.

The final major objective is to investigate whether tourism development can act as a regional growth-pole or key industry for regional growth. This is done by initially considering the relevance of unbalanced growth and growth pole theory. Then the possibility is specifically examined of whether input-output analysis can be used to identify this potential and how it can be done. In order to make the matter concrete, input-output analysis is applied to Yunnan to identify whether tourism has the capacity to be a leading growth sector there.

The concluding chapter summarises and qualifies the main findings from this study and considers the future prospects for tourism development in China, a country which has made extraordinary progress in the expansion of its tourism industry in just a few (two) decades.

Chapter 2

Tourism Development and Changing Policies in China: An Overview

2.1 Introduction

The development of tourism in China since 1978 has been extremely rapid. Possibly few, if any, countries in the world have experienced as fast a rate of growth in tourism as China. In a relatively short period, China has gone from a situation where its international tourism industry was insignificant to one today where it ranks amongst the ten top nations. At the same time, its domestic tourism industry has undergone considerable transformation and growth, and in terms of the number of tourists involved, domestic tourism is China exceeds that of its inbound tourism many times over.

The purpose of this chapter is to outline the tourism policy and administrative changes in China which have facilitated the growth of its tourism industry, and then to trace out the pattern of growth of inbound tourism to China and trends in the components of this tourism. A similar exercise is undertaken for domestic tourism and the composition of the total Chinese tourism market is analysed. Comparisons are made between the growth rates of segments of the total tourism market in China using trend analyses which also enable some projections to be made, albeit tentatively. Some environmental and other sustainability obstacles to China's continued tourism growth are identified. Such obstacles need to be given increasing attention by policy-makers if the development of China's tourism industry is to be sustained.

2.2   Policy Changes and the Administration of Tourism in China

2.2.1   *Tourism before 1978 in China*

Travel for leisure in China dates back thousands of years with emperors, scholars and monks being frequent travellers in ancient times (Zhang, 1995). International travel to China, with Marco Polo being one of the famous forerunners, developed quickly from the middle of the 19th century when the old kingdom of China was forced to keep in contact with the outside world after a series of treaties allowing foreigners to live, do business and engage in religious activities in China. Travel agencies dealing with both inbound tourism to China and Chinese going abroad were set up in the 1920s and were concentrated in Shanghai (Yang and Jiang, 1983). However, wars in the 1930s and the 1940s stopped pleasure travel both in and to China.

From the announcement of the People's Republic of China (PRC) in October 1949 to the implementation of the "open door policy" in 1978, due to the prevalent hostility between the capitalist and communist worlds, people from the west could visit China only with a special permit, mainly for the purpose of diplomacy (Uysal *et al.*, 1986). People with relatives in China could apply through the China Travel Service for a travel permit. Therefore, there was hardly any international tourism in China before 1978. Outbound travel was limited to government officials and diplomats, and domestic tourism hardly existed.

2.2.2   *Encouragement of international tourism in China since 1978*

In 1978, the Chinese Communist Party held the Third Plenary Session of its 11th Congress. This Congress paved the way for China's economic recon- struction and reforms. Nevertheless, during the early reform era (1978 to 1985), tourism was still regarded mainly as an instrument of foreign affairs rather than as a means for economic gain. For example, compatriots and overseas Chinese paid much less than foreigners for the same service. In

1987, inbound tourism development was declared to be a desirable economic activity for the purpose of earning foreign exchange and was included in the national plan for social and economic development for the first time (Zhang, 1995). A less hostile official view towards domestic tourism also emerged. When China started lifting restrictions on entry to many locations in 1978, the pent-up demand for inbound tourism to China was released after more than 50 years of impediments and restrictions. All the 30 localities/ regions of China soon considered tourism to be a potentially powerful earner of foreign exchange, and all tried to increase their supply of tourist facilities accordingly (Tisdell and Wen, 1991a).

The scale of the tourist industry in China had expanded considerably by the end of 1998. According to the official statistics, fixed assets of the tourism industry in China totaled 257.4 billion RMB in 1998 (NTA, 1999). Direct employment of tourism industry was 1.8 million and another 9 million people were indirectly engaged in the tourism industry. Over 16,266 enterprises engaged in tourism and earned 144.14 billion RMB in revenue. The revenue of 5,782 tourist hotels with a total of 0.76 million rooms reached 79.68 billion RMB, and their profit was 5.56 billion RMB. There were 6,222 travel agencies in 1998, with a total revenue of 25 billion RMB and a profit of 334 million RMB (NTA, 1999).

Around 20 percent of international tourists arriving in China participate in organised tours and tour packages supplied by travel agencies. Three major travel agencies in China are CTS, CITS and CYTS. Overseas Travel Service, the predecessor of China Travel Service (CTS), was set up in 1949 mainly to receive ethnic Chinese visitors. China International Travel Service (CITS) was established in 1954 for non-Chinese. China Youth Travel Service (CYTS) was established to receive young visitors. With their headquarters in Beijing and branches over China, they have changed their purpose of servicing overseas Chinese and foreigners primarily from socialist countries when they were established, to facilitating trips for international tourists, promoting the development of tourist areas, and marketing tourism in China.

The process of liberalising the administration of inbound tourism to China began as early as 1978. In that year "the process for obtaining group tourist visa was eased and CITS began marketing general tours through foreign

operators, and working with them to design their own China programmes"
(Bailey, 1995: 21), but initially liberalisation was slow.

2.2.3   The administration of tourism in China

The Bureau of Travel and Tourism (BTT) was established as part of the
Foreign Affairs Ministry as a policy-making body in 1964. The National
Tourism Administration of China (NTA) was set up in 1981 in Beijing under
the State Council to replace BTT as the highest administrative body for
tourism in China. Its purpose is to concentrate on the macro-management of
tourism and provide development plans for tourism for the whole of China.
NTA supervises the Tourist Association, Hotel Association, Domestic Tourist
Association and has ten functional departments, including: general
administration; policy and law; planning and statistics; resource development;
travel service and hotel management; general "coordinative" affairs; marketing
and promotion; finance and foreign currency control; personnel, labour and
education; and international liaison. With branches in provinces, cities and
counties throughout China, NTA exercises macro-administration of the
tourism industry in China and implements national tourism policies.

Increased decentralisation of tourism administration occurred in China
from the late 1980s onwards. In the 1990s, provincial governments and
municipalities have been allowed more power in decision-making about
tourist projects. For example, all projects related to tourism, such as hotels
and amusement parks, needed to be authorised by NTA in the 1980s. However,
from the early 1990s onwards, it was agreed by NTA that projects with a
total investment of less than 1 million RMB did not have to be agreed to by
NTA and reported to it. This decentralisation may have assisted localities in
making timely decisions related to tourism development, but has made macro-
administration of tourism nationwide more difficult. Nevertheless, these
changes mirror the increasing decentralisation of economic decision-making
in China.

According to Bailey (1995: 21), there have been complaints from officials
of China's NTA that their ability to coordinate the development of China's
tourism industry is hampered by their lack of control over transport (aviation,

rail and road). Certainly general coordination between transport and tourism development is desirable but given bounded rationality there are also limits to the workable span of control of most organizations (cf. Tisdell, 1996). Furthermore, with China's continuing reform process, the role for central coordination is tending to diminish further.

NTA has fruitfully organised themes for certain years to promote special tourist itineraries in China, such as Tourism Year of Dragon '88, Visit China Year '92, China Landscape '94, China Folklore '95, China Holiday Resort '96, Visit China '97, and Ecotour China '99. Joint efforts from a wide range of participants have proven to be the key to the success of these tourist themes.

2.3   Features of the Growth of Inbound Tourism to China

2.3.1   Overall growth of inbound tourism to China

This book concentrates on the study of the development of international inbound tourism in China for three major reasons: (1) it is an important source of overseas income for China; (2) according to the National Tourism Administration of China (abbreviated as NTA in this book), the average daily expenditure of inbound tourists in China is much higher than that of Chinese tourists (NTA, 1997); (3) statistics at regional levels are usually only available for inbound tourism. Therefore, such terms as tourism, tourist, arrival, and receipts all refer to international tourism from hereon in this book unless otherwise stated.

Note that "tourism receipts" refers to the income in foreign currencies earned from providing services and commodities to inbound visitors in China. "Tourist nights" means the accumulated number of nights tourists stay in China's hotels. "Tourist arrivals" or "number of tourists" coincides with the concept of "arrivals of tourists from abroad" (WTO, 1992), including foreigners, overseas Chinese who hold Chinese passports, and compatriots who live in Hong Kong, Macau and Taiwan. Although Hong Kong was returned to China in 1997, due to China's "One Country Two Systems" policy for this "Special Administrative Region", Hong Kong is supposed not to change its status for at least 50 years. Hence, visitors from Hong Kong are still counted as part of international arrivals in China's statistics. This helps to maintain consistency of statistics over years. Note that WTO statistics for international tourist arrivals to China include visitors from Taiwan but exclude those from Hong Kong and Macau. Therefore, there are some differences between WTO statistics and those of NTA. NTA statistics and definitions are used here unless otherwise stated.

The strong growth of tourism in China is partly indicated by the rapid growth in the number of inbound tourists, receipts, and hotel rooms as shown in Table 2.1.

Table 2.1 Inbound tourism growth in China, 1980–1998.

	Arrivals (m)	Arrivals as percentage of 1980 (%)	Receipts ($m)	Receipts as percentage of 1980 (%)	Number of hotels	Hotels as percentage of 1985 (%)
1980	5.70	100.00	617	100.00		
1981	7.77	136.26	785	127.23		
1982	7.92	139.02	843	136.63		
1983	9.48	166.26	941	152.51		
1984	12.85	225.47	1131	183.31		
1985	17.83	312.86	1250	202.59	710	100.00
1986	22.82	400.33	1530	247.97	974	137.18
1987	26.90	471.96	1862	301.78	1283	180.70
1988	31.70	556.05	2247	364.18	1496	210.70
1989	24.50	429.84	1860	301.46	1788	251.83
1990	27.46	481.79	2218	359.48	1987	279.86
1991	33.35	585.09	2845	461.10	2130	300.00
1992	38.12	668.68	3947	639.71	2354	331.55
1993	41.53	728.54	4683	759.00	2552	359.44
1994	43.68	766.39	7323	1186.87	2995	421.83
1995	46.39	813.81	8733	1415.40	3720	523.94
1996	51.13	897.02	10200	1653.16	4418	622.25
1997	57.59	910.35	12074	1856.89	5201	632.54
1998	63.48	1013.68	12602	1942.46	5782	714.37

Source: NTA, various years.

Between 1980 and 1998, China's inbound tourists rose in number by more than 10-fold and its nominal tourist receipts by over 19-fold. Between 1985 and 1998, the number of China's hotels showed a 7-fold increase. According to NTA, China's inbound tourism receipts (in current terms) grew at an average annual rate of 18.1 percent from 1980 to 1998, while the annual rate of growth for inbound tourist arrivals was 14.4 percent, in spite of a large reduction in both arrivals and receipts in 1989 as a result of the Tiananmen turmoil in Beijing (Table 2.1). On average, these growth rates far exceeded the high growth rates for China's GDP. So from this perspective, tourism showed itself to be a leading growth industry. By 1998, China was ranked the sixth nation in the world in terms of tourist arrivals and seventh in its tourist receipts in the World Tourism Organisation (NTA, 1999:1).

2.3.2 Observations on tourism growth to China

Changes in the annual growth rate of inbound tourist arrivals and of receipts for China are shown in Fig. 2.1. These help to highlight the fact that while international tourism growth to China has been considerable, it has also been variable and adversely affected by particular events at times.

Although Fig. 2.1 indicates that tourism has been growing rapidly in China, growth in arrivals and receipts was sluggish in 1982 and 1998, and was negative in 1989. Consider the likely reasons.

Tourism in China started to grow rapidly from very low levels in the late 1970s, and its growth rate appeared very high at the initial stage. However, infrastructure, especially the supply of hotel rooms, was in serious deficiency in the early 1980s, limiting further expansion of tourism (Tisdell and Wen, 1991b). Therefore, after strong growth in 1981, 1982 showed less than 10 percent increase in arrivals and receipts. Nevertheless, the reason is not completely clear. Rapid inflation, some economic instability and a pause in reforms with attendant uncertainty may have played a role (cf. Jackson, 1992: 23–24).

The cause of the 1989 downturn is clear. Both arrivals and receipts suffered a reduction of more than 20 percent in 1989 compared to 1988

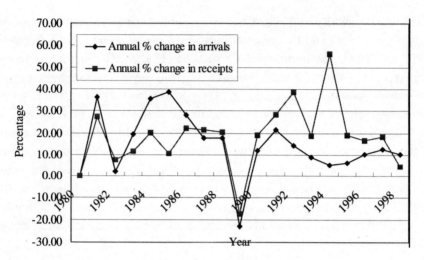

Fig. 2.1 Annual growth rate of international tourist arrivals and receipts in China, 1980–1998.

Source: Calculated from Table 2.1.

when the Tiananmen tragedy in Beijing and unrest in other areas of China resulted in cancellation of some travel bookings. Considering the growth trend of arrivals from 1984 to 1988, there were over 12 million fewer tourists than might otherwise have visited in 1989. Moody Investors Service lowered China's investment status from A3 to Baal (Earle, 1991). Banks and other financial guarantors in the major sources of investment to China were all adversely affected, leading to higher funding costs, less foreign investment in tourism facilities, and reduced business travel (Cheng, 1990).

Foreign arrivals were 4.3 percent lower in numbers in 1998 compared to the previous year (NTA, 1999), mainly because of economic depression in the Asian market. The Asian financial crisis, started in late 1997, and reduced disposable incomes in many Asian countries, resulting in a generally lower outbound tourism demand in this region. Significantly lower number of arrivals from China's major tourism source countries such as Japan, Korea, Malaysia, Philippines, and Thailand, contributed to the low growth rate of tourism in 1998.

The time series for percentage growth in tourism receipts and in the number of inbound tourists shown in Fig. 2.1 exhibit some positive but not perfect correlation. In fact, in 1994 there is a significant divergence between these series. In 1994, there was a 56.4 percent rise in tourism receipts compared to 1993 but the percentage growth rate of tourism arrivals fell. This jump in receipts can largely be attributed to a change in the method of estimating receipts from foreign tourists. The figure for tourist expenditure was for the first time obtained by surveying departing tourists, a procedure recommended by the World Tourism Organisation. Basic measurement methods for tourism receipts or expenditure are: direct observation, survey of tourists or households, simulation, and bank returns in a regulated economy. Before 1994, receipts were estimated by tourist revenue in Foreign Exchange Currency (FEC), a special currency issued at currency exchange as a substitute for RMB (Renminbi), the non-convertible Chinese domestic currency, in order to keep international tourists relatively isolated from the domestic market and to maintain the official exchange rate that seriously overvalued the RMB. Because there was private exchange directly from foreign currencies to RMB through a *de facto* black market exchange rate that benefited foreign currency holders, international tourists were able to use RMB rather than FEC. It was commonly agreed that tourist receipts in China calculated from tourist income in the form of FEC severely underestimated China's total tourist receipts. With the abolishment of FEC in 1994 and the new survey method, tourist receipts started to be reported more accurately.

It therefore seems likely that prior to 1994 China's foreign tourism receipts were significantly understated. Note also that the statistics for receipts are in nominal or current terms calculated at the prevailing exchange rate. Most inter-period comparison would therefore call for adjustment to allow for inflation and anomalies in the exchange rate. To make such adjustments is not easy. Fortunately, they also turn out to be irrelevant for the interregional comparisons which form a significant part of the analysis in this book. However, if no adjustment is made for the factors just mentioned tourism expenditure trends can prove to be misleading if based on nominal receipts for China. Therefore most of the analysis of trends in this chapter concentrates on the number of tourist arrivals.

2.3.3   Statistical trends in inbound tourism

Figure 2.2 plots the number of inbound tourists to China in the period 1978–1998. A linear trend line has been fitted by ordinary least squares to these observations and gives an excellent fit ($R^2 = 0.97$). It indicates that there is a tendency for the number of inbound tourists to China to increase by about 2.93 million per year.

It can be seen that in the Phase of Policy Readjustment in China (1981–1983) (Jackson, 1992) and for a couple of years subsequently inbound tourism was below the trend. It subsequently climbed above the trend line crashing with the Tiananmen tragedy and subsequently took about three years to return approximately to the trend, then remained near the trend line

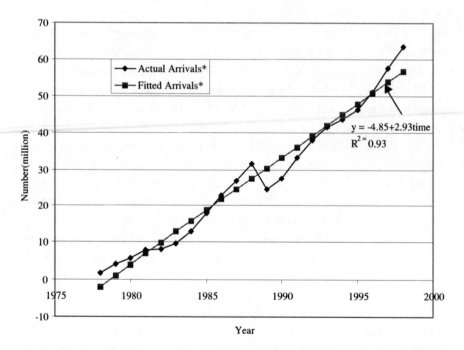

Fig. 2.2 Actual and fitted number of arrivals of inbound tourists to China, 1978–1998.

Source: Based on NTA data.

* Based on actual observations, 1978–1998.

for several years before rising above it in 1997 and 1998. Total tourist arrivals to China in 1998 remained above trend despite a slow down in their proportionate rate of growth and an even greater deceleration in the proportionate growth of tourism receipts.

Observe that the trend line shown in Fig. 2.2 implies that the average proportionate rate of growth in China's inbound tourism is declining. That hypothesis is also supported by fitting a trend line to observations on the annual percentage rates of change in the number of inbound tourists.

When the relationship

$$y = \alpha + \beta x^{-1}$$

where y is annual percentage growth rate and x represent time is fitted by least squares, the relationship is

$$y = 1.19 + 116.32/x \qquad [R^2 = 0.77]$$

This is illustrated in Fig. 2.7 introduced later.

It seems likely that on average inbound tourism to China will not sustain the proportionate growth rates of the past and a long-term slowdown in the proportionate rate of growth of this tourism might be expected, even though short-term deviations are quite possible. In view of these results, a degree of caution seems necessary in relation to the WTO (2000) prediction that China will become the top nation for international tourism in the world by 2020. This matter will be discussed further later in this chapter.

2.4 An Analysis of the Composition of China's Inbound Tourism

2.4.1 *Market segmentation of inbound tourists to China*

Market segmentation is the process of classifying customers into groups with different characteristics or behaviour. One of its purposes is to divide potential consumers into separate groups by identifiable means so as to charge different prices to customers with different intensity of desire for a particular tourist product (Holloway, 1981). Hall (1992) identified three main sets of characteristics, namely geographic, demographic and psychographic in the segmentation of travel markets. Geographical segmentation deals with origin or destination of tourists; demographic factors cover age, sex, occupation, income level, religion, education, health condition and so on; psychographic segmentation relates to motivations, expectations and images.

As explained earlier in this chapter, inbound tourists to China are segmented into three groups by NTA, namely "Foreigners", "Overseas Chinese" and "Compatriots". Proportions of these three groups of inbound tourists to China for the period 1978 to 1998 are reported in Table 2.2.

Compatriots account for the overwhelming proportion of this market, ranging from a low of 86.3 percent in 1978 to a high of 93.9 percent in 1988, as indicated in Table 2.2. The market share for foreigners varied between a low of 5.8 percent in 1988 and a high of 13.19 percent in 1996. The proportion of Taiwanese visitors in the total, after showing a rapid increase initially, has since 1990 been relatively stationary.

Visitors from Taiwan reached over 2 million arrivals and spent US$2.2 billion in 1998 (NTA, 1999), and NTA started to list them as a separate category from 1988 onwards, although they are still included in the category of "Compatriots" (Table 2.2). Taiwanese were allowed to visit China from 1987 onwards. After a suspension of cross-strait travel for almost 40 years starting in 1947, visitors from Taiwan reached an initial peak in 1993 at 1.5 million (NTA, 1995), but decreased after the robbery and murder of a Taiwanese tour group in 1994 in Zhejiang, and subsequent restrictions on travel to China imposed by Taiwan.

There is little seasonality in number of compatriots visiting China. August through October are traditional holiday months with amiable weather in most parts of China. While the early part of the year sees few foreigners visiting because of the cold weather in northern China the Chinese Lunar New Year boosts the number of compatriots visiting China.

It is worthwhile to compare the expenditure levels of different segments of inbound tourists to China. Visits from Hong Kong and Macau accounted for over 85 percent of total arrivals in 1998 but for only 45.3 percent of total tourism expenditure, while Taiwanese, accounting for only 3.4 percent

Table 2.2 Composition of inbound tourists to China, 1978–1998.

	Proportion (%)			
	Foreigners	Overseas Chinese	Compatriots	(Taiwanese[a])
1978	12.69	1.00	86.31	
1979	8.62	0.50	90.88	
1980	9.28	0.60	90.12	
1981	8.69	0.50	90.81	
1982	9.65	0.54	89.81	
1983	9.21	0.43	90.37	
1984	8.83	0.37	90.80	
1985	7.68	0.48	91.84	
1986	6.50	0.30	93.21	
1987	6.42	0.32	93.25	
1988	5.81	0.25	93.94	1.38
1989	5.96	0.28	93.76	2.21
1990	6.36	0.33	93.31	3.45
1991	8.13	0.40	91.47	2.84
1992	10.51	0.43	89.06	3.46
1993	11.21	0.40	88.39	3.68
1994	11.86	0.26	87.88	3.18
1995	12.69	0.25	87.16	3.30
1996	13.19	0.3	86.51	3.39
1997	12.90	0.17	86.93	3.68
1998	11.20	0.19	88.61	3.43

[a]Also included under compatriots.
Source: Calculated from data of NTA, various years.

of total arrivals, contributed 17.4 percent of the total tourism receipts (Table 2.2 and Fig. 2.3). This pattern was usual in the 1990s mainly because Taiwanese visitors mostly stayed longer in China than visitors from Hong Kong and Macau. Short but frequent cross-border trips from Hong Kong and Macau to mainland China are the norm. In addition, visitors from Hong Kong and Macau are considered to have a lower per capita economic impact than those of higher spending Westerners or Japanese (Roehl, 1995).

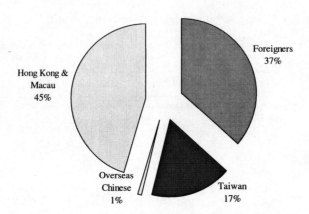

Fig. 2.3 Composition of China's international tourism receipts, 1998.
Source: NTA, 1999.

This is mainly because a high percentage of these compatriots stay with relatives and friends. The average daily expenditure in 1998 was US$141.63 for foreigners, US$134.46 for Overseas Chinese, US$117.73 for Hong Kong visitors, US$94.22 for Macau visitors, and US$127.15 for Taiwanese (NTA, 1999: 49).

2.4.2   Change in the number of foreigners visiting China

The relative proportion of foreigners in the total number of arrivals to China decreased from 1985 to 1989, and has been increasing in the past ten years, although there was a decrease in 1998. Annual absolute change in the number of foreigners to China since 1978 is shown in Fig. 2.4, and a comparison of the annual percentage growth rate for the number of foreigners and compatriots to China is provided in Fig. 2.5.

2.4.3   Comparison of growth rates for number of compatriots and foreigners visiting China

The proportionate growth in the number of compatriots visiting China was higher than that for foreigners during most of the 1980s but this situation

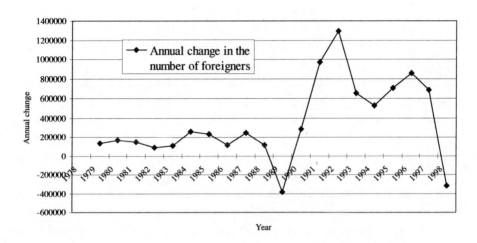

Fig. 2.4 Annual change in the number of foreigners visiting China, 1978–1998.

Source: Based on NTA data.

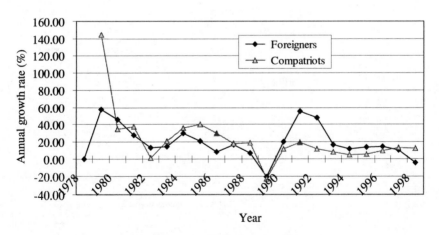

Fig. 2.5 Annual growth rate (%) for the number of foreigners and compatriots visiting China, 1978–1998.

Source: Calculated from data in Tables 2.1 and 2.2.

was reversed in the 1990s. However, during the political unrest in China in 1989, arrivals of compatriots declined by 22.84 percent and those of foreigners by 20.7 percent. In 1998, there was a decrease in foreign arrivals of 4.31 percent due mainly to the Asian economic crisis, but the number of compatriots visiting rose by 12.36 percent.

Long-term analysis of the comparative trends suggests, however, that while the percentage long-term growth rate for the number of arrivals of compatriots was initially above that for foreigners, it is now below that for the number of arrivals of foreigners. The trend lines fitted by ordinary least squares are shown in Fig. 2.6.

Note that the R^2-value for number of foreigners is very low at 0.29. This actually indicates that the relative value of the unexplained variance is high in this case or that the relative volatility of foreign inbound tourism *is quite high*. This volatility is much greater than for the number of arrivals of compatriots, that is a value of $1 - R^2 = 0.71$ needs to be compared to one $1 - R^2 = 0.33$ for arrivals of compatriots.

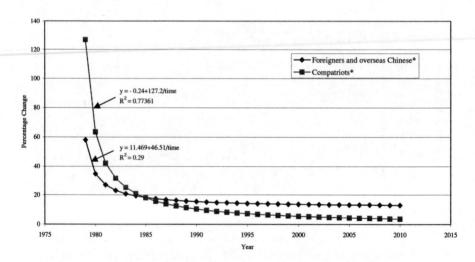

Fig. 2.6 Estimated growth trends in number of compatriots and foreigners and overseas Chinese tourists to China.

Source: Based on NTA data.
* Based on actual observations, 1978–1998.

2.4.4   Composition of foreign arrivals in China

Table 2.3 provides some information about the composition of foreign arrivals in China. Asia is the prime source of arrivals followed by Europe and then Asia. Since 1986 the Asia share has tended to rise, although there was some reversal in 1998 with the Asian financial crisis. Also the proportion of European travellers although fluctuating considerably was generally up in the 1990s compared to the 1980s. By contrast, the proportion of North American travellers was down. The composition of foreign visitors to China seems to exhibit considerable variation.

Table 2.4 provides a more detailed account of foreign visitors to China in 1998 by country of origin giving information on the top 15 source nations. Japan is the main source followed by Russia and the USA. Visitors from Russia and Mongolia are mainly involved on cross border trade. Most Asian countries registered a substantial decline in the number of their tourist visiting China in 1998 due to the Asian financial crisis.

Table 2.3 Composition of international arrivals in China, 1986–1998.

	1986 (%)	1988 (%)	1990 (%)	1992 (%)	1994 (%)	1996 (%)	1998 (%)
1. Foreigners:							
a. Asia	50.9	51.3	52.38	46.13	58.74	60.27	58.24
(Japan)	32.6	32.1	26.51	19.76	22.02	22.96	22.12
(Singapore)	3.3	3.6	4.1	3.81	4.47	4.25	4.45
b. Europe	19.5	22.9	25.54	37.94	25.52	24.21	24.40
(United Kingdom)	5.4	5.2	4.52	3.24	3.22	3.17	3.42
(Germany)	3.3	3.7	3.21	3.03	2.87	2.65	2.69
c. North America	23.5	20.9	17.37	12.37	12.22	12	13.34
(United States)	19.7	16.3	13.35	8.64	9.07	8.55	9.53
d. Oceania	5.5	4.1	3.63	2.63	2.62	2.57	3.16
(Australia)	4.9	3.3	2.87	1.89	2.11	1.97	2.62
2. Compatriots as % of total arrivals	93.21	93.94	93.31	89.06	87.87	89.9	88.61

Source: Based on data of NTA, various years.

Table 2.4 Major tourist generating foreign countries for China 1998 in terms of number of arrivals in China[a].

Rank	Country	Arrivals (millions)	Change over 1997 (%)	
1.	Japan	1.5721	−0.6	1.5816
2.	Russia	0.6920	−15.0	0.8141
3.	USA	0.6773	9.9	0.6163
4.	ROK	0.6328	−19.0	0.7812
5.	Mongolia	0.3648	6.4	0.3429
6.	Singapore	0.3164	−0.1	0.3167
7.	Malaysia	0.3001	−16.9	0.3611
8.	Philippines	0.2565	−7.3	0.2767
9.	UK	0.2429	6.6	0.2279
10.	Canada	0.1960	12.6	0.1741
11.	Germany	0.1919	3.9	0.1847
12.	Australia	0.1864	18.9	0.1568
13.	Thailand	0.1443	−14.3	0.1684
14.	France	0.1380	5.1	0.1313
15.	Indonesia	0.1046	−29.0	0.1473

[a]Taiwan is not included since it is not regarded as a separate country by China.
Source: NTA (1999: 12–13).

Two-thirds of foreigners visiting China between 1985 and 1987 took package tours, but this decreased to one-third in 1989, and business travel comprised 50 percent of foreign trips to China (Gormsen, 1995). Foreign sources that historically dominated the volume of visitors became less important, while new origins, including Russia, Korea and the Southeast Asian countries, became more important in the late 1980s and in the 1990s, resulting in a more diversified market. In 1992, visitors from the former USSR became the largest single foreign source of visitors, although the proportion of excursionists, visitors arrived in China and returned to their home countries on the same day, was high. Per capita expenditures of tourists from the West are likely to be much higher than those from emerging markets such as Russia, Korea and the Philippines (Roehl, 1995).

2.5 Growth of China's Domestic Tourism Industry

2.5.1 Basic data and trends with inbound tourism comparisons

Domestic tourism in China has grown quickly. By the end of the 1990s, the number of domestic tourist trips annually had tripled compared to those in the 1980s. International tourism was given priority for development in the 1980s due to limited infrastructure and domestic service industries still remained a low priority for China being regarded as unproductive. However, in 1992, the Central Committee of the Chinese Communist Party and the State Council made the important decision to increase the relative size of tertiary industry in the Chinese economy. In line with this changed policy direction, a positive attitude was then adopted towards the development of domestic tourism. With increasing disposable

Table 2.5 Domestic tourism in China, 1984–1998.

Year	Trips (million)	Yearly change (%)	Expenditure (billion yuan)	Yearly change (%)
1984	200			
1985	240	20.0	8.0	
1986	270	12.5	10.6	32.5
1987	290	7.4	14.0	32.1
1988	300	3.4	18.7	33.6
1989	240	−20.0	15.0	−19.8
1990	280	16.7	17.0	13.3
1991	300	7.1	20.0	17.6
1992	330	10.0	25.0	25.0
1993	360	9.0	50.0	100
1994	524	45.6	102.35	104.7
1995	629	20	137.57	34.4
1996	639.5	1.67	163.84	19.1
1997	643	0.55	211.23	28.92
1998	694	7.8	239.12	13.2

Source: NTA, various years.

personal income and improving supply of tourist facilities, China has started encouraging domestic tourism, which exhibits the following characteristics: highly diversified segments, the coastal regions and large metropolitan areas are principal generating markets, per capita tourism expenditure is low, and domestic tourist consist of independent travellers and those organised by working units. However, the relative lack of attention to domestic tourism in China is reflected by shortage of statistics on domestic tourism.

Nevertheless, some statistics are available from NTA on domestic tourism. Table 2.5 sets out the number of trips taken annually by domestic tourists in the period 1984–1998. In this period, the number of domestic tourism trips has increased almost seven-fold and expenditure at a much faster rate. However, because the expenditure figures are in current or nominal values

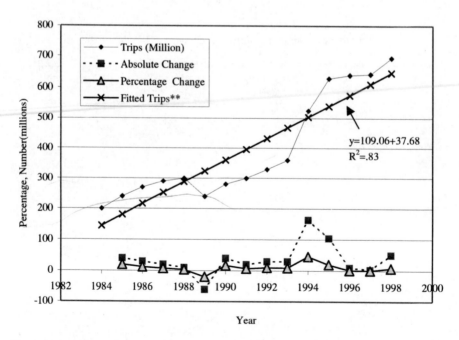

Fig. 2.7 Number of domestic tourism trips, China 1984–1998 and changes in these.

Source: Based on NTA data.

** Based on actual observations, 1984–1998.

rather than real ones adjusted for inflation, these figures overstate the increase in real tourism expenditure by domestic tourists, even though real expenditure is likely to have risen by more than seven-fold.

Figure 2.7 graphs the actual number of tourist trips in China in the period 1984–1998. Using ordinary least squares, a linear trend line has been fitted to these observations as identified in Fig. 2.6. From this figure, it can be seen that the number of domestic trips was above this trend line for most of the 1980s but with the Tiananmen tragedy in 1989 collapsed to well below the trend line and did not return to it until 1994. Since then, actual figures have remained above the trend line. The trend line indicates that the number of domestic trips in China is increasing by about 38 million a year, that is by about 13 times the annual increase in inbound arrivals, according to the trend shown in Fig. 2.2.

While the annual number of domestic trips greatly exceeds the annual number of international tourist arrivals, domestic tourists spend much less than international tourists per head.

2.5.2 Relative composition of all tourism in China

Table 2.6 provides some information on the overall composition of tourism in China. More than 90 percent of all trips are accounted for by domestic tourists, with foreigners accounting for around 1 percent of the total and compatriots around 8 percent of the total. The share of tourism "trips" accounted for by domestic tourists has fluctuated between 89.65 percent and 93.96 percent in the period 1984–1998, and has actually fallen to some extent compared to 1984.

2.5.3 Growth rate of domestic tourism compared to inbound and their volatility

Perhaps somewhat surprisingly, the annual number of domestic tourism trips displays a high degree of volatility. While this may be apparent from Fig. 2.6, it is clearer from Fig. 2.8. It reports trend curves which were fitted to the data for proportionate (percentage) annual changes in the number of

Table 2.6 Composition of total tourism market, China 1978–1998 in terms of arrivals and domestic trips in millions and percentages.

Year	Total international arrivals	Foreigners	Domestic travellers	Total international & domestic	Domestic as % of total	International as % of total	Foreigner as % of total
1978	1.81	1.81	0.23				
1979	4.20	4.20	0.36				
1980	5.70	5.70	0.53				
1981	7.77	7.77	0.67				
1982	7.92	7.92	0.76				
1983	9.48	9.48	0.87				
1984	12.85	12.85	1.13	200	93.96	6.04	0.53
1985	17.83	17.83	1.37	240	93.08	6.92	0.53
1986	22.81945	22.82	1.48	270	92.21	7.79	0.51
1987	26.902267	26.90	1.73	290	91.51	8.49	0.55
1988	31.694804	31.69	1.84	300	90.44	9.56	0.56
1989	24.501394	24.50	1.46	240	90.74	9.26	0.55
1990	27.461821	27.46	1.75	280	91.07	8.93	0.57
1991	33.349761	33.35	2.71	300	90.00	10.00	0.81
1992	38.114945	38.11	4.01	330	89.65	10.35	1.09
1993	41.526943	41.53	4.66	360	89.66	10.34	1.16
1994	43.684456	43.68	5.18	524	92.30	7.70	0.91
1995	46.386511	46.39	5.89	629	93.13	6.87	0.87
1996	51.127516	51.13	6.74	639.5	92.60	7.40	0.98
1997	57.587923	57.59	7.43	643.8	91.79	8.21	1.06
1998	63.478401	63.48	7.11	694	91.62	8.38	0.94

Source: Based on NTA data.

domestic trips and in the number of inbound arrivals. The relative degree of variation from the trend line for inbound tourism is only $1 - R^2 = 0.33$ but for domestic tourism it is $1 - R^2 = 0.85$. Why the number of domestic trips should exhibit such a high degree of volatility is unclear. Note also from Fig. 2.7 that initially the growth rate of inbound tourism to China exceeded

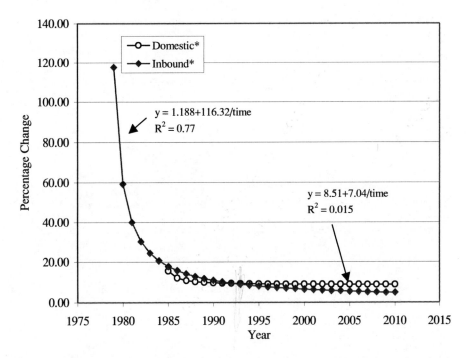

Fig. 2.8 Estimated growth trends in inbound number of visits and domestic tourist trips in China.

Source: Based on NTA data.
* Based on actual observation, 1978–1998.
** Based on actual observation, 1984–1998.

that for domestic tourism but after 1994 the position was reversed. This reversal might in part reflect China's decision in 1992 to place greater emphasis on the growth of service industries. Moreover, observe that if these trend lines apply and are extrapolated, domestic tourism trips approach a growth rate of 8.51 percent per annum but the growth rate of inbound tourism only 1.19 percent per annum.

However, a somewhat different comparative picture emerges if the growth rate in the number of foreign visitors is compared with that of domestic tourism trips. As can be seen from Fig. 2.9, the trend in the proportionate rate of growth for the number of foreign visitors to China has throughout the

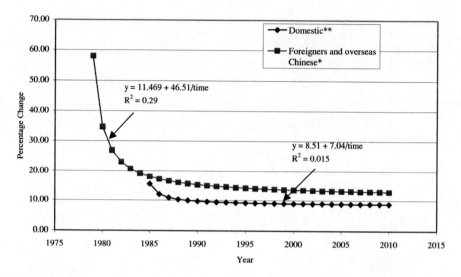

Fig. 2.9 Estimated growth trends in domestic tourist trips and number of visits by foreigners and overseas Chinese tourists, China.

Source: Based on NTA data.
* Based on actual observation, 1978–1998.
** Based on actual observation, 1984–1998.

observed period remained above that for the number of domestic trips. Moreover, if the trend is extrapolated, the growth rate of foreign arrivals approaches 11.5 percent per annum compared to 8.5 percent for domestic tourism trips. If such a growth rate was to be sustained for foreign arrivals, it is conceivable that the WTO prediction that China will become the world's top country for international arrivals by 2020 could be satisfied.

Note that overseas Chinese have been included with foreign arrivals in Fig. 2.9. They are relatively small in number and are a diverse category. Their visiting pattern is positively correlated with that of foreigners. Observe also that $1 - R^2 = 0.71$ is relatively high for foreigners, considerably higher than for compatriots but lower than for domestic tourism, This indicates that on the whole the number of visits by foreigners is more volatile than that for compatriots.

2.5.4   Caution needed in projecting trends

One should, however, be very cautious about projecting the trends identified above. To do so is purely a mechanical approach. Furthermore, the projections depend on the type of function fitted to the data.

In fact, linear functions provided a reasonably good fit to the data on total inbound arrivals in China and to the total number of domestic tourism trips. If one accepts these trends, then the proportionate increase in both cases would decline with the passage of time and eventually approach zero. If on the other hand, the inverse exponential function fitted to the data on annual percentage change is preferred, proportionate growth rates tend to a positive constant.

In reality much can change in the future, particularly in two decades, and the level of tourist activity depends on a complex interdependent system of factors. Further substantial growth in China's tourism industry (both domestic and inbound) is likely in the foreseeable future, but it is doubtful if one can confidently predict more than this.

2.6   Notes on Outbound Tourism from China

While outbound tourism from China is not a significant focus of this book, some observations about it are in order. Until 1990, travel of Chinese abroad was mostly limited to visits for official or commercial purposes rather than for holiday or recreation. However, in 1990, China began to relax its policies on outbound travel and visits to some Southeast Asian countries were allowed for tourism purposes.

The total number of Chinese outbound travellers was 8.4 million in 1998, of which 5.2 million were for business and the rest for private purposes. Outbound tours organised by travel agencies reached 1.8 million (NTA, 1999). Major destinations for Chinese outbound travellers are Hong Kong, Macau, Thailand, Singapore, Malaysia, the Philippines, Russia, Australia, New Zealand, Republic of Korea and Japan. Most of the remaining outbound Chinese travellers are same-day cross-border visitors. Cross-border same-day tours to Russia, Korea and Mongolia in the north, and the Vietnam, Laos and Burma in the south are popular. They attract Chinese who otherwise would hardly have a chance of travelling abroad.

Note that the WTO does not usually count same-day cross-border travellers as tourists. Nevertheless, even if Chinese statistics are used, it is clear that a major surplus of inbound travellers over outbound travellers exists for China. Whereas China had 8.4 million outbound travellers in 1998, it had 63.5 million international arrivals. The balance is very much in China's favour, and more so financially than the relative number of outbound and inbound travellers might suggest.

It seems possible that there is some suppressed demand for outbound travel from China due to regulations on such travel and administrative obstacles to outbound travellers. Greater liberalisation and continuing rises in income could result in a substantial rise in the number of China's outbound travellers. Nevertheless, China's international tourism account is likely to remain in positive balance for some time to come. Consequently, tourism and China's tourism industry will continue to make a net positive contribution to China's foreign exchange earnings. These earnings in turn are likely to continue to be valuable in supporting China's future economic growth.

2.7 Environmental Concerns and Sustainable Tourism, Especially Ecotourism, in China

Both economic growth and growth in tourism can be two-edged swords as far as the sustainability of tourism is concerned. While economic growth, as pointed out in Chapter 1, can stimulate the development of tourism, if this growth destroys or degrades the assets which help to attract tourists and results in severe man-made pollution, it can eventually deter tourist. As a result of its rapid rate of economic growth since China began its economic reforms, China has experienced increased air and water pollution and many of its natural and heritage items have come under increased pressure.

Although environmental protection in China under the centrally planned system was far from adequate, decentralisation of political and economic control since the economic reforms began in 1998 have come at an environmental cost. With the reduced power of the central government, local governments have been permitting polluting activities which adversely affect neighbouring regions and reduce overall national welfare. Property rights have become weakly defined in parts of China, leading to exploitation of resources. Relaxation of state control over resources can result in *de facto* open-access property. New laws do not always keep pace with the economic transformation, and law enforcement is not ensured. Consequently, many of China's water resources have been polluted, and air quality has deteriorated seriously. Most of the large cities in China have air quality of a much lower standard than the one set by the World Health Organisation. Loss of forests in China has been so serious that in 1992 only 13.6 percent of China's area was covered by forest and woodland — the area decreasing from 20.1 percent in 1979 (Bingham, 1993). Only 4.5 percent of municipal waste water in China receives treatment (Bingham, 1993). Soil erosion, flood and droughts, pollution and shrinking biodiversity are growing problems in China. China's fresh water supply per capita is expected to fall below 1,500 cubic metres by 2025. The World Bank considers countries with less than 2,000 cubic metres of water per capita to have serious economic problems (World Bank, 1992).

The United Nations Conference on Environment and Development held in June 1992 proposed sustainable development as the goal for development in the future. Sustainable development was declared in 1996 to be China's national development strategy in the Ninth 5-Year Plan (1996 to 2000). In March 1994, China approved and promulgated *China's Agenda 21: White Paper on China's Population, Environment, and Development in the 21st Century*. At its Fourth Session in March 1996, China's Eighth National People's Congress examined and adopted the Ninth 5-Year Plan of China for National Economic and Social Development and the Outline of the Long-Term Target for the Year 2010. The Constitution of China stipulates that "the State protects and improves the living environment and the ecological environment, and prevents and remedies pollution and other public hazards" (State Council China, 1994). China has enacted and promulgated many special laws on environmental protection as well as on natural resources. In many special laws on environmental protection, the environmental quality standards and pollutant discharge standards are compulsory standards, and those who violate these compulsory environmental standards are supposed to bear the corresponding legal responsibility. But there has been a tendency in the past not to enforce such laws fully. At present, there are nationwide more than 2,500 environmental protection administration departments above the county level with a total staff of 88,000 engaging in environmental administration, monitoring, inspection and control.

While China recognises the seriousness of its environmental problems, has and is developing polices to deal with these, it is difficult to make rapid progress with environmental protection in a developing country such as China. Emphasis on material wealth, economic self-interest at the local level and by individuals and corruption do not facilitate the process. So far, however, the adverse environmental consequences from China's economic growth have not prevented massive growth in tourism in China. Overall, China's economic growth seems to have facilitated such tourism expansion despite its adverse environmental side-effects.

Apart from the adverse environmental impacts of other industries on assets used for tourism, growth in tourism itself can also endanger resources used to attract tourists. In the earlier stages of China's reform period, tourism was regarded as a "green industry" friendly to the environment.

However, China has now developed a more realistic assessment of the relationship between tourism and the natural environment. The tourism industry is no longer regarded as being necessarily environmentally friendly and the importance of sustaining tourism is being increasingly recognised. China has progressed from a situation where tourism was regarded as environmentally benign to the stage where both possibilities for environmental deterioration and conservation are emphasised. It is clear that while at the point of delivery for example, hotels and entertainment, the tourist industry may appear to be "smokeless", this ignores the environmental impacts of items like energy, transportation and water required for tourists as well as waste products, such as sewage, produced by tourists. The need for appropriate planning and associated government measures to protect the environment in tourism development has taken root.

China plans to increase the share of tertiary industry in its GNP and aims to "develop non-polluting environment friendly 'green tourism'" (Information Office, 1996: 12). This is evident, for example, from *China's Agenda 21: White Paper on China's Population, Environment and Development in the 21st Century* (State Council, 1994: 58), an important document which will influence China's planning and policies to achieve sustainable development in the 21st century. It recommends that "new routes for tourist attractions should be opened up and tourism resources should be protected to promote pollution-free and environmentally-sound tourism. Tourist-oriented road transportation facilities, airports and related services (including catering establishments) should be constructed. Appropriate ways should be found to solve problems in sewage disposal, refuse collection, goods transportation, waste disposal and to strictly control sources of hazardous pollution at scenic spots".

Encouragement of nature-based tourism is increasingly seen in China as a way to support conservation of biodiversity. Although a variety of definitions of ecotourism exist, as will be discussed in detail in Chapter 6, they all to a certain extent link tourism with conservation, especially the natural environment, but also in some cases with the conservation of culture and cultural artefacts. All definitions stress the need for sustaining assets on which tourism depends. Sustainability is central to most discussions involving ecotourism.

Ecotourism is to be promoted in China as a means to conserve biodiversity and nature generally and pilot projects are to be developed for this purpose (State Council, 1994: 177). This direction is not only indicated in *China's Agenda 21* but is supported by *China: Biodiversity Conservation Action Plan* (National Environmental Protection Agency, 1994). Xishuangbanna Prefecture in Yunnan, an area internationally recognised as being very rich in biodiversity, has been targeted as one of the areas for ecotourism development. Nature-based tourism is promoted using the ecological resources of the Xishuangbanna State Nature Reserve, as will be discussed in Chapter 8.

While China adopted the Environment Protection Law and the Forest Law in 1979, specifying goals of maintaining 30 percent of its forest cover and prohibiting logging in protected areas, China's forest cover currently is 13.92 percent or a total forest area of 134 million square hectares. By 1995,

China had designated 11,333 square kilometres of smoke-and-dust control zones, and 1,800 square kilometres of up-to-standard noise control zones (Information Office of the State Council of China, 1996). However, it is clear that more than two decades after the Forest law was adopted, achievement falls far short of the goal.

The first nature reserve in China was established at Dinghu Mountain, in Guangdong Province in southern China in 1956 to provide a living laboratory for the Chinese Academy of Sciences. Changbai Mountain Area in northeast China was established as a biosphere reserve in 1960 to conserve temperate and mountain flora and fauna. By the end of the 1980s, there were altogether 59 nature reserves in China. Zhangjiajie National Forest Park in Hunan Province, China's first national park, was designated in 1982. By early 1995, 20 national parks existed in China, of which 17 were situated in non-coastal areas.

China has experienced uneven regional development since commencing its economic reforms and this has resulted in incomes in the coastal provinces rising considerably above those in the interior. Tourism development is now being pursued as a means to encourage economic growth in a number of the interior regions and promotion of ecotourism is a part of this strategy. In fact, all of China's inland provinces showed substantial rises in the number of tourist arrivals between 1986 and 1998. The fact that two provinces in China's inland area abundant in cultural and natural tourism resources — Yunnan and Shannxi — have joined the top ten earners of tourism receipts since 1994 (NTA, 1995 to 1997) indicates that inbound tourists to China are being increasingly attracted to non-coastal areas and may be looking for new touristic experiences. It is becoming increasingly important for China to improve its tourist products to compete with other destinations, and the development of ecotourism may stimulate further tourism growth in China.

There are also other problems which can interfere with China's tourism development. Security problems can threaten China's profile as a safe tourist destination. For example, visitors from Taiwan decreased following the robbery and murder of a Taiwanese tour group in 1994. Cases of theft, fire, traffic accidents, disease, murder and so on have involved tourists and consequently on occasions have negatively influenced tourism to China. Other social and cultural impacts of tourism, such as commercialisation of ethnic cultures, change in traditional family and moral systems, shift in ideological attitude, and life-style alteration (Tisdell, 1996), have been observed in China partly as a result of the interactions between locals and tourists. Political unrest can have a very negative impact on tourism and in 1989 involving bloodshed in Tiananmen Square.

Long-haul travel decisions are deeply influenced by the advice of friends and relatives, and the attitude of travel agencies. With the novelty of China starting to wane in the late 1980s (Roehl, 1995), China has to supply better quality tourism products and services to continue to attract potential tourists. According to an NTA survey, 26.8 percent of respondents complained about transportation in China, 23.1 percent were not satisfied with shopping, while 70 percent of all interviewees regarded prices in China as reasonable (NTA, 1992). Improvements in infrastructure and expansion of tourist activities, including more reliable travel schedules and products and services of higher quality are required. Handicapped by an image of poor service, China needs to improve its tourism services.

• While ecotourism can bolster conservation of biodiversity, it is also possible for inappropriately planned nature-based tourism to hamper conservation (Tisdell, 1996). Problems of deterioration of tourist resources and alienation of local communities resulting from tourism growth need to be addressed also.

Concentration of tourism on the coastal areas, especially coastal cities, has resulted in congestion and deterioration in some popular tourist sites, and has added to regional disparity across China (Wen and Tisdell, 1996). Analysis of NTA data for 1998 reveals, for example, that 80.15 percent of international tourists arrived in its 12 coastal regions and, therefore, only 19.85 percent in its 18 inland regions. The disparity was even greater for tourism receipts with the coastal region accounting for 84.76 parcent of those. Nevertheless, China designated seven key tourism localities during its Seventh 5-Year Plan (1986 to 1990) — Beijing, Shanghai, Jiangsu, Zhejiang, Guangdong, Guangxi and Shannxi — but only one is located in the interior. Among the 12 Tourism and Vacation Zones approved by the state in 1993 with special preferential policies, including Jinshi Beach in Dalian, Shilaore

Beach in Qingdao, Tai Lake in Wuxi, Tai Lake in Suzhou, Sheshar Mountain in Fujian, the River Zhi in Hangzhou, Wuyi Mountain in Fujian, Meizhou Island in Fujian, Dianchi Lake in Kunming, Nanhu Lake in Guangzhou, Silver Beach in Beithai, A-Long Beach in Sanya, only Dianchi Lake is located in the interior (Anon, 1992a). In contrast, a survey conducted in 1991 of both domestic and international tourists about their most favoured attractions found that more than half were located in the interior (Anon, 1992b). Narrow views on Chinese tourist resources, such as "the landscape of China, at least in the eyes of most Westerners, is actually the landscape of Guilin" (Raffery, 1993), have been promoted. How to develop tourist resources in the inland areas and to disperse tourists from the crowded coastal areas has become an issue that influences both the quality of Chinese tourism and the welfare of non-coastal localities. This is discussed in several chapters of this book, for example, Chapters 3, 4 and 6.

The nature of tourism is always changing and can be subject to evolutionary processes. This needs to be taken into account in the development of tourism in China. As Plog (1973) warned, destination areas may lose their qualities of attraction of tourists over time. Butler (1980) proposed the famous staged model of exploration, development, consolidation, stagnation, decline and rejuvenation to depict the tourism development process, in which such principles as "product life cycle" and "carrying capacity" are applied (Butler, 1991). The destination life cycle has become one of the focuses for tourism research (Keller, 1987; Smith, 1992). Although criticism of the life cycle and carrying capacity hypotheses exists (Getz, 1992; Lindberg *et al.*, 1997), it is generally agreed that tourism has important impacts on a destination and that the evolution of sites is determined by both economic, environmental and social forces (Haywood, 1986).

Adopted from the agricultural/biological context, the concept of tourism carrying capacity has been defined as "the maximum number of people who can use a site without an unacceptable alteration in the physical environment and without an unacceptable decline in the quality of the experience gained by the visitors" (Mathieson and Wall, 1982: 21). This concept has been applied in diversified contexts such as ecology, sociology, and tourism. However, from the view point of some economists, the optimal level of tourism use of *arel.*

a location would occur when the utility obtained by an additional tourist exactly equals the loss of enjoyment caused to existing tourists by having one more tourist involved (Wanhill, 1980; Tisdell, 2000, Vol. 2, Part IV). But this is just one view of social optimality, and it does not take account of various sustainability aspects of a site (Tisdell and Wen, 1997).

The above are just a few of the environmental and other sustainability issues which China faces in developing its tourism industry. These challenges are not necessarily unique to China. But they may be more acute for China as the leading less developed nation in tourism development.

2.8   Concluding Comments

This chapter has traced the spectacular rise of tourism in China since China commenced its economic reforms in 1978. Initially, China's emphasis was on the expansion of inbound tourism as a vehicle for its economic growth. But subsequently attention was also given to the expansion of domestic tourism as China's attitude towards the potential contribution of its domestic service industries to its development changed from being negative to being positive. While the proportionate rate of growth of domestic tourism now exceeds that of inbound tourism for China, the percentage rate of growth of arrivals of foreigners still surpasses that for the number of domestic trips.

In terms of the number of trips annually, China's domestic tourism is absolutely well in excess of its inbound tourism and grows annually by a much larger absolute amount. But the disparity in tourism receipts for China from domestic and inbound tourism is comparatively much less.

Although both domestic and inbound tourism in China's case continue to grow strongly, with inbound *foreign* tourism rising at a very rapid percentage rate, percentage growth rates seem to be declining. Nevertheless, the Chinese tourism industry is bound to register further gigantic expansion. This will intensify the sustainability issues raised above.

As mentioned briefly above, the regional distribution of tourism in China is extremely uneven. The nature of this inequality will be given particular attention in Chapters 4 and 5. Such regional inequality is likely to be of particular concern if it reinforces regional economic inequality in China which is already marked. The next chapter will consider economic inequality in China. This will pave the way for examining the extent to which the growth of tourism in China has reinforced or ameliorated economic inequality.

Chapter 3

Regional Economic Disparity and Tourism Development: Theories and the Chinese Case

3.1 Introduction

In the previous chapter, it was mentioned that considerable inequality exists in China in both regional development of its tourism and in its economic development. This chapter provides a broad overview of theories of regional development and regional economic inequality, and relates these in general terms to regional income inequality in China. In doing so, it discusses the historical and current pattern of such inequality, especially between China's coastal and interior areas, and examines government policies which have shaped this pattern. The question is then debated of whether regional economic inequality really matters from an economic policy point of view, and whether or not government intervention should be considered as a means to modify the spatial distribution of economic development, particularly in China, by encouraging key or leading industries, such as tourism, in the interior of China. This chapter is a prelude to considering impacts of tourism development on regional economic disparities in China, in particular, whether tourism development adds to such inequalities or moderates these, a central concern in Chapters 4 and 5.

3.2 Theories of Regional Development and Inequality: An Overview

Theories about regional development are complex and diverse. Gunnar Myrdal (1957), Harry Richardson (1976), William Alonso (1980), and

John Friedmann (1966 and 1985), amongst others, were significant contributors to the literature on regional development. Some leading theories, such as the dependency theory, strategies of self-reliance, and the New International Economic Order, differ from each other in terms of varying emphasis on domination, linkages and distribution. Theories about high technology production complexes, employee-ownership and de-industrialisation, and the encouragement of small businesses as job creators, have had varying degrees of influence on regional policies.

Richardson (1969, Chapter 1) discussed three ways of analysing the economic implications of the spatial dimension. The first type of analysis recognises the existence of space and the impact of distance on the economic interrelationships between different regions. It assumes that the location of population, industry and resources is fixed, while space is a friction measured by the extent to which transport costs reduce commodity flows. The second type of analysis treats space as a matrix for the placement of economic activities. It is a more generalised spatial analysis, emphasises the heterogeneity of the spatial system, attempts to explain commodity flows, and forms the basis of inter-regional trade theory. This approach is in fact an extension of the first because it makes allowance for changes in location of some resources. The third type concentrates on the interrelationship between regions in the national economy. Regions are treated as integral parts of a multi-sector economy.

Theories of regional growth can be roughly divided into two categories according to their emphasis on different factors as economic constraints. In the first group, the growth of inputs required for the production of goods and services is assumed to be the major constraint on the regional growth rate. Capital (K) and labour (L) are major indicators of inputs in this group (natural resource inputs are ignored). The Cobb-Douglas production function with constant returns to scale, expressed as $Y = AK^aL^{(1-a)}$, has been often used as a supply-side model for regional growth. Capital moves from regions with low rates of return to those with high rates, and labour migrates in response to wage differentials across regions. The second group of theories supposes that the supply of all necessary inputs for production is not perfectly elastic, such as in many neoclassical models where full employment of productive factors occurs, while the growth of demand for a region's output, particularly the growth of its exports, is regarded as the essential determinant of regional development (Borts, 1960). Demand from within a region, as well as demand for the region's exports, significantly shape the economic growth of a region.

Richardson (1969, Chapter 3) listed six major approaches to the study of regional growth. Harrod-Domar models are applicable to regional analysis if aggregate growth theories can be adapted to regional studies and lack of effective demand is the major problem for the region. It is expected from these models that labour will tend to flow from low to high income regions to take advantage of higher money wages and greater employment opportunities, and capital may flow in the same direction since investment opportunities may be greater in the high income regions. Therefore, it will be necessary for the government to intervene to make capital flow from high to low income regions, if balanced growth across regions is the objective. Harrod-Domar models are often applicable to regional analysis because they are demand-oriented and lagging regions normally suffer from unused productive factors, especially labour.

The second approach is via neoclassical models. Concentrating on the supply side, these models assume a continuous function linking output to inputs of the two factors: capital and labour. The rate of growth in income is determined by three elements, namely capital accumulation (K), increase in labour supply (L) and technical progress over time (t). A typical production function for the *i*th region is: $Y_i = f_i (K, L, t)$. The export-based theory of growth states that the growth of a region is dependent upon the growth of its export industries, and economic activities for other than exports are induced by the change of export performance. Exports alone are elevated to become the sole exogenous influence on demand and other possible factors are neglected.

The sectoral approach begins with the Clark-Fisher hypothesis that a rise in per capita income is accompanied by a decline in the proportion of resources employed in agriculture, and a rise in manufacturing and later in service industries. Rising incomes are inevitably accompanied by a transfer of resources to sectors with higher income elasticity of demand, usually manufacturing and services. The regional growth and industrial structure approach assumes a region may grow either because it has industries that are growing fast naturally or because it is gaining an increasing proportion of a given industry or industries, regardless of whether these industries are growing or not. In addition, there are theories of whether per capita income for different regions will converge or diverge in the long run.

These models are to a large extent adapted from models originally developed for national economies. Hence the deficiencies of these models are at least as serious for regions as for a nation. The condition that each region is treated as an open economy, which enables inter-regional flow analysis to be grafted on to the regional models, is not always satisfied. A closed region may grow not only because of a fast rate of expansion in its stock of inputs, labour and capital, but also because it employs its existing inputs more productively through inflows of technology, management or other productivity-raising advances from elsewhere or inside (Richardson, 1969, Chapter 12). Lagging regions usually suffer from unused labour but have shortage of capital. Hence the assumption of continuous full employment associated with neoclassical models is less appropriate to problems of regional disparity. Balanced growth or equilibrium is stressed in these models. However, because it is easier for income leakages and movement of capital to occur across regions than national boundaries, opportunities for dynamic disequilibrium are considerable. Furthermore, there are risks that the initial income inequality between regions will be magnified if regions remain net debtors or creditors for long periods of time.

Regional economic disparity, principally in the form of differences in average per capita income, is a major topic in regional economics studies. Both equilibrating and disequilibrating powers work within any economic system, leading to either expanding or shrinking disparities among regions within a nation. An understanding of theories about both convergence and divergence of regional income seems to be necessary in order to analyse the dynamics of regional economies.

3.2.1   Inverted-U paradigm and balanced development

Some researchers believe that regional inequality will disappear over time as the factors of production move across regions. The best known theory in this group of balanced development is the inverted-U paradigm. Kuznets (1955) introduced the highly acclaimed inverted-U hypothesis, stating that income inequality between individuals tends to increase first and then decline with the progress of economic development, but did not apply it to regional development. This hypothesis has been extended to typify changes in regional income inequality within nations. Some writers believe such inequality follows an inverted-U path. International cross-sectional data and national time series data suggests increasing economic inequality in early stages of economic development as a consequence of concentration of income and income-generating factors in some regions of a nation, and decreasing at later stages when diffusion of income and income-generating factors prevails across a nation (Williamson, 1965). Neoclassical logic, which stresses the tendency toward equilibrium and the ability of the adjustment mechanism in factor markets to smooth out regional disparities in income, has been applied to explain the inverted-U in relation to regional income inequality (Alonso, 1980).

Economic inequality frequently exists between urban and rural areas. The literature, mainly based on the experience of industrialised countries, argues that for countries or regions proceeding through stages of economic development, population and economic activities are dispersed during the phase of agriculture, but urbanisation polarises the region into a core and a periphery during the process of industrialisation. Then during the post-industrialisation phase deconcentration commences as a result of diseconomies of scale (Williamson, 1965; Alonso, 1980; Jones, 1991). This path of development corresponds to an "inverted-U" hypothesis.

However, other studies raise doubts about the validity of the stage of the inverted-U hypothesis when applied to regional income inequality. For instance, increased regional income inequality in the US in the late 1970s and 1980s (Braun, 1991), raised doubts about the explanatory and predictive power of the inverted-U model. Fan and Casetti (1994) propose that theories of polarisation, polarisation-reversal and spatial restructuring offer more powerful explanations of changes in regional income inequality. According to their study of the US, polarisation reversal is not the same as the equilibrium predicted by neoclassical regional growth models. It is primarily a result of capital seeking locations with promise of lower costs and higher profits and not indicative of uniform factor returns across regions. Empirical studies in the US indicated that the dominant factor associated with the change of regional per capita income throughout 1880–1950 was changed in the relative importance of agricultural to manufacturing employment within each region (Richardson, 1969, Chapter 3). Regional divergence and convergence can be explained as a response to the concentration and diffusion of income and income-generating factors (Williamson, 1965), or as a consequence of polarisation, polarisation-reversal and spatial restructuring (Fan and Casetti, 1994).

Simplistic application of pure neoclassical economic theories may lead to the conclusion that a free market system necessarily results in the elimination of regional gaps, sooner or later. However, neither the Walrasian general equilibrium analysis, which assumes a one point, non-spatial economy, nor the Keynesian aggregate general equilibrium that divides the national economy into several sectors, has a geographical frame of reference. Myrdal (1957: 144) argued that the emphasis of many economists on the likelihood of convergence stems from treating the concept of stable equilibrium as if it had "teleological significance" rather than as "very abstract, almost crude and usually unrealistic theoretical assumption". It is therefore worthwhile exploring the views of those who advocate theories of unbalanced regional development.

3.2.2   Unbalanced economic development across regions

Some writers claim that inequality between and within regions is unavoidable. Contrary to the neoclassical economic theory that the market will bring about a Pareto optimum of spatial equilibrium in the distribution of economic activities, some writers have pointed out that a permanent unequal functional regional economy typically consists of a central urban core and a surrounding (largely rural) periphery (Hughes and Holland, 1994). Perroux (1970) contended that the natural tendency within any economy was towards polarisation, dominance and dependence. He argued in his doctrine of polarisation that a market economy brings a concentration of development in particular centres rather than a balanced development in space. In Perroux's view of the dynamic economy, regional balance never occurs and it should not occur because "there never has been a historical case of economic evolution where one does not observe clustering, cumulative, and propulsive effects that generate development. History has handed down its verdict: there is no other way of development" (Perroux, 1988).

Perroux's works, along with contributions of Friedmann (1966 and 1985) and Higgins (1988), suggest that it is unnecessary to make an impassioned plea for the elimination of regional gaps. Based on the finding that large cities are often more efficient and innovative than other regions, mega-city supporters argue that investment flowing to non-urban areas is likely to waste scarce capital and thereby slow the rate of national economic growth, and the country will be less able to redistribute income and remedy poverty (Jones, 1991). A natural level of regional disparities or "optimal regional differences" (Perroux, 1988), may persist within an economy. Gunnar Myrdal argued that backwash effects often outweigh spread effects to the lagging areas, and the movements of factors are usually disequilibrating, favouring the rich regions at the expense of the poor. Backward regions fail to attract new economic activities because their "limited advantages, say cheap labour, do not exert sufficient attractive force to outweigh these external economies found at centres of agglomeration" (Myrdal, 1957: 348).

A basic element in the regional income framework is that large regions tend to have lower marginal propensity to import than small areas, and that factor reduces the propensity of regions to import from another (Richardson, 1969: 273). This is mainly because large regions have a more diversified economic structure and tend to have less need of imports to satisfy essential demands, and the transport costs and lack of contact between markets and suppliers reduces trade. Gunnar Myrdal showed that regional disparities in the less developed European countries tended to be large and increasing, but small and diminishing in the more advanced economies (Higgins, 1988). Fan and Casetti (1994) found in the US that income inequality from as early as the 19th century between states in the traditional core is low, but higher between these and the peripheral states, and also between peripheral states as well. A decline in regional inequality occurred in the US in the 1960s and

1970s when income rose in peripheral states. In the 1980s, however, there was an increase in inequality between low income states and overall increase in regional inequality.

"Unbalanced growth" proponents regard regional disparity as a natural process of economic development, but often overlook the potential of regional disparities to create social and political problems that must be addressed in any democratic society, and especially so in a country where the gaps between regions correspond closely to provinces and municipalities. Improvement in mass communications bring developments in high growth regions to the attention of residents in backward regions. In many developing economies where there is not free movement of factors of production, and the national economy is heavily influenced by government policies, increasing economic inequality can threaten long-term political stability or social goals of the nation. The next section will therefore examine regional economic disparity in China in order to assess the applicability of both "inverted-U" and "unbalanced growth" theories to the Chinese economy.

3.3   Regional Income Inequality in China: History and Current Situation

This section analyses the change in China's regional inequality, considering household income, consumption, productivity and availability of infrastructure, since the establishment of the People's Republic of China in 1949. Arguments about income inequality in socialist countries have drawn on such fields as economics, sociology, geography, history and so on. Marxists believe that the origin of inequality lies in the private ownership of the means of production and that workers are exploited to produce profit for the owners of these means (Marx, 1956, Vol. 2). Orthodox socialists aim to eliminate inequality and to achieve a classless society (Lampton, 1983), but some scholars argue that inequalities can be expected in socialist systems as a result of political prestige, price distortion, subsidies and other non-market factors (Nelson, 1983; Szelenyi and Mancin, 1987).

3.3.1 Income inequality between 1949 and 1978 in China

Many researchers believe that China made significant progress in reducing inequalities in basic consumption, income, education and availability of other basic services between 1949 and 1976 under Mao Zedong's regime (Lampton, 1983). Adelman and Sunding (1987) claimed on the basis of their estimates for the Lorenz curve depicting China's income distribution during 1952 and 1983 that "the level of inequality in China is one of the lowest in the world".

Explanations of relative economic equality in China in the pre-reform era (1949–1978) include mainly consideration of three factors. First, the guiding slogan or an aim of the Chinese Communist Party used to be to eliminate "three disparities" — namely, the disparities between urban and rural areas, between factory workers and peasants, and between manual labourers and intellectuals. The ideal society was considered to be one without any inequality in relation to profession, location or gender.

Secondly, by denying private ownership of factors of production, income from property rights was almost eliminated. Wage rates for urban and government employees were mainly determined according to working years, position, occupation and location without substantial variation. Low prices were set for agricultural products, which were sold to the government for redistribution to the urban population on a controlled allocative basis. Although urban residents had some privileges in access to their allocated amount of food materials and cash income, their overall income level was just above subsistence and differences in income were almost negligible.

Thirdly, Mao's regime squeezed the agricultural sector and personal consumption in order to accumulate capital to build up heavy industry (Tisdell, 1993), and there was insufficient wealth left to create a large income gap. A double squeeze on agriculture occurred. There was a direct outflow of capital represented by the net balance of purchases and sales of the agriculture sector, the deteriorating domestic terms of trade and to a limited extent, the transfer of human capital from the rural areas through migration (Yotopoulos and Nugent, 1976, Chapter 15). Wage rates in the urban areas were generally kept at a very low level, leaving the urban population living at subsistence level. The Great Leap Forward in the late 1950s and the Cultural Revolution from 1966 to 1976 plunged the economy into chaos, and there was hardly any real increase in capital accumulation in the 1960s and 1970s (Yeh, 1996). Any absolute inequality in income given the low level of production and consumption in pre-reform China would, therefore, have been so low as to be insignificant.

3.3.2   Income inequality since 1978

China entered its era of economic reform in 1978 under the late leader Deng Xiaoping. *A priori*, the process of transition from a planned economy to a market economy dismantles artificial equalisation of income as the realignment of resource allocation and prices by the market brings changes to the distribution of income across sectors, regions and households. Therefore increased income disparities can be expected. Nevertheless, differing opinions have been expressed about the effect on income inequality of China's economic reforms, such as dismantling of market barriers. Some researchers suggest that the reduced politically-related rents along with free movement of factors of production after the economic reforms led to less inequality in China (Szelenyi and Mancin, 1987), while others argue that income differentials have grown with increasing income from property rights, profits from private enterprises, and a regressive rather than progressive system of net taxation, as well as widening wage gaps (Tsui, 1991; Khan *et al.*, 1993). Tisdell (1993) suggested that the centre-periphery paradigm was relevant in analysing China's recent regional development. Jian *et al.* (1996) noticed that real income across provinces in China did not change in the period 1952–1965, but regional inequality increased between 1965 and 1978, but then started to equalise initially from 1979 onwards with economic reform, which raised rural productivity. However, regional income started to diverge again from 1990 onwards because the growth of the coastal area was markedly faster than that of the interior.

Closer examination reveals that diminution of income differentials occurred during the period 1979 to 1984 across China, principally as the result of shrinking income difference between the rural and urban areas (Adelman and Sunding, 1987; Tsui, 1991). The reforms commenced with the implementation of the "household responsibility system" in the countryside which encouraged rural families to increase and improve their producti ... in order to raise their income by selling a portion of their output at market price, which was higher than the contract price set by the State (Tisdell, 1993). Raising procurement prices for agricultural products in the late 1970s improved the terms of trade for agriculture and brought a significant decline in urban-rural inequality (Adelman and Sunding, 1987). Rapid growth of township and village enterprises provided employment and consequently extra income for the rural areas. Relaxation of control over factor allocation and migration permitted an exodus of surplus labour from the agriculture sector, whose income from the industrial and service sectors contributed to higher rural incomes. Income in rural China grew rapidly with freer allocation of resources by individual households and the ending of the policy of depriving the agriculture sector to benefit heavy industry.

Although inequality between rural and urban areas decreased from 1979 to 1984 and led to lower income inequality across China, this inequality subsequently increased. The terms of trade for agriculture deteriorated from around 1984 and urban incomes increased rapidly, reversing the earlier trend (Tsui, 1991). Khan *et al.* (1993) argued that while inequality in the distribution of income within rural and within urban China is less than that for most developing countries, the distribution of income in the nation as a whole is more unequal now than in other Asian developing countries because of the large difference between income in rural and urban areas. There was also a growing consensus among observers that the benefits of reform were not equally distributed throughout China (Khan *et al.*, 1993).

Fiscal decentralisation is considered to have contributed to growing interregional inequalities in China (West and Wong, 1995). This is because, instead of extracting large surpluses from the rich localities to transfer to poor regions as happened in the pre-reform era, the central government has reduced its capacity to effect equalisation across regions, and all the localities have moved toward a higher degree of self-financing, leading to relatively lower budgetary revenue for poor areas. Reynolds (1987) suggested that rapid international trade growth in China since 1978 exacerbated interregional inequality because, for example, the richest 15 provinces accounted for 43 percent of the population and generated 75 percent of exports, while the poorest nine provinces accounted for only 8 percent of exports yet contained 37 percent of China's population.

Inequality within China's rural sector has been changing. The World Bank found that the Gini ratio for rural China declined steadily between 1978 and 1982 but rose steadily thereafter, indicating increasing rural inequality (World Bank, 1985). Growing regional inequality in the rural sector was driven by economic reforms, which increased the share of cash income from sales of produced agricultural output and increased opportunities for non-agricultural income in the countryside. Income stratification or variation in rural areas has widened as a result of differences in location, household productivity, and non-agricultural activity, particularly that of township and village enterprises (Knight and Song, 1993; Hare, 1994).

The widening gap between the basic wage set by the State and non-wage income (including bonuses, earnings from the operation of individual enterprises plus income from property rights) also raised differences in income levels in urban areas (Tisdell, 1993). Economic reform in China has been reducing central controls on prices, input-output of enterprises, distribution and consumption of commodities, while the non-state sector, especially the private sector, has been growing quickly, leading to greater disparity in both personal income and regional productive capacity.

Increasing disparities in income and other economic variables both within and between regions since 1984 have been accompanied by rising income inequality within and between rural and urban areas, and rising income inequality within and between coastal and interior China (Zhang and Tam, 1991; Tsui, 1991; Jones, 1995). Chen and Fleisher (1996) argue that there was convergence of per capita income within the coastal and non-coastal groups between 1978 and 1993, but not between them. By using an augmented Swan-Solow growth model, they predicted that China's overall regional inequality was likely to decline modestly but that the income differential between the coast and non-coastal regions was likely to increase. The increasing economic inequality between coastal and inland regions has been discussed from a variety of angles (Reynolds, 1987; Tsui, 1991; Hare, 1994). The widening economic gap between coastal and non-coastal regions has become one of the most noted phenomena in the study of regional economic inequality in China. The relative economic position of these two areas of China will now be considered.

3.4   Inequality Between Coastal and Inland Areas

3.4.1   Growing income disparity between the coastal and inland areas

China's coastal area consists of three municipalities and nine provinces, namely Liaoning, Hebei, Beijing, Tianjin, Shandong, Jiangsu, Shanghai, Zhejiang, Fujian, Guangdong, Guangxi and Hainan provinces (Taiwan is not included in this study). The remaining 18 localities are grouped as the inland area, also referred to as the interior or non-coastal area. Some researchers prefer to call those the East and West regions (Chai, 1994). The shaded region in Fig. 3.1 shows the 12 municipalities and provinces conventionally considered to be coastal ones. The "coastal" region constitutes the economic core of China. Please note that Hainan was separated from Guangdong in 1988 to become a Province, and figures presented in this book for Hainan before 1988 are estimated unless otherwise stated. Although Chongqing was declared in 1997 a municipality directly under the ruling of the central government instead of Sichuan Province, it is treated as part of Sichuan in this book to keep data consistency.

This spatial division into those coastal and inland areas is used by the Chinese government in its official publications as well as its five-year plans (Liu and Zhang, 1987).

The practice of dividing China into major regions started in 1949 in order to implement the policies of the central government. Four stages of regionalisation either by political need or level of economic development have been observed in China (Liu and Zhang, 1987). The first stage was from 1949 to the middle 1950s when China was roughly divided into only the coastal and inland areas according to the difference in their economic strength, a situation left from the past when the coast developed early industry and high productivity. The second stage commenced in 1958 when

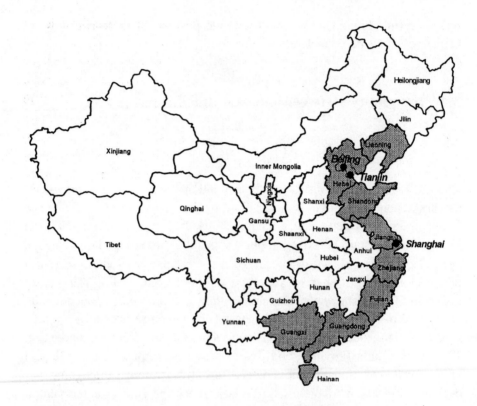

Fig. 3.1 Map of China in which the "coastal" region is shaded.

the government divided China into seven administrative regions, namely northeast, north, middle north, northeast, south, northwest, and southwest areas. In the early 1960s, China was divided into three frontiers, with heavy investment in the "third frontier" (the rural areas in the southwest) as a strategy to counteract the possibility of attack during the cold war, and the coastal area as the first frontier was neglected for the reason of its close vicinity to the then potential enemies of the US and the former Soviet Union. The fourth stage, starting in the middle 1980s, was to divide China into three regions including the East coast (which coincides with the "coastal area"), middle inland and the West.

A retrospective examination of China's regional development indicates that industrialisation started from the East coast in the middle of the 19th century when China was forced to open up to the outside world and accept the spread of industrialisation from Western countries. Agricultural production, manufacturing industries, textile industries, silk and flour industries, were established mainly in the Yangtze River Delta with Shanghai as the centre, and the Pearl River Delta with Guangzhou as the centre. Metallurgical, chemical, and machinery industries concentrated in the Northeastern region with Shenyang as the centre, whereas Qingdao and Tianjin were centres for coal and iron mining, chemical and textile industries (Liu and Zhang, 1987). Before the establishment of the People's Republic of China in 1949, the East coast had become the economic centre of China with light industry and commerce in the Yangtze River area and heavy industry in the Northeastern region.

Uneven distribution of resources between different regions is a basic feature of China's reality. Jia and Tisdell (1996) suggested that its coastal area is rich in human resources and technological capability, with high levels of productivity, high living standards, and a rapid rate of capital accumulation. Although the coastal region is endowed with the advantages mentioned above, it is handicapped by lower per capita mineral resources, but this is more than compensated for by price distortions in the Chinese economy favouring processing industries along the coast. The coastal region supports around 40 percent of China's population on 14 percent of the nation's land area, and has been producing over half of China's national income in recent years (SSB, various years). Table 3.1 compares major socio-economic features of the coast and the interior.

Table 3.1 Economic and demographic indicators for the "coastal" region of China as a percentage of those for China as a whole.

	GDP	Population	GDP per capita
1992	57	41	138
1995	58.33	41.26	141

Source: SSB, various years.

GDP per capita for the coastal area was over 30 percent higher than the national average. Table 3.1 also indicates that the gap between the coastal and non-coastal area has expanded slightly. However, the measure of GDP does not reflect the real income remaining after net inter-regional private and public transfer. Chai (1994) made use of the price-level corrected national income utilised (NIU) to compare the average per capita income of the East and the West, concluding that the average income of the East region was only 50 percent higher than that of the Western region in 1978, but was twice as much as that of the West in 1991, resulting on average in over a 2 percent per year increase in the East-West income-gap during that period of time.

3.4.2 Principal reasons for the expanding disparity between coastal and inland China

The reasons for the widening economic gap between China's coastal and non-coastal area are complicated. As stated by Chen and Fleisher (1996), "currently wealthy provinces, for example, Shanghai and Guangdong, are also those offering better access to the transportation facilities that facilitate both exports and domestic sales. Being coastal provinces, they also have, through historical emigration patterns, the closest ties to overseas Chinese, who have been the most important source of direct foreign investment and business knowledge. According to conventional wisdom these ties have contributed significantly to these provinces' recent phenomenal growth rates".

Discussion of the factors contributing to this economic disparity between coastal and interior China intensified with China's economic reform commencing in 1978. The development strategy of a country dominates its regional policy. China's adoption of high growth policy in 1978 terminated its heavy industry development policy. Hence, the policy rooted in the "cold war" of investing in inland China in order to build up the "third frontier" to avoid potential attack from the Pacific shifted to the "ladder step" doctrine with the commencement of China's economic reforms. The "ladder step" doctrine postulates that optimal investment allocation is to the regions where capital productivity is highest and that development efforts should maximise regional comparative advantage by concentrating in the East coast, or the top ladder, where higher capital productivity occurs due to its inherent strong economic capacity, accessibility and externalities. Later this development should be diffused to the second and third step of the ladder, namely the central and western regions.

To institute this policy, the "top ladder" not only had restrictions on its development eliminated in China's new economic era, but had preferential policies to facilitate its high growth. Four Special Economic Zones along the East coast were established beginning in August 1980, and 14 coastal cities were opened in April 1984. The Yangtze River Delta, the Pearl River Delta and the Minnan Delta (in south Fujian Province) were opened in 1985. Economic development zones were established in Shandong Peninsula and Liaodong Peninsula (in East Liaoning Province) and later extended to the entire coastal area (Hu, 1989: 113). Preferential investment and taxation policies were implemented in these areas, accompanied by flexible employment policies, more powerful and efficient local bureaucracy, heavy national investment in infrastructure, and so on, reinforcing the advantages of the coastal area in attracting investment and accelerating economic growth.

The Maoist development strategy sought regional industrial balance and political benefits by directing a large proportion of state investment into the interior from 1949 to 1979. Almost two-thirds of the major investment was allocated to the interior during the first 5-year plan (or "15", from 1953 to 1957), with 472 out of the 694 national projects for that period located in the interior. About 44.1 percent of the total national investment was in the inland during "25", and it increased to 68.5 and 57.5 percent respectively during "35" and "45" (Yang, 1990). However, although a basic production structure was established from 1949 to the late 1970s relying on heavy state investment in the inland areas, this "blood transfusion" to the inland areas did not alter the low economic efficiency of industries in these areas. For example, the so-called "third front" program — largely a defence-related plan was implemented from 1964 till the late 1970s. Highly centralised and requiring enormous state investment, it utilised two-thirds of the nation's entire industrial budget for the construction of large scale, remotely located factories which offered little to develop local economies. Some provinces, such as Guizhou, became even more vertically oriented and dependent on the state as a result of misdirected state investment. The ability of capital to produce a profit in the inland areas was only a fraction of that in the coastal areas. For example, the profit earned per hundred yuan of investment in Shanghai in 1978 was 12 times that for Inner Mongolia, 9.8 times that of Guizhou, and 6 times that of Shanxi (SSB, 1985). Both capital and skilled personnel from the East coast were diverted to support various inland projects, leaving old industrial plants on the coast short of necessary inputs for further development, and the competition among plants with similar requirements for factors of production, especially raw materials, became so serious that some big plants on the coast had to operate at half capacity (Yang, 1990).

This trend of investment in favour of inland China was reversed from 1979 onwards when the government abandoned its "balanced" growth strategy. Reform was accompanied by decentralisation of economic control and reduced barriers to the movement of goods and factors of production, leading to accelerated growth in areas where inputs have higher productivity — the East coast. The coastal regions were favoured by both domestic and overseas investment. They received over 90 percent of the US$68 million foreign direct investment (FDI) in China over the period of 1979 to 1990 (SSB, 1991) as well as more than half of the domestic investment. The East coast attracted investment due to its business environment, high favourable externalities, accessibility, overseas connections and its geographical proximity to China's major overseas investors. The realised foreign direct investment (FDI) received by the coastal region in 1995 was over seven times that of the interior (SSB, 1996). Recent statistics reveal that China has approved a total of 120,000 foreign-funded enterprises with a total foreign investment of US$135 billion, but the central and western parts of China obtained less than 10 percent of the total volume, and the average amount of investment per project in the inland is only US$847,000, less than the national average of US$1.37 million as a result of labour-intensive processing projects in the inland (Anon, 1996b).

The income tax rate for Special Economic Zones was in the early 1990s 15 percent, and 24 percent for coastal open cities, but 33 percent for most inland areas. The coastal areas were empowered to make decisions on projects involving less than US$30 million foreign investment, but only up to US$10 million in the inland (Yin and Li, 1995). In addition, fewer industries in the inland are allowed to use foreign capital than on the East coast. In addition, China's ongoing financial reforms have restricted the ability and willingness of banks to extend new loans in regions where default rates on old loans are unacceptably high as is the case in much of inland China (Chen and Fleisher, 1996). To enhance the investment environment in the coastal area, local authorities are given an increasing share of taxation revenue and other types of income to improve infrastructure.

Fiscal decentralisation and change in redistribution policy after 1978 severely eroded the ability of the central government to redistribute financial resources to the interior. During the Mao Regime, under the fiscal system of "Tong shou tong zhi" (control over revenue and spending), the central government extracted a large proportion of revenue collected from provinces with high incomes through differential revenue-sharing rates with the individual provinces, and distributed some of these funds as subsidies to the poor localities, mostly located in the interior. For example, Shanghai and Liaoning kept only 10 percent and 18 percent of their revenues in 1972, respectively, whereas Yunnan, Guizhou, Guangxi, Anhui, Xinjiang, Qinghai, Gansu and Tibet retained all their revenues and received subsidies from the central government (Lardy, 1978). The new fiscal responsibility system implemented after 1978 allows a surplus province to contribute a fixed amount of its revenue to the central government and a deficit province to receive a fixed amount of subsidy, no matter how big its actual deficit. Consequently, the degree to which inter-provincial transfers can level the distribution of consumption relative to production and to transfer investment funds away from the coast to the interior has been undermined. Coastal provincial governments can use their newly gained budgetary authority and provincial monetary surplus to develop their localities instead of remitting a large portion of their provincial income to the central government to support regions with lower productivity. Chai (1994) argued that the rate of extraction from the surplus Eastern region had declined drastically since 1978, but the rate of subsidy has increased very little for the Western provinces, adding to economic disparity between these two regions as well as encouraging localism or even duplications of investment.

There are some other factors that also influence the East-West disparity. (1) The non-state sector, consisting of the collective and private sectors, is located mainly along the coast and this sector grew twice as fast as the state sector in the 1980s (Yang, 1990). This helped to increase the relative economic strength of the coastal region. Coastal areas account for more than half of all employees and three-quarters of the operating revenue of township and village enterprises in China (Hare, 1994). (2) There are sharp differences in labour supply and demand conditions between the coastal and interior regions in China as a consequence of uneven regional economic growth and population distribution since the early 1980s. The demand for labour has been relatively strong in the coastal areas, particularly in the large cities and the Special Economic Zones, whereas the reverse is the case in the interior (Yeh, 1996). Inland China is to a great extent a primary producer, while the coastal area is a secondary producer, hence the generally increasing gap of labour productivity between the agricultural and non-agricultural sector from the early 1980s, accompanied by a faster rate of employment shift out of the primary sector along the coast, results in increasingly lower annual value-added per employee in the interior compared to the coastal area (Chai, 1994). (3) The export-orientated strategy in the reform era benefits the coastal region more than the interior because of the easier accessibility of the East coast to China's main international markets. This gives the coast an advantage in comparison to the interior in obtaining imports and raw materials and in exports of products from China.

3.5   Does Regional Inequality Need to be Considered for Policy Purposes?

As discussed earlier in this chapter, economists have diverse opinions about whether elimination of regional economic disparity is desirable and whether it occurs naturally. Contrary to neoclassical economic theory which assumes that income distribution will be reduced through market forces as resources relocate to reflect the marginal productivity of factors of production, studies have indicated that this does not always happen because of market imperfections, social impediments, regional imbalances or other reasons. A "steady state" of income distribution which does not reflect marginal productivity can exist as a result of market imperfections (Kaldor, 1955), and many governments show little sign of interest or competence in remedying regional inequalities (Jones, 1991).

All land and resource development has a spatial dimension. The integration of space into development analysis has come to be acknowledged as a significant extension of traditional ways of thinking. As proposed by Higgins (1988):

> "One might conclude that any nation wishing to reduce regional disparities should adopt policies designed to accelerate growth of the national economy; or one might conclude that in order to accelerate growth of the national economy, one should adopt policies designed to reduce regional gaps. It is not easy to demonstrate the validity of one of these conclusions and the invalidity of the other. Indeed, both may be true; diminishing regional gaps and higher rates of growth may reinforce each other. My own historical studies of interactions between regional and national development, however, lead me to believe that the more unshakable truth lies in the second proposition."

On *a priori* grounds, it may be expected that labour flows could be more equilibrating than capital flows because labour tends to move from low to high income regions, which offer higher money wages and greater employment opportunities. However, against the conventional impression that capital tends to move from higher income to lower income areas, it may "tend to flow in the opposite direction since investment opportunities (certainly when viewed subjectively) may be greater in the high income region. In this case, capital flows will be disequilibrating, accelerating the rate of growth in the richer regions and slowing it down in the poorer one .... If capital flows are disequilibrating and if equilibrium growth is the objective, it will be necessary to intervene to make capital flow from high to low income regions" (Richardson, 1969: 330). Studies have shown that returns on investment are higher in the metropolitan areas than in small towns or in rural areas in China (Jones, 1991). As a consequence, unless initial regional income levels are identical, equal growth rates will widen absolute income differentials across regions. Greater regional inequality is expected when growth rates are higher for the relatively more developed areas due to their strong attractiveness for inputs.

Regional development policy seeks the attainment of social objectives throughout terrestrial space. As argued by Chai (1994): "The issue of widening income gap between East and West China poses a serious threat to the stability of China's economic reform program and hence her prospect of becoming Asia's next economic giant and the world's new growth centre. It is well know that the Eastern region is mainly populated by the Han Chinese whereas the Western region mainly by the ethnic minorities. As the experience of the former Soviet Union and Yugoslavia show, the rising income disparity between the Han Chinese and the ethnic minorities is likely to fuel the ethnic conflict generated by the increased democratisation and local aspiration under the reforms".

Perroux (1970) pointed out that "growth does not appear everywhere at the same time. It becomes manifest at points or poles of growth with variable intensity; it spreads through different channels, with variable terminal effects on the whole of the economy". He further suggests that imbalances are a natural phenomenon in the growth process, and some areas serve as centres or poles, from which centrifugal forces emanate and to which centripetal forces are attracted. The link between the location of economic activities and the development of a system of regions, or the micro- and macro-levels of economic performance, should be stressed because both point locations and regional systems are covered in growth pole studies (Friedman, 1985). Perroux's concept of regional difference originated from the normal economic environment of the market system, in which certain industries or regions perform better than others due to some advantages with which they are endowed (Perroux, 1988). In places where markets are incomplete and hence cannot work on the entire economy, as in the case of China, regional disparity is then a combination of natural economic factors and policy influences. For example, China's mounting regional inequality is in fact a result of a variety of factors many of which are of a political rather than of an economic nature. Hu Angang, an outspoken Chinese economist, warned of the dangers of the creation of wealthy provinces, which may not share the fruits of their economic success with Beijing and the underdeveloped inland area (Hu, 1995).

Although regional disparity is sometimes regarded as a natural con-sequence of economic development, regional disparities create social and political problems that must be addressed in any democratic society, and especially so in a country where the gaps among regions correspond closely to provinces and municipalities. Uneven regional and urban development is necessary in many circumstances to maximise national product if the marginal product of a resource is to be equalised for all regions (Tisdell, 1993). However, in many developing economies, where there is no completely free movement of factors of production, and the national economy is heavily influenced by public policies, deteriorating income inequality within a nation may threaten the long-term political stability or social goals.

"The goals of rational spatial policy should be the creation of truly functional economic areas, which will provide employment opportunities not merely in primary production (farming, mining, forestry, fishing) but in industry and in service activities, thus utilising to the full the varied potential productivity of a work force. Furthermore, by creating a sense of "community" there can be a far better protection of regional economy than is possible if "outside" enterprises without any local roots "mine" the natural resources and pollute the rivers and the air" (Johnson, 1970: 419). It may take longer for the economy to generate adequate spread effects, and inequality will persist in the economy if backwash effects dominate in the economy (Myrdal, 1957). Reduction of chronic regional socioeconomic disparity does not seem to be a high policy priority in many large developing countries where many other socioeconomic problems are usually present. Nevertheless, growing regional inequality needs to be seriously addressed in China.

When the market system is not very well established, as is still the situation in today's China, the conditions for the "inverted-U" paradigm are not satisfied. Since increasing regional inequality has become a political threat to the China (Hu, 1995), some policies seem to be required in order to reduce regional disparity. Patterns of development for densely settled regions, such as linking urban and rural areas very closely, as pioneered in Japan and Taiwan, and encouraging off-farming activities that involve an alternative development spectrum of employment opportunities in the rural areas, have provided another model that does not necessarily require high levels of urbanisation (Jones, 1991). While this type of linkage has not been a specific focus of policies in China, rural industrialisation in the form of township and village enterprises has been encouraged. This together with the household responsibility farming system has increased rural income. The slogan "leave agriculture but not the village" has obtained force in China.

Increasing regional and sectoral inequality since the late 1970s and its possible influence on social and economic stability have become serious concerns in China. China's shift from fostering inland development to encouraging coastal development appeared to be based partly on a choice of faster growth now over improved equity. In a study on the level and quality of service provision in China, West and Wong (1995) found that there is large disparity across regions with service provision in poorer regions falling far short of desired targets. Regional disparities "not only directly affect the welfare and living standard of the populace, but also the lower investment in human resources in poor provinces such as Guizhou is likely to doom their economies to a lower growth path unless corrective action is taken".

The increasing economic gap between coastal and interior China makes the minorities, who live mostly in the interior, more disadvantaged compared to the Han Chinese. There are 55 minority nationalities recognised by the Chinese government. With an overall population of over 73 million in 1995, they account for 6 percent of China's total population, but the areas where they live make up well over half of China's total area. "The importance of the minorities to China's long-term development is disproportionate to their population" (Gladney, 1994: 185). The concept of autonomy has been defined in the 1982 Constitution and the Law on Regional Autonomy for Minority Nationalities implemented in 1984. The disparity between Han and minority is even greater than that for the economy because of a dominance of Han people even in minority areas. There was a major conference on disparities between the East coast and the minority areas in 1995 and most delegates saw economic backwardness as affecting social stability (Hu, 1995). With memory of disturbances in the minority areas, China has been trying to reduce tensions and possible disintegration through policies aimed at accelerating economic growth in minority areas, including a flexible and light taxation system, price subsidies and priority in the appropriations to local governments. Nevertheless, with economic growth in China, regional disparity in China increased in the 1990s. Income inequality between the Han and minority areas rose, as did that between the minority areas (Mackerras, 1996). In addition, environmental degradation is threatening the sustainability of income in minority areas (Longworth and Williamson, 1993).

It has become urgent to identify policies that have the potential to reduce regional inequality in China. Although the Ninth 5-Year Plan (1996–2000), adopted in September 1995, included the amelioration of regional income disparity as one of its key targets, it is difficult to implement policies to reduce regional disparity in China. This is because policy-makers believe that there is incompatibility between efficiency and equity goals, and it is not clear what aspects of equity society prefers. Consequently, "equity-efficiency and spatial policy have to be viewed in the rather messy reality of politics and administration, where corruption, political patronage and sheer inefficiency are part of the everyday reality of planning" (Jones, 1991). However, China is unlikely to revert to a regional economic development policy which overtly favours inland areas as it did in the Maoist era. To do so would be at odds with its post-reform emphasis on the pursuit of economic efficiency and China's desire to make greater use of market systems. Nevertheless for political reasons, it cannot ignore the economic backwardness of its interior. But some compromise is possible within the new economic paradigm. For instance, the development of industries may be envisaged which are profitable for China but in which the inland has a comparative advantage. In such a case, economic efficiency will not be compromised by equity considerations. Some types of tourism may satisfy these conditions. In Yunnan Province, for example, tourism has been selected as a key industry for economic development. Some provinces and local governments have selected growth pole theories as a guide in policy making. The growth pole paradigm and its role in promoting economic growth in the less developed areas, especially in the non-coastal and rural regions, need to be carefully discussed, and this is done in Chapter 9.

3.6   Concluding Remarks

Post-Maoist economic policy for development has been concentrating development on the coast in the hope that this development will radiate out to China's interior at a later stage. High growth policy can be compatible with regional equity in the long run because it has the capacity to improve labour productivity and employment, to generate redistribution benefits to the lagging areas, and to modernise industrial structure for the entire nation. Because China has chosen a regionally unbalanced growth strategy since 1978 as its development strategy, regional disparity is unavoidable at the early stage of its economic development according to economic theories. However, there is little sign that benefits from growth along the coast have diffused widely. Instead, it has been noticed that the spread effect from the coastal to the interior area appears to have been limited during the post-Maoist period (Jia and Tisdell, 1996). The reasons for this lack of trickling-down effects in the Chinese economy since 1978 are complicated.

Excessive regional inequality is a hurdle to the integration and further economic growth of China as a whole. The issue of how to reduce the gaps between coastal and inland China needs to be discussed urgently. While economists disagree on the likely directions of inequality at a later stage of economic growth, the hope that economic growth will naturally trickle down to the interior over time may not be satisfied. Hence, selection of proper economic strategies seems to be necessary for achieving the goal of narrowing regional disparity. However, instead of stripping privileges from special economic zones to prevent the growing gap between the rich and poor widening further, as suggested by some Chinese economists (McGregor, 1996b), assisting China's inland to develop industries in which it has a comparative advantage may serve as a better alternative in reducing regional disparity. For example, the interior region of China may have a comparative advantage in catering for some types of tourism, for example, ecotourism or culturally-based tourism. Development of such types of tourism would then have the advantages just mentioned.

From this chapter, it can be seen that China's regional development has been very uneven with its inland economically deprived compared to its coastal region. Furthermore, its reform policies have favoured the economic growth of its coastal regions. But the spread of benefits from economic growth in its coastal region to the inland have been slow and weaker than hoped. This has presented China with a political dilemma. This bind may cause political instability (and certainly causes dissatisfaction in its interior) where minority populations are relatively high. At the same time the Chinese government no longer favours state intervention in resource allocation and is increasingly reluctant to alter income distribution directly or is more restricted in its possibilities for doing so. This leaves the Chinese government with few options for supporting economic development in the interior and supplementing incomes there. Nevertheless one option may be to encourage the development of profitable industries in which the interior has a comparative economic advantage, if not in relation to the industry as a whole, then significant portions. The tourism industry may be one such industry. But we need to know much more about the regional and geographical spread of tourism and its attraction to different locations before we can assess the potential of the development of the tourism industry to assist in the above respect. We need to ask questions such as the following: Does tourism favour centralised or decentralised economic development? Where does tourism concentrate geographically? Is it urban-centric or rural-centric? Does tourism in China concentrate on the coast rather than inland? Does its expansion in China favour coastal or inland areas? To what extent has the inland benefited from the growth of tourism in China? What types of tourism are attracted to China's inland? Can some inland areas successfully use the tourism industry as a key industry or growth pole for their economic development? These are all the questions which will be considered in subsequent chapters.

Chapter 4

Spatial Distribution of Tourism in China: Its Nature, Determinants and Consequences

4.1 Introduction

China's tourism industry is a large and rapidly growing one. In the second half of the 1990s, it accounted for about five percent of China's GDP (SSB, 1997). In view of the size and potential "fluidity" of the tourism industry, it clearly has considerable potential to influence regional economic development. Furthermore, it is an industry worth studying in its own right. The spatial distribution of tourism is bound to play a significant role in shaping the regional distribution of the Chinese economy, especially if the multiplier effect of tourism and its influence on related industries are taken into account.

The main purpose of this chapter is to determine whether and to what extent tourism is concentrated on China's coastal region (core or economic centre) compared to its inland (its economic periphery). The spatial distribution of China's tourism industry is analysed in order to understand whether the development of tourism in China in recent times has seemingly added to or ameliorated the regional inequality across China, and particularly between its coastal and inland region. The spatial distribution pattern of tourism in China is analysed by using indicators from both the tourism demand- and supply-side. Gini coefficients, Lorenz curves, regression analysis, and other statistical analyses are used. The spatial inequality of tourism in China is measured and socio-economic reasons for this inequality are considered. The analysis in this chapter is focussed on the spatial distribution of inbound tourism in 1986. As will be apparent from Chapter 5, which includes data for 1998 and other years, the basic spatial pattern has not altered although some trends in the skew are apparent.

The spatial distribution of demand-side tourist indicators such as number of tourists, tourist receipts and so on, are considered first, followed by the distribution of supply-side tourism variables such as number of hotel rooms, number of hotel employees and number of employees in tourism. China's 12 coastal localities are compared with the remainder of China (its inland) in the initial analysis.

It should be noted that two competing hypotheses exist in the literature about the impact of tourism on economic decentralisation. One view is that it promotes decentralisation (Sessa, 1983; Yannapoulos, 1988) and rural development (Christaller, 1963). An alternative view is that it fosters economic centralisation because it favours urban centres and centres of economic growth (McKee and Tisdell, 1990). Empirical results for Malaysia (Oppermann, 1992b), New Zealand (Pearce, 1990), and Turkey (Tosun, 1999) favour the hypothesis that tourism is a centralising force. Here it will be shown that the empirical results for China favour the centralisation hypothesis as far as inbound tourism is concerned. Furthermore, inbound tourism shows greater relative concentration in the centre compared to the periphery than economic activity as a whole.

4.2 Distribution of Demand-Side Factors in China's International Tourism

Tourism models concentrating on spatial aspects of tourism are concerned with the origin-destination linkage and emphasise destinations and spatial scale, along with demand and income generation. From the viewpoint of geography, four categories of models are identified: travel and tourism space, origin-destination, tourism industry core-periphery models and dynamic models. Core-periphery models often analyse the influence and control of multinational companies (Hills and Lundgren, 1977). However, these models usually ignore tourism distribution within countries because they concentrate on differences between industrial and developing countries. By contrast, a major focus of this book is the distribution of tourism within China.

Overseas tourists are attracted to China by curiosity, by its amazing cultural heritage, by the opportunity to visit relatives and to do business. After the implementation of the "open door" policy in China in 1979, all the 30 localities of China, including three municipalities, 22 provinces and five autonomous regions, considered tourism to be a powerful foreign-exchange earner, and the supply of tourist facilities increased accordingly. International recognition for tourism resources in China reached its zenith in 1991 when UNESCO issued the World Heritage List Certificate for seven sites in China, namely the Great Wall, the Palace Museum, the Mausoleum of Qin Shi Huang, Mount Taishan, Mount Huangshan, the Peking Man Site, and the Dunhuang Grottoes.

It is the distribution of tourism across regions, especially between the East coast and the interior that is the focus of this chapter. Table 4.1 provides

Table 4.1 Economic, demographic, and demand-side indicators for 12 coastal regions in China with comparisons for the whole of China, 1995.

	China total	Sum of the 12 coastal localities	The proportion of the 12 to the total for China
Socioeconomic indicators:			
GDP	5,763.3 (billion yuan)	3,361.5 (billion yuan)	0.583
Population	1,202.2 (m)	496 (m)	0.413
GDP per head	4,794 (yuan)	6,777.5 (yuan)	1.414
Tourism indicators on the demand side:			
Tourism receipts	8,249.9 (US$ m)	7,213.3 (US$ m)	0.874
No. of inbound tourists	17,281,300	13,775,900	0.797
Number of tourist per 1,000	14.37	27.77	1.93
Tourism receipts per capita	6.86 ($)	15.4 ($)	2.24
Hotel revenue	63,608 (yuan m)	56,038 (yuan m)	0.881

Source: Based on data in NTA (1996) and SSB (1996).

data on the demand-side indicators of international tourism in China and 12 coastal areas. For comparative purposes, socio-economic data are expressed in similar terms.

In this book, note that "tourism receipts" refers to the income in foreign currencies earned from providing services and commodities to inbound visitors in China. "Tourist arrivals" or "number of tourists" coincides with the concept of "arrivals of tourists from abroad" (WTO, 1992), including foreigners, overseas Chinese who hold Chinese passports, and compatriots who live in Hong Kong, Macau and Taiwan. "Tourist nights" means the accumulated number of nights tourists stay in China's hotels.

Table 4.1 indicates that China's 12 coastal localities account for a much higher proportion of its tourism receipts (0.874), number of inbound tourists (0.797) and hotel revenue (0.881) than they do for GDP (0.583) and population (0.413). Their tourism receipts per capita are more than twice those for China as a whole, whereas their GDP per capita is not quite one and a half of that for all China. Thus there is *prima facie* evidence that demand-side tourism variables are *even more biased* in favour of the coastal areas than are the socio-economic variables. Therefore, international tourism in China is reinforcing relative regional economic inequality rather than reducing it.

Large disparities exist between coastal and inland China for the demand-side tourist indicators (Table 4.1). Twelve coastal regions obtained most of China's tourism receipts and account for most of China's tourist arrivals. The direct economic impact of inbound tourism to China appears to favour the coastal area most markedly. Hence, tourism to coastal China exhibits greater concentration than the already skewed distribution of general economic activity towards the coastal areas as discussed in Chapter 3. Out of the 13 localities with tourism receipts of over US$100 in 1995, only three were in the interior, namely Yunnan (8th), Shaanxi (10th) and Sichuan (12th). In 1995, only 2 out of the 15 cities receiving more than 200,000 international tourists were inland cities (NTA, 1996). A complication that needs to be pointed out is that China's statistical data for cities sometimes include nearby counties under city-administration. Consequently, tourism receipts for cities also include some income earned by rural places. It is hard to say what proportion of tourism receipts earned by cities should be considered as rural tourist income, but it is still clear that most tourism income in China is concentrated in its cities. China's tourism is to a considerable extent urban-centric.

International tourism demand is heavily concentrated in a few coastal cities. Eight coastal cities, namely Beijing, Shanghai, Shenzhen, Guangzhou, Zhuhai, Xiamen, Quanzhou and Hangzhou, accounted for 63.71 percent of the total tourism receipts and 53.2 percent of total international tourists in 1995 (NTA, 1996). Eleven out of the 13 cities with over US$100 million in tourism receipts in 1996 were coastal cities. Together their total tourist receipts in 1996 were US$5.45 billion, accounting for 51 percent of that for the whole country (NTA, 1997). The only two non-coastal cities in the above category were Xian and Kunming. City-based tourism is also dominant in inland provinces such as Guizhou, where Guiyang, its capital city, accounted for 72.4 percent and the second largest city, Anshun, accounted for 21.4 percent of its inbound tourists, respectively, in 1993. Guiyang retained 94.1 percent of the income from inbound tourists and 94.3 percent of domestic tourism revenue (NTA, 1994). In addition, Xian (the capital city of Shaanxi) and Kunming (the capital city of Yunnan) accounted together for 22 percent of receipts and 21 percent of tourists respectively for the entire inland regions in 1996 (NTA, 1997).

In short, international tourism demand in China demonstrates predominant concentration in the 12 coastal localities, especially coastal cities. Inland and rural areas are less able to attract tourists. The next section will consequently discuss the spatial distribution of tourism facilities in China in order to compare tourism demand and supply in China.

4.3 Distribution of Supply-Side Tourism Factors in China

Now consider the spatial distribution of tourism facilities in China. Table 4.2 gives major indicators for tourist supply in the coastal and in the inland region. "Hotel rooms" refers to actual number of hotel rooms that are suitable for international tourists, and "hotel beds" indicates the aggregate number of beds available in these hotel rooms.

Table 4.2 Supply-side indicators and some ratios of China's international tourism, 1995.

	China total	Sum 12 coastal localities	The proportion of the 12 to the total for China	Sum of 18 inland localities	The proportion of the 18 to the total for China
Supply-side tourism indicators:					
Hotel rooms	486,054	336,907	0.693	149,147	0.307
State-owned hotel room	311,360	1901,34	0.61	121,226	0.39
Proportion of state hotel rooms	0.64	0.56	NA	0.81	NA
Hotels with more than 500 rooms	73	67	0.918	6	0.082
No. of tourism employees	1,115,800	835,600	0.75	280,200	0.25
No. of hotel employees	868,600	662,800	0.76	205,800	0.24
No. of state hotel employees	509,001	348,580	0.68	160,421	0.32
No. of travel agencies	3,826	2,384	0.623	1,442	0.377
1st category travel agencies	360	257	0.714	103	0.286
Relevant ratios:					
Hotel revenue per room	0.131 (US$ m/room)	0.162 (US$ m/room)	1.24	0.061 (US$ /room)	0.47
Hotel revenue per employee	73200 ($)	82140 ($)	1.12	44510 ($)	0.61
Net profit per hotel employee	4,800 (yuan)	5,100 (yuan)	NA	–1,430 (yuan)	NA
Fixed asset per hotel employee	125.7 (1,000 yuan)	137.18 (1,000 yuan)	1.09	88.81 (1000 yuan)	0.71

Source: Calculated from SSB, 1996.

Supply of tourism facilities and services is concentrated on the coastal areas according to Table 4.2. Sixty nine percent of hotel rooms and 76 percent of hotel employees were distributed in the coastal areas in 1995, along with 75 percent of the total employees working in international tourism. These proportions changed to 70, 73 and 72 respectively in 1996 (NTA, 1997). Table 4.2 indicates that hotels in the coastal area had superior economic performance compared to their interior competitors. The coastal areas manifested greater labour productivity, or hotel revenue per hotel employee, higher revenue per room, and higher net profit per hotel employee in 1995 than the interior. Hotel occupancy rates and the proportion of star-rated hotel rooms were also higher for coastal areas (NTA, 1997). It follows that the coastal areas have an above average income per hotel room in China and more tourists per hotel employee. Furthermore, tourist receipts in the coastal area per inhabitant are about twice those for China as a whole, as is the number of tourists per inhabitant of the coastal area (NTA, 1990–1997). Thus, all relevant tourist indicators show considerable skew in favour of the coastal area of China compared to the inland.

Comparing Tables 4.2 and 4.1, it is obvious that tourism supply-side indicators are more biased towards China's coastal localities than some major socio-economic indicators. Whereas the 12 coastal localities accounted for 58.3 percent of China's GDP and 41.3 percent of its population, they contained 69.3 percent of hotel rooms in China, 91.8 percent of the larger sized hotels (hotels with over 500 rooms), 76 percent of the hotel employees and 75 percent of employees in the international tourism in China (Tables 4.1 and 4.2).

Coastal areas obtained the major fraction of economic benefits from China's inbound tourism in 1995, such as receipts (87.4 percent) and tourist arrivals (79.7 percent), and the majority of input, including employment (75 percent) and travel agencies (62.3 percent). Twelve coastal areas obtained 88.1 percent of the total hotel revenues from the supply of 69.3 percent of hotel rooms. Figures in other years show similar results (NTA, various years). The distribution pattern within the Chinese tourism industry indicates that the regional allocation of tourism facilities is not proportionate to economic benefits from tourism operations. The proportion of resources used by the tourism industry in the inland in relation to "economic benefits" is higher than in the coastal region.

4.4 Lorenz Curve and Gini Coefficient Analysis

4.4.1 *More sophisticated methods*

More sophisticated analysis of the regional distribution of tourism in China requires the use of more powerful techniques than those involved in the above simple comparison between the inland and coastal region. Using these techniques, each province and each administratively autonomous city, for example, Beijing, Shanghai, can be considered in the distribution as independent entities. This more sophisticated analysis makes possible the use of the Lorenz curve and the Gini coefficient, the size of which is reflected in the nature of the Lorenz curve.

As pointed out by Gunaratne (1998), many different measures of income distribution and inequality have been developed. These include distribution models by V. Pareto (the Pareto Model), O. Ammon and L. March (Gamma function), D. McAlister (Lognormal Distribution), S. Singh and G. Maddala (Singh and Maddala Model) and other researchers (Gunaratne, 1988). Measures of income inequality include the Gini coefficient, the Lorenz curve, the coefficient of variation, the variance of the logarithm of income, Theil's index, Hirschman's index, and Kolm's ratio.

All of these measures and concepts can be adopted to take account of the spatial distribution and regional inequality of tourism variables. The Lorenz curve and the Gini coefficient are selected in this chapter to analyse further the spatial distribution of tourism in China due to their analytical strength and the availability of data. Developed as measures of income inequality, they can be adapted to reflect the level of regional disparity for the distribution of tourism and other variables. The Lorenz Curve, Gini coefficient, Kakwani interpolation method, cross-sectional data and other tools can be combined to better understand the characteristics of a distribution.

It might be noted in advance, however, that the sophisticated techniques reinforce the thesis that inbound tourism to China shows a high degree of spatial inequality and is highly concentrated geographically, its main concentration being in the coastal region, the economic core of China.

4.4.2   Lorenz curve analysis

Suggested in 1905 by Lorenz, the Lorenz curve is widely used to analyse the size distribution of income and wealth. It describes the relationship between the cumulative percentages of income of persons or other entities arranged in ascending order of their income (Kakwani and Podder, 1976). Assuming a straight line approximation between any two points, the Lorenz curve plots the cumulative proportion of total income received by income earners along the vertical axis and the cumulative proportion of income earners along the horizontal axis (Lorenz, 1905). The slope of the Lorenz curve is positive and increases monotonically.

Since the Lorenz curve captures the deviation of individual incomes from perfect equality, it has been employed as a convenient graphical device to display the essence of inequality in the inter-temporal and inter-spatial distribution of wealth. When the Lorenz curve of one distribution lies strictly inside that of another, it can be safely inferred that the former is more equal than the latter; but when the Lorenz curves of two distributions intersect, it cannot be judged which of the two distributions displays greater equality using the Lorenz curve method itself, but can only be determined by subjective ranking in terms of social welfare (Gunaratne, 1988, Chapter 2). The Lorenz curve can be adapted to measure the distribution of variables other than income.

Here, the degree of inequality in the distribution of tourist receipts in China is illustrated by using a Lorenz curve. This is done by constructing a Lorenz curve depicting the distribution of receipts in 1995 by localities (regions). The 30 localities have been divided into 10 groups by the ascending distribution of the percentages of receipts they earned in 1995. Table 4.3 gives the ten groups of localities and their proportion of receipts.

If the distribution is completely even among these groups, an increase of ten percent in the relevant variable should correspond to the addition of an extra group, resulting in the diagonal as the Lorenz curve. However, since the

Table 4.3 Proportion of 1995 tourism receipts of the 30 localities (regions) of China by ascending order.

Groups	Name of localities	Share of receipts of each locality (%)	Aggregate share of each group (%)	Accumulated share of groups (%)
1	Ningxia	0.01		
	Qinghai	0.03		
	Tibet	0.14	0.18	0.18
2	Shanxi	0.25		
	Gansu	0.25		
	Jiangxi	0.30	0.8	0.98
3	Guizhou	0.35		
	Anhui	0.38		
	Jilin	0.50	1.23	2.21
4	Hebei	0.51		
	Henan	0.73		
	Heilongjiang	0.73	1.96	4.17
5	Hunan	0.79		
	Hubei	0.89		
	Xinjiang	0.90	2.58	6.75
6	Hainan	0.98		
	Inner Mongolia	1.10		
	Guangxi	1.47	3.55	10.3
7	Sichuan	1.52		
	Tianjin	1.61		
	Shaanxi	1.69	4.82	15.12
8	Shandong	1.86		
	Yunnan	2.00		
	Liaoning	2.29	6.15	21.27
9	Zhejiang	2.86		
	Jiangsu	3.15		
	Fujian	5.87	11.89	33.15
10	Shanghai	11.39		
	Beijing	26.46		
	Guangdong	29.00	66.85	100.00

Source: Calculated from NTA, 1996.

distribution can rarely be absolutely equal, a typical Lorenz curve of the distribution would be a curve falling below a 45 degrees line. The closer the Lorenz curve is to the diagonal line, the more equal the distribution, and vice versa.

The Lorenz curve for inbound tourist receipts for China in 1995, plotted on the basis of Table 4.3, is shown in Fig. 4.1 by curve OCB.

When the distribution is completely equal, the Lorenz curve corresponds to the diagonal OB, which is called the line of equality or egalitarian line. In the case of complete inequality the Lorenz curve consists of the sides OA and AB of the triangle OAB, which implies that one group receives the entire income. Greater inequality is represented by an increase in the area between the Lorenz curve and the diagonal OB, an area which represents the degree of concentration. The same exercise is conducted for the distribution of hotel rooms (Table 4.4 and Fig. 4.2) and GDP in 1995 (Table 4.5 and Fig. 4.3).

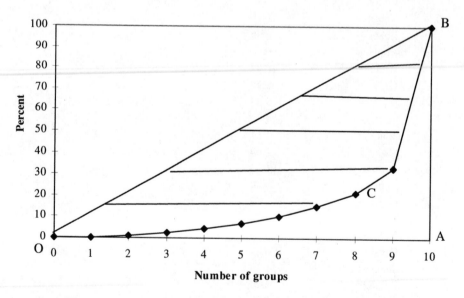

Fig. 4.1 Lorenz curve for receipts of the 30 localities (regions) of China, 1995.
Source: Based on Table 4.3.

Table 4.4 Proportion of 1995 hotel rooms of 30 localities by ascending order.

Groups	Name of localities	Share of rooms of each locality (%)	Accumulated share of each group (%)	Accumulated share of groups (%)
1	Qinghai	0.30		
	Tibet	0.37		
	Henan	0.38	1.05	1.05
2	Ningxia	0.42		
	Inner Mongolia	0.98		
	Gansu	1.04	2.44	3.49
3	Jilin	1.23		
	Shanxi	1.25		
	Tianjin	1.27	3.75	7.24
4	Xinjiang	1.43		
	Heilongjiang	1.60		
	Hunan	1.72	4.75	11.99
5	Jiangxi	1.89		
	Shaanxi	2.02		
	Hebei	2.30	6.21	18.2
6	Anhui	2.43		
	Yunnan	2.71		
	Liaoning	2.72	7.86	26.06
7	Fujian	2.83		
	Hainan	2.95		
	Guizhou	3.26	9.04	35.1
8	Guangxi	3.32		
	Hubei	3.75		
	Shandong	3.81	10.88	45.98
9	Sichuan	3.93		
	Zhejiang	4.43		
	Jiangsu	5.16	13.52	59.5
10	Shanghai	5.98		
	Beijing	10.76		
	Guangdong	23.76	40.5	100

Source: Calculated from NTA, 1996.

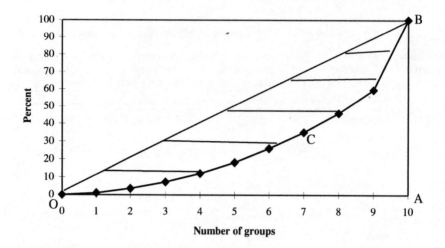

Fig. 4.2 Lorenz curve for hotel rooms of the 30 localities (regions) of China, 1995.
Source: Based on Table 4.4.

Smaller areas are found between the diagonal OB and Lorenz curve OCB in Figs. 4.2 and 4.3 respectively for hotel rooms and GDP than that in Fig. 4.1 for receipts. Both the Lorenz curves in Figs. 4.2 and 4.3 would be located inside that in Fig. 4.1. This implies that inbound tourism receipts show more regional inequality than hotel rooms. The earlier conclusion is also reinforced that the distribution of tourism is much more concentrated and regionally unequal than the distribution of economic activity. Estimates of concordance confirm that coastal concentration is the main source of this inequality.

4.4.3   Gini coefficient

The Gini ratio, as proposed by Gini in 1912, measures the relative degree of departure of a population from a state of perfect equality. It has a value of zero for absolute equality and unity for complete inequality. Gini introduced his measure of inequality as a function of the Gini mean difference, which is defined as the mathematical expectation of the absolute difference of all the possible pairs of variable-values of income, y (Gunaratne, 1988: 62).

Table 4.5 Proportion of 1995 GDP of the 30 localities (regions) of China by ascending order.

Groups	Name of localities	Share of GDP of each locality (%)	Accumulated share of each group (%)	Accumulated share of groups (%)
1	Tibet	0.10		
	Qinghai	0.29		
	Ningxia	0.29	0.68	0.68
2	Hainan	0.63		
	Gansu	0.96		
	Guizhou	1.09	2.68	3.36
3	Inner Mongolia	1.45		
	Xinjiang	1.45		
	Tianjin	1.60	4.5	7.86
4	Shaanxi	1.74		
	Shanxi	1.90		
	Jilin	1.96	5.6	13.46
5	Jiangxi	2.09		
	Yunnan	2.09		
	Beijing	2.42	6.6	20.06
6	Guangxi	2.79		
	Anhui	3.48		
	Heilongjiang	3.50	9.7	29.76
7	Fujian	3.75		
	Hunan	3.81		
	Hubei	4.15	11.71	41.47
8	Shanghai	4.27		
	Liaoning	4.85		
	Hebei	4.96	14.08	55.55
9	Henan	5.21		
	Zhejiang	6.14		
	Sichuan	6.13	17.48	73.03
10	Shandong	8.68		
	Jiangsu	8.95		
	Guangdong	9.34	26.97	100

Source: Calculated from NTA, 1996.

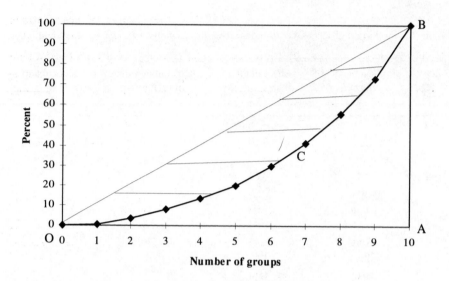

Fig. 4.3 Lorenz curve for GDP of the 30 localities (regions) of China, 1995.

Source: Based on Table 4.5.

Mathematical details about the Gini coefficient are available, for example, in Gunaratne (1998). However, in this context, it is sufficient to observe that the Gini coefficient is equal to the ratio of the area between a Lorenz curve and its diagonal, and the area of the triangle containing the Lorenz curve. For instance, in Fig. 4.3, the Gini coefficient is found by dividing the hatched area by the area of triangle OAB. The magnitude of the Gini coefficient rises with the degree of inequality of the variable under consideration, and varies between zero for complete equality to unity for the greatest possible degree of inequality. The Gini coefficient is lower the less is the concavity (bulge) of the Lorenz curve (Schnitzer, 1974).

Here observations are discrete, so Gini coefficients are estimated using the formula provided by the *Macmillan Dictionary of Modern Economics* (Pearce, 1992: 172):

$$G = 1 + (1/n) - (2/(n \times n \times y_0)) \times (y_1 + 2y_2 + 3y_3 + \ldots + ny_n)$$

where G represents the Gini coefficient, n is the number of observations, y_0 is the mean of observations, and y_1, y_2, ... to y_n represent individual observations in decreasing order of size. The calculation of Gini coefficients was done by listing groups of data for 30 localities in descending order before multiplying them by the corresponding weights valued from 1 to 30. The results are reported in Table 4.6.

Table 4.6 Gini coefficients of selected economic and tourism variables in China, 1995.

	GDP	GDP per head	No. of tourists	Tourism receipts	No. of hotel rooms	No. of hotel employees	Hotel income
Gini coefficient	0.407	0.311	0.6704	0.7439	0.5204	0.5813	0.7432

Source: Based on data in NTA (1996) and SSB (1996).

Analysis of the Gini coefficients further reinforces the fact that even though general economic activities are already unevenly distributed in China (as indicated by high Gini coefficients for GDP and GDP per capita), tourism exhibits an even higher regional disparity. Demand-side indicators for tourism in China display a higher regional disparity than that for general economy and that for the supply of tourism facilities and services.

While the same Gini coefficient can correspond to diverse distribution patterns, the concentration pole can be determined by examining the Gini coefficient together with Tables 4.3 to 4.5. This clearly demonstrates the concentration of the relevant variables on the coastal areas. Furthermore, tourism is more concentrated on coastal areas in China than general economic activity. Higher Gini coefficients for tourism demand than those for tourism supply indicate that coastal areas obtain a larger fraction of tourism receipts compared to the quantity of their inputs than interior areas, and economic gains from tourism are more concentrated on the coastal localities than is tourism supply.

The use of the Gini coefficient has limitations in relation to income distribution because it gives more weight to transfers near the mode of the distribution than at the tails. In addition, it does not distinguish between different locations of income inequality say within one industry because it is a one-parameter measure. More generally, Gini coefficients in themselves are not able to tell where inequality among different variables is located (Bronfenbrenner, 1971). In considering spatial distributions, Gini coefficients should be combined with other methods of analysis. That is why in this chapter the Lorenz curve is employed to compensate for the limitation of the Gini coefficient in clarifying how the concentration of the variables of China's tourism industry is distributed.

4.5 Regression Analysis of Factors Affecting the Spatial Distribution of Tourism

Can the regional distribution of inbound tourism in China be explained by a simple model or relationship? In this section, multiple regression analysis is used to explore some such possible relationships, even though this analysis is at most indicative rather than definitive.

Regressions were run to analyse whether there might be a relationship between selected regional variables and regional tourism receipts. Thirty localities were treated as 30 observations. GRP (gross regional product), GRP per capita (GRPpc), utilised foreign direct investment (inv) and export per capita (exppc) are regarded as socioeconomic variables that may influence international tourism receipts. The number of first category travel agencies (1st), total hotel rooms (room) and total hotel employment (emp) were included as supply-side variables while tourist arrivals (arr) were included as a demand-side variable. Two groups of dummy variables (D1 and D2) were assigned to capture the roles of location and presence of tourist attractions in tourism generation. For D1, three localities — Beijing, Shanghai and Guangdong — the major gateways for international tourism to China, are consequently assigned 1 and the other 27 localities 0. Dummy variable two (D2) represents the presence of significant tourism attractions. A problem however is that the magnitude of this variable is to some extent subjective. Seven places with rich tourism resources (Beijing, Jiangsu, Zhejiang, Guangxi,

Hainan, Yunnan and Shannxi) were assigned 1 to incorporate the importance of sightseeing tourism, which is a major type of international tourism in China.

Regression analysis of cross-sectional data may face problems such as heteroskedasticity, multicollinearity, and so on. Tests are available to detect their presence. Heteroskedasticity is avoided by using a heteroskedasticity-consistent covariance matrix in the command of regressions. Testing for multicollinearity is also necessary because it may invalidate regression analysis. Tests for multicollinearity include computing a matrix of partial correlations, regressing each variable against all other independent variables. The matrix of partial correlation between independent variables is shown in Table 4.7.

Some of the correlations in Table 4.7 are higher in absolute terms than the traditional critical level of 0.80 (–0.80), indicating the possibility of multicollinearity in the data. In addition, correlation between dependent variable receipts and some independent ones are very high, especially for arrivals (the correlation coefficient is 0.897), hotel employment (0.923), export (0.817), and the first category travel agency (0.938). Correlation coefficients were calculated from data in NTA (1996) and SSB (1996). Following this testing, parameters for linear, linear-log, log-linear and double log forms were estimated because the relationship between tourism receipts

Table 4.7 Correlation coefficient matrix of regional variables.

	Arr	GRP	Inv	Room	Exppc	D1	1st	Emp	GRPpc	D2
Arr	1									
GRP	0.506	1								
Inv	0.895	0.700	1							
Room	0.318	0.352	0.273	1						
Exppc	0.734	0.302	0.648	0.607	1					
D1	0.779	0.266	0.598	0.605	0.933	1				
1st	0.716	0.28	0.535	0.741	0.796	0.852	1			
Emp	0.977	0.561	0.878	0.453	0.751	0.796	0.79	1		
GRPpc	0.418	0.33	0.454	0.614	0.875	0.726	0.56	0.46	1	
D2	–0.103	0.041	–0.13	0.342	–0.17	–0.111	0.09	0.03	0.18	1

Source: Calculated from data in NTA (1996) and SSB (1996).

and other independent variables seemed to be linear from direct observation of the data series. After comparing four groups of regression results, which are excluded from this book to avoid an unnecessary increase in its bulk, the double log model was selected because of the statistical significance of the estimated coefficients. Double log models were then constructed with receipts as the dependent variable and variables that are neither highly related to receipts nor highly correlated to other variables as independent variables. Various combinations of explanatory variables were postulated and tested in the double log functional form. The most satisfactory model is presented below:

$$\text{Ln receipt} = 0.3482 \ln (\text{GRPpc}) + 0.3879 \ln (\text{inv}) + 0.2889 \ln (\text{room}) + (1.7360) (\text{D1})$$
$$\qquad\qquad (1.329) \qquad\qquad\quad (3.684) \qquad\quad (1.267) \qquad\quad (5.217)$$

T-ratios: $+ 0.3322 (\text{D2}) - 3.7298$
$\qquad\qquad (1.134) \qquad\quad (-1.573)$

The null hypothesis is that there is no linear relationship between the dependent variable and each independent variable. Because the estimated values of the parameters in this model are statistically significant at the .05 level, the null hypothesis can be rejected. $R^2 = 0.8074$, R^2 (adjusted) = 0.7673, are statistically significant at .05 level (one tailed test); $F = 20.128$, d.f. = 29, statistically significant at .05 level (one tailed test); and Ramsey reset specification tests show that the specification for this model is significant at .05 level.

In this model, tourism receipts are heavily related to the presence of major entry gateways, D1, and to a much lesser extent to utilised foreign investment, GDP per capita, the number of hotel rooms and D2. Three major entry points, all located in the coastal areas, have been contributing around 62 percent of China's total tourist receipts since the mid-1980s (NTA, various years). However, the importance of entry may be exaggerated because other economic factors such as investment and export performance are also heavily concentrated in these three localities. Hence, D1 is not only a variable for entry but also a reflection of the combined strength of the three top economic giants in China, although the problem of multicollinearity is not present. China's 110 airports handled 40 million travellers in 1994, 90 percent of whom were served by the top 40 airports including Beijing's Capital Airport and Guangzhou Baiyun Airport where capacities have long been exceeded (*China News Digest Computer Network*, 2 August 1995). But Beijing's airport has recently been upgraded. It is worth noting that the entry-point factor may become less important in the future. In the late 1990s, China began construction of several airports to decentralise airport entry, and improve access to non-coastal areas.

Tourism receipts are not closely related to regional gross product but to regional GRP per capita mainly because of the influence of population distribution, especially given that almost 80 percent of tourism receipts are earned by 12 coastal localities whose population is only 40 percent of the national total (Table 4.1). It is logical for investment and hotel rooms to be positively related to receipts because foreign direct investment contributes to business travellers, who usually spend more than other tourists on average, and income from hotel rooms comprises around 30 percent of China's total tourism receipts (NTA, various years).

Tourism receipts seem to be much more closely related to the entrance factor (D1) than tourism attractions (D2) partly due to the fact that Shanghai and Guangdong together earn around 40 percent of the total receipts but are not considered to be rich in tourist attractions. D2 reflects the level of tourist resources, including some Ricardian-type tourist attractions, located in both the coastal and inland areas of China. Tourism resources, frequently consist of both immobile resources, such as land, scenery and host cultures, which are relatively scarce and unique, and mobile resources, such as capital and labour. Murphy (1985) identified three basic characteristics of tourist resources: (1) they are a combination of human and physical resources; (2) the physical resource may have seasonality in nature; (3) the search for the 4Ss — sun, sand, surf and sex (Matthews added servility to this list in 1978). It is possible that a particular tourism site may give rise to a pure economic surplus, or a rent, which is defined as a payment to a factor in excess of what is necessary to keep it to its present employment (Pearce, 1992). However, the relatively low correlation coefficient between receipts and D2 possibly indicates a low contribution of the resource-factor to tourist income. Because the model does not differentiate between different types of tourists, for example, business travellers, leisure–tourists and VFRs, and so on, it is not a very discriminating one — it may be too aggregative.

Regressions were run on the same set of data with receipts per capita (recpc) as the dependent variable. After excluding multicollinearity and heteroskedasticity, a new double log model is:

Ln recpc = 1.0091 (agencies) − 0.7358 ln (inv) + 0.7681 ln (invpc) + 0.9127 (D1)

   (3.296)   (−7.211)   (4.867)   (2.366)

T-ratios: + 0.3307 ln (exppc) − 4.1578
              (1.787)   (1.309)

Because the estimated values of the parameters in this model are statistically significant at the .05 level, the null hypothesis that there is no linear relationship between the dependent variable and each independent variable can be rejected. $R^2 = 0.8482$, R^2 (adjusted) = 0.8086, statistically significant at .05 level (one tailed test). The calculated F value (from mean) is 21.423 with six degrees of freedom for the regression and 23 degrees of freedom for the error, which is statistically significant at a five percent significance level. A test of significance for the model as a whole was also conducted via a Ramsey RESET test. Including Y^2, Y^3 and Y^4, the calculated F value is 1.3690 for the regression with 3 and 20 degrees of freedom respectively. It is therefore statistically significant at a five percent significance level.

While both export per capita and direct foreign investment per capita are related positively to receipts per capita, direct foreign investment is negatively related to receipts per capita due to the influence of the population distribution across regions. D1 and the number of travel agencies both relate positively to receipts per capita, reflecting the tendency for receipts per capita to correlate with entry ports and supply of tourist facilities.

4.6   Further Discussion of Influences on the Regional Distribution of International Tourism in China

Because of its aggregative nature and the presence of multicollinearity, the above functional quantitative analysis of factors which may influence China's regional distribution of inbound tourism is not entirely satisfying. While this analysis highlights major entry points as being very important for the spatial distribution of tourism, it does not give an adequate insight to the pull of tourist attractions, the importance of China's overseas family connections and certain aspects of foreign direct investment. The discussion in this section is designed, therefore, to bring attention to their regional influences which may otherwise not be fully appreciated.

Because three major components of tourism, namely the tourist, the product (including facilities, activities and other natural and human resources), and the tourist industry, can be related in many different ways, the spatial distribution of tourism is influenced by many factors. Tourism development relies on a variety of factors, including the tourism resource-base, the general social, economic, political environment and so forth, and concentration in certain spatial aspects is regarded as unavoidable (Pearce, 1987; Smith, 1989). Tourist assets are not distributed uniformly over the geographical space and as accessibility varies, tourist demand, service, and employment in tourism as a result seem to be differentiated by place. Oppermann (1994) provided insight into the concentrated distribution of tourism in New Zealand in the 1980s, attributing this regional imbalance to the decreasing length of stay of international tourists, the change in the market composition when the shorter staying Japanese and American segments increased in the 1980s, and the changing spatial preferences of most overseas visitors towards a greater concentration on Auckland and less frequent visits to most other areas. These three major factors "caused a spatial concentration process of tourist activity with Auckland being the big winner while all other locations lost out to a varying degree" (Oppermann, 1994).

Heavy concentration of inbound tourism along China's coast is a result of favourable conditions from both demand- and supply-side tourism factors. Factors such as international entry in the coastal provinces, the location of some major tourist attractions, strong family connections with overseas Chinese, and international business connections, all help to explain the existing pattern. The difference in the composition of state hotels and hotel operation may have favoured the coastal areas as well.

4.6.1   *Entry ports factor and tourist attractions*

Entry points play a major role in tourism concentration along the coast. The three biggest gateways to China (Beijing, Shanghai and Guangzhou) are all located in the coastal area, and their combined portion of tourist nights in 1994 was 42.2 percent of the national total and they obtained more than half of China's international tourism receipts (NTA, 1995). In addition, most of China's large cities are located along the coast, adding to the concentration of tourism in the coastal areas as tourism in China is heavily city-based. In fact, 12 of the 14 cities receiving over 20,000 tourist nights in 1994 were in China's coastal area (NTA, 1995). Easy access and short distances to China's major coastal tourist resources make the coastal areas more attractive than the interior for many inbound tourists.

By contrast, distance is a constraint for many inbound tourists considering the inland areas. The full cost of tourism is a sum of its market prices plus the value of time foregone by tourists from other uses. Consequently, time may be regarded as both a resource and a cost for recreation (Becker, 1965). It has been noted that time for the journey may have a positive utility on short, scenic trips, but this utility declines and becomes negative as the journey becomes longer and more tedious (Walsh *et al.*, 1990). Globally, most tourist arrivals for a destination are generated from nearby regions. For example, over three quarters of all international arrivals to the Americas are intra-regional (WTO, 1994). The time budget for an average international traveller in China is 11 days and this prevents most inbound visitors from visiting places distant from major entry points or going to sites with difficult access. Therefore, more than half of all international tourists visit one to three cities in China, 27.4 percent visit four to six cities, whilst only 15.9 percent visit more than seven cities (NTA, 1992). Long distances to the interior of China from major entry ports, which are located mainly on the coast, imposes an extra hurdle on visits by inbound tourists to China's inland.

There are some famous tourism attractions (historical, artistic and cultural) in the coastal area, including those at famous sites in Beijing, Suzhou and Hangzhou. Furthermore, new investment in tourism development has been concentrated along the coastal areas "to consolidate tourist attraction of traditional destinations in China" (NTA, 1996: 15). Although the peripheral areas towards the West are rich in cultural and natural attractions (Gormsen, 1990), tourism promotions often neglect the interior, resulting in limited appreciation of the diversity of tourism resources across China and the impression amongst foreigners that the interior is remote and tedious for travel by foreigners (Raffery, 1993).

4.6.2   Connection with overseas Chinese

China's coastal areas have a stronger connection with overseas Chinese and compatriots than its interior. Emigration out of China used to be rare, and was restricted in early times mainly to Fujian traders or pirates. The first major period of emigration from China occurred in the late 14th century and early 15th century when traders and vessels from China travelled the southern seas as far as Africa (Lyman, 1974). The fall of the Ming to the Manchurian Qing Dynasty in the 17th century resulted in a wave of emigration to Taiwan and Southeast Asia. It was not until the mid-19th century that treaties forced upon China by European powers made emigration legal. The majority of Chinese going abroad chose to work in Southeast Asia and America and were from Guangdong and Fujian. In addition, two million fled to Taiwan before 1949 with the victory of the Chinese Communist Party in sight (Andrews, 1992). The most recent wave of emigration began in the late 1970s to the US, Canada and Australia. Because the East coast of China has been the major source of Chinese emigrating overseas, it has strong ethnic links with Chinese compatriots and therefore enjoys a higher portion of family-related visits than the interior. For instance, the 12 coastal localities obtained 79.14 percent of the total nights spent by foreigners to China, while 96.75 percent of nights spent by overseas Chinese and 93.34 percent of those for compatriots were concentrated in the coastal areas in 1994 (NTA, 1995). Twelve coastal localities received 93 percent of tourist nights spent by overseas Chinese and 91 percent of those by compatriots in 1995 (NTA, 1996). The majority of these tourists are business travellers and VFRs — tourists visiting friends and relatives (NTA, various years).

Guangdong received 70.6 percent of tourists arrivals from Hong Kong in 1994, while Guangdong and Fujian received 38 percent of those from

Taiwan (NTA, 1995). The history of emigration from the Pearl River Delta dates back 1,000 years. There are now more than ten million Chinese descendants abroad with roots in this province. Guangzhou claims to have 679,843 residents with close relatives in Hong Kong and Macau (Anon, 1984). Eighty-five percent of Taiwan's 21 million people are descendants of Chinese who emigrated from Fujian Province and other places along the coast between the 1600s and 1949. These have been the major single source of international arrivals in China since 1990 with more than one million annual arrivals since Taiwan lifted the ban on visits of Taiwanese to mainland China at the end of 1987. Taiwanese visitors show a heavy concentration on Fujian, Shandong, and Zhejiang where they have close family connections. By contrast, a large percentage of foreigners visiting areas of inland China, such as Inner Mongolia, Ningxia, Gansu, Qinghai, Tibet and Yunnan, have an interest in seeing more exotic landscapes and cultures (Gormsen, 1995). Concentration of tourists in certain areas as a result of ethnic, cultural or other linkages is also observed in other countries, including Greece, where 80 percent of British visitors concentrate in Kerkyra, the Dutch flock to Kriti, and the Scandinavians favour the Dodecanese (Chiotis and Coccossis, 1992). VFR tourists account for 17 to 27 percent of all inbound travel and up to 50 percent of all domestic trip nights in Australia (Bureau of Tourism Research, 1994).

4.6.3   Foreign direct investment in the coastal areas and business travel

The presence of business travel to China seems to be associated with foreign direct investment (FDI). FDI in China experienced three waves of high growth in 1984, 1988 and 1993, respectively. Due to factors discussed in Chapter 3, FDI is concentrated on the coastal areas. Furthermore, 35 to 40 percent of direct foreign joint venture investment in China has been in property development, including hotels, resorts, golf courses, office space and so on (Lew, 1995), improving the business and leisure environment on the coast. In 1992, 90 percent of the 17,000 enterprises with foreign investment were located on the coast (SSB, 1993). These factors attract business travellers to the coast where they constitute a stable source of tourists for this area.

Over 50 million ethnic Chinese not resident in mainland China possess liquid assets of US$1.5 to US$2 billion in mainland China (Anon, 1992c). The share of compatriots in the total FDI rose from around 60 percent in 1984 to around 82 percent in 1993 (SSB, 1986 and 1995). Hong Kong and Taiwan account for two-thirds of actual direct investments to China (SSB, 1996). More than 25,000 firms in Taiwan have invested a total of US$10 to US$20 billion in the mainland (McGregor, 1996), creating constant business trips. Hong Kong places 80 percent of its investment in China in Guangdong (Lew, 1995). Besides cultural and family links, compatriots enjoy extra benefits in investment such as a shorter waiting time for approval and greater tax deductions than many local businesses in China.

As a product with a relatively high income demand elasticity, tourism exhibits major fluctuations with natural, political and socioeconomic variations. But tourism undertaken for different purposes has different demand elasticities, and business travel exhibits lower elasticity than other types of tourism (Bull, 1995). For example, the proportion of foreigners visiting China for sightseeing is higher than that for compatriots visiting friends and relatives. The former suffered greater relative reduction in 1988 and 1989 when there were student demonstrations and political turmoil in China (NTA, 1990) than did travel of Chinese compatriots, many of whom travel for business or family visits (Gormsen, 1990).

4.7 Discussion on State-Owned Hotels, Hotel Operations and Regional Distribution

It was suggested earlier that one factor which may help to attract inbound tourist to China's coastal regions is the greater presence there of more modern and better managed hotels than in the interior where a higher proportion of hotels are state-owned and managed. But to some extent also the differences in the composition of the stock of China's hotels in the coastal region and in the interior region are a consequence of the concentration of tourist-demand in the coastal region and the large absolute increase in tourism to this region which has required considerable new investment in hotels. Furthermore, given its greater contact with the outside world, one might expect management of hotels in coastal areas to be more cosmopolitan than in the interior.

Nationwide, 74.3 percent of hotels in China were owned by the state in 1989, whilst in the interior 80.3 percent of the hotels were state-owned, and 71.5 percent of the hotels in coastal areas fell into the same category (NTA, 1990). The average nationwide proportion of state hotel rooms in 1995 was 64 percent, but was 81 percent in the interior and only 56 percent in the coastal areas (Table 4.2). The coastal localities have been developing hotels with investment from sources other than the state so the proportion of state-owned hotels on the coast has fallen. By contrast the proportion of state-owned hotels increased in the interior, partly due to a weaker non-state sector in the interior. Non-state-owned hotels are those owned by collectives, individuals or jointly owned by the state and the collective, and hotels with foreign investment including sole foreign venture, joint ventures and Sino-foreign co-operative management. Non-state-owned hotels usually enjoy flexible import policies and favourable foreign exchange quotas, have better connections with international hotel chains as well as advanced management systems. Consequently, they are more competitive in marketing and have staff with superior training.

Even within the state hotels sector, lower "productivity" of hotel employees can be observed in the interior compared to the coast (Table 4.8). Average arrivals per hotel employee were lower in the interior than that in the coastal areas.

Furthermore, the top six tourism income-earners, all in the coastal areas, obtained 78.94 percent of the nation's total tourism income in 1992 with only 40.57 percent of China's hotel employees, while the lowest six localities, all located in the interior, received 0.62 percent of tourism income by employing 4.41 percent of the nation's hotel staff (NTA, 1993). In 1995, the top six receipt earners, all in the coastal areas, accounted for a total 78.7 percent of China's international tourist receipts at 60.93 percent of hotel employees, while the lowest six receipt earners, all in the interior, received 0.98 percent of income and accounted for 3.87 percent of hotel employment (NTA, 1996).

Table 4.8 Ratio of hotel arrivals to hotel employees in state hotels (1,000 per hotel employee).

	1986	1988	1990	1992	1994
Beijing	6.59	15.34	9.71	14.25	1.90
Tianjin	4.79	3.18	2.00	2.63	3.88
Hebei	5.48	0.45	0.42	1.04	1.35
Liaoning	15.35	1.14	1.07	1.81	1.69
Shanghai	6.40	22.46	12.19	14.57	13.84
Jiangsu	8.95	8.69	6.78	6.57	4.52
Zhejiang	7.31	11.59	8.57	10.80	8.64
Fujian	11.11	15.91	14.76	20.05	16.76
Shandong	2.32	0.92	0.84	2.08	2.35
Guangdong	8.89	33.25	27.55	34.55	22.76
Guangxi	20.93	9.65	12.14	13.69	8.36
Hainan	2.38	1.78	1.56	15.69	8.77
Coastal average:	**8.375**	**10.36**	**8.13**	**11.48**	**12.19**
Shanxi	9.88	0.75	0.74	1.48	0.95
Inner Mongolia	3.88	0.33	0.30	1.32	4.14
Jilin	8.91	0.67	0.83	1.65	1.84
Heilongjiang	10.73	0.67	0.68	1.51	1.45
Anhui	2.31	0.62	0.80	2.61	1.59
Jiangxi	2.52	0.68	0.29	1.35	1.21
Henan	8.77	0.87	0.84	1.43	1.59
Hubei	6.53	1.18	1.33	3.44	2.74
Hunan	10.85	0.63	0.60	2.46	2.49
Sichuan	18.14	1.88	2.15	3.78	3.26
Guizhou	2.20	1.37	1.11	4.10	6.13
Yunnan	21.47	4.47	4.69	8.30	11.30
Tibet	1.37	2.79	3.33	7.25	27.46
Shaanxi	5.46	6.89	6.05	7.86	7.20
Gansu	11.57	1.39	1.25	3.00	1.99
Qinghai	47.37	2.58	2.14	1.42	1.32
Ningxia	7.79	1.05	1.80	0.54	0.42
Xinjiang	1.24	1.53	1.63	8.09	4.16
Inland average	**10.01**	**1.69**	**1.7**	**3.42**	**4.51**

Source: Based on NTA, various years.

Large hotels are concentrated on the coast. Only six of the 73 hotels with more than 500 rooms in 1995 were located in the inland areas (Table 4.2). A major feature of tourism supply activity is the heavy preponderance of fixed costs in relation to total costs. It is easier for big hotels to realise economies of scale and achieve higher operation efficiency. Some hotels, mainly small-sized ones owned by the state in the interior, had low levels of income, resulting in lower revenue per unit of fixed assets of the hotel sector in most interior areas compared to the coast (NTA, 1996: 122–123). Higher cost per hotel guest in the interior may be attributed to such factors as lower productivity due to X-inefficiency (Leibenstein, 1986), operations below minimum economic scale (as inland hotels are not on the minimum of their long-run average cost curves, whereas those on the coast are more likely to be), and lower occupancy rates, which means that the inland hotels are likely to be at a point on their short-run per unit cost curves above those on the coast.

The different ratios between tourism receipts and employees reflect higher overall economic efficiency in tourism operations in coastal areas. This might be attributable to more tourist arrivals on the coast, coastal advantages of higher capital to labour ratios, labour supply of better quality, better management, and more market-oriented management instead of labour-absorbing management under political pressure as sometimes happens in the inland areas where employment opportunities are limited. The higher proportion of state-owned hotels in the interior compared to the coast may be a source of X-inefficiency in hotels in the interior and make them susceptible to feather-bedding, that is the practice of over staffing. Furthermore, the higher proportion of larger-sized hotels in the coastal areas (combined with greater capacity utilisation) usually result in economies of labour-use because cost per bed tends to fall with the size of the hotel as measured by the number of its beds. Lack of basic infrastructure, dynamic entrepreneurs and appropriately trained personnel in the interior makes it difficult for non-coastal areas to compete with coastal regions.

There have been warnings about the possible oversupply of hotels in China relative to basic tourism infrastructure since all the 30 localities started investing on tourism facilities in the early 1980s (Tisdell and Wen, 1991b).

Nevertheless, the fever for hotel investment continues even in areas less frequented by tourists, for bureaucracies are budget-maximisers who are inclined to underestimate costs of and overestimate demand for their preferred policies to encourage new projects (Mueller, 1979). It was particularly common in China in the 1980s for local governments to initiate hotel construction projects in an effort to obtain loans at low interest rates, the repayment of which was softly controlled. In most cases, the idea is to provide extra tourist facilities as inducements to tourists but these supply-led strategies often fail in their purpose.

The ability of central government to perform macro-management on the economy has been severely undermined with the reduction in the proportion of revenue received by the central government. From 1952 to 1978, this accounted for 35 percent of national income on average (Liu and Yang, 1989), but dropped from 37.2 percent of national income in 1978 to 19.3 percent in 1988 (Dai, 1992). Although the State Council issued rules to restrain the construction of buildings, especially hotels, in September 1987 so as to curb hotel oversupply, local government continues to invest in hotels, and market signals do not work well in the inland where the old economic system is relatively stronger, leading to increased imbalance between demand and supply in some peripheral areas.

4.8 Concluding Comments

Economic inequality in China has generally increased since China began its economic reforms in 1979 (see Chapter 3 for details). Economic activity has become even more skewed towards China's coastal areas since 1979 and overall regional economic inequality has increased. It might be thought that China's substantial tourism development would play a role in moderating this regional economic inequality but inbound tourism has in fact exacerbated it. Both demand-side and supply-side indicators for the Chinese tourism industry support the hypothesis that the coastal region has in comparison to the interior gained most from the development of tourism in China. Whether this inequality is declining and is likely to be moderated in the future remains to be seen. It will be considered in the next chapter.

The heavy concentration of tourism on China's coastal areas and their higher economic gains from tourism mean that inland areas are less able to profit from their rich tourism-resources and the efficiency of their hotel operations is lower, leaving them even more disadvantaged than their coastal competitors. Thus, in China, tourism development may not have helped the rural areas and inland areas catch up with more developed areas. Within such interior areas as Guizhou, a state-controlled tourism industry, which results in powerful urban control of tourism planning, investment and development, hampers locally initiated commercial tourism development.

Note that statistics on tourism receipts reflect just the direct economic injection from tourism to local economies. When the income-multiplier effect is taken into account, leakages from tourism receipts in the inland China are most likely higher than along the coast because coastal areas have a larger and more dynamic economy and better ability to supply local consumption goods for tourists. Thus the economic disparity of coastal tourism compared to the interior is likely to be magnified after regional leakages are taken into account. Spatial concentration of tourism has also been observed in other countries. Tourism is concentrated predominantly on the West coast of Malaysia, coinciding with the hubs of other economic activities. Thus tourism in general — at an aggregate level — has not helped to redistribute wealth within Malaysia (Oppermann, 1992b).

The above suggests that the tourism industry may not be as effective in promoting decentralisation of economic activity as sometimes believed. The results here supports the view that the tourism industry may reinforce existing hubs of economic activity, rather than promote spatial decentralisation of economic activity (Oppermann, 1992b; McKee and Tisdell, 1990). Furthermore, the rather romanticised view of Christaller (1963), a pioneer of regional economics, that tourism in the modern urbanised world is likely to be oriented towards rural rather than urban areas, is not supported by observations from China on inbound tourism. This chapter makes a significant contribution by highlighting such issues and it provides the first in-depth study of the regional distribution of tourism in China.

Nevertheless, before drawing any firm conclusion about the role of international tourism in influencing the regional distribution of the Chinese economy, the following issues need to be addressed: Has this concentration of tourism on China's East coast remained stable over the years? Has this concentration remained the same or is it changing? The situation concerning the influence of tourism development on regional economic activity in China may well be much more complex than is indicated by a cross-sectional view, particularly when domestic tourism is accounted for. The following chapter will examine trends in the regional distribution of inbound tourism of China over time, and make use of the limited data available on China's domestic tourism.

While the above findings are significant ones, one must be careful not to draw erroneous conclusions from them. In particular, it cannot be concluded that the growth of inbound tourism (and tourism generally) in China has failed to assist economic development in China's interior. On the contrary, as will be seen in the next chapter, tourism in China's inland area has expanded greatly, and is helping to contribute to the interior's economic development. This is so despite the fact that the coastal region seems to have been relatively favoured by the general development of tourism in China.

Chapter 5

Trends in the Regional Distribution of Tourism in China and their Implications

5.1 Introduction

International tourism in China has grown rapidly since 1979 (Wen and Tisdell, 1996; Chapter 2). From 1980 to 1998, China's inbound tourist arrivals and tourism receipts grew at an average annual rate of 17 and 15 percent respectively. Total international arrivals reached 63.5 million in 1998, and China's international tourism receipts were US$12.6 billion. This amounted to 6.9 percent of China's total foreign exchange revenue in 1998 (NTA, 1999).

While it has been well recognised that Chinese economy is heavily concentrated on the coastal region (Tisdell, 1996), greater spatial inequality of tourism (based both on demand- and supply-side indicators) is present than occurs for the socio-economic variables. Thus inbound tourism appears to reinforce the regional socio-economic inequalities in China (Wen and Tisdell, 1996). International tourism seems to be contributing to greater economic disparity between coastal and inland China as is evident from the previous chapter.

Given the extent to which growth has occurred in the Chinese economy and in inbound tourism to China, those regional disparities may well have altered. Consequently the purpose of this chapter is to investigate the change in the spatial distribution of international tourism in China from 1986 to 1998, and to analyse factors that have contributed to this change.

5.2 Overall Changes in Spatial Distribution of Tourism in China

In this book, as stated previously, China's coastal area is assumed to cover three municipalities and nine provinces. These 12 coastal localities are hatched in the map of China shown in Fig. 3.1. The other 18 provinces (shown in Fig. 3.1) are categorised as its inland area.

5.2.1 Trends in concentration of international tourism on the coastal area of China

Although 40 percent of China's population lives in its coastal area, this area accounts for over 55 percent of China's GDP (SSB, 1993–1998). Thus the distribution of China's economy is significantly biased in favour of the coastal area compared to the inland area. International tourism in China is even more heavily concentrated on the coastal area than the general economy, leaving the inland area more disadvantaged (see Chapter 4). Nevertheless, the relative dominance of coastal areas in Chinese tourism has varied over the years. Table 5.1 shows the proportion of major tourist variables accounted for by China's 12 coastal areas.

Table 5.1 Tourism indicators for 12 coastal localities in China as a percentage of national totals, 1986–1998.

	Receipts %	Number of tourist arrivals %	Number of hotel employees %	Number of hotel rooms %
1986	93.5	85.7	83.3	78.1
1988	87.3	89.1	78.3	79.0
1990	89.2	88.4	77.6	70.8
1992	89.5	84.0	77.4	71.2
1994	89.3	81.4	76.9	71.5
1996	85.6	78.6	72.7	70.1
1998	84.8	78.9	72.9	70.2

Source: Calculated from data in NTA, 1987–1999.

Although the absolute numbers for such indicators as tourist arrivals, receipts, hotel rooms and hotel employees in the coastal areas of China have been increasing (NTA, various years), their proportionate share fell between 1986 to 1998 as apparent from Table 5.1. The declining relative dominance of the 12 coastal areas in tourism corresponds to the increasing relative importance of inland areas in tourism, and suggests the possibility of a relatively smaller gap between the coastal and inland areas in the economic benefit derived from tourism. The trends in the spatial distribution of tourism in China are well captured by variations in the Gini ratios.

5.2.2   Trends in Gini coefficients for the regional distribution of tourism

The Gini ratio, as pointed out in the previous chapter, measures the relative degree of departure of a population from a state of perfect equality. It has a value of zero for absolute equality and of unity for complete inequality. As the degree of inequality rises so does the Gini coefficient. The same method of measurement is used here as in the previous chapter.

Table 5.2 presents Gini coefficients for major tourism indicators for China for every second year from 1986 to 1998 but not yearly, mainly because this calculation is quite time-consuming. Since tourism variables mostly show

Table 5.2 Gini coefficients for major tourism indicators in China, 1986–1998.

	Receipts	No. of tourist arrivals	No. of hotel employees	No. of hotel rooms
1986	0.8374	0.7577	0.7344	0.6344
1988	0.7297	0.7276	0.5766	0.5978
1990	0.7988	0.7412	0.5941	0.5236
1992	0.7472	0.7049	0.6090	0.5361
1994	0.7446	0.6706	0.5815	0.5208
1996	0.7443	0.6701	0.5812	0.5203
1998	0.6903	0.6428	0.5810	0.5128

Source: Based on data of NTA, various years.

limited variation in a period of two years, these estimates are suitable for capturing trends.

The trend in the value of Gini coefficients for all the four tourist indicators for China from 1986 to 1998 is downward, indicating a reduction in the relative spatial concentration of tourism. The distribution of hotel rooms has become more dispersed, possibly reflecting the effort of all localities to expand hotel supply in the hope of promoting tourism (Wen and Tisdell, 1996). Concentration of tourism demand on the coast, depicted by high Gini ratios over years, is greater than for the supply of tourism facilities, partly because of expansion in supply of tourist facilities and services in some inland areas without adequate consideration of demand (Wen and Tisdell, 1997), or in the hope of attracting more tourists.

It should be noted that a Gini coefficient can remain constant but the ranking of entities subject to inequality may alter Kendall's coefficient of concordance (W) (Seigal, 1958) can, however, be used to test if changes in rankings have occurred. When the authors' applied this test to the intertemporal data studied in this chapter, they found very high coefficients of concordance. Thus the ranking of regions did not alter significantly with the passing of time and the skew was continually in favour of the coastal region.

It is important to note that Gini coefficients for the whole of China reflect only systemic inequality. There is frequently greater inequality between some regions and lower inequality between others within a nation, and change in this type of inequality may differ from that indicated by the systemic inequality. For example, with an increase in systemic inequality, there may be: (i) an increase in the inequality between high-income regions and low income regions; (ii) a higher inequality within the high-income or low-income regions while that between the two groups remains relatively stable; (iii) a combination of both (i) and (ii). Therefore, it is insufficient to analyse changes only in systemic inequality as indicated by Gini coefficients for the regions of China as a whole because grouping 30 localities with great diversity may seem arbitrary. Detailed analysis of alterations in inequality within the coastal area and inland area is a necessary part of identifying changes in both inter- and intra-regional inequality in tourism in China.

Trends in the spatial distribution of tourism in China's coastal area and in its interior will now be considered in turn.

5.3   Changes in Spatial Distribution of Tourism within China's Coastal Area

Gini coefficients for major tourism indicators within China's coastal area for the period 1986–1998 are shown in Table 5.3.

Table 5.3 Gini coefficients for major tourism indicators for 12 coastal localities in China.

	Receipts	Number of tourist arrivals	Number of hotel employees	Number of hotel rooms
1986	0.6648	0.5693	0.6384	0.5199
1988	0.5878	0.6138	0.4433	0.5121
1990	0.5915	0.6259	0.5234	0.4743
1992	0.5940	0.6203	0.5529	0.4820
1994	0.6003	0.5946	0.5131	0.4640
1996	0.5938	0.5887	0.4879	0.4643
1998	0.5716	0.5484	0.4876	0.4384

Source: Based on data of NTA, various years.

Gini coefficients for major tourist indicators within the coastal area listed in Table 5.3 are much lower in general than those for the whole of China listed in Table 5.2, implying a much more even relative distribution of tourism within the coastal area than for China as a whole. A general reduction of Gini ratio for each tourism indicator within the coastal area from 1986 to 1998 reflects a trend towards greater spatial dispersion (relatively) of tourism variables (both supply-side and demand-side variables) within China's coastal area. This conclusion is supported by change in the proportions of major tourist indicators accounted for by specific coastal localities as reported in Tables 5.4 and 5.5.

Table 5.4 Percentages of tourism receipts of each locality within coastal areas.

	1986	1988	1990	1992	1994	1996	1998
Beijing	45.47	34.15	32.91	30.25	31.71	27.77	26.14
Tianjin	0.75	1.77	1.40	1.46	1.66	1.87	2.21
Hebei	0.12	0.40	0.45	0.31	0.54	0.91	1.10
Liaoning	0.91	3.90	4.01	2.86	2.63	2.76	2.88
Shanghai	3.85	16.70	15.52	16.29	13.42	14.43	13.35
Jiangsu	5.07	3.44	3.45	3.14	3.50	3.91	5.80
Zhejiang	2.31	2.36	2.85	2.63	2.85	3.60	3.96
Fujian	3.17	2.93	2.60	4.05	7.06	6.84	7.14
Shandong	0.68	2.83	2.45	1.74	1.77	2.42	2.41
Guangdong	35.85	25.90	28.54	31.57	31.78	32.53	32.26
Guangxi	1.75	3.95	4.01	2.84	1.89	1.90	1.71
Hainan	0.07	1.67	1.80	2.85	1.17	1.05	1.06

Source: NTA, various years.

Table 5.5 Percentages of hotel employment of each locality within coastal area.

	1986	1988	1990	1992	1994	1996	1998
Beijing	21.06	19.14	19.98	19.25	18.43	15.65	14.50
Tianjin	1.86	2.99	1.81	1.56	1.84	2.16	2.35
Hebei	1.18	2.75	2.09	1.72	2.24	2.36	2.82
Liaoning	0.78	6.98	4.29	3.43	3.28	5.18	6.13
Shanghai	12.47	12.08	10.26	9.55	8.63	8.01	6.49
Jiangsu	5.31	5.20	4.53	4.09	5.30	8.30	9.16
Zhejiang	2.66	3.48	2.97	3.45	5.00	7.43	9.59
Fujian	4.96	5.28	4.61	4.19	3.96	4.35	3.63
Shandong	2.72	3.92	4.11	3.06	4.56	5.72	7.72
Guangdong	43.89	30.27	38.59	42.77	39.79	33.28	30.49
Guangxi	2.88	4.66	2.72	3.69	3.16	4.02	4.76
Hainan	0.23	3.25	4.04	3.25	3.79	3.54	2.35

Source: NTA, various years.

From Tables 5.4 and 5.5, the dominance of three major gateway localities in international tourism, Beijing, Shanghai and Guangdong, is apparent. Together they account for around 75 percent of the total receipts for the 12 coastal localities. However, Beijing's relative proportion of receipts decreased from almost half of the total receipts of the coastal area in 1986 to 26.4 percent in 1998 as shown in Table 5.4, while that of Shanghai and Fujian increased considerably.

Table 5.5 indicates that employment in the international hotel sector along the coast is becoming relatively more dispersed with the proportion of hotel employees accounted by the major destinations, such as Beijing, Shanghai, and Guangdong, on the decrease, although Guangdong retains its dominance. Hainan and Liaoning have shown a large increase in their share of hotel employment in recent years.

Hence, a generally higher degree of dispersal of tourism distribution has occurred along the coast according to the analysis based on Gini coefficients and major tourist indicators for both the demand- and supply-side of tourism between 1986 and 1998. Now consider the change in the spatial distribution of tourism in China's inland area during the same time period.

5.4   Changes in Spatial Distribution of Tourism Indicators within China's Inland Area

It can be deduced from Table 5.1 that between 1986 and 1998 both tourist receipts and arrivals in inland China increased as a proportion of their totals for China by around 8 percent. Thus tourism to China's inland increased in relative importance compared to its coastal area. But, what happened to regional inequality of tourism within China's interior?

Gini coefficients of tourism variables shown in Table 5.6 for the interior area of China are generally lower than those for both the whole of China and in comparison to its coastal area. Therefore the spatial distribution of tourism in China's interior is relatively more even than in its coastal region and shows

Table 5.6 Gini coefficients of major tourism indicators for 18 inland localities in China.

	Receipts	Number of tourist arrivals	Number of hotel employees	Number of hotel rooms
1986	0.5293	0.5911	0.5958	0.2857
1988	0.5437	0.5316	0.4082	0.3277
1990	0.5771	0.6144	0.3649	0.4996
1992	0.5301	0.4005	0.3952	0.3338
1994	0.4563	0.4343	0.3596	0.2832
1996	0.4554	0.4338	0.3578	0.2828
1998	0.4432	0.4521	0.3828	0.3684

Source: NTA, various years.

greater equality than in China as a whole. The lowest Gini ratios are found in the supply of hotel rooms, indicating a potential over-supply, along with possible low productivity and low hotel occupancy rate in localities not frequented by international visitors (Wen and Tisdell, 1997). The generally declining Gini ratios from 1986 to 1988 highlight a tendency for international tourism within China's inland area to become spatially more dispersed with the passage of time.

Yunnan and Shaanxi provinces have been the top two earners of international tourist receipts in the interior. Their combined receipts accounted for over one third of these total receipts for inland China in the 1990s (NTA, various years). However, Inner Mongolia increased its receipts by 18-fold from 1992 to 1998, resulting in a sharp increase in its proportion of the total receipts of the inland area.

The relative proportion of hotel employment accounted for by Shaanxi decreased by 33 percent from 1986 to 1998, although its relative proportion of receipts decreased by less than 2 percent. By contrast, the relative proportion of employment of Heilongjiang and Sichuan increased despite the decrease in their proportion of receipts over the same period, indicating a disproportionate distribution between the earning of tourist receipts and the number of employees (NTA, various years).

5.5   Coefficient of Variation

First suggested by Karl Pearson (Pearson, 1896), the coefficient of variation (CV) measures the relative degree to which a variable is distributed around its mean value,

$$CV = \sigma / \mu$$

where $\mu = E(Y)$ is the mean of the independent variable, and σ is the standard deviation of the distribution.

Defined as the ratio of the standard deviation to the mean, "it standardises for the scale of the variable concerned, so that comparisons between the degree of dispersion of variables with widely differing typical values is possible" (Pearce, 1992: 66). The higher the value of CV for regional variables, the greater is the degree of regional inequality. The coefficient of variation compensates for the possible bias in the Gini coefficient. Its application provides an additional useful measure of regional inequalities. Table 5.7 lists coefficients of variation for the regional distribution of tourism variables in China as a whole.

Coefficients of variation are found to be generally decreasing over the years, and lower for the supply-side tourist indicators than those for the

Table 5.7 Coefficients of variation of the regional distribution of some tourism indicators in China.

	Receipts	Number of tourist arrivals	Number of hotel employees	Number of hotel rooms
1986	2.82	2.27	2.18	1.82
1988	2.01	2.16	1.47	1.63
1990	2.08	2.02	1.74	1.42
1992	2.10	2.07	1.88	1.47
1994	2.12	2.06	1.73	1.65
1996	2.08	2.03	1.68	1.61
1998	2.06	2.04	1.63	1.60

Source: Calculated from data provided by the NTA, various years.

demand-side in China. This is in accordance with the earlier finding in this chapter, based on trends in Gini coefficients, that inequality in the regional distribution of tourism in China decreased from 1986 to 1998, and that inequality in the demand of tourism has been higher than that in the supply of resources supporting tourism. Trends in the inequality of four tourist indicators as measured by their CV-values, listed in Table 5.7 accord with those depicted by Gini ratios as listed in Table 5.2. These results further support the hypothesis that the regional distribution of international tourism is becoming relatively more dispersed with the passage of time.

5.6 Regional Convergence in Tourism Versus Divergence in the General Economy

The purpose of this section is to compare trends in the spatial distribution of inbound tourism variables in China with those for major socio-economic indicators such as the distribution of population and incomes.

Economic dynamics result in changes in regional economic inequality. Changes in regional economic disparities with the process of economic development have been studied in both industrialised countries, including the United States and Canada (Rauch, 1993; Fan and Casetti, 1994), and for LDCs (Kundu, 1975; Ikemoto and Limskul, 1987; Ghuman and Kaur, 1993). The possible convergence of OECD economies has been examined (Dowrick and Nguyen, 1989).

Measures of regional divergence and convergence are frequently categorised into four groups (Braun, 1988; Fan and Casetti, 1994):

1. Lorenz curve measures, such as the Gini ratio and the dissimilarity index;
2. dispersion measures, such as the standard deviation and coefficient of variation;
3. information theoretic measures, such as the entropy measure; and
4. other indices such as Atkinson measure, Nelson index, and Theil index.

Due to the availability of data and the predictive power of this index, the Gini ratio is selected here to measure the change in regional disparity of the general economy and tourism in China. Gini coefficients are calculated for both indicators of the general economy and tourism in China in the following sections to estimate the extent of regional divergence or convergence in China's general economy and in tourism since the early 1980s.

5.6.1 Regional divergence in the Chinese economy

Gini coefficients for China show no sign of regional convergence for the major demographic/economic variables listed in Table 5.8. On the contrary, a slight trend towards greater regional economic divergence occurred in regional income from 1986 onwards and in the same period, Gini coefficients for regional income per head remained approximately stationary. However, compared to the pre-1986 period regional economic inequality in China increased considerably, following its economic reforms (Chen and Fleisher, 1996). Note that Gini coefficients are lower for per capita regional income when compared to those for population and regional income. This is a consequence of the coexistence of high populations and high gross regional incomes in some coastal localities, such as Jiangsu and Shandong (SSB, various years).

Nevertheless, Chen and Fleisher (1996) claimed that there was conditional convergence of per capita production across China from 1978 to 1993. Convergence is conditional on physical investment shares, employment

Table 5.8 Gini coefficients for major socioeconomic indicators.

	1982	1986	1988	1990	1992	1994	1998
Population	0.383	0.390	0.385	0.384	0.387	0.391	0.394
Regional income	0.287	0.375	0.384	0.380	0.387	0.389	0.396
Regional income per capita	0.201	0.295	0.285	0.284	0.285	0.284	0.289

Source: Calculated from data of SSB, various years.

growth, human-capital investment, foreign direct investment and coastal location. Other research suggests that regional income in China converged from 1978 to 1984 with the rise in rural productivity, but started to diverge again from around 1984 onward, because the coastal areas grew much faster than the interior, even though the convergence continued within the coastal localities (Jian *et al.*, 1996). Results reported in Table 5.8 show a weak tendency from 1986 onwards to regional divergence and are consistent (but not strictly so) with the research of Jian *et al.* (1996). In addition, maintenance of economic inequality between the East coastal areas and the inland areas is occurring simultaneously with the rising economic power of southern China, especially Guangdong, and the economic decline of northeast China, including Heilongjiang, Jilin and Liaoning. Gini ratios for two groups — the 12 coastal and 18 interior localities — are therefore calculated in order to analyse the trend in regional distribution of socio-economic variables within each group.

Gini ratios for regional income and population, reported in Table 5.9, are generally higher for the inland group, but lower for income per capita, as compared with those for the coastal group. This is mainly a result of less

Table 5.9 Gini coefficients for coastal and inland China for selected years from 1982 to 1998.

	12 coastal areas			18 inland areas		
	Regional income	Population	Regional income per capita	Regional income	Population	Regional income per capita
1982	0.235	0.318	0.319	0.409	0.357	0.175
1986	0.297	0.363	0.317	0.384	0.396	0.122
1988	0.309	0.358	0.300	0.383	0.393	0.115
1992	0.322	0.360	0.283	0.367	0.391	0.126
1995	0.324	0.355	0.233	0.397	0.389	0.143
1998	0.323	0.357	0.237	0.399	0.391	0.146

Source: Calculated from data of SSB, various years.

conformity between the distribution of population and regional income within the coastal group. For example, Shanghai has been contributing over 9 percent of the coastal group's income with around 3 percent of the group's population since the 1980s, while Hebei contributed 9 percent of income on 13 percent of the group's population (SSB, various years). Slight convergence in income per capita is observed for the coastal areas from 1982 onwards, but a weak divergence for the inland areas started from 1988 onwards. To conclude, generally increasing Gini ratios for China as a whole suggest that overall weak regional divergence of the Chinese economy has occurred since 1980, mainly as a result of expanding inequality between the coastal and inland areas. Even though slight convergence is present among the coastal localities, increasing divergence between inland areas contributed to this growing inequality.

The "inverted-U" paradigm and balanced growth theories suggest that regional inequality within nations increases in their early stages of economic development as a result of concentration of income and income-generating factors, and decreases in later stages with diffusion of income and income-generating factors (Williamson, 1965; Robinson, 1976). Observations in this chapter suggest that China is most likely to be still on the lower branch of the inverted-U with rising income disparity across regions. This result is compatible with the "inverted-U" hypothesis.

However, given that the Chinese economy has been strongly influenced by governmental policy decisions rather than market forces, economic theories developed according to the Western experience may not be directly applicable to economic phenomena in China. In addition, the study of regional income inequality although empirically rich is subject to considerable theoretical disputes. It may be naive to expect polarisation-reversal or convergence to happen automatically in China because some developing countries may never reach the levels of income where regional income disparities tend to narrow. Regional income disparities in such countries are wider than those characteristic of developed countries in the past, and convergence may depend on effective government intervention (Jones, 1991). It is therefore interesting to consider whether there are indications of convergence in the Chinese economy as far as its tourist sector is concerned.

5.6.2 Convergence of tourism in China as indicated by Gini coefficients

In contrast to lack of convergence in the general economy, relative convergence is observed in Chinese inbound tourism over the period 1986–1998. A general decline in the Gini coefficients for major tourism indicators is apparent in Table 5.2, indicating a trend towards a reduction in regional concentration of international tourism. Gini coefficients for tourism variables for the coastal area (Table 5.3) and inland area (Table 5.6) show a similar trend towards decreasing concentration within both coastal and interior areas. Comparing the Gini ratios for four different tourist indicators for the whole of China, coastal and inland areas, those for the whole of China are generally the highest while those for the interior the lowest, leading to the conclusion that the disparity between coastal and interior China is the major reason for the high degree of regional inequality in inbound tourism in China.

5.6.3 Convergence of tourism in China indicated by the absolute values of some major tourist indicators

Consideration of the absolute growth in the value of tourism variables in both coastal and inland China may further facilitate the study of spatial convergence of international tourism in China. Figure 5.1 compares the number of hotel rooms in the 12 coastal and 18 inland localities over the years.

The supply of hotel rooms has been increasing in both coastal and inland areas since 1986 as indicated in Fig. 5.1. The highest growth rate in the number of hotel rooms occurred between 1988 and 1990, when the number of hotel rooms for the coastal areas increased by 65 percent, from 125,813 in 1988 to 208,159 in 1990, while that for the inland areas increased by 154 percent, from 33,672 to 85,668 in the same period. Total hotel rooms in the inland areas increased from less than 30 percent of that in the coastal areas in the early 1980s to around 43 percent in 1996 (based on data of NTA, various years), indicating a convergence in the number of hotel rooms between the coastal and inland areas.

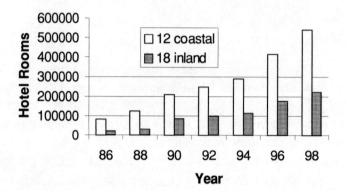

Fig. 5.1 Number of hotel rooms in 12 coastal and 18 inland localities, 1986–1998.
Source: Based on NTA, various years.

The highest growth rate for inbound tourist arrivals in the period 1986–1998 occurred between 1986 and 1988, when tourist arrivals increased by 5 and 3.4 times 1986-levels in the coastal and the inland areas respectively, as indicated in Fig. 5.2. The political unrest in 1989 in China precipitated a larger proportionate reduction in the tourist arrivals in 1990 in the coastal areas (–10%) than it did in the inland (–4%). There was a 3 percent reduction in the number of arrivals for the East coast in 1994 as compared to that in 1992, while an increase of 12 percent occurred in the inland areas in the same period. Tourist arrivals in the inland areas increased from less than 12 percent of that in the coastal areas in 1986 to over 27 percent in 1996 (based on data of NTA, various years), indicating a convergence in the relative number of tourist arrivals for the coastal and inland areas.

A higher concentration of tourism in the coastal areas than that of the general economy, as indicated by higher Gini ratios for tourist indicators than those for the general economy, may well lead to the conclusion that tourism has added to regional disparity instead of fulfilling the goal of promoting economic growth in the inland area. If expanding economic divergence across regions has become a threat to national stability in China (Hu, 1995), it seems pertinent to understand what contribution the tourism industry, as a sector that is growing quickly with high multiplier effects,

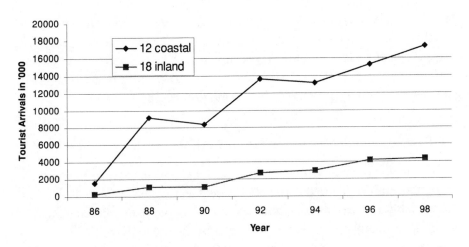

Fig. 5.2 Tourist arrivals in inland and coastal China, 1986–1998, in thousands ('000).

Source: Based on NTA, various years.

may make in reducing regional disparity. The trend in relative convergence in the tourist industry between coastal and inland China is obviously an encouraging phenomenon because it shows the potential for international tourism to counteract regional economic disparity in China. Therefore factors contributing to the trend in regional convergence of tourism require more attention in order to identify ways in which the tourism industry can make a larger contribution to reducing regional economic divergence in China.

5.7 Discussion About Regional Convergence in Chinese Tourism

The reduction in the relative concentration of international tourism on the coastal areas of China since the mid-1980s is a product of various forces. This section examines major factors contributing to the spatial convergence of tourism in China. These are: China's "opening up" which cleared barriers to tourists visiting its interior; improvements in and greater supply of tourist facilities in the interior encouraged inland trips; improved productivity of the tourism industry in the interior made its tourism more profitable; changes in tourism demand and tourist mix, especially increasing demand for ecotourism, enticed more tourists to visit the inland areas; and growing domestic tourism contributed strongly to tourism in the interior of China.

5.7.1   The opening up of China

International tourists were only free to visit designated places open for foreigners in China in the late 1970s and early 1980s, and there were considerable restrictions on foreigners visiting some parts of China, mainly in the interior. Entry permits were issued by the government, after careful checking, in order to control tourist inflow to areas that were regarded by the Chinese government as unsuitable for foreign tourists (Tisdell and Wen, 1991). This type of entry control prevented many foreigners visiting the interior. However, with the progress of China's opening up, restrictions have gradually decreased. There were only 122 areas, mainly on the East coast, open to foreign tourists in 1982, but more than 500 by 1990 and 1060 by 1994 (NTA, 1995). Entry ports to China were less than 50 in the early 1980s, with the majority of them located in the coastal areas, but more than 200 border points all over China were open in 1995, allowing easier entry to the interior (NTA, 1996). Today in fact tourists can travel freely in China. The proportion of China's international tourists visiting its interior increased from 11 percent in 1988 to 20 percent in 1995 (NTA, 1989 and 1996). Thus the process of opening the interior to tourism undoubtedly has contributed to the increasing visitation to the inland by inbound tourists.

5.7.2   Improvement of tourism facilities in the interior

Heavy concentration of international tourism in a few coastal localities from 1979 to the mid-1980s can be attributed partly to the lack of supply of tourist facilities in the interior. Tourist supply was predominantly concentrated in Beijing, Guangdong and Shanghai in the early 1980s, for historical and political reasons (Wen and Tisdell, 1997). Their combined hotel beds accounted for almost 70 percent of the national total in 1985 (NTA, 1986). Inconvenient transportation, communication and other infrastructure difficulties, combined with unsatisfactory hotel facilities, discouraged tourism in the interior.

With continuing tourism development throughout China, the interior has been able to expand and upgrade its tourism facilities so as to meet the demand of international travellers better. Tourist supply, as indicated by the number of hotel rooms and employees, has been growing in the interior. The interior increased its share of total hotel rooms in China from 22 percent in 1986 to 28.5 percent in 1994, and then to 29.9 percent in 1996 (NTA, various years). With increasing supply of tourist facilities of improved quality in non-coastal localities and more entry points to China, travellers are more likely to be less concentrated on the coastal area to become more dispersed throughout China.

5.7.3   Hotel operations and the state-owned hotels

The economics of hotel operations in the interior have improved relative to those for coastal hotels since the mid-1980s. For example, hotel income per room in the interior was less than 20 percent of that in the coastal areas in 1985, but was 28 percent in 1990 and almost 40 percent in 1996 (NTA, various years). The rising productivity of hotels in the interior may be attributed mostly to the improved performance of state hotels in the interior and to the increasing proportion of non-state hotels, which usually exhibit greater efficiency than state hotels.

Hotels in China are classified into domestically owned hotels, including state-owned, collectively and privately owned hotels, and foreign investment hotels, including solely foreign owned, joint-venture and cooperative hotels. In general, state-owned hotels are more common in the interior compared to foreign-owned hotels which are more frequent in the coastal area. State hotels, or hotels owned by the state, often suffer from lower productivity compared to the non-state ones. Differences in hotel performance between the coastal and interior area are apparent from Tables 5.10 and 5.11.

Table 5.10 Ratio of total hotel revenue to hotel employees.

	1986	1988	1990	1992	1994	1998
Coastal average (1,000 RMB per hotel employee)	2.21	6.54	28.54	43.58	75.29	83.24
Inland average (1,000 RMB per hotel employee)	1.24	3.59	16.23	25.73	43.68	45.27
Ratio of inland to the coastal average	0.56	0.55	0.57	0.59	0.58	0.54

Source: Based on data of NTA, various years.

Table 5.11 Ratio of total hotel arrivals to employees.

	1986	1988	1990	1992	1994	1998
Coastal average (1,000 per employee)	2.21	6.54	4.92	5.79	7.56	22.04
Inland average (1,000 per employee)	1.15	3.5	2.78	3.36	4.55	13.86
Ratio of inland to the coastal average	0.52	0.53	0.56	0.57	0.60	0.63

Source: Based on data of NTA, various years.

Hotel revenue (unadjusted for inflation) per employee has been increasing for both coastal and inland China, but the relative ratio between the two groups, has hardly changed (see Table 5.10). Nevertheless, this indicates that since 1986, hotel employee productivity in the inland has kept pace with increases in the coastal area as measured by revenue per employee. However when measured by number of tourists per hotel employee, productivity per employee has risen at a faster rate in China's interior than in its coastal area (see Table 5.11). Nevertheless, productivity ratios still remain much higher on the coast compared to the interior of China.

State hotels account for a larger proportion of hotels in the inland than in China's coastal area. The average nationwide proportion of state-owned hotels in relation to all hotels in 1995 was 66.6 percent, but this proportion is 81.36 percent in the interior. More than 70 percent of hotel revenue in China's interior was accounted for by state hotels, but only a little over 40 percent in the coastal area (NTA, various years). State supplied tourism facilities account for most excess supply in the Chinese tourism industry, especially in the interior, where the state sector dominates the industry. But even in the interior, the proportion of state owned hotels is starting to decline.

5.7.4 Growth in ecotourism

As mentioned previously, increasing numbers of tourists are seeking new travel alternatives and are prepared to pay extra to obtain the desired "green" travel experience (Millman, 1989). Nature-based tourism is growing by up to 30 percent whilst general tourism has increased at an average annual rate of 4 percent (Lindberg, 1991). Ecotourism could provide opportunities for rural areas to achieve sustainable development (Wearing and Neil, 1999: 136).

China is promoting ecotourism and the National Tourism Administration of China designated 1999 as the year of "Ecotour China". Abundant ecotourism resources are located mainly in the inland areas of China. By the end of 1995, 199 nature reserves had been established in China, covering an area of 71.85 million hectares, or 7.19 percent of China's territory (Information Office of the State Council of China, 1996). Fourteen marine nature reserves with state status had been declared, along with 710 forest parks, 60 large botanical gardens and 512 historic and scenic sites (Information Office of the State Council of China, 1996), and further protected areas have been established more recently (*Peoples Daily*, overseas edition, 30 December, 1999).

Ecotourism can play a role in ameliorating regional disparity in China because the majority of its ecotourism resources are located in its interior. Rich ecotourism resources are distributed in inland areas of China and there is increasing tourist demand in rural places such as Xishuangbanna in Yunnan Province in southeast China (Tisdell, 1995). China has taken steps to limit the speed of resource depletion in an effort to conserve its environment and promote ecotourism (Tisdell, 1999).

5.7.5   *International tourist arrivals: Source and their spatial dispersion*

The origin of tourists influences to a great extent the location of tourism, especially in China. International tourists to China show different spatial distribution patterns. Compatriots, especially those from Hong Kong, concentrate on the East coast more than tourists from other places, and they enter China frequently for short visits, mainly for business. They are relatively low in hotel registrations as well. By contrast, foreigners are proportionately well represented in the periphery. For example, 98 percent of tourists to Lhasa in Tibet were foreigners, and were very interested in tourist activities involving ecotourism, nature and culture (Gormsen, 1990). Changes in the composition of overseas tourists by origin have also contributed to tourism development in the interior of China.

Of the total 63.48 million inbound arrivals in China in 1998, slightly over 7 million were foreigners, 0.12 million were overseas Chinese, and 56.25 million were compatriots, who live in Hong Kong, Macau, and Taiwan (NTA, 1999: 1). Table 2.3 reports the composition of international tourist by classification by China's method since the mid-1980s.

Table 2.4 provided details of arrivals of foreigners from Asia which has been the dominant source of foreign tourists to China. Changes have occurred in the percentage of tourists coming from different countries. For example, Japan and the United States were the most important source of foreign tourists for China in 1986. However, the share of each decreased by over ten percent respectively between 1986 and 1998. Furthermore, market shares of Europe, North America and Oceania declined. The total share of Chinese compatriots has generally decreased as well. In contrast, tourists from East Asian countries (except Japan) have been on the increase, as are tourists from countries of the former Soviet Union countries rose compared with earlier years (NTA, various years).

Different types of tourists have a varied effect on spatial tourism distribution. Oppermann (1992a) divided tourists into four categories, namely those who exhibit inactive, little active, active and very active travel behaviours. Those "active travellers", who stay in at least four different overnight localities during a trip exhibit a dispersed spatial behaviour according to Opperman's definition. Consequently, targeting this group may achieve the goal of more even regional development through a more uniform distribution of tourism expenditure. However, as discussed later, this is not the only way of achieving spatial dispersion of tourism.

Tourist activity and average expenditure by different types of tourists in China vary. Foreigners are relatively active and are higher spending travellers in China compared to Chinese compatriots. They were more dispersed spatially and spent $1,063 on average per trip as compared to $345.80 for tourists from Hong Kong and Macau in 1990 (NTA, 1992). Even with the decreasing proportion of higher spending foreigners from North America and Japan, foreigners still showed the highest average expenditure (NTA, 1997). Daily expenditure per tourist was $147.96 for foreigners in 1996, $145.90 for overseas Chinese and $120.60 for compatriots (NTA, 1997). Because foreigners tend to be more dispersed in their travel, are more likely to visit the interior and show greater interest in ecotourism than other tourists, their increasing visits may expand demand for ecotourism in China.

Chinese data do not identify inbound travellers to China by purpose of visit. Nevertheless, it is estimated that 60 percent of arrivals are for leisure and 40 percent for business, and the latter concentrate overwhelmingly on the East coast (Bailey, 1995). Visiting friends and relatives (VFR) visits are included in the leisure-share because much of the quasi-domestic travel by people from Hong Kong and Macau has a VFR element. There have been attempts to exclude the quasi-domestic element of visits from Hong Kong and Macau, and consequently the adjusted arrivals in 1993 for China was 20 million as estimated by the World Tourism Organisation, and 15 million by the Travel Business Analyst of Hong Kong (Bailey, 1995). A survey conducted on international travellers departing China revealed that the composition of international tourists to China by purpose was 57 percent for sightseeing, 12.3 percent for holiday, 20 percent for business, and 5.4 percent for visiting friends and relatives (NTA, 1992).

Oppermann (1992a) used a Travel Dispersal Index to reflect both the spatial and sectoral effects of intra-national travel behaviour employing five variables, namely length of stay, number of overnight destinations, number of different types of accommodation, transportation and travel organisation.

A low Travel Dispersal Index was found among short-staying, inactive travellers who usually join bigger tourist groups and frequent less destinations than active travellers. The degree of concentration among the former is much higher and their economic impact is less dispersed. In his survey in Malaysia, Oppermann (1992a) found that tourists from Germany and the United Kingdom had the highest Travel Dispersal Index, while those from ASEAN countries tended to concentrate in major gateways. In the case of China's international tourism, in contrast to Chinese compatriots, especially those from Hong Kong and Macau, who concentrate overwhelmingly in Guangdong for short but frequent trips mainly for business and VFR, foreigners are more dispersed throughout China. Twelve coastal areas received 85.7 percent of total international arrivals to China in 1986, 83.6 percent in 1992, and 79.72 percent in 1995 (NTA, various issues), indicating reduced relative concentration of international tourists on the coast and growing relative tourist dispersal.

Average length of stay may influence the number of places a tourist visits within a country. Pearce suggested that an increase in "length of stay results in more places being visited, not more time being spent in the same number of places". He argued that visitors who stay shorter "opt for the most accessible sites and what are perceived to be the main tourist attractions. Those on longer visits take in other secondary and small centres and attractions" (Pearce, 1990: 38). Tourists to New Zealand stay on average 19.7 nights and visit 5.4 places, compared to 4.5 nights and 1.5 places for those to Malaysia (Oppermann, 1992b). The average length of stay is the highest for free independent travellers who account for less than 40 percent of total arrivals to China and stayed on average 15.5 days (NTA, 1992). The average length of stay of international tourists in China in 1995 was 3.29 days, with 4.27 days for foreigners, 4.04 for overseas Chinese, 1.99 for visitors from Hong Kong and Macau, and 2.62 for Taiwanese (NTA, 1996).

Ecotourism is a form of recreational tourism and usually appeals more to longer-staying tourists than short-staying business or VFR tourists (Boo, 1990). With the changing structure of arrivals to China, there is increasing scope for development of ecotourism. It provides considerable potential for tourism development in the inland regions.

5.8   The Dispersal of Domestic Tourism

The statistical measurement of tourism data started only in the 1920s and concentrated on international tourism data (Simmons, 1984). Details of domestic tourism are not available in the official Chinese statistics, hence most discussion in this book is based on international tourism. However, in the worldwide tourism market, domestic travel accounts for around 90 percent of the total tourism volume (WTO, 1995). Furthermore, an understanding of Chinese domestic tourism is necessary in order to provide a more complete study of tourism in China.

Domestic tourism has grown rapidly in China in recent years as indicated in Chapter 2. Domestic tourism used to be dominated by business trips paid for by employers in China in the 1980s. It often took the form of organised package tours, such as round trips for employees and "travel meetings", that is conventions, exhibitions and so on. Hence it came to be viewed by some as a legitimate excuse for squandering public funds to satisfy those in power. However, from the early 1990s, with increasing discretionary income and time, trips taken by individuals rose, and domestic tourism in its real sense has emerged in China (NTA, 1994). Domestic tourism is "transforming from a state of spontaneous travel to being marketed and organised by travel services" (NTA, 1993: 23).

Expanding domestic tourism is a normal phenomenon with increasing income and leisure time (Smith, 1989, Chapter 1). GNP per capita in China was expected to increase from US$400 to US$1,300 by the year 2000 as indicated in the Ninth 5-Year Plan (1996–2000) (Anon, 1995), and purchasing power measured by per capita consumption in Shanghai was US$2,530 in 1994, compared with US$1,700 for Guangdong and US$1,325 for Beijing (Hiscock, 1995). With increasing discretionary income, more leisure time and mobility in China, domestic tourism is expected to grow further.

Although there are no specific data on the number of domestic tourists received by each locality, the number of Chinese staying at hotels, calculated by subtracting hotel guests from overseas from the total hotel guests, serves as a proxy for regional distribution of domestic tourists. Among the top ten receivers of domestic hotel patrons, the coastal areas, including Guangdong,

Zhejiang, Beijing and Jiangsu, accounted for only 23.4 percent of the national total domestic hotel patrons. By contrast, the top ten receivers of international hotel patrons accounted for 80 percent of the national total. Among them, only two were inland localities, namely Yunnan and Shaanxi, who received together only 7.6 percent of the total international hotel patrons (NTA, 1999). Therefore, domestic tourism is much more dispersed throughout China, and the inland areas obtain a higher proportion of travellers and tourism receipts when domestic tourism is included in the discussion.

Table 5.12 shows a much higher proportion of hotel patrons from overseas present in the coastal area than that in the interior in 1995. While 77 percent of the 40.5 million hotel guests received in the coastal areas were Chinese, but 93 percent of 36.3 million hotel guests received by the interior were Chinese. The interior hosted 52 percent of the total domestic hotel guests in 1995 (Table 5.14). The interior of China therefore receives a higher proportion of hotel-based tourism nationwide (than that evident from inbound tourism) when domestic tourism is taken into account.

Travel agencies in China are divided into three categories. Category A travel agencies are those liaising with foreign tour operators directly and receiving international arrivals to mainland China. Category B travel agencies only receive international arrivals and co-ordinate with the Category A travel agencies or other departments concerned. Category C travel agencies only handle domestic tourism. Category A travel agencies are concentrated heavily on the coastal areas, whereas 42 percent of the 2,801 Category C travel agencies were distributed in the interior in 1996 (NTA, 1997), indicating the higher level of domestic tourism than international tourism in China's interior.

Table 5.12 Overseas patrons received by hotels in China, 1995.

	Total hotel guests (000)	Guests from overseas (000)	Overseas guests (%)	Chinese (%)
China total	76,746.6	11,814.6	15.39	84.61
Coastal (12)	40,491.4	9,296.3	22.96	77.04
Inland (18)	36,255.2	2,518.3	6.95	93.05

Source: Based on data of NTA, 1996.

The difference between domestic and international tourists influences spatial distribution of tourism demand. First of all, the distance factor may be a greater constraint for international tourism in the inland areas. The full cost of tourism is a sum of its market prices plus the value of time foregone from other uses. Time is an important resource, especially for tourism activities (Becker, 1965). It has been noted that time for a journey may have a positive utility on short, scenic trips, but the utility declines and becomes negative as the journey becomes longer and more tedious (Walsh *et al.*, 1990). Unlike inbound tourists, especially businessmen from Hong Kong and Taiwan who are inclined to visit popular coastal cities because of tight time budgets, Chinese tourists (mainly from coastal regions and large metropolitan areas) may have a greater desire and more opportunity to visit rural and inland areas, and so relatively contribute more to rural development. The time budget for an average international traveller, who stays in China for 11 days, prevents him/her from visiting places distant from major entry points or sites with difficult access. Pearce (1990) noticed that short-staying visitors concentrated more on major destinations. More than half of international tourists visit one to three cities in China, 27.4 percent visit four to six cities, whilst only 15.9 percent visit more than seven cities (NTA, 1992).

Secondly, the tourism expenditure pattern of a domestic tourist typically consists of 26.3 percent on transportation, 20.8 percent on shopping, 17.9 percent on accommodation, 18.7 percent on food and beverages, and 16.3 percent on others, while the major outlay by an international visitor is for accommodation, amounting to 25 percent, with the next two major items being transportation (20.6 percent), and food and beverage (19.2 percent) (NTA, 1995). Thus China's domestic travellers spend relatively more of their budget on travel in China than do its international travellers. Time constraints and travel distance are less serious for Chinese tourists compared to international arrivals, therefore Chinese tourists are more dispersed than international ones (NTA, 1995). When domestic tourism is taken into account, China's tourism is less concentrated on the coastal area.

The dispersal of tourists over wider areas, rather than crowding of tourists into a few cities, helps more regions to obtain economic gains from tourism. Dispersal of tourism can occur in different ways, such as:

- raising the degree of dispersal of individual travellers;
- raising the number of tourists who have a high dispersal tendency; and
- scattering tourists geographically.

It is still debatable whether a decrease in the interregional concentration of tourism demand over time is highly desirable, owing to the possibility that it may mean a transfer of demand from a previous centre to its immediate neighbours without necessarily increasing the entire market. In some cases, peripheral regions may not experience the major share of tourism growth even with greater dispersion of tourism. It has been observed in the United Kingdom that a wider spatial distribution of tourism from the early 1990s appears to have been a transfer of part of London's share to the geographically proximate regions of the Heart of England, Thames, Yorkshire and so on (Pack *et al.*, 1995). Nevertheless, it is still desirable to have a more dispersed regional distribution of tourists from the viewpoint of regional development, especially in China, because increasing crowding in some coastal areas and the existence of under-utilised tourist facilities in the interior.

While inbound tourism to China more than reinforces China's economic skew in favour of its coastal region, this does not seem to be so for domestic tourism. If studies of the numbers of domestic hotel guests are taken as an indicator of the regional distribution of Chinese domestic tourism, domestic tourism appears to ameliorate the skew. However, a higher proportion of domestic Chinese tourists may stay with friends and relatives on the coast than in the inland. This is because Han Chinese tend to reside in China's coastal core whereas minorities comprise a high proportion of the population in China's inland. Nevertheless, it seems safe to conclude that the expansion of Chinese domestic tourism is of particular economic benefit to China's inland areas. Unfortunately, paucity of Chinese data on domestic tourism rules out a detailed analysis of trends in the spatial spread of that tourism.

5.9   Regional Economic Impact of Tourism Does Not Depend Solely on Regional Relativities

Even though the skew of inbound tourism in favour of China's coastal region has been reduced in recent years, it remains very marked and inbound tourism continues to reinforce the bias of China's economic activity in favour of its coastal region. This is because inbound tourism is even more skewed than general economic production towards the coastal region of China.

Now it might be thought that because of this skew the expansion of inbound tourism to China would not be supportive of economic development in China's inland. But this conclusion does not necessarily follow. As a matter of fact tourism to inland China since 1986 has expanded in terms of receipts and tourist arrivals at a faster rate on average than in its coastal region. This is why the percentages of the tourism variables shown in Table 5.1 for the coastal region have on average declined since 1986.

It follows that if the economic leakage from tourist receipts in the inland happened to be constant or ever increasing somewhat, the growth in inbound tourism to China as a whole would have provided a positive stimulus to economic growth in China's inland. The following factors could be relevant in assessing the ability of inbound tourism to stimulate economic growth in inland China:

(i) Although the share of the inland region in inbound tourism receipts is relatively low at just over 15 percent of the total receipts (using the 1998 figure — see Table 5.1), this inland share may be higher than for many other industries in China.

(ii) Tourism is a rapidly growing industry, and although some other industries may show a greater skew in favour of the inland, they may be growing at a slow or slower rate.

(iii) There may be few economic growth opportunities for the inland. Therefore, even relatively small possibilities for economic growth may be worth pursuing.

(iv) Although the proportionate share of China's inland in total inbound tourist receipts remains small, it has increased substantially in a decade and scope may exist for its further increase.

(v) The growth in tourism in China's inland region has not been uniform. It has been rapid in some provinces, such as Inner Mongolia, Xinjiang, Tibet and Yunnan. Therefore, even if some areas of the inland are limited in their potential for tourism development, it has a high potential in others. Aggregate figures conceal such differences.

Naturally, there may be significant economic leakages from tourism in inland regions. But we cannot assume that they will be of such a magnitude as to annul positive impacts of tourism growth on inland regional development. Most other industries in the inland will also exhibit regional economic leakages and many of these may be stagnant or show little economic growth. Neither a skew of tourism in favour of the economic central core nor a high degree of economic leakages from tourism in peripheral areas, would be sufficient in themselves to rule out tourism as a growth-inducing industry for peripheral areas. While these elements do reduce the positive economic impact of tourism growth on the development of peripheral areas, they need not negate it completely. Furthermore, this discussion indicates that one must consider more than regional relativities in assessing regional economic growth.

5.10 Parting Detailed Snapshots by Regions of Proportionate Growth of Visits by China's Inbound Tourists

While the earlier analysis of trends in China's inbound tourism growth and changes in its spatial inequality in China are useful, this analysis may mask significant differences in tourism growth between individual provinces. The extent, however, of disparities in tourism growth between provinces are apparent from Table 5.13. It shows the proportionate change in the number of inbound tourists visiting China's tourist regions between 1986 and 1998 as well as variation in tourism receipts from this group. This table indicates that international tourist arrivals in the inland area of China increased by 16.9-fold in this time but by only 12.2-fold in the coastal area. Likewise receipts in the inland rose faster than on the coast (41.5-fold compared to 17.6-fold) and the disparity was such as to indicate rising real receipts from inbound travellers in the inland of China.

It might be observed that total arrivals for China as a whole as reported in Table 2.6 are higher than the sum of the arrivals in each locality as set out in Table 5.13. This is because data for the former are collected at entry

Table 5.13 Regional arrivals and receipts from inbound tourists, China 1986 and 1998 with growth ratios, classified into coastal and inland areas and shown by descending order of growth ratios of arrivals.

Region	Arrivals 000		Growth ratio	Receipts $m		Growth ratio
	1986	1998	98/86	1986	1998	98/86
Total 30	**1782.6**	**21678.3**	**12.2**	**611.3**	**10761.5**	**17.6**
Total Coastal (12)	**1527.7**	**17374.0**	**11.4**	**571.8**	**9120.7**	**16.0**
Hainan	?[a]	394.2	?[a]	0.4	96.3	240.7
Shandong	11.7	608.2	52.0	3.9	219.5	56.3
Hebei	12.0	326.9	27.2	0.7	100.1	142.9
Zhejiang	36.0	819.6	22.8	13.2	361.2	27.4
Tianjin	16.5	304.9	18.5	4.3	201.8	46.9
Liaoning	22.2	410.7	18.5	5.2	262.4	50.5
Jiangsu	88.0	1154.0	13.1	29.0	528.8	18.2
Fujian	102.0	1217.8	11.9	18.1	651.1	36.0
Guangdong	723.0	7886.5	10.9	205.0	2941.9	14.4
Shanghai	147.7	1527.1	10.3	22.0	1217.9	55.4
Beijing	257.0	2200.9	8.6	260.0	2384.0	9.2
Guangxi	111.6	523.3	4.7	10.0	155.7	15.6
Total Inland (18)	**254.9**	**4304.3**	**16.9**	**39.5**	**1640.8**	**41.5**
Xinjiang	0.9	162.9	181.0	2.3	82.5	35.9
Inner Mongolia	2.7	369.0	136.7	0.4	125.5	313.8
Tibet	1.4	96.4	68.9	0.4	33.0	82.6
Hunan	6.0	348.6	58.1	1.1	156.1	141.9
Guizhou	3.9	151.3	38.8	0.4	48.3	120.8
Heilongjiang	12.3	383.3	31.2	3.2	120.9	37.8
Yunnan	31.5	760.9	24.2	6.5	261.0	40.2
Anhui	7.8	184.2	23.6	0.4	51.2	128.0
Jiangxi	6.0	114.9	19.2	1.4	42.8	30.6
Henan	15.0	274.7	18.3	2.0	101.4	50.7
Hubei	20.4	295.6	14.5	4.0	88.3	22.1
Gansu	9.0	102.4	11.4	2.1	30.2	14.4
Sichuan	42.0	454.0	10.8	6.6	172.0	26.1
Qinghai	1.8	16.6	9.2	0.0	2.8	92.0
Ningxia	0.6	5.1	8.5	0.0	1.4	473.3
Shaanxi	77.4	540.5	7.0	6.5	247.2	38.0
Jilin	9.0	31.4	3.5	1.5	37.8	25.2
Shanxi	7.2	12.5	1.7	0.7	38.3	57.1

[a]Note: Hainan was not a separate province in 1986. Its arrivals for 1986 are uncertain but the growth ratios of its arrivals could be of the order of 200.

Source: Calculated from data of NTA (1987) and (1998).

points to China whereas the latter information is collected by hotels, travel agencies and so on at the provincial level. This results in inbound tourists who do not use these tourist facilities being omitted in the provincial count. Discrepancies also occur in tourism receipts reported at national and local level but these are in the opposite direction to those for arrivals. Tourism receipts earned from tourism services provided by central government ministries and departments, such as those affiliated with NTA and the Ministry of International Economic Cooperation and Trade, are not included in the statistics of tourism receipts for any locality but are regarded as a part of national tourism receipts, resulting in a higher level of tourism receipts reported at the national level compared to the sum of such receipts for the 30 localities. However, the arguments in this book about comparative regional differences are not invalidated by such discrepancies.

An interesting feature apparent from Table 5.13 is that those tourism areas with higher levels of tourism in 1986 did not sustain the highest proportionate growth. Also proportionate rates of growth varied widely from a low of 1.5-fold for international arrivals in Shanxi to a high of 181-fold for Xinjiang in inland China, to the very high but uncertain figure for Hainan. Although growth ratios were very high between coastal regions, they were extremely so in China's inland area. Furthermore, inland provinces registered both the highest and the lowest ratios of tourism growth in China between 1986 and 1998, Hainan excluded, Shanxi and Jilin had the lowest growth ratios in China and that for Guangxi on the coast was relatively low.

The remoter provinces of China situated in its interior displayed the largest tourism growth ratios. These ratios are extremely high for Xinjiang, Inner Mongolia and Tibet. Although Yunnan's activity did not expand relatively by so much, its growth was sufficient for it to displace Shaanxi by 1998 as China's leading inland tourism province. On the coast, Hainan and Shandong experienced exceptionally high growth of their tourism industries. The high growth rate for Hainan seems to represent a coastal "outlier".

The details in Table 5.13 make it clear that while tourism expansion in several inland provinces was spectacular between 1986 and 1998 (and well above the average for China as a whole), several inland provinces lagged seriously in increasing their visits of international tourists. Reasons for the varied tourism growth experiences of the individual provinces/cities in China would be worthwhile investigating but are beyond the present study.

Figure 5.3 helps highlight some of the general relationships implied by Table 5.13. The logarithms of the growth rates of coastal provinces/ administrative cities and the inland provinces are shown in Fig. 5.3 in descending order corresponding to Table 5.13. However, Hainan has been excluded from the coastal group because it is regarded as an outlier. Linear regression lines provide a good fit to the data and these are also shown. The regression line for the inland provinces lies well above that for the coastal areas, confirming the higher growth ratios of arrivals in the inland compared to the coast. Furthermore, the downward slope of the regression line for coastal areas is less than for the interior showing that on average growth ratios in international arrivals for inland areas are more unequal than for coastal areas.

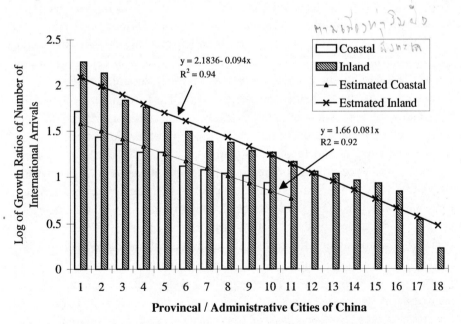

Fig. 5.3 Logarithms of growth ratios of international arrivals for inland provinces and coastal areas of China, 1998 relative to 1986; based on Table 5.13. Note that Hainan has been excluded.

Although several inland provinces of China did experience spectacular growth in tourism between 1986 and 1998 and tourism in the inland region as a whole expanded proportionately more than in the coastal region, one should nevertheless not lose sight of the fact that inbound tourism in China's interior still accounts for less than 20 percent of China's international arrivals and its international tourism receipts. In 1998, inbound tourism to China remained highly concentrated on its coastal region.

5.11   Concluding Remarks

The fact that the share in tourism of the non-coastal area of China increased along with growth in aggregate tourism demand for the whole country implies that relatively greater spatial dispersal of tourism development is occurring. This is a desirable change in a country with severe economic inequality across regions. The relative convergence of international tourism as compared to the lack of economic convergence between coastal and interior China, combined with the potential of tourism to be a growth pole, suggests that tourism growth might eventually reduce regional economic inequality in China. Nevertheless, further research is needed to compare the spatial distribution of domestic tourism with international tourism, and to complete a more detailed study of the regional distribution of tourism paying attention to more detailed spatial features of China.

Compared to central or core regions, peripheral areas have less economic flexibility, suffer more serious consequences from seasonality, and experience higher income leakages. While "central tourism regions have a choice to a certain extent about what segment of the tourism market to cater for, the periphery has to develop the few segments that are attracted by their limited resources" (Hohl and Tisdell, 1995). Inland China has resource advantages for ecotourism compared to its coastal area where mass tourism is more significant. A better understanding of what ecotourism is and how to conserve tourist resources in the process of tourism development is crucial for the long-term viability of tourism, especially in the inland areas of China where ecotourism is important. The next chapter therefore concentrates on issues involving ecotourism.

Chapter 6

Ecotourism: Its Nature, Sustainability, and Other Issues

6.1 Introduction

In the previous chapter, it was suggested that ecotourism, broadly defined, has been an important factor in the expansion of the level of tourism in inland China. This is especially so if ecotourism is defined to include tourism which relies both on natural and cultural manifestations in natural areas as does the definition of Hector Ceballos-Lascurian introduced later in this chapter. China's inland areas have a greater presence and variety of cultures of minority groups than does its coastal region, as well as diverse natural attractions, as for example outlined in depth for the inland province of Yunnan in Chapter 8.

Regional areas containing abundant or special natural areas can target ecotourism to promote their local economy. The development of ecotourism may reduce economic gaps between regions. This is particularly pertinent to Chinese economic development — an important focus in this book. However, tourism faces new challenges in this era. On one hand, international tourism keeps on increasing at an annual rate of around 4 percent per annum, adding over 400 million extra tourists every year (WTTC, 1995). On the other hand, global pollution and environmental changes, accompanied by damage from the tourism industry itself, have reduced the natural resource-base for tourism. At the same time, tourists are demanding experiences of higher quality and of greater diversity, and demand for ecotourism is growing.

Ecotourism or ecological tourism, is a term that has been applied in different ways often without a clear definition. Various definitions of ecotourism exist in the literature and a broadly accepted definition of ecotourism does

141

not yet exist. The extent to which ecotourism can be separated from tourism generally or the extent to which a separate tourism industry can be identified is uncertain. Considerable fuzziness exists about the boundaries. In many countries, including China, ecotourism is regarded as a sustainable type of tourism, especially for regional areas. But in many cases, ecotourism is unfortunately used as an excuse for encroaching on natural areas where other types of industry are perceived as threatening the long-term existence of the resource-base. Can ecotourism truly be tailored in a fashion that proves to be both environmentally protective and economically viable? Is ecotourism favourable to the conservation of tourist resources or just another way to invade pristine areas? To answer these questions, a better understanding of the definitions of ecotourism is important.

It is therefore necessary to define ecotourism adequately in order to provide economic and other measures of its importance and consider its potential for economic development. Lack of a clear definition can be expected to provide inappropriate measurement and inadequate policy advice. Policy proposals for developing or managing ecotourism must take account of the participants (stakeholders) in ecotourism and these are identified and discussed. The sustainability of ecotourism depends not only on the participants in it but is also influenced by the nature of ecotourism, which varies according to the definition used. Furthermore, the sustainability of ecotourism is affected by market and government failures. All of these aspects are discussed in this chapter with further related discussions occurring in the next chapter. Even though the main focus is on general principles and the international context, where possible, examples and illustrations from China are introduced.

6.2 The Boundary of Ecotourism

6.2.1 *Ecology and ecological systems*

Before defining ecotourism itself, one needs to look first into the terms "ecology" and "ecological system" because they define the domain in which ecotourism is performed. There are basically two groups of definitions for these two terms in the literature — one set is broad and the other is narrow. The broad definition for ecology is: "A science to study the relationship between the distribution of human groups with reference to material resources and the consequent social and cultural patterns" *(Webster's New 20th Century Dictionary of the English Language, second edition, 1962)*. An ecological system has been defined as "A community of organisms, interacting with one another, plus the environment in which they live and with which they also interact" *(The Macquarie Dictionary, 1981)*. These two descriptions relate ecology and ecological systems to the environment and include both physical and non-physical factors that interact with one another. There is nothing external to this system, and there is no way of viewing any type of tourism except as a part of an ecosystem. There is no difference between ecotourism and other forms of tourism if it is positioned in this broad ecological system because the entire cosmos is covered, and the boundary of ecotourism overlaps that of tourism completely.

Some people hold the opinion that ecotourism is a subset of tourism which takes care of the environment while the other types of tourism do not. However, ecotourism itself cannot survive indefinitely in a situation where non-ecotourism activities keep on depleting resources as a result of the interchanges of material and energy between and among ecotourism, non-ecotourism activities and the ecological system. This indicates that there is inherent interdependence between the broad ecological system and tourism (including ecotourism) and suggests that it is not only the responsibility of ecotourism to protect the environment but also the entire tourism industry's mission to promote a better resource situation in order to facilitate a sustained development. There is no way to isolate ecotourism from other tourist activities with which it shares the same ecological resources and interacts. Placing ecotourism in its broadest context will help to encourage ecological consciousness within the entire tourism industry and will counteract the misunderstanding that it is just the duty of ecotourism to conserve the environment.

Further discussions are based on narrow definitions of ecotourism and the following set of definitions are therefore adopted: Ecology is "the scientific study of the interrelationships between living organisms and the environment (including the other living organisms present) in which they live. Without qualification the term tends to be confined to plant ecology" (Clark, 1985). The narrow meaning of "ecological system" is: "A system made up of a community of animals, plants and bacteria and its inter-related physical and chemical environment" *(Webster's New 20th Century Dictionary of the English Language, second edition, 1962).*

In this set of definitions, ecology and the ecological system are confined to living things and their environments. However, in practice ecotourism is often used to refer to tourism practised in natural areas little disturbed by human activities. This distinguishes ecotourism from urban-based or heavily anthropologically moulded tourism. Nevertheless, the natural environment is not the only factor involved in ecotourism. Some non-natural elements such as social, cultural, economic and political factors interweave with the natural setting and cannot be separated from the closely related living environment, and so are included in the ecotourism system. It is therefore appropriate to expand discussions beyond the territory of narrowly defined ecological systems even though these are the major focus in this book.

6.2.2   Definitions of ecotourism

There is no universally accepted definition of ecotourism. But a few scholars have been trying to distil the basic elements of ecotourism beginning in the early 1980s. The word "eco" comes from the Greek "oikos", meaning home. One of the earliest and most quoted definitions was put forward by Hector Ceballos-Lascurian, who set up a travel agency called "Ecotours" in 1984, serving people interested in nature and Mexican culture. He defined ecotourism as "tourism that involves travelling to relatively undisturbed or uncontaminated natural areas with the specific objective of studying, admiring and enjoying the scenery and its wild plants and animals, as well as any existing cultural manifestations (both past and present) found in these areas" (cited by Boo, 1990). While it is self-evident that this type of ecotourism can only exist in well-preserved areas, and the experimental and educational factors are mentioned, the definition does not mention the responsibility of the ecotourism industry for environmental conservation. As a matter of fact, it is just a good definition for nature tourism but not satisfactory for eco-tourism because conservation is not addressed by it.

Many authors use the term "nature tourism" and "ecotourism" inter-changeably, such as Lindberg (1991) and McNeely *et al.* (1992), while some limit it to tourism based primarily on living natural things. It is difficult to draw a clear cut line between ecotourism and nature tourism because of the fuzziness in judging whether a tourism activity is environmentally consump-tive or not. The common ground between ecotourism and nature tourism lies in the fact that they both rely on natural areas. Ecotourism differs however from nature tourism in its role of minimising negative effects on environment and providing economic and educational incentives to maintain or to improve the resource base. On the other hand, nature tourism is just a branch of tourism activity that makes use of natural areas but not necessarily in an environmentally sensitive way. Nature tourism may refer to everything from the use of the environment to attract visitors and sell tourist destinations without regard for environmental impacts, to experiences and products that sustain both tourism and environment (Wright, 1994).

After discussions at such international conferences as the IUCN Parks Congress in Venezuela and the Ecotourism Conference in Belize in 1992, conservation has been added to the definition for ecotourism. Hence most recent studies emphasise the role of ecotourism in conservation as a way to differentiate ecotourism from nature tourism. The 4th Congress on National Parks and Protected Areas, held in Venezuela, 1992, defined ecotourism as "responsible travel to natural areas that sustains the well-being of local people and conserves the environment". Zell (1991) stated "I define eco-tourism as ecologically responsible tourism". Valentine (1992) also proposed ecotourism as "a direct contributor to the continued protection and manage-ment of the protected areas used", arguing that all ecotourism must be at least nature-dependent, as opposed to simply taking place in a natural environment.

Wen and Tisdell (1995) use a Venn diagram to demonstrate the conceptual relationship of four groups of tourism:

A Entire tourism
B Nature-based tourism
C Tourism taking care of the environment
D Ecotourism

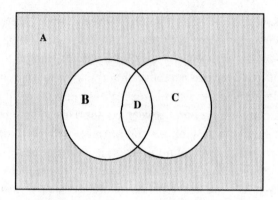

Fig. 6.1 Boundary for four types of tourism.

A modified form of this Venn diagram is shown in Fig. 6.1.

The National Ecotourism Strategy of Australia (1994) defined ecotourism as "(N)ature-based tourism that involves education and interpretation of the natural environment and is managed to be ecologically sustainable". This definition recognises that the "natural environment" includes cultural components, and that "ecologically sustainable" involves an appropriate return to the local community and conservation of the resource in the long run. Wright (1994) mentioned some principles for ecotourism: it should not degrade the resource and should be developed in an environmentally sound manner; it should provide long-term benefits to the resource, to the local community and industry; it should provide first-hand, participatory and enlightening experiences; it should involve education among all parties — local communities, government, non-governmental organisations, industry and tourists; it should encourage all-party recognition of the intrinsic values of the resource; it should involve acceptance of the resource on its own terms, and in recognition of its limits, which involves supply-oriented management; it should promote understanding and involve partnerships between many players, which could include government, non-governmental organisations, industry, scientists and locals; it should promote moral and ethical responsibilities and behaviour towards the natural and cultural environment by all players.

Miller and Kaae (1993), and later Orams (1995), developed a continuum of ecotourism paradigms in order to analyse the diverse definitions and connotations associated with ecotourism. At one pole of this continuum is the view that all tourism has negative impacts on the natural resources, hence ecotourism is impossible. At the other pole, humans are regarded as a natural part of the environment and tourists are not responsible to consider other living organisms. Definitions of ecotourism are considered as "lying in a position somewhere within a range that lies inside these polar extremes" (Orams, 1995).

From what has been argued above, it may be concluded that three basic characters are found in ecotourism (Wen and Tisdell, 1995):

- ecotourism involves travel to relatively well-conserved natural areas;
- it takes particular care of the environment and promotes conservation;
- its purpose is to provide non-consumptive experience and to educate participants.

With respect to education, a distinction can be made between simple observation and more in-depth learning. Individuals can tailor their educational experience to meet their own interests to varying degrees. Learning in tourism in the form of an educational guided-tour is regarded as more rewarding and intellectually challenging than other tours. The role of tour guide involves both teaching and acting. He/she is a motivator, ambassador, entertainer, disciplinarian, and group leader (Holloway, 1981). A characteristic of ecotourism is the greater focus on participation in activities rather than destinations compared with mass tourism (Hall and Weiler, 1992), leading to more environmentally responsible attitudes and behaviour during and after the ecotourism experience.

In the case of China, it is commonly accepted that ecotourism is nature-based, and culturally based ecotourism amongst minorities is becoming a major part of inland tourism. However, the conservation part of ecotourism needs to be further emphasised. Although it is difficult to estimate the importance of ecotourism in China, it may be reasonable to guess that a higher proportion of ecotourism exists in the inland areas than coastal China because more nature and cultural based tourism occurs in inland China.

6.3   Principal Participants in Ecotourism

Ecotourism involves basically a combination of environmental, social and economic factors, which cannot all be categorised as business attributes. Many tourism problems can be attributed to the business-only outlook of tourism enterprises. The sooner it is understood that ecotourism is a compound system involving both marketable and non-marketable components, the more successful ecotourism development will be. Broadly speaking, those who participate in ecotourism and influence its scale as well as direction can be divided into four groups: the business sector, ecotourists, the government sector and non-government organisations. They are considered in turn in the following sections.

6.3.1   Ecotourism industry — the business sector

The business sector is the backbone of ecotourism in the sense that it provides economic incentives and links resources with consumers. It includes travel agencies, accommodation, transportation and other sections that cater for ecotourism arrangements. The market mechanism directs this section and price adjustment influences this system.

From an economics point of view, it may be possible to measure the size of the industry by considering either the supply side or the demand side. The supply-side approach might be based on a survey of businesses involved in ecotourism, designed to measure the economic involvement of each in ecotourism and from whether tourist organisations perceive themselves to be involved in ecotourism. Such an approach may however be costly and since many tourist organisations tend to be involved in ecotourism as well as other tourist activities, the boundaries between the two may be difficult to delineate. This is apart from the difficulty posed by businesses that engage both in tourism and non-tourism activities. The demand-side approach involves surveys of tourists or potential tourists to determine their involvement in ecotourism or their demand for it. However, it is hard to measure the number of ecotourism agencies or ecotourists due to limited resources and the fact that tourism is usually a mixed experience. Despite the difficulties in

Table 6.1 Estimated value of ecotourism worldwide, 1980–1989 ($ billion).

Year	80	81	82	83	84	85	86	87	88	89
Estimated value	4.0	4.0	4.0	4.0	4.5	5.0	6.0	7.5	9.0	10.0

Source: Smith and Jenner, 1991.

estimating the market share of ecotourism, some estimates have been made. Table 6.1 gives the estimated value of ecotourism from 1980 to 1989 by Smith and Jenner (1991).

WWF estimates that $12 billion out of the $55 billion earned from tourism by developing countries in 1988 was due to ecotourism (EIU, 1992). Almost all the 1,420 national parks in the tropics, covering 175 million hectares, promote tourism (McNeely and Thorsell, 1987). The Australian Tourist Commission estimated that 18 percent of international tourists in 1990 were ecotourists, and that this sector would grow by 30 percent annually, a rate of growth almost three times as great as the tourism industry on average (Hill, 1994). In the WWF airport survey of 436 tourists in five South American countries, almost half reported that the presence of protected areas was the "main reason" or "very important" in their decision to visit the country, and more than half went to at least one park on their trip (Boo, 1990: 3). The number of international visitors to Costa Rica's national parks more than doubled between 1984 and 1989. Over 40 percent of the international tourists surveyed in 1988 mentioned that protected areas were primary or important in their travel decision (Boo, 1990). Ecotourism income accounted for only 7.8 percent of the export earnings and 4.5 percent of GDP of Belize in 1981, but increased to 42.3 and 24.8 percent, respectively, in 1990 (Cater and Lowman, 1994: 70).

Hill (1990) cited a 1985 marketing survey for the Costa Rican Tourism Institute, which predicted a 300 percent increase in nature-based tourism to Costa Rica by the year 2000 if the political stability in the region is maintained. Smaller scale, more specialised tourism, such as ecotourism, shows more promise in this area. Ecotourism is growing in Latin America. Dominica adopted a deliberate ecotourism strategy in the 1970s to depart from previous mass tourism activities. Costa Rica is benefiting from its stability, biodiversity and the interaction with a comprehensive protected area system. Mexico and Cuba have the potential of becoming important ecotourism destinations owing to their resources and proximity to the North America market. However, it is still too early to predict whether these countries will become models of sustainable tourism in the long run (Weaver, 1994).

Within the travel and tourism industry two movements are taking place in response to the growing interest by consumers and travellers in protecting the environment. These are ecotourism and the growing incorporation of "green" measures in tourism and hotel operations. The ecotourism product must be done well, with a sense of mission, or not at all. Ecotourism suppliers must take responsibility for standards of education and training because clients are looking for quality experiences. In the context of tourism facilities, development and operating costs will continue to rise in response to environment requirements. Without standards, profitability, especially in the longer term is marginal, minimal, and more likely non-existent (Dowling, 1992). With their special features as discussed above, ecotourists are a new challenge to both tour operators and policy-makers. They demand experiences different from mass-tourists and have more interest in participation and self-improvement in unspoiled areas. How to arrange programs which both satisfy ecotourists and conservation and how to educate them are matters that have to be tackled.

There has been insufficient economic study of the demand for ecotourism and its relationship with other forms of tourism. It needs to be recognised that the same tourist may engage in ecotourism as well as in tourism activities other than ecotouristic ones. Thus the demand for ecotourism may either by complementary or competitive with other forms of tourism. Such relationships have not yet been investigated by economists. This contrasts with detailed econometric analysis of the demand for international tourism for example by Witt and Martin (1987), which examined complementarity and substitutability of tourism between countries.

Tour operators, or tour wholesalers, are "manufacturers" of specific tourism products. They supply either inclusive tours or the quintessential components for tourism as profit-maximising agents. Government intervention and a legal code of conduct to protect host destinations are necessary (Hudson,

1996). Hockings (1995) surveyed tour operators in Queensland, Australia, finding that 72 percent of operators incorporated some form of interpretation in their programs, especially the larger ones with over 1,000 clients yearly, and that marine parks in Queensland put effort into development and into running courses for staff education. Ecotourism customers want operators who commit themselves to making their operations "green". The Japan Association of Travel Agents has organised a Committee for Environmental Protection. It will be developing a code for environmental travel and is seeking to establish the JATA Foundation for environmental protection and conservation. The Ecotourism Association of Australia has developed an accreditation scheme for tourism operators who offer environmentally sensitive products. The scheme will allow the targeting of operators who are fraudulent in their claims about the environmental attributes of their products.

6.3.2 Ecotourists (The Motivation of Ewtourists)

It is difficult to define an "ecotourist" because people go to natural areas for a variety of purposes and their interaction with the natural resource varies from careless observation to responsible study. Both theoretical and empirical studies have nevertheless supported the notion that ecotourists are a distinct market segment (Eagles, 1992). The term "ecotourist" can vary in its level of environmental impact or its degrees of "green" (Plant and Plant, 1992), in its level of intensity of interaction with the environment (Valentine, 1992), and level of physical challenge (Butler and Waldbook, 1991). The survey of Weiler and Richins (1995) on ecotourists revealed that most of them are "extreme, extravagant and elite", and that an ecotourist is "keen to be environmentally responsible, to have an intense level of interaction with the environment, and to be physically and intellectually challenged. She is also young, well-off, well-educated, with few responsibilities and therefore is able to spend a portion of her considerable disposable income and leisure time on an Earthwatch expedition".

Gunn (1994: 93) stated that an ecotourist "wants an in-depth, authentic experience; considers the experience worthwhile, personally and socially; abhors large tour groups on a strict itinerary; seeks physical and mental challenge; wishes interaction with locals; cultural learning; adaptable; often prefers rustic accommodations; tolerates discomfort; seeks involvement but not passive behaviour; prefers to pay for experience rather than for comfort". Ecotourism customers are often considered to be repeat travellers who have already been to popular tourist destinations. They are visitors who are tired of visiting modern cities or man-made resort complexes. They seem to be much more concerned with seeking both personal and interpersonal rewards and opportunities rather than with escaping personal and interpersonal environments. They want novelty and quality, and have a greater need for intimate contact with both the natural and the built environment as well as local people (Weiler and Hall, 1992).

Behavioural psychology and humanistic psychology, in which a person's behaviour is assumed to be rooted in his or her response to an external environment, consider that tourists require very diversified structures from the tourism industry and that tourism has the potential for self-development of the individual (Botterill, 1989). Krippendorf (1987) identified three streams of lifestyle. The first group takes work as the focus of life and lives for work. Leisure is, as a result, of little importance for this group. Although decreasing in importance, this group comprised 10 to 20 percent of the population in 1980. The second group is characterised by a hedonistic lifestyle. Those individuals who work in order to live. Leisure is a counterpart to everyday life. By 2000, about 45 to 60 percent of the population were expected to belong to this group. The third group is described as "the new unity of everyday life". They try to combine work and leisure and look for fulfillment throughout all sectors of life. Tourism motivations for them include broadening their horizons and going back to nature. The share of this group was predicted to rise from 20–30 percent in 1986 to 30–45 percent in 2000.

Plog (1973) developed a psychographic model to group tourists into psychocentrics (self-inhibited and non-adventuresome, preferring familiar atmosphere and package tour), mid-centrics and allocentrics (adventurous and confident, seeking novel destinations and independent tour arrangements). In the process of destination succession, allocentrics are usually the first wave and the psychocentrics the last. Psychocentrics tend to be conservative and cautious in their choice of holidays, wishing to maintain familiarity in their experiences, while allocentrics are more adventurous, looking for new experiences. According to Maslow's hierarchy of needs, individuals work their way through a hierarchy of needs. The five levels are basic needs, safety needs, social needs, ego needs and self-actualisation. One would expect ecotourism to typically involve needs toward the top of Maslow's hierarchy, and hence postmaterialist values.

Cohen postulated that there were four types of tourists with a combination of novelty and familiarity. The "organised mass tourist" is the "least adventurous and remains largely confined to his environmental bubble" during his trip. Pursuit for novelty increases from "the individual mass tourist" to the "explorer", whereas the "drifter" is "almost wholly immersed in his host culture" and ventures furthest away from the beaten track (Cohen, 1972: 167–169). Psychographic characteristics, particularly those relating to the core motivations, values or personality characteristics of individuals, are relevant in analysing ecotourists. Iso-Ahola (1982) suggested that two motivational forces influence leisure-behaviour simultaneously — escaping from the everyday environment and the seeking of intrinsic rewards from participating in leisure activities. Individuals seek the optimal level of stimulation which is neither too boring nor too mentally exhausting. A study of Canadians revealed that the ecotourist is less family- and city-oriented, and more interested in travelling to different cultural, historical and environmental sites. Social motivations pertaining to simpler lifestyle, rediscovery of self and so on are more important to the ecotourist than tourists as a whole (Eagles, 1992). Authenticity is also an important feature of ecotourist experiences (Cohen, 1972). A large proportion of ecotourists appear to be "DINKS" (double income no kids) or "empty-nesters" — couples whose children have left home. Ecotourists are most common among individuals between 20 and 40 years of age, with higher education (Beal, 1996). Ecotourists are psychographically amicable and broad-minded, intelligent, self-assured and sociable. They are more likely to be members of conservation organisations, and to purchase environmentally friendly products such as biodegradable detergents than non-ecotourists.

Although it is difficult to estimate the volume of ecotourists in China, a higher percentage of ecotourists may be found in the inland areas because a higher proportion of nature- and culture-based tourism resources occur in the inland areas than the on East coast.

6.3.3   Government sector

The government is actively involved in the administration, legislation and the financing of national parks, nature reserves and so on. Public ownership of land, forests and water bodies is common. For example, the US Federal Government owns 20 percent of all land and 25 percent of all forests with a total market value of between $0.5 and $1.5 trillion. One-quarter to one-third of the property in North America is owned by the public (Borcherding, 1991). The power of government to direct ecotourism is difficult to exaggerate. However, government is also influenced by voters, parties, bureaucracies and interest groups, each of which may be assumed to be a maximising agent, trying to seek benefits over its rivals. The extent to which government promotes ecotourism depends on the competition between pressure groups whose income comes from ecotourism, and opposing groups, such as on occasions, conservationists striving to protect the environment.

A few governments have recognised the potential growth of rural tourism. About A$1 million from the Federal Budget per year in Australia was made available for rural tourism programs for four years from 1994. A$10 million for a National Ecotourism Strategy to finance the development of ecotourism infrastructure, monitoring of impacts and integration in regional development, and the Regional Tourism Development Program, provided A$23 million over four years from 1994 to local authorities, organisations and regional tourism associations (Commonwealth Department of Tourism, 1994). Canada established the National Round Table on the Environment and the Economy and the Tourism Industry Association of Canada. Both are engaged in promoting sustainable tourism.

Some governments have established codes in order to monitor ecotourism. Ecotourism codes have been developed in the United States, Canada and Australia, providing both general and specific guidelines for the ecotourism administration body, tour operators and ecotourists (Wright, 1994). A number of policies, codes and principles oriented towards natural or cultural resources have been introduced by government bodies, associations and industries, including the World Travel and Tourism Council, Pacific Asia Travel Association, ITT Sheraton Corporation, Canadian Pacific Hotels and Resort, New Zealand Tourist Industry Federation and so on. Tourism codes tend to focus on the biophysical or cultural resources and regulate the conduct of both tourists and other players. Codes of ethics based on values are mixed with codes of practice or specific guidelines.

The Government of Kenya has played an active role in promoting ecotourism. A complete ban on hunting was declared by the Kenya government in 1978, bringing an end to big game hunting and ivory seeking. Ex-guides and trackers began to develop ecotourism under the slogan of "come shooting Kenya with your camera". Eight percent of Kenya's national territory is protected by 52 parks and reserves, most in the Great Rift Valley. In 1965, the Department of Tourism was created as part of the Ministry of Tourism and Wildlife. The Kenyan Wildlife Service ensures the protection and management of ecotourism resources both within and outside the protected areas (Dixon and Sherman, 1990)

As discussed in Chapter 2, government agencies in China, including the Ministry of Forestry, have recognised the potential of ecotourism for promoting local economies and conservation (National Environmental Protection Agency, 1994).

6.3.4 Non-profit groups

With increasing concern about environmental conservation, many recreational, historic, professional, ethnic, health and religious organisations are becoming involved in resource management, ecotourism research, policy-making and safeguarding of the environment. They often champion the interests of local communities and the long-term development of ecotourism, sometimes working jointly with policy-makers and communities to deal with ecotourism problems arising from business operations or from visitors. In the US for example, the National Parks and Conservation Association developed public education workshops on ecotourism and corridor issues with the National Parks Service Cooperative. The Lackawana River Corridor Association, and the Rails-to-Trails Conservancy, also work to improve ecotourism facilities (Gunn, 1994: 92). In China, universities and research bodies often work together with government and travel businesses to monitor ecotourism development.

6.4   Can Ecotourism Grow Sustainably?

Sustainable development is a term that was given popularity by the report of the World Commission on Environment and Development (WCED, 1987). Sustainable development envisages a situation in which lasting livelihoods are provided with minimal resource depletion, little environmental degradation, cultural disruption and social instability. Tourism has been influenced by the "sustainability movement". However, *Our Common Future* makes no reference to tourism, nor did the Global Forum of the official UNCED meeting, thereby reflecting some ignorance of tourism by public sector agencies.

A working definition of sustainable development in the context of tourism is taken by Butler (1993) as: tourism which is developed and maintained in an area (community, environment) in such a manner and at such a scale that it remains viable over an indefinite period and does not degrade or alter the environment (human and physical) in which it exists to such a degree that it prohibits the successful development and well-being of other activities and processes. But he regarded sustainable tourism as "tourism which is in a form which can maintain its viability in an area for an indefinite period of time". It is worth noting that "sustainable tourism", which relates to whether the tourism industry itself is sustainable, in the face of changing supply and demand, is different from the role of tourism in sustainable development (Tisdell and Wen, 1997).

Nevertheless, "if there is growth, no matter how small and no matter how small the base starting point is, the end result is non-sustainability. With any positive rate of growth we run up against the finiteness of the environment" (Gowdy, 1994b: 172). As an economic activity, ecotourism depends intrinsically on "good" natural environments. This implies that ecotourism undoubtedly has an impact on the environment, and that changes in environments are likely to have more serious effects on ecotourism than on other industries or other types of tourism. This fragility of ecotourism makes its sustainable development risky when the factors to be addressed in the following sections are taken into account. *Challenge*

6.4.1 Global environment deterioration

There has been worldwide concern about large-scale environmental degradation and depletion of natural resources. As observed by Gowdy (1994b: 155), "It is clear that the current level of economic activity is rapidly destroying the natural world upon which we ultimately depend for life itself". One can understand that once the general environment on which ecotourism depends is under attack, ecotourism itself will be negatively affected in terms of the quality of its product and in the amount of resources available to it.

Such environmental changes as increasing solid waste, air and water pollution, climate change, deforestation, wildlife extinction and so forth have reduced the scope for ecotourism to develop and will have further adverse environmental implications if the present trend continues. Take coral reefs, an important tropical ecotourism resource, for example. Two-thirds of 632 reefs surveyed in 1982 have been degraded in the Philippines, and only 2 of 8 reefs in Tanzania recommended for national park status in 1968 were of acceptable quality for this status in 1983 (Jenner and Smith, 1992) as a result of sediment accumulation, fertiliser use and habitat damage. At the Great Barrier Reef Marine Park in Australia, environmental damage to such areas by tourists, including scuba divers, is a concern (Davis and Tisdell, 1995).

6.4.2 Resource encroachment from other industries

Ecotourism resources are threatened by encroachment of agriculture, forestry and other economic activities that benefit from the same resource bases. In China, pollution and deforestation due to low efficiency of energy use is another danger. China uses over three times as much energy as the United States per dollar of output, and eight times as much as Japan (Bingham,

1993). Several industries compete with ecotourism for limited resources, and in general they damage and deplete the natural environment at a faster rate and in a more harmful manner. Mining, forestry, and agriculture, to name a few, are among the competitors for the same slice of resources.

Illegal collection in protected areas, logging and wildlife poaching threaten the future of ecotourism in some areas. In Thailand, around 50 percent of the mangrove forests have disappeared since 1960 due to charcoal processing and due to the conversion of mangrove areas to shrimp ponds. An annual reduction of 100,000 to 200,000 square kilometres in the tropical rainforest habitat is occurring worldwide (McNeely and Dobias, 1991). Natural resource depletion has also occurred in China, such as in Xishuangbanna, as will be discussed in Chapter 8 of this book. Other industries rely on their well-established lobbying system and usually have stronger economic power to gain access to natural resources than the ecotourism industry. In contrast, it takes longer for ecotourism to earn a profit, or profit may not be the goal, and the total benefit is not completely reflected in the market price for eco-tourism. Therefore, the possibility of encroachment from competing resource-users is a serious threat to ecotourism.

There are usually alternative uses for ecotourism resources. Hence economic returns from different uses determine to a large extent whether an area is used for ecotourism or used for other industries. Studies have been completed to compare monetary gains from alternative possible uses of natural areas. One was conducted comparing the net value of Amboseli National Park, Kenya, for the viewing of wildlife and for agriculture. It turned out to be $40 per hectare for wildlife viewing, but only $0.8 per hectare for potential agriculture (Western, 1982). Amboseli National Park and the Masai herders reached a compromise. Net monetary gain from use of Masai land is $500,000, the grazing compensation from the park to the Masai result in an income 85 percent greater than from cattle herding alone (restricting wildlife to the boundaries and excluding all cattle would result in a decreased population of both) (Sherman and Dixon, 1991). A cost-benefit study on the Virgin Islands National Park calculated its total benefit/cost ratio to be 11.1 to 1 (Boo, 1990: 17). Ecotourism is usually a more sustainable resource-user than its economic alternatives.

6.4.3   Inappropriate tourism development

Tourism has been one of the fastest growing industries in recent decades. The annual international flow of tourists was 450 million in 1990 and receipts from international tourism exceeded $250 billion (WTO, 1992). Travel and tourism in the 1990s had already become the world's largest industry, with an output of US$3.4 trillion, accounting for 10.9 percent of world GDP, 212 million jobs and 11.4 percent of investment (WTTC, 1995). Nevertheless, in this process of its fast growth, mass tourism has been sending tourists to environmentally sensitive areas without enough consideration for their re-source bases. Cases like the closure of polluted tourist beaches in the Great Britain and deterioration in China's most popular tourist areas due to tourist activity (Tisdell and Wen, 1991a) are not rare. Ecotourism itself is one of the causes of environmental degradation when it is not properly planned. Adventure expeditions and mountaineering in the Himalayas have produced deforestation, environmental deterioration, social fragmentation and cultural change (Puntenney, 1990). In some places, ecotourism operators do not con-tribute to the maintenance of national parks but take it for granted that national parks are provided for their business, and this has led to overcrowding and deterioration in some parks (Boo, 1990). Tourists with insufficient educa-tion in protecting natural areas can also pose a danger to the places they visit by engaging in improper activities such as collecting natural items, feeding and disturbing wildlife.

The travel market has become increasingly specialised and segmented with the development of different styles of leisure and tourism (WTO, 1986). Ecotourism utilises resources from relatively inaccessible rural areas and expands tourism supply in this regard, but often leaves the issue of sustaina-bility unanswered. There has been in recent years a proliferation of marketing in the travel area with terms prefixed with "eco" to increase the attraction of products, while the consumers do not necessarily know what they are obtaining nor its impact on the environment, or how the product differs from others, if there is any difference indeed. Masterton (1991) clams that "eco" is to a certain extent an abuse of this potential market or "eco-exploitation". Misuse of the term "ecotourism" in the promotional materials of some operators may have resulted in an erosion of the environmentally responsible

ecotourism image in some areas. It has been recognised that tourism has the
potential to act as a force to conserve natural resources (Budowski, 1976),
but most tourism efforts has been for advancing economic objectives rather
than conservation. Romeri (1985) warned that there is difficulty in ensuring
environmental awareness with accompanying responsible actions owing to
the complexity and multiple facets of tourism.

It is necessary to determine whether ecotourism is truly a sustainable
option. This requires consideration of the different interests involved at various
spatial and temporal levels. It is often believed that the smaller scale, dispersed
nature of ecotourism with less sophisticated demands will enable a much
higher degree of local participation than conventional mass tourism. However,
any influx of tourists creates some environmental impact. For example, the
number of annual visitors to the Kakadu National Park grew from 38,000 to
328,000 between 1981 and 1990, imposing a considerable strain on park
management (Knapman, 1991). The Ngorongoro Conservation Area in
Tanzania is home to 23,000 Masai but regulations have restricted their possibilities for livestock-keeping and agriculture as well as access to grazing areas
and essential water sources. Tourism in this area results in rubbish, track
erosion, disturbance to wildlife and the destruction of vegetation and archaeo-
logical sites (Olerokonga, 1992). If the finite limits of environmental tolerance
are crossed, the in-built mechanisms to absorb impact and make adjustments
will collapse. Therefore, a crucial issue in ecotourism is to control any development within the adaptation thresholds of the local environment (Prosser,
1994).

6.4.4   *Economic expectations for ecotourism*

Ecotourism is seen as an income-earner for some protected areas and as a
means to provide financial support for conservation and a contributor to
income for everyday operations. Although the prefix "eco" in ecotourism is
generally considered as referring to ecological concerns, it has been suggested
that the "more important underlying premise is economic benefit", and without
economics and profitability, ecotourism will "go nowhere" (Pearson, 1994).
Efforts that are entirely conservation-based in areas where other economic

development opportunities are rare will diminish possibilities for success. Most conservation victories which are not driven by economics tend to occur in countries with high standards of living. Chairman of the Adventure Travel Society, James Pearson, who believes that local communities will have little interest in developing a viable and sustainable ecotourism industry, states that the Society is "strongly committed to the development of profitable local businesses" (Pearson, 1994).

However, if ecotourism is targeted to maximise its monetary benefit, conservation may become of reduced importance and natural resources may be sacrificed for financial benefit. When ecotourism becomes income-oriented and conservation loses its priority, there is a danger that there will be little difference between ecotourism and other types of tourism which are environmentally consumptive. This unfortunately can be the fastest way to bring ecotourism to its end. Benefits from ecotourism, if properly developed and managed, can include economic diversification in rural and non-industrialised regions, long-term economic stability, the tendency for higher dollar expenditures because of longer length of stay by ecotourists, demand for local goods and services, infrastructure development and an increase in foreign exchange earnings (Lindberg, 1991). Furthermore, if ecotourism can currently earn little income, this does not mean that this situation will persist. Future demand for ecotourism in an area may increase due to a rise in income levels of future tourists and it may be wise to conserve the area to cater for these future demands. In many developing countries, there are pressures to obtain income from natural areas, and ecotourism is expected to make profit from its environmentally acceptable operation. While it is important to make ecotourism financially viable to ward off threats to protected areas from other industries, but not at the price of (excessive) damage to the environment on which ecotourism depends.

Tourism is often viewed as commercialised activity driven by profit-oriented enterprises, while recreation and park service areas are seen as welfare-oriented products. But ecotourism cannot be viewed as just another profit maximisation activity. Although it is encouraging to see that ecotourism is potentially profitable in itself, the monetary gain from ecotourism could become a misleading criterion for the total benefit of ecotourism. On top of economic considerations, ecotourism is also valuable for conserving biodiversity and natural scenery, protecting other non-tourism benefits from natural areas, educating people and so on. All the benefits from ecotourism, including its positive externalities, cannot be captured by the mere financial income from it. The optimal scale of ecotourism could be under-estimated if monetary profit were taken as the only consideration. Excessive emphasis on the ability of ecotourism to be an income-earner could lead to the belief that ecotourism and protected areas exist primarily for profit. If ecotourism cannot make a profit, this view just mentioned may discourage the establishment of nature reserves or it may result in ecotourism being replaced by other economic activities often less advantageous for conservation, such as agriculture or grazing, and thus degradation of natural resources could occur. Doubts have been cast on the ability of ecotourism, usually small in scale and sensitive to the environment, to cope with the pressure of growing numbers of tourists and to counteract expanding environmental deterioration.

6.4.5 *Ecotourism and local communities*

Tourism development introduces a different world to many local communities and can influence them dramatically (Luloff *et al.*, 1994). Tourism is a form of development that encourages contact between people of different backgrounds (Smith, 1977). Residents not only have to realise that they and their life-style are objects of attraction, but also obtain contact with other cultures that they would not have known without tourism (Young, 1973). There are usually five types of responses to tourism from the local residents according to Cohen (1972): resistance, retreatism, boundary maintenance, revitalisation and adoption. Conflicts in images can occur in terms of the projected and actual behaviour of tourists, the facilities supplied and character of the destination, the means of image transmission, and the spatial scale of the image promoted. Such contradictions can result in disillusionment with the product on the part of tourists, and future decreases in demand. The degree of support or hostility on the part of the local community depends upon their participation in, effects on and returns from the process of tourism development. Tourist literature refers to destination attributes as possessing diversified appeals to different types of tourists, but tourist behaviour may change over time within one specific destination (Cohen, 1972).

Several authors have discussed the cultural impact of tourism (Smith, 1977; Lea, 1988). Furnham (1984) suggested that the amount of difference between the cultures is directly proportional to the amount of culture shock and changes that may arise. As a result, certain types of society may be much more vulnerable to the pressure from cultural exchange brought about by tourism than others. However, the common accusation that tourism necessarily wrecks culture ignores the potential for culture to absorb tourist demands in conservative and creative ways. This absorption depends upon the degree to which the tourists consume the host culture and the local culture embraces the tourists (Zurick, 1992). Cohen (1987) claimed that the independent explorer tourist has less impact on host cultures than mass tourists due to their small numbers and a sympathetic attitude. The growth of ecotourism has seen increasing numbers of tourists visiting remote isolated places where cultures are most vulnerable to change. Hence their impact may be greater than their sheer numbers suggest. Ecotourism has the potential of extending tourism development into frontier regions, and it is tied to the hierarchy of gateways and to the development of a periphery-frontier closely associated with other regional developments (Zurick, 1992).

Haywood (1988) called for responsible and responsive tourism planning as far as the community is concerned. It is unrealistic to think that most communities can exert enough control over market forces to maintain environmentally sustainable development, or to assume that local interests will necessarily be compatible with the long-term health of ecosystems. Barriers to a community-based approach include: lack of overall vision for the community and region; a lack of interest or awareness of tourism on the part of local residents, a lack of trained human resources to ensure local economic benefit from tourism; cultural barriers between hosts and guests and between planners and residents; differing time requirements for local planning and the political commitments of government; and a lack of investment capital within the community. In Hawaii, community opposition to tourism development is reflected in a 1989 conference on the impact of tourism "Contrary to the claims of its promoters, tourism ... has not benefited the poor and oppressed native Hawaiian people. Tourism is not an indigenous practice, nor has it been initiated by the native Hawaiian people … . Its primary purpose is to make money. Such tourism is a new form of exploitation … which perpetuates poverty … sexism and racism … is detrimental to the life, well-being and spiritual health of native Hawaiian people… all is not well in 'paradise' " (Patterson, 1992).

The relationship between parks and local people has been given increasing attention (Boo, 1990; Place, 1991). It has been suggested that local participation from the beginning of conservation projects is critical to their success (Budowski, 1982). Saglio (1979) gave an example of a successful project called "Tourism for Discovery" in Senegal — the secret lies in the fact that it entailed local participation in building, managing and operating traditional lodgings and excursions for foreign visitors in an effort to present genuine West African culture.

The transition of communities from an economy based on resource extraction to one based on the preservation of the ecosystems around them involves major social changes. Only if rural people in developing countries are able to replace the direct exploitation of biological resources with income from tourism based on the continuing presence of those resources, national parks may be successful and their potential in regional development in some rural parts be realised. Ecotourism offers LDCs the prospect of capitalising on their comparative advantage in natural assets. The Kenya Wildlife Service has launched a programme to ensure that landowners outside the national parks benefit from wildlife tourism based on animal watching, game bird shooting and game cropping (EIU, 1992: 73). Monteverde Reserve in Costa Rica and the Community Baboon Sanctuary in Belize are two examples of successful privately owned ecotourism companies (Boo, 1990). Ecotourism in Belize has been found to contribute to local economic benefits and conservation, and is a source of financial support for protected area management (Lindberg *et al.*, 1996). When communities adopt tourism as part of their economic and physical planning strategies, they must examine the effectiveness the image of their attractions in a competitive market, target most appropriate visitor niche markets and exploit the synergistic opportunities that tourism can provide locally (cf. Murphy, 1992).

Relying on small-scale, locally managed facilities and activities, eco-tourism is supposed to be able to avoid the commonplace negative effects of mass tourism on destinations, and to promote balanced growth in tune with local, environmental, social and cultural concerns. However, ecotourism needs to be an integral part of regional planning networks and to be supported by the local communities in order to survive in the long run, and it is not the panacea for all tourism ills (Cater and Lowman, 1994). Failures in eco-tourism because local residents are not involved in the decision-making pro-cess have been observed (Ioannides, 1995). Place (1991) analyses the impact of Tortuguero National Park in Costa Rica. Before the park was set up, Tortuguero was based on the exploitation of biological resources for sub-sistence and for sale to the international market. The establishment of Tortuguero National Park in 1975 withdrew many of the forest and marine resources, including forestry and "turtling", on which the local people had been relying.

6.4.6 Criticisms of ecotourism development

The long-running debate about the role of ecotourism in development involves both advocates and critics (Bryden, 1973; Sinclair, 1991). Criticism of eco-tourism has emphasised its potential negative impacts on its resources. Moore and Cater (1993) pointed out that the marketing of ecotourism does not ac-knowledge the impact of ecotourism on resources and the management of resources does not acknowledge the impact of protection policies on tourism operators and their clientele, and both have failed to consider adequately the long-term impact on the physical, social and economic environment and visitor experiences. Ecotourism faces the pressure of both financing itself and conserving its natural resource base (Tisdell, 1995 and 1996). Ecotourism can add to environmental deterioration, local cultural shift and negative in-come distribution due to the fact that ecotourists in most developing countries are higher income groups and foreigners, and the country or region hosting ecotourists may not be able to appropriate very much economic gain from them. Losses from ecotourism can even result in reduced expenditure on natural conservation to cover the losses. The main losers from ecotourism can be local people when ecotourism is controlled by outside developers and locals do not obtain adequate economic benefits such as employment.

Tourism can cause environmental degradation in natural areas, especially if it is not properly managed and results in over-crowding, because congestion may not only reduce the amenity value of the tourist site but also the ecological functions and values of the environment (Davis and Tisdell, 1995). For example, national parks in the United States are facing deterioration and degradation, congestion and so on, and the repair bill is estimated to approach $6 billion by 1996 (Mitchell, 1994). According to Jafari (1990), "It is only during recent years that tourism has received some serious [government] attention". Obviously ecotourism resources are under attack from both external and internal factors, and the future of ecotourism is bleak if no positive actions are taken at this stage to conserve such resources for future generations. Global cooperation, appropriate national policies and careful planning are required to make sure that a sustainable resource-base for ecotourism is preserved.

6.5   Market and Government Failure in Ecotourism

It is therefore necessary to observe how two systems, namely markets and the government, interact within ecotourism. The resources used for ecotourism are to a large extent collective goods to which people may theoretically have common access, and cases of both "tragedy of the commons" and "tragedy of the enclosure" may occur (Gowdy, 1994b: 77). Collective interest and group rights may be guaranteed by tradition, morality or dictatorship. On the other hand, individual tourists and tour-operators may try to maximise their own benefits from the resources to achieve a higher level of satisfaction, and their aims often conflict with the purpose of conservation. Hence, market failure and government failure may have a considerable impact on ecotourism development.

6.5.1   Market failure in ecotourism

"Market failure occurs when market prices fail to reflect the true social value of goods" (Gowdy, 1994b: 83). If the preference of every individual affected by the provision of goods was accurately reflected in the market-place, there would be no need for any non-market power to intervene, except possibly to improve the distribution of income. However, for the use of natural resources, the price mechanism may fail to achieve a social optimum due to the existence of externalities and other factors. The "invisible hand" cannot function well for ecotourism because property rights are incomplete and the market does not reflect all the costs and benefits arising from public goods or common access. Factors relating to ecotourism which cause market failure are outlined below.

(a) Externalities

Marshall (1890) and Pigou (1920) were among the first economists to bring attention to externalities. Marshall mentioned only the benefits enjoyed by economic identities without payment, and Pigou made it clear that not only benefits but also costs can accrue from externalities. Kapp (1950) anticipated the immense consequences of economic growth on the environment via externalities. Externalities, or spillover effects, or external economies/diseconomies, arise when "activities of economic units (firms and consumers) affect the production or consumption of other units and where the benefits or costs which accrue to these units do not normally enter into the gain and loss calculations" (Kula, 1992). Adverse externalities on ecotourism could include acid rain which destroys ecotourism resources while positive externalities might include better-educated participants and consequently more conservation-minded individuals after ecotourism trips.

(b) Public goods, common property and free access

When the provision of a good to one person does not reduce its availability to others and exclusion is impossible, a public good is identified. An individual will not be willing to pay for public goods because he/she is automatically provided with such a product whenever it is supplied. There is a free-rider problem, as occurs for example, in the maintenance of fresh air or the preservation of a gene reservoir. Conservation of ecotourism resources sometimes suffers because of this problem.

An ecotourism resource is a communal property if it is managed by communities of individuals on the basis of rules and regulations that are enforced by tradition, morality and legality. When such common property arrangements or enforcement break down, the situation reverts to open-access, a situation where access to the resource is open to all without restriction. Open-access can be a source of destruction of ecotourism resources.

(c) Non-monetisation of benefits

Many social and cultural aspects of ecotourism cannot satisfactorily be expressed in monetary form but nevertheless have social value. They include factors such as ethnic tradition, traditional festivals, artistic heritage and so on. They might either become commercialised or be ignored if left to market forces. In either case, this could result in the loss of valuable ecotourism resource.

(d) Justice and equity

While economic efficiency is the guiding principle in the market-place, distributive justice and equity are also fundamental issues which need to be addressed in relation to local communities and future generations in developing ecotourism.

6.5.2   *Government failure in ecotourism*

Believers in free markets doubt the efficiency of government as a substitute for market mechanisms in dealing with environment. Some even blame the political mechanism for the failure of market forces because the government fails to organise suitable systems for the operation of markets. Even worse, inappropriate governmental interference causes markets to perform worse than if they were left alone. The libertarian school of environmental economics holds the view that no government intervention is necessary except in establishing and enforcing property rights, and individual economic incentives are reliable as means to settle other issues (Bennett, 1991). While it is possible that these liberals exaggerate market power, political mechanisms do have their own shortcomings in ensuring the stewardship of the environment. Major possible sources of government failure in ecotourism are listed below.

(a) Costs of bureaucracy

Short-sightedness or special interests of some public officials and managers of public property, together with insufficient information and lack of incentive, can increase the cost of running public enterprises by 20 to 100 percent (Borcherding, 1982). Separate government departments are often involved in the management of natural resources, national parks and related industries, and there is often a delay in handling problems, resulting in lack of efficiency and in economic loss. Borcherding (1991: 102) reported that absolute return on the marketable rights of land and forest resources owned by the US Federal Government was negative one billion US dollars. However, this is not surprising given that these resources supply many non-marketable benefits.

(b) Interest groups

Many participants, including local villagers, developers, tour operators, researchers, and policy-makers, are involved in ecotourism, with diverse goals and different degrees of bargaining power. They form pressure groups to maximise their specific benefits. Very often the interests of influential groups, who are not necessarily the biggest portion of the affected population, prevail over those of others, so sometimes sacrificing the majority's interest.

(c) Interests of officials

Government politicians are usually seeking re-election and political funding, and can be easily influenced by lobbyists who represent the interests of voters or fund-donors, and so their ability to make socially appropriate judgements is sometimes compromised. Hardin (1968) was among the earliest to analyse possible misallocation and political misconduct involved in the management of open-access property.

There is no universal single means for managing ecotourism resources that is bound to avoid market failure, government failure or administrative failure. Maybe a blending of market, political and administrative mechanisms (Tisdell, 1993) is needed for management purposes and the alternatives must be examined in each circumstance. It has been recognised that "tourism must be developed and managed in a controlled, integrated and sustainable manner, based on sound planning" (WTO, 1994: 3).

As is well known, China has undergone major economic reform since 1978, the main impact of which has been to foster the use of market mechanisms as means to manage the resources of the economy and reduce the role of the government sector in this respect. While the government sector continues to play an important role in China in the management of tourism resources, market mechanisms have also become more important. It is therefore important to realise that both markets and governments may fail in managing resources to promote social welfare "adequately", for example, to maximise social welfare in the Kaldor-Hicks sense. Such failures can result in socially insufficient conservation of resources or assets used for tourism and in the lack of sustainability of tourism. In inland China, where ecotourism is an important component of tourism, the possibility of such failures needs to be carefully considered and policies devised to offset these shortcomings.

6.6 Concluding Remarks

Two intersecting trends of the time, the rapid growth of the $2.75 trillion world tourism industry and the growth of environmentalism as reflected in the high level of international participation in environmental concerns, have stimulated the growth of ecotourism. Although a variety of definitions of ecotourism exist which set different boundaries to the coverage of the term, all closely link tourism with the conservation of the environment, especially the natural environment, but also in some cases the conservation of cultures and cultural artefacts. All definitions stress the need for sustaining the assets on which tourism depends. Sustainability is central to most discussions involving ecotourism.

The framework for ecotourism studies covers the interrelationship between ecotourism and its resources, which comprised of the natural, social, cultural and economic systems. The coexistence of ecotourism and the resources depends on profits from ecotourism being compatible with the continuous conservation of its resource basis. Ecotourism undoubtedly has the power to bring about both favourable and unfavourable changes to its resources.

The development of ecotourism is influenced by the business sector, the government, non-profit groups and ecotourists themselves. The major players in tourism all have a stake in sustainable tourism and their interests are often tied together to ensure sound environmental practice. It is noted that the development of ecotourism cannot be safely left to markets because of market failure and that market failures in other parts of the economy can influence the development of tourism. Some government intervention, planning and coordination are required to help correct some of these failures. However we have to be aware that government (political) failure and bureaucratic failure can also occur. Win-win situations arise where sound environmental and business practices coincide, but all interests will be compromised if resource degradation deters tourists (Cater and Lowman, 1994: 10).

Monetary gain from ecotourism can be a misleading criterion for measuring the economic benefit of ecotourism, and could furthermore lead to degradation of its resources. It is important to make ecotourism financially viable but not at the price of (excessive) damage to the resources on which it depends. Economists usually favour pricing mechanisms to "correct" market failures. For example, when the social marginal cost of an ecotourism activity exceeds its private marginal cost, an additional charge or price to that which usually would prevail may be imposed on the activity to bring private and marginal social cost into line (cf. Clarke *et al.*, 1995). But apart from the serious difficulties involved in extending social cost accurately, the user-pays principle can be limited by the transaction costs involved in collecting fees and in some cases it can result in exploitative monopoly-pricing (Tisdell, 1995). Furthermore, other mechanisms, such as environmental education, can sometimes be more effective and cost-efficient in reducing socially adverse environmental spill overs.

Demand for, benefits and threats from ecotourism may be best managed through an integrated approach that encourages wide community participation and coordination at the local level. Sustainable development includes the human dimensions, and a solution is frequently not sustainable if local populations are denied involvement in the development potential of their community. People and environment are usually viewed as exogenous variables, but in the people-centred approach, they are endogenous. As the immediate beneficiary or victim of ecotourism, local communities are closely affected by the long-term development of ecotourism.

The next chapter considers methods that can be used for evaluating natural resources suitable for ecotourism since there is often a conflict between conservation of natural resources and the desire to exploit resources for economic gain. Since the transformation of natural landscapes by "development" can be irreversible or to a large extent irreversible, considerable care must be exercised in deciding whether it is socially desirable to transform natural resources in order to increase some types of production, or conserve these for ecotourism or other ends. Factors which should have an important bearing on this decision are outlined in the next chapter. As China becomes more market- and profit-oriented, these considerations are likely to be of growing importance. In practice, as will become clearer from Chapter 8, China still has a considerable way to go, as do most countries, in meeting the ideals of ecotourism (cf. Lindberg *et al.*, 1997).

Chapter 7

Evaluating Resources for Ecotourism, Particularly in China

7.1 Introduction

This chapter mostly involves a discussion of the evaluation of resources for use in ecotourism, an important issue given the development needs of China. Land used for ecotourism competes with alternative possible uses. Therefore, it is important that alternative land-use be appropriately evaluated from an economic point of view. In particular, indirect or non-market values ought to be taken into account in the *total* economic evaluation of alternative land uses as well as the sustainability of alternative land-uses. Systems of evaluation (and rewards) based only on direct economic benefits appropriated by land holders involve restricted evaluation and can result in the economic misallocation of resources. Such an approach disadvantages activities with high indirect values such as ecotourism.

As discussed in the previous chapter, ecotourism, strictly defined, is compatible with the conservation of indirect values (non-use values) of a natural area. This can make it an attractive alternative to other land uses such as agriculture which, to a considerable extent, are incompatible with retention of the conservation values of a natural area. However, landholders are more likely to appropriate a greater proportion of the economic benefits from agricultural activity than from conserving an area and using it for ecotourism. Hence, agricultural development is favoured in comparison to conservation of an area. One fundamental issue in ecotourism development is that those who exploit natural resources, for example, for agriculture, can obtain benefits without having to pay the full cost (both economic and social) of depletion, while some of these costs, paid either now or in the future, are transferred to the society as a whole.

173

Although returns from tourism are higher than in agriculture in many cases (Dixon and Sherman, 1990), tourism should not be used as an excuse for further encroaching on protected areas. Current financial returns from ecotourism represent only a part of the direct use value of land, and other direct, indirect and potential returns from both consumptive and non-consumptive uses of resources should be taken into account as well (Blane and Jackson, 1994). Furthermore, the potential negative effects of ecotourism should not be neglected when making the assessment of land-use (Jacobson and Lopez, 1994). At the micro-level, evaluation of tourist resources is important for both properly pricing and conserving natural resources.

In considering the most economic use of an existing natural land area, it is rudimentary to consider the impact of alternatives on *total economic value*, or the direct plus indirect economic value from an area. If no use of a natural area is permitted, then its total value in practice will consist purely of its indirect value. If ecotourism is developed and if this does not compromise the indirect values of the natural area (or only does so minimally), the total economic value obtained from the natural area can be expected to increase. Such use, apart from providing benefits to tourists, may also benefit local residents.

Because unpriced values, particularly indirect values, are so important for assessing whether an area should be used for tourism (especially ecotourism) rather than in an alternative way, it is necessary to give attention to the nature and determination of such values. This subject will be reviewed, first in the context of welfare economics generally, and then actual techniques for measuring these values will be discussed. Because China is an important focus in this book, possibilities and limitations involved in using such techniques for evaluation purposes in less developed countries are outlined.

7.2 Welfare Economics and Ecotourism: A Review

7.2.1 *Environment and resource: Externality and market failure*

Neoclassical economic thought treated the environmental impacts of economic activity as minor until the 1960s. Followers of Pigou suggested that a limited degree of government intervention is necessary because of the presence of externalities. But members of the Chicago School of Economics opposed government intervention and promoted property rights as an alternative (Coase, 1960). The laissez-faire view is that if market forces are extended as widely as possible and operate properly, few serious environmental or resource problems will occur and little direct government intervention is necessary.

However, Neo-Malthusian economists, including Mishan (1967), Hermann Daly (1968), and Perrings (1987), among others, put greater stress on environmental problems. It has been realised that economic profit maximisation criteria have been used rather indiscriminately to decide on optimal resource use in the past. With the shift towards the recognition of alternative objectives of resource use, such as conservation and social equity, economic theory and methodology have to be adapted to suit the growing multiple objectives of resource use (Hohl and Tisdell, 1993). The conflicts between individuals and society are related to the liberal versus communal value dispute, and conflicts between the human sphere and the biosphere are related to the anthropocentric versus bio-centric value dispute (Hohl and Tisdell, 1993).

Externalities, both favourable and unfavourable, arise from the activity of an individual or firm when it imposes costs or benefits on others but does not have to pay fully or to be paid for those. In the case of an activity of an agent that involves a net loss for society, the agent does not bear the full cost. Therefore, it is usually carried out on a greater scale than is optimal from the viewpoint of society. Externalities were ignored by mainstream economics until the 1930s when Pigou published *The Economics of Welfare* in 1932. Even at a much later time, in some cost/benefit analysis of projects, externalities were not considered (Little and Mirrlees, 1974).

Market price is commonly accepted as the best available valuation for marketable goods and services, although it is not the perfect measurement. The presence of things that have not been bought and sold in markets and are therefore unpriced has resulted in complicated problems. Sinden and Worrell (1979) made use of the term "unpriced" for certain goods and services when they have no monetary prices because the price system does not measure people's relative desire to consume and willingness to produce the goods and services. The public good nature of some tourist resources creates market failure, because "until congestion sets in the price for use of the good is zero. This is typical of many environmental goods and means that their 'true' value (total economic value) has been underestimated" (Davis and Tisdell, 1996). It is almost impossible for market price, if there is one, to capture the total economic value of such unpriced goods as environmental resources, and it is more elusive for the total value of non-market goods such as natural resources to be properly reflected. Some feel it is impossible to place values on these goods, some others think they can only be compared by assigning monetary prices. Is it possible to determine comparative values for unpriced things and can valid comparisons be made without always resorting to monetary prices?

Since "all over the world local biospheres are being irreparably damaged for a monetary gain which is a fraction of the value of these resources" (Gowdy, 1994b: 84), efforts have been made to tackle the evaluation of natural resources. The contribution of economics would be to deliver a valuation of the direct and indirect costs of the materialisation of an environmental threat, and then to compare the expectation of these costs with the net benefits of those human activities that give rise to environmental damage. Daly and Cobb (1989) constructed an Index of Sustainable Economic Welfare, taking non-renewable resources and environmental damages into account. Evaluation of natural resources will facilitate the appropriation of a substantial proportion of the rents from the users of public goods (Lindberg, 1991). Environmental economics and valuation can play a key role in helping to incorporate concerns about biodiversity loss into the traditional decision-making framework. Munasinghe (1993) used both economic valuation of environmental impacts and multiple attribute evaluation techniques in his case studies to examine the impacts of projects on national parks and to eliminate projects with unacceptable environmental consequences.

7.2.2 *Market and public solutions to externalities*

It has often been argued that the problem of externalities is not attributed to market failure, but to the legal framework within which society operates. The free market proponents suggest that if ownership titles regarding resources are assigned to either the polluters or the affected private transactors, who are rational maximising agents, they are provided with an incentive to negotiate a result between the parties involved. The failure to undertake these transactions implies that the costs of carrying out further transactions exceed the potential benefits, and the re-assigning of property right is appropriate only if it serves to eliminate transaction costs. In practice, the nature and extent of these costs, the information level, and the type of externality dominate initial considerations.

The market mechanism was previously believed to be a responsive and inexpensive means for allocating resources. Many economics textbooks suggest that an economic optimum will be achieved through the operation of market price when consumers, who are usually sovereign, maximise their utility and suppliers maximise their profits (Brown, 1975). Nevertheless, market failure occurs mostly due to the presence of externalities or spillovers (externalities), public goods and common property issues.

Government intervention has been suggested as a means to overcome market failures in relation to resource-use and conservation. The World Conservation Strategy (IUCN, 1980) suggested more government involvement in resource-use but less reliance on the market. But government intervention is subject to a cost as well as political and administrative failure. Supporters of free markets argue that the extent of market failure has been exaggerated and it can be countered by creating conditions, such as private property rights, to improve market operations. Consequently, neither market mechanisms nor an interventionist approach can be solely relied on. The best approach is likely to be a blending of a variety of mechanisms (Tisdell, 1993).

7.3 Evaluating Ecotourism Resources: Existing Methods and Limitations

7.3.1 Argument about values

Debate on the environment is fundamentally related to the determination of its value. For any scarce resource, there has to be decisions about which of the potential users should obtain the satisfaction of the resources and to what extent, and this decision is dependent on the kind of underlying preferences, preferability and values (Hohl and Tisdell, 1993), although economists may disagree on what these concepts really mean.

The word "value" is used variously and somewhat indiscriminately because there is a lack of consensus on its precise meaning within and between disciplines and applications (Rescher, 1969). As a variable property of things which is determined by desiderata involved, value is derived basically from the capacity to satisfy and has a capacity to make a favourable difference to someone's life. Value is the intrinsic worth of a commodity. It has been common since the time of Aristotle to separate the use value, the capacity to satisfy human wants, from the value in exchange, which is the worth of a commodity in terms of its capacity to be exchanged for another commodity. In classical economics, use value is a prerequisite for commodities to have value in exchange (Pearce, 1992: 446). Adam Smith (1976) argued that the costs of producing a commodity, such as wage, profit, and rent, determine the exchange value, or the "natural price" of the commodity, around which actual prices fluctuate in the short-term as a result of demand variation. Ricardo (1819) developed the Labour Theory of Value, which argues that the value of a commodity depends on the relative quantity of labour necessary for its production. Marx (1956) developed the labour theory of value into a theory of surplus, and refers to value as "social character of labour" involved in production.

Neo-classical economics concentrates on the value of exchange to come to the conclusion that marginal utility helps determine the price of a commodity, and market price is determined by the interaction of demand and supply, with utility maximisation for the consumer verses the profit maximisation for the producer. Classical economics agrees that individual value is a function of both utility and disutility which occur in the course of deriving satisfaction from a certain good or service to meet the want or need of a human being. A society combines the aggregated individual valuations and arrives at a social valuation. Consequently, several problems associated with value in the economics arena arise, including the following.

(1)   Market economic values are determined by the exchange of goods and services in organised markets through the price mechanism. Market prices are therefore just the best available indicators of how people feel about the *relative* values of things or people's *relative* desire to consume and willingness to produce the goods and services, rather than the measurement of value itself (Sinden and Worrell, 1979), even though adjustments are necessary where markets are distorted to yield shadow prices. Prices, where they exist, do not necessarily measure the whole value of goods or services that are traded in the market place.

(2)   Non-market values are not exchanged in any market because no market exists for the goods and service to which the value is attached. When there is no monetary price in existence, in other words, there is no market for such items as many environmental goods, it becomes more difficult to measure the value of the object of concern.

(3)   It is not just human needs that determine the valuation by an individual. An individual's valuation is influenced by his/her perception of the thing being evaluated in relation to the needs, and "his perceptions are strongly influenced by the attitudes of his social group" (Sinden and Worrell, 1979: 15). He/she evaluates different alternatives in terms of their utility and the opportunity cost of obtaining them to reach a decision, on which his/her environment and social group exerts influence.

(4)   The valuation of individuals can be so diverse that it is impossible or too expensive for society and institutions to aggregate them or to reinforce the decisions made by people in power or experts according to the Pareto optimality, leaving part of the society worse off. Etzioni (1988) suggests that it is important for individuals to interact socially to ensure harmony between private and public values and reduce the prevalence of "evil" values. Some of a society's needs and resources are inherent in its own make up in addition to the needs, resources and knowledge of its individual members, and there is always the gap between the valuation of individuals and society, leaving the question of choice.

Value may be either instrumental or intrinsic value. Instrumental value, or use value, is attributed to something that is valued as a means and achieves a purpose of an outside entity (Hohl and Tisdell, 1993). Use value includes direct use value (utilitarian value), which refers to commercial uses such as fishing; indirect use value, which is the benefit derived from ecosystem functions such as forests protecting water-sheds; and option value. Option value which was first proposed by Krutilla (1967), is the value of the option of using it in the future in the face of rapid economic and technical changes that create unforeseen opportunities arising in the future, like an insurance value. Intrinsic value, also referred to as non-use value, is the reference entity being an end in itself and is attributed to something that is valued as an end, for itself and in its own right (Hohl and Tisdell, 1993). Many authors use the term non-use value instead of intrinsic value to avoid the potential confusion between the economic and philosophical meanings of the latter. Non-use value is divided between a bequest value and existence value (Randall and Stoll, 1983). Bequest value relates to the value of conserving certain natural assets for future generations to enjoy and represents the willingness to pay for keeping access for future generations by handing on the environment in the same condition if not better than present. Existence value refers to the value of a certain object for its own sake independent of any use or recreational benefit which could arise from that existence, recognising that the individuals will value natural assets regardless of whether they are likely to visit or make use of these assets (Krutilla. 1967).

However, there is as yet no consensus amongst economists as to a terminology and definition for non-market economic value components. Approaches defining components of total value may be internally coherent but impossible to render operational guidance. Total economic value does not capture intrinsic value, or the "primary values" (Turner and Jones, 1991), upon which all ecological functions are contingent. The total value of an ecosystem exceeds the sum of the values of the individual functions. Although economic value involves a much wider perspective than the parallel notion of commercial value, it does not embrace all of value. The concept of economic value is regarded as restrictive in scope because of the anthropocentric nature of economic assessment, which emphasises what can be gained from the point of view of *Homo sapiens* only (Doeleman and Watson, 1988; Tisdell, 1990). Economics has no decision criteria to offer when purely intrinsic values are in conflict (Hohl and Tisdell, 1993).

Geohistorically speaking, human beings are relatively recent arrivals in a planetary environment already shared by plenty of other species. However, human beings have developed technological powers to manipulate the environment with far-reaching impacts. It is suggested to include an additional ethical basis to the economic valuation of environment (Elliot and Gare, 1983). This ethical basis allows scope for constructing non-anthropocentric, or non-economic environmental value, which rates value from the point of view of animate and inanimate beings (Passmore, 1974). Therefore, the non-anthropocentric dimension of value-heritage value, which is not related to the usefulness of human beings, comes to supplement economic values. Heritage value considers values from the point of view of Gaia, the living earth. It exists in respect and recognition towards nature as well as all forms of lives. It can be found not in economic calculation of relative usefulness but in philosophical thinkings of respect toward nature (Elliot and Gare, 1983). Only from an ethical perspective may a non-anthropocentric or non-economic environmental value, which measures value from the viewpoint of all animate and inanimate beings, be understood (Passmore, 1974). Such an ethical approach would set certain minimum standards of a non-negotiable nature to conserve critical natural assets regardless of price. It does not oppose economic value, but when "minimum standards are at risk of being violated, economic calculation should thus be excluded" (Doeleman and Watson, 1988). Attention to heritage value is reflected in campaigns about conservation, where support is given for the sake of natural assets instead of human beings.

Option value relates to unforeseen opportunities that will arise in the future from rapid technical and economic changes and from which human beings will be able to exploit resources in ways that cannot be envisaged currently (Krutilla, 1967). Bishop (1982) suggested that option value would be positive for a project that is able to eliminate the uncertainty of supply. Option value is conceived as a risk aversion premium and is negative for risk-averse individuals with the uncertainty about future income (Hartman and Plummer, 1987). It is actually the difference between option price, or the maximum willingness to pay for the option of consumption, and the expected consumer's surplus. In other words, it is the difference between an *ex-ante* option and an *ex-post* expected consumer surplus. Some researchers have redefined the concept of option value as option price, which is the maximum sum an individual is willing to pay to preserve the option of visiting a natural environment with the existence of demand uncertainty (Freeman, 1984). Quasi-option value is regarded as the value of information that arises after a choice has been made, or a benefit from adopting better decision making procedures rather than a component of economic welfare (Fisher and Hanemann, 1987).

Brown (1984) distinguished three realms of value, namely conceptual realm, relational realm, and object realm. McNeely (1988) divided the value of biological resources into direct and indirect values. The former consists of consumptive use value and productive use value, while the latter includes non-consumptive use value, option value and existence value. Direct and indirect uses are often mutually exclusive (but up to a point may be compatible with the use that is non-consumptive of the resource, such as ecotourism). Attempts to isolate option, bequest and existence value are more problematic with existing valuation techniques. Environmental values are divided into three groups according to the type of function they perform: utilitarian, user and intrinsic values (Tunstall and Coker, 1992). For the utilitarian component, the utilitarian functions are associated with commercial production, and direct or indirect market mechanisms can be used to put a monetary value on them.

Individual value is defined by Sinden and Worrell (1979: 57) as a function of both utility and disutility which occurs in the course of deriving utility: $V_i = U_i - DU_i$, where V_i is the value of matter I, U_i is the utility and DU_i is the disutility occurred when obtaining U_i. Social value is: $U_{ig} - = f (PU_{ig}, W_g)$, where U_{ig} is the utility I to group g, PU_{ig} is the potential utility of I to group g, W_g is the wants and needs of group g (Sinden and Worrell, 1979: 64). A society combines the aggregated individual valuations and arrives at a social valuation. Nonetheless, the valuation of individuals can be so diverse that it is impossible or too expensive for society and institutions to aggregate them or to come to reinforce the decisions made by people in power or experts according to Pareto optimality, leaving part of the society worse off. Some of a society's needs and resources are inherent in its own make up in addition to the needs, resources and knowledge of its individual members (Sinden and Worrell, 1979: 16). There is always a gap between the valuation of individuals and society, leaving the question of choice.

From the social viewpoint, after taking both use and non-use values which reside in the host nation or globally, total economic value of sustainable use of biodiversity becomes the sum of use value (both nationally and globally), option value, bequest value, and existence value. The present value of total economic value of sustainable use of resources minus cost should equal or exceed the present value of benefit from development minus the cost of development (Pearce and Moran, 1994). If the national gains are greater than the costs, or even greater after capturing some of the global values, the nation will have incentive to preserve biodiversity (Lindberg, 1991). The individual land user needs to get part of the national or global gains from conservation, otherwise the private gains and losses will still be applied. This divergence between social, global and private returns explains loss of biodiversity to a large extent.

If there are no data or not enough data to value preservation, the opportunity cost of preservation, or the net present worth of development calculated as a net social benefit with recognition of both consumer's and producer's surplus, can be applied (Tintner and Patel, 1966). There have been controversies over the concepts and application of the consumer's and producer's surplus (Currie *et al.*, 1971). The traditional Marshallian definition is different from that presented by Hicks (1941). Mohring (1965) points out the inaccurate computation of net social benefit in cases when only one interpretation is considered. The aggregation of consumer's and producer's surplus into an estimate of net social benefit assumes implicitly that consumers have the same weight for each unit of gain.

7.3.2 Techniques for measuring both marketable and non-marketable values

History has witnessed attempts to extend the theoretical concepts and measurement techniques of welfare economics and microeconomics to the valuation of non-market goods and services that characterise many natural systems and economic sectors, such as ecotourism. However, "conceptual and empirical methods for placing monetary values on non-market goods and services are quite imperfect" (Hufschmidt *et al.*, 1983), especially when it comes to understanding measuring effects of activities on the non-physical environment, such as culture, ethnicity and the social system.

Efforts in putting an economic value on natural resources can be divided into two major groups (Gowdy, 1994a). The first group tries to place market value on unpriced resources by calculating the amenity value of resources, and such valuation methods as travel cost, the contingent valuation method and surrogate market approach are applied. The second group attempts to place a value on natural resources as productive assets by determining the effect of the reduction in natural capital on future economic growth, hence measures such as "natural resource account" and "net national product" have been developed to take the negative consequences of economic growth into account.

The valuation of non-market environmental goods has expanded into a major area of research since the mid-1970s. Valuation techniques for the environment can be classified broadly as market-oriented and consumer-survey oriented. In the market category, costs and benefits can be valued by actual market or surrogate market prices. In the survey orientated methods, direct questioning for willingness-to-pay is constructed, and net-social-benefit is developed from consumers' surplus or the combined consumers' and producers' surplus as an indicator of social value (Hufschmidt *et al.*, 1983). With various aspects of values and their use, some researchers regard people's willingness to pay, or what they are willing to give up to have certain consumption, as the most reliable evidence of their relative valuation (Sinden and Worrell, 1979). Existence, option and bequest values can also be assessed from users' willingness to pay, although the sample population is not a specifically defined user group, but the whole society instead. However, willingness is influenced by the ability to pay. The classical questionnaire problem arises when respondents answer in terms of what they think they ought to be doing from an ethical point of view. For example, when the object of price is identified as revenue generation in the decision-making of tourist entities, it is usually justified with explanations encompassing conservation in some surveys (Rogers, 1995).

Valuation techniques can also be categorised as direct approach and indirect approach. Direct valuation approaches, with the contingent valuation method as the most widely applied method, are based on responses to hypothetical valuation questions and aim at eliciting preferences from questionnaires and experiments. Indirect valuation approaches are based on actual behaviour and seek to elicit preferences for the environmental elements from the actual market to which environmental features are related in certain ways, including such methods as travel cost, hedonic pricing, and voting in a referendum.

Two major categories of techniques are applied for estimating the value of resources, namely the conventional market approach and the surrogate market approach (Pearce and Moran, 1994). The conventional market approach makes use of market prices or shadow pricing to measure the changes in opportunity cost and in the sum of consumer's and producers' surplus when environmental factors are involved, including the dose-response and the replacement cost technique. The surrogate market approach looks into markets for private goods and services that are often related to the non-marketable environmental attributes in question. The value of the environmental resources is estimated by the expenditure on goods that are substitutes or complements to the resource. In the surrogate market approach, environmental factors of concern are evaluated from the consumers' preferences for both the marketed good and the non-marketed good, usually environmental good, when purchasing private goods, such as hedonic pricing, household production function approach, and travel cost method. The hedonic pricing approach is based on the assumption that the price of a product is related to all the characteristics of this product, and the price of certain characteristics can be isolated by differentiating the price of that product. By making use of market data from transactions in private goods and services, which are complementary to the aspect of the resource in question, a value can be assigned to a particular non-marketable resource (Freeman, 1986).

Other methods to measure unpriced value include: cost based approaches, including opportunity cost, expenditure (to be avoided) based, mitigation-cost and replacement cost, shadow project and relocation cost; multiple-objective method; market price interpretation; direct questioning for willingness-to-pay, where the direct willingness to pay can be measured by entry fee or other fees charged for facility or site, and questionnaires can be used to measure indirect willingness to pay for environment or conservation; net-social-benefit (develops consumers' surplus or both demand and supply curve to estimate the combined consumers' and producers' surplus as an indicator of social value. Dixon and Hufschmidt (1986) made use of production functions to prove that many environment conservation programs have positive net returns. Random utility models (RUMs) or discrete choice models, especially suitable when the demand for recreation is dependent on the quality of substitutes, are applied in measuring a particular site among a set of sites treated as substitutes (Bockstael *et al.*, 1991). Human capital, or the foregone earnings approach, uses market prices and wage rates to value the potential contribution of an individual to society.

Valuation methods can be categorised into three groups according to the way data are collected (Sinden, 1992):

- Observed data from actual market exchanges, including the market value, where market prices are used to value products which are marketed directly or indirectly, travel cost, cost saving, replacement cost and opportunity cost methods.
- Observed data from related markets, such as hedonic pricing, input valuation, interpretation of past decisions, and valuing proxy goods. The surrogate market price approach uses prices of substitutes or complementary goods to value an unpriced environmental good or service, including wage differential (wages for similar jobs in different locations to value implicitly the quality of environment), property value, and travel cost.
- Questionnaire data: survey techniques to help determine performances of consumers and therefore place values on environmental goods and services, such as contingent valuation method, costless choice, and Delphi.

The decision on which valuation technique(s) to apply for a particular case is a matter of making compromises between the strengths and weaknesses of different techniques. John Gowdy (1994a) compared various valuation methods by showing that they have both strength and weakness. The methods should be valid and reliable, institutionally acceptable, and not only technically but also financially feasible. More than one measure can be applied and a more comprehensive outcome may arise by comparing different results. The most frequently used and presumably theoretically acceptable and practically applicable methods are the travel cost and contingent valuation method (CVM) (Walsh, 1986), which are to be discussed in more detail in this chapter.

7.3.3 Travel cost method

To evaluate the environment using surrogate markets and survey techniques, travel-cost approach is one of the methods that are relatively feasible in practice. First suggested by Hotelling to the National Park Service (Prewitt, 1949) to assist in outdoor recreation management and developed by Clawson, travel cost has been reviewed extensively and used widely to derive a demand curve for recreational goods (Clawson, 1959; Clawson and Knetsch, 1966; Forster, 1989). Initially developed to value the benefits received by consumers from their use of an environmental good, it attempts to measure the real value of a recreational site or the actual willingness of users to pay, which includes both user charts if there is any, and the total consumer surplus enjoyed by users of resource. From observed consumer behaviour, a model for predicting site use can be developed, and additional variables can be incorporated in the original regression to reflect other effects.

Travel cost measures recreation and the educational value of a site by substituting journey costs for willingness to pay for the recreational or educational experience (Stabler and Ash, 1978), that is, the costs associated with travelling to a site are taken as a proxy for the value of the visit. As an indirect method, it requires only visitor statistics on the number and origins of visitors and on the populations of areas of origin. Surveys are conducted to obtain information on the origins of site visitors.

Usually costs include travel cost, admission fees, on-site expenditure and the costs of capital equipment which facilitates consumption of the good (Hanley and Spash, 1993). A demand curve is estimated using travel costs as a substitute for market prices. Distance is used as a proxy for price with the restrictive assumptions that all users obtain the same total benefit, which is equal to the travel cost of the marginal user, whose consumer's surplus is zero; the demand curves for zones of different distance have the same slope, that is, people in all zones would consume the same quantities of the activity in given monetary costs (Sinden and Worrell, 1979). After the recreation site has been identified, the surrounding area is divided into concentric zones of increasing distances, representing increasing levels of travel cost. The basic travel cost method is captured by this formula:

$$Q_i = f\ (TC,\ X_1,\ X_2,\ \dots\ X_n),$$

where Q_i is the visitation rate (number of visitors from zone i per 1,000 population in zone i), TC is travel cost, $X_1, X_2, \dots X_n$ are a number of socio-economic variables including income, education level, age and so on (Hufschmidt *et al.*, 1983: 217).

The travel cost method has been used in valuing protected areas such as national parks and World Heritage Areas, as well as in the modelling of outdoor recreation (Hanley and Spash, 1993; Beal, 1995). It is applicable when travel cost is a significant determinant of recreation use. The study of Trice and Wood (1958) on recreation benefits in California was among the earliest applications of this method. It made distinctions between benefits on-site and of travel to and from the site. The relationship between the environment and marketed goods is used to derive the value of an environmental asset (Bennett and Carter, 1993). By regressing visitation rates on travel cost, the impact travel cost has on visitation rates can be tested, and the inclusion of other variables other than travel cost may eliminate effects which are not related to travel cost on the visitation rate.

The travel cost method is based on three assumptions. First, the response of average individuals to a user fee of a given magnitude is assumed to be the same as their response to a travel cost of the same size. Secondly, the relationship between travel costs and the number of trips taken is linear, which means that there is no competition from other sites. Finally, the visitation rates are not affected by capacity constraints. It estimates the willingness to pay for a recreation site on information of money and time spent on getting to the site. Only use values are considered here, and when the on-site time is not the sole object of a trip, the problem of multiple purpose trips arises in applying this method to valuing sites that are visited as part of a wider experience.

Widely applied with encouraging results, travel cost requires substantial data, such as socioeconomic characteristics of the visitors, direct travel expenses, environmental quality attributes for this particular site and its substitutes and time costs. Major limitations for travel cost method are the following:

- In practice, the travel cost approach is site-specific by measuring the benefits from one particular site but not from recreation in general (Freeman, 1979). Travel cost estimates the willingness to pay for a recreation site on information of money and time spent on getting to the site. There needs to be the assumption that all travel costs occur specifically to visiting the site being valued, and costs not directly relevant to the valuation must be separated (Sinden and Worrell, 1979: 374). Therefore, travel cost works best "when applied to the valuation of a single site, its characteristics and those of other sites remaining constant" (Pearce and Moran, 1994: 70).
- Perhaps the most mentioned weakness of this method is that it is restricted to measuring the on-site recreation benefits from a resource. When the on-site time is not the sole object of a trip, the problem of multiple purpose trips arises in applying this method to value sites that are visited as part of a wider experience. Tisdell (1991) noted that the economic value of an attraction does not solely depend upon visits to it with the so-called "meanderers". Recreation incorporates often more than one activity in the same trip such as shopping or visiting friends that may not necessarily be considered as recreational in nature. For sites where major clienteles are local users who do not travel, this method is not as appropriate as when recreation benefits accrue to visitors who travel to reach the site. Although there have been suggestions of allocating travel cost over all sites visited (Mendelsohn *et al.*, 1992), its applicability is still in doubt, especially when the off-site benefits may be "equal to or greater than the on-site recreation benefits" (Ward and Loomis, 1986). Mendelsohn *et al.* (1992) suggested combining a number of popular sites as a single joint site to

overcome the multi-site problem. This method involves the problem of researcher-designed values in defining the group of sites.

- Besides monetary travel cost, time is another factor affecting recreation activities. The role of time is critical to the estimation of travel costs because both the time spent en-route and that spent at the site contribute to the total travel cost as a consequence of the opportunity cost of time. Cesario and Knetsch (1970) pointed out that there may be a consistent bias in the demand curve as a result of the assumption that the disutility of distance is solely a function of money costs. Therefore, the trade-off between time and monetary costs should be observed and reflected in demand function. A classical demand curve can be created on the basis of visitation rates, from which the consumer's surplus from the recreation site can be estimated. In the case of zero or minimum entrance fee to a recreational site such as a national park, demand for it is not infinite because of the cost involved in getting to and from the site. The farther away potential visitors of a site live, the less is their expected demand for the site, and vice versa.

- The unit of value is based on kilometres per visitor day, or the like, which needs to be converted to monetary units by cost per kilometre (mile) multiplier (Smith and Kavanagh, 1969). Such procedure is based on the assumption that all users incur the same monetary cost per unit of distance and the disutility of time is constant. However, constant cost does not always apply to various distances, and it has been noted that time for journey may have a positive utility on short, scenic trips, but the utility declines and becomes negative as the journey becomes longer and more tedious (Walsh *et al.*, 1990). Cesario and Knetsch (1970) recommended that the cost of travel time be estimated as proportion of the wage rate and added to other travel cost. But Walsh *et al.* (1990) argued that travel to and from a site may have consumptive value itself, thus both the benefits and costs of travel time would be estimated. The assumption that the value of the enjoyment of a visit must be higher for those who incur greater travel costs to travel for longer distance was tested at ten coastal sites in Britain with the result that "there was a positive relationship between the travel costs involved and the value put on the enjoyment of the day's visit at only two sites" and it was suggested that "travel cost method cannot generally be advised as a means of valuing coastal recreational benefits and that its use in any other context would need to be validated using survey data" (Tunstall and Coker, 1992).

- The travel cost method relates more to the general amenity value or aesthetic value than to the "intrinsic worth" of the resource because only the user population are usually questioned and if certain resource does not have value for the use population or present generation, it does not necessarily has no value for the society or future generations. The travel cost method does not measure the total economic value by excluding option, existence and bequest values. Only use values of a particular site are considered. However, empirical studies have indicated that non-use value can even exceed the total use value (Pearce and Moran, 1994), hence the strength of this method in measuring recreational resources whose non-use values are dominant is questioned. Its appropriate functional form of the demand function being estimated is under question as well (Smith, 1989). All users obtain the same total benefit, which is equal to the travel cost of the marginal user, whose consumer's surplus is zero. Individual difference in behaviour and valuation of recreation activities is masked in the process of the data aggregation by zones (Brown and Nawas, 1973), but is not able to differentiate such variables as income or quality. Seckler (1966) mentioned that the income of travellers influences the utility they may obtain from recreation activities, and therefore the slope and position of demand curves change for different zones not only because of distance but also different income groups although Sinden (1974) argued that some recreation activities but not all of them would be affected by income. Stovener and Brown (1968) pointed out that demand curves could be adjusted to incorporate income effects.

There are some other methods that are used in the valuation of resources together with travel cost approach. As a comparison, the contingent valuation method is discussed in the following section.

7.3.4   *Contingent valuation method (CVM)*

Dating back to Davis (1963) and Bradford (1970), CVM is a direct valuation method for estimating the value of a range of unpriced resources based heavily on surveys in which carefully designed questions are structured to find personal valuations of changes in the availability of a good. Developed and tested by resource and environmental economists in the US since the early 1960s, it has been applied in valuing environmental goods and has been the subject of methodological research (Cummings *et al.*, 1986). It was recommended by the US Department of the Interior in 1986 for valuing natural resource damages and by the US Water Resources Council in 1979 as a preferred method for measuring outdoor recreation benefits (Tunstall and Coker, 1992). Cummings *et al.* (1986) stated that its results are likely valid when familiar environmental goods are used, and respondents have some prior knowledge regarding the environmental change in question.

CVM can be applied to give values in money terms to uses that had previously been regarded as intangible. It is based on the neoclassical approach of the measurement of the willingness to pay that when the market is in equilibrium, the price for a product is a reflection of the consumer's willingness to pay. When there is no market, consumers are asked how much are they willing to pay for a certain well-defined hypothetical environmental good with the help of questionnaires. But when one looks carefully at the neoclassical paradigm which starts with the possibility of choice, that is, the consumer has to choose one good or another, and when degradation of the environment occurs, there is no option to choose, hence neoclassical welfare theories are not fulfilled in this situation. Requiring that the values expressed by participants can be meaningfully represented by economic welfare theory, CVM provides Hicksian measures of changes in economic welfare. These measures depend on the existence of a continuous utility function that depicts individuals' preferences in various structural conditions.

Disagreement on CVM ranges from the reliability of the sample to the psychological and cognitive processes of response formulation (Schkade and Payne, 1994). This method is based on the assumption that perfect knowledge of the good, the circumstances in which the good is supplied with the alternatives available, and the respondents are sufficiently familiar with or informed about the subject to make a correct valuation. But in practice there are limitations to the information available to be conveyed in questionnaire, and people are unaccustomed to valuing unpriced goods and they often find valuation questions hard to answer. There is evidence that the structure of valuation question and especially that offering a starting value for the interviewee can affect the responses (Cummings *et al.*, 1986). The possible biases in the CVM, such as strategic bias, information bias, embedding problem, instrument bias, and biases arising from hypothetical answers have been discussed extensively (Forster, 1989; Tisdell, 1991).

"Strategic bias" occurs if there is a "free rider" problem in surveys when the intentions indicated ex-ante (before the change) do not describe accurately the ex-post (after the change) behaviour if no penalty or cost is associated with a discrepancy between the two (Pearce and Moran, 1994). It therefore occurs when the individuals tend to understate their true preferences when they have to pay or over report if the price is not tied to an individual's willingness to pay response. The fact that the amount and kind of information provided may affect response has been described as "information bias" (Samples *et al.*, 1986) and it should be noticed that this method can only be valid for specified tourism resource as defined in the specific survey because different results may arise in other definitions and specifications, and some even concludes that contingent valuation method will not offer real solutions to the problem of the unpriced environment (van der Straaten, 1992: 90). Hypothetical bias arises if the declared intention of the respondents cannot be regarded as accurate guides to their behaviour due to the hypothetical nature of the market, and it is argued that the specific attitude tested by willingness to pay must correspond to the specified behaviour (Fishbein and Azjen, 1975).

Kneese (1984) mentioned the inclination of people to allocate everything to their environmental account when dealing with a hypothetical situation and thus do not notice other possibilities to improve the environment. It is also plausible that respondents are able to separate general situations from a certain localised problem. In this case a part-whole bias arises, and there is no difference to ask respondents what they are willing to pay for loss of tropical forest or a certain location. Embedding occurs if the value of the good being studied is embedded in the value of the more encompassing set of goods and services reported by the respondent. The quality and quantity of information influence the responses. Responses are influenced by the way interviews are conducted, the starting point of bidding, and aggregation bias. To take advantage of its ability to value not only the current availability of a recreational good but also resources under changing or hypothetical conditions, it is necessary to be able to define or predict the environmental resources or changes that may occur so that realistic contingent valuation method scenarios can be presented to the respondents in the survey. Embedding occurs if the value of the good being studied is embedded in the value of the more encompassing set of goods and services reported by the respondent. Some researchers claimed that the ability of CVM to provide estimates which are in accord with the decision-making situation at hand is limited (Bennett and Carter, 1993).

In addition, willingness to pay (WTP) to secure a benefit or to avoid damage is different from willingness to accept (WTA), or compensation to forgo a gain or tolerate a cost. Economic values captured by measuring WTP are likely to be a mix of potential use and non-use values. Typically, WTA is larger than WTP as a result of both higher damage compared to comparable gain and limited substitutes for environmental goods (Hanemann, 1991). WTP, as measured by the consumer's surplus under aggregate demand curve, implies that individuals are the best persons to make judgments about recreation resource, they are able to make the best decisions about the effects of environmental quality if they want to make such decision. WTP is a function of prior knowledge, hence the validity of responses is influenced by the degree of information the respondents have, and heavily affected by the design of questionnaire and the way survey is conducted. In practice however, there is not complete information, individuals are willing to allow government agencies to make decisions. However, WTP is influenced by both willingness to pay and capability to pay, which is determined by income levels (Hufschmidt *et al.*, 1983). The poor may not be willing to pay for environmental programs that have the potential of improving social welfare significantly just because they have no ability to pay. Randall *et al.* (1983) argued that it is possible that a lower level of the willingness to pay is indicated by the respondents.

While CVM is useful in determining general and recreational values of natural resources, it is liable to be much less useful in determining "productivity" values (Tisdell, 1995) because the general public does not possess sufficient knowledge of the productivity influence of change in resources. In this case, experts are more reliable than the general public. As the only means available for valuing non-use values, CVM's reliability is influenced by the degree of randomness, sampling procedure and the interview or questionnaire. The use of CVM to value the existence of single discrete species has been viewed with skepticism (Stevens *et al.*, 1991) mainly due to the argument that respondents to a CVM survey may be unable to give meaningful answers because the intrinsic right for wildlife to exist is independent of humankind's attitudes.

7.3.5 A comparison of the travel cost and contingent valuation methods (CVM)

Contingent valuation and the travel cost method are applied to the problem of valuing non-market recreation benefits derived by visitors (Hanley, 1989). Optimistic views in estimating non-market values agree that the CVM and travel cost methods will suffice, and the new challenge is to learn how to adjust past studies to estimate non-market values for future policy analysis (Walsh *et al.*, 1989).

Non-use values do not require a choice but people experience satisfaction from environmental resources without actually using them, so the CVM framework is used in measuring such behavioural indicators as conversation and the adaptations people make as they learn (Smith, 1989). CVM measures both use and non-use values whilst travel cost measures only use values. The former is able to provide ex-ante measures whilst hedonic pricing and travel cost are ex-post estimates and indirect approaches because they do not rely on the direct answers as to how much the correspondents would be willing to pay (or accept) but allow reference values. Contingent valuation survey responses are combined with travel cost method data on actual market behaviour to estimate jointly both the parameters of the underlying utility function and its corresponding ordinary demand function (Cameron, 1992).

In addition, the travel cost method measures the expectation of visit enjoyment before the visitor commits him/herself to incur the travel cost, while CVM measures the enjoyment of the visit during the course of the visit as it is being experienced. The same result can be yielded only when the visitor has a clear intention of visiting a specific place and is able to accurately judge the enjoyment of visiting that site before setting out. For example, a value of A$86 million per year was derived in 1991–1992 to the management and research of the Great Barrier Reef Marine Park by using the contingent valuation method (Driml, 1994), which includes an annual willingness-to-pay by both the Australian population and international tourists, but excluding the value placed on it by people outside Australia who are not actual visitors to Australia.

7.4 Application of Valuation Techniques in LDCs and Ecotourism

7.4.1 Valuation of resources in LDCs

Although it has been argued that people in traditional societies are more prone to preserve ecological systems than those in developed countries who rely on the world's resources as a whole (Klee, 1980), with the widely accepted notion of the "global village" or "spaceship" (Boulding, 1966), the entire world, particularly the developed world, has developed the concept of conservation out of self-interest as well as altruistic reasons, or both. In addition, demand for improved environment is income-elastic, hence countries with low per capita income will concentrate on raising material income rather than improving environmental quality (Victor, 1972). Major reasons for undertaking valuation of resources, especially in LDCs, include the following points:

1. Natural resources are likely to be treated as free goods if they have no prices attached to their access. Therefore, they may be treated as worthless and be over-exploited, resulting in a classic case of market failure (Tietenberg, 1992; Gowdy, 1994b). Placing a value on resources admits that they frequently have real and even substantial value.

2. Sinden and Worrell (1979) suggested that valuation could assist general understanding and decision-making in many ways, such as examining which alternative uses of resource contributes more to welfare. As noted by Ward and Loomis (1986: 164), "to allocate resources efficiently in the economic sense, managers require information on relative values and costs of recreational outputs and resource inputs, respectively".

3. Valuation provides incentive for investment in projects based on the use of natural resources. For instance, it provides a means for comparing the importance of recreation as a resource use with that of other resource uses.

In addition, a challenge comes from the undeniable fact that biodiversity is frequently distributed in areas with the fewest economic means to implement a preservation program (McNeely, 1988). Development of markets and the market system, the rapid technological change, the development of institutions that removes local control over resources, high discount rates to projects with foreign investment, corruption, and so on, have undermined the ability of the LDCs to alter their customs or adjust to new practices to preserve resources effectively (Tisdell, 1990). They usually lack the institutional basis for applying pollution-control measures, and prices rarely reflect the real cost of production — often raw materials are under-priced, encouraging the expansion in the subsidised area. Natural systems suffer increasing stress from population expansion, economic growth, and deteriorating global environment, and in turn deteriorating natural systems deter further economic development.

Some argue that environmental spillovers are smaller in quantity in LDCs than in industrialised countries given their lower level of industrialisation, and that they have considerable capacity for assimilating negative environmental spillovers (Little and Mirrlees, 1974). However, high rates of discount in LDCs result in little consideration in the future impacts of projects. Private companies give greater weight to profit making than to environmental concerns. When projects are implemented by foreign companies, less concern will be given to environmental factors due to the distance of the principals from the areas affected (Tisdell, 1990). For example, markets and market reforms are not sufficient to deal with Asia's economic growth and economic problems accompanied by rapid urbanisation of and the likelihood of increased international and trans-boundary conflicts over use of natural resources. Rapid economic growth in the Asian-Pacific region provides economic hope for the region's low-income countries but raises international environmental dilemmas and could be unsustainable. Environmental pollution in China, for example, causes 95 billion yuan in economic losses per year — 6.75 percent of its GNP (Bingham, 1993). Hence institutional and other reforms, as well as high-income countries supporting the environmental conservation efforts of low-income countries, are needed (Tisdell, 1995).

Travel cost and CVM have been applied to valuing natural resources in both industrialised and developing countries. For example, consumers' surplus attached to current non-consumptive use of protected areas by foreign visitors in Kenya, estimated by contingent valuation survey of expressed preference, stands at $450 million per annum — more than doubling the best available estimate of opportunity cost and appears to justify current resource use (Moran, 1994). Protected areas and their inhabitants are not only the principal focus of the tourist industry for Kenya, but also a source of wonder and value for a global population of non-users, and there is frequently little coincidence between those that benefit and those that pay for the continued existence of such areas (Navrud and Mungatana, 1994).

7.4.2   Valuation and resource use related to ecotourism

It was not until the 1950s and 1960s that the valuation of natural resources used for recreation and tourism received widespread attention (Clawson and Knetsch, 1966). It also became clear that there are many parks in the developing world, that wildlife viewing is becoming an important part of the global trend of increasing ecotourism, and that sustainable management of wildlife resources could provide a significant and much needed revenue source for developing countries in the future.

There is no common agreement about whether economic valuation of environmental goods is desirable. In view of the complex nature of ecosystems, any attempts to develop a realistic economic valuation method to include the package of values of environmental resource are likely to be difficult. Both conceptual and empirical methods for placing monetary values on non-market goods and services are far from perfect (Tisdell, 1996), especially when it comes to measuring the effects of activities on non-physical environment, such as culture, ethnicity and the social system.

Conservation, as defined by IUCN (1980), is in fact a form of economic development. It means wise use which contributes to sustainable development instead of non-use (McNeely, 1988). Assessment of values and costs of conservation can provide a basis for determining the total value of biological systems, which can be so considerable that "conservation itself should be seen as a form of economic development" (McNeely, 1988: 4). Direct use values of natural resources include ecotourism, genetic material for pharmaceuticals, sustainable forestry, and crop breeding. The question of why natural resources, especially tourism attractions, might be valued is raised in the context of gaining economic returns from using those resources.

It has been suggested that resources deployed for non-consumptive purposes may provide the best use when both conservation and economic benefit are considered. There have been numerous studies on evaluation of natural resources and recreation using a variety of techniques. Walsh (1986) summarised these studies in the US, and Sinden (1992) provided a review of studies in Australia. Support for the use of valuation methods in governments indicates the wide acceptance of these techniques (Walsh, 1986). Travel cost and CVM methods were used to evaluate the economic value of six different ecotourism activities in Pennsylvania, USA, where the consumers' surplus value in 1988 dollars amounted to more than $1.28 million annually — twice the total expenditures of approximately $640,000 in these sites (Shafer *et al.*, 1993).

Attempts to place a financial value on natural attractions have ranged from estimating the financial value of wildlife in East Africa, in which an elephant is worth $14,375 per annum, or $900,000 over its life in terms of tourist expenditure (Olindo, 1991), to calculating the willingness to pay to visit tropical rainforest (Tobias and Mendelson, 1991). Hodgson and Dixon (1988) looked into the issue of logging versus fishing and tourism in Palawan, the Philippines, from the point that the sedimentation from logging damaged coral reefs and the fishery. They evaluated the gross revenues with and without a hypothesised ban on logging; the result shows that the revenue from fishery and tourism with a logging ban exceeded that without the ban by $17.5 million.

Krutilla and Cicchetti (1972) compared the net social benefits of two alternative uses of Hells Canyon in America — construction of a dam for hydroelectric power or preservation of the canyon for recreation — through threshold and sensitivity tests, and achieved the conclusion that preservation for recreation was the more desirable alternative. Artificial reefs, used as part of ecotourism dive packages, provide significantly greater economic return than commercial fisheries because the annual gross revenue from the commercial fishery of one open-access dive tour artificial reef is 4 percent of the annual pre-tax profit of dive tours operating on this same reef, while the estimated daily catch from this reef is equivalent to the estimated annual sustainable yield (Brock, 1994).

Nevertheless, there has been a vicious circle in sustaining the viability of natural areas, including national parks and natural reserves. Generally low entrance fees to natural areas cannot compensate for investment in maintaining and enhancing the natural areas, and the perverse result is that relatively poor host countries (such as China) subsidise tourists from wealthy places, who comprise a large proportion of all ecotourists and the generation of small revenues from natural areas provides little political or fiscal rationale for government to strongly support funding for further development of natural areas. The fundamental question arises of how to price natural areas in order both to make them financially viable and to achieve equity goals. Little infrastructure is solely for tourism use, but it is possible to identify tourism as a major call on certain facilities in a specific area and as a marginal cause of increased maintenance costs.

Theoretically, price is a derivative of a demand curve, which is shifting over time with changes in fashion and lifestyle, although supply is relatively fixed. If the marginal social cost of ecotourism is higher than the private marginal cost, the optimal fee will be higher. Environmental and social consequences add more obstacles to the socially optimal charge on ecotourism (Clarke *et al.*, 1995). Nevertheless, the user-pays principle can be limited by the cost of collecting charges, and it may be socially optimal from an economic viewpoint not to charge. Monopoly may occur in fee collecting (Tisdell, 1995). A study by Rogers (1995) concluded that the concept of "value for money" was frequently mentioned as an underpinning rationale by price-makers in an investigation into the pricing practice in tourist attractions in the United Kingdom.

Ecotourism should not be used as an excuse for further encroaching on protected areas where other forms of depletive activities have been abandoned. Current financial returns from ecotourism are only a part of direct use, and other direct, indirect and potential returns from both consumptive and non-consumptive uses should be taken into account in the meantime (Blane and Jackson, 1994).

7.4.3 *Limitations of valuation methods in their application, especially in China*

Although widely applied in valuing unpriced resources, the currently available valuation methods have their limitations, especially when applied in developing countries such as China. They usually require a considerable amount of information to approximate valuation of recreation sites. For example, travel cost requires substantial data, such as socioeconomic characteristics of the visitors, direct travel expenses, environmental quality attributes for the particular site and its substitutes, time costs, and so forth. CVM is based on the assumption that respondents have perfect knowledge of the good, the circumstances in which the good is supplied and the alternatives available. It is supposed that respondents are sufficiently familiar with or well informed about the subject to make a "correct" valuation. There is evidence that the structure of valuation question and especially the starting value offered to the interviewee can affect the responses (Cummings *et al.*, 1986). The possible biases in CVM, such as strategic bias, information bias, embedding problems, instrument bias, and biases arising from hypothetical answers have been discussed extensively (Forster, 1989).

In practice, there are limitations to the information available and what can be conveyed in questionnaires. Shaw (1984) pointed out that problems arise in the valuation of wildlife in tourism when people do not fully understand the role of wildlife in recreational experiences and when we have a poor understanding of the ecological significance of specific wildlife populations. Many people are unaccustomed to valuing unpriced goods and find valuation questions hard to answer. The quality and quantity of information influence the responses, and responses are influenced by the way interviews are conducted, the starting point of bidding, and aggregation bias.

For ecotourism sites, which are usually secondary to other recreational destinations, it is hard to derive a demand curve for a particular site through the travel cost or contingent valuation method. Multiple destination trips challenge the validity of valuation methods. As will be discussed in Chapter 8, in Yunnan Province of China, many ecotourism sites are a part of a multi-destination trip and it is difficult for their value to be properly derived by methods such as TCM.

Incomes of travellers influence the utility they may obtain from recreation activities, and therefore the slope and position of demand curves derived by the travel cost method change for different zones not only because of distance but also different income groups (Seckler, 1966). Because of the big income difference between an average Chinese traveller and foreigner, it is difficult to obtain a unified demand curve for a tourist site used by both domestic and international tourists. In any case, the unified curve may be of limited relevance for policy purposes.

How to evaluate ethnic cultures remains a thorny problem. Ecotourism in some parts of China utilises minority cultures as there are 55 minority nationalities recognised by the state in China, with an overall population of about ten percent of China's total, covering well over half China's total area. Both the inequality between the Han and minority areas and among the minority areas widened in the 1990s with economic growth in China (Mackerras, 1996). With memory of disturbances in the minority areas, China has been trying to reduce possible ethnic disharmony and attempts of secession by introducing preferential policies for minority areas, including measures to encourage tourism development. Nevertheless, minority cultures have been exposed to tourism without sufficient social evaluation, and environmental degradation and cultural commercialisation have been observed in minority areas as a result of tourism (Swain, 1995).

There are other ways to make social decisions such as by voting instead of putting dollar values on the resource. However, problems raised by Arrow (1951) limit their application to the evaluation of tourism resources. A cautious attitude is necessary when applying valuation techniques to tourism resources.

7.5   Conflict Between Ecotourism and the Maximisation of Total Economic Value and Nature Conservation

Economists *per se* usually suggest that land use should be organised so as to maximise its total economic value (TEV), that is the total of its direct and indirect economic values, whether appropriated by the landholder or not. But in practice at least two problems exist for this point of view:

1. Not all landholders (including holders or managers of potential lands) are in a financial position to act in this manner.
2. Economic value is determined solely with reference to human beings (usually on the basis of their willingness to pay) and thus is anthropogenic. It therefore does not satisfy the values of "deep ecologists", that is those with strong ecocentric values who believe that nature conservation may have value independently of human wishes (cf. Tisdell, 1991, Chapter 1). An example of this viewpoint is the "land ethic" of Aldo Leopold (1966).

Two problems in the development of ecotourism can be related to those points of view, and both are currently relevant in China and in most less developed countries. Because of financial constraints, managers of protected lands are being placed under considerable pressure to develop ecotourism as a means to supplement their finances (Tisdell, 1999). In their attempt to appropriate revenue from ecotourism, they may expand tourism beyond the level which maximises TEV and/or compromise the conservation values of the protected area. In the first case the social economic consideration in (1) above is not satisfied, and in the second case, nature conservation is compromised. It should be noted that even maximising TEV can compromise nature conservation given, the type of views mentioned in (2) above.

It may be useful to illustrate just one aspect of this problem. In Fig. 7.1, let curve OABC represent the net revenue which a protected area can earn from ecotourism development, and let the curve DEF represent the conservation value of this area, may be indicated by an index. In this case, ecotourism in the protected area could be developed up to an intensity of X_1, without compromising the conservation value of the area. But the need for finance to manage the protected area may lead its managers to expand ecotourism beyond this level. Because of shortfalls in their funding, they may be tempted to expand the intensity of ecotourism to level X_2, the level which maximises their net revenue thereby compromising conservation values. This is a serious problem in China (Tisdell, 1999).

In Fig. 7.1, ecotourism intensities between X_1 and X_2 constitute a conflict zone. Note also that if the curve OABC were to be interpreted so as to be TEV, Fig. 7.1 would illustrate the possible conflict between maximisation of TEV and nature conservation.

Of course the situation for the development of ecotourism is very favourable when a situation like that illustrated in Fig. 7.2 occurs. In this case, the net revenue curve from ecotourism peaks before the ecotourism intensity

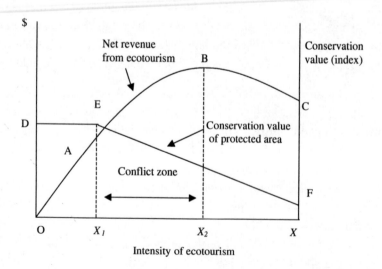

Fig. 7.1 Possible conflict between ecotourism development and nature conservation.

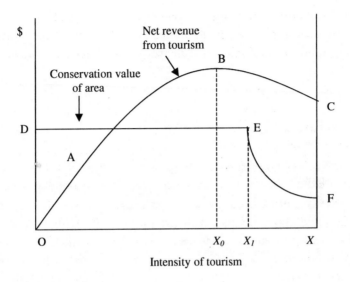

Fig. 7.2 A case in which ecotourism development is unlikely to compromise nature conservation.

compromises nature conservation. Maximising net returns from ecotourism should not compromise nature conservation in this case.

Uncertainties about the type of relationship shown in Figs. 7.1 and 7.2 may further complicate the management situation. In addition, curves of this nature are not designed to throw light on sustainability issues because they do not address dynamics. Nevertheless the problems which they illustrate are real ones.

There is another important way in which the development of ecotourism can compromise nature conservation. The development of ecotourism in China has in the past involved a financial investment by the managers of a protected area. Unfortunately, ecotourism development does not always turn out to be profitable. Hence, instead of reducing the financial problems of the managers of a protected area, it may add to those problems. Consequently funds normally intended for protecting nature may be diverted to loan repayments or to cover losses on ecotourism investments and nature conservation suffers (Tisdell, 1995).

These problems are relevant throughout China (cf. Lindberg *et al.*, 1997) and to most LDCs. They are of particular relevance in inland China where ecotourism (and cultural tourism) are relatively important drawcards for tourists.

7.6 Conclusion

The neoclassical economic notion of value concentrates on the existence of exchange relations between valuable goods. Total economic value of an environmental resource is composed of its instrumental and intrinsic value, or use value and non-use value. Valuation techniques have been developed in an effort to capture unpriced values of natural resources to prevent or at least slow down resource depletion. There is no common agreement over whether and to what extent economic valuation of environmental goods is desirable. In view of the complex nature of ecosystems, attempts to develop a realistic economic valuation method to include the package of values of environmental resources are likely to be difficult.

In most countries, natural conservation has occurred on land of little direct economic value or of little use value. Such land is usually uneconomic for agriculture or very marginal, for instance, even though the situation may alter with technological progress. Tourism can often be developed specifically in locations with little alternative economic use, such as sites with a picturesque landscape but with no mineral resources and with little agricultural value, as in some parts of China.

Tourism represents a direct use of natural resources but often not a very consumptive one. Up to a point, tourism is compatible with the conservation of natural resources. This is particularly so for ecotourism, bearing in mind that it is a type of tourism that is supposed to be careful of the natural environment (see Chapter 6 for details). Provided that such care is taken, the conservation values of a land area may be retained but in the light of the discussion of the previous section can also be compromised. Nevertheless, ecotourism may maintain greater conservation value than alternative forms of direct economic use of an area, or tourism of an exploitative kind.

Ecotourism can result in a win-win outcome, or be the only available alternative to worse land uses from a conservative point of view.

As pointed out in this chapter, ecotourism or nature tourism has tended to develop on land which has little *direct* economic value for alternative economic activities such as agriculture or mining, that is land with little *direct* opportunity cost in terms of alternative economic activities forgone. In some cases however, the historical pattern of land-use may not be a socially optimal one from an economic point of view. This is because, in some instances, conservation of land area plus its use for ecotourism/tourism may give a higher total economic value than the *positive* direct opportunity cost of its use in alternative economic activities, such as agriculture. However, in such cases, without public intervention, the area concerned is likely to be used for these alternative economic activities such as agriculture, rather than conserved.

Thus important choices concerning land use are required. Unfortunately, prices and markets do not provide an adequate guide to such choices because of market failures, particularly in relation to indirect or non-use values. Both the non-existence of market prices and, to a lesser extent, the inability of market prices to reflect the complete set of values bestowed by natural resources have resulted in underestimation of resource loss compared with the benefit from growth.

Reconciling and operationalising sustainable development in economic, ecological and social contexts poses formidable problems. The central issue for the world has become how to continue development in a fashion that preserves the long-term productivity of natural systems for sustained development while minimising deterioration in environmental quality. In the face of poverty, increasing population and widening inequality, countries, especially LDCs, tend to use natural resources to assist economic growth at the price of imbalance in natural systems. Because of the strong connection between natural system imbalance and social-economic imbalance, growth by depleting natural systems can lead to environmental and socio-economic deterioration, and contribute to further poverty as well as expanding the gulf between the rich and poor.

Conservation is believed to be able to contribute to economic development, and conserved resources may be utilised for sustainable development.

However, some forms of pragmatism hold dangers for conservation because they rely on seemingly rational and objective economic evaluation, which is often made on the grounds of short-term commercial benefits. Moreover, there are no private property rights in natural resources in many countries, leaving conservation to the total mercy of bureaucrats. The "tragedy of commons" can be frequently observed, resulting in deterioration of resources, including those in China.

Tourism, especially ecotourism, is often regarded as a type of sustainable use of resources. However, careful examination indicates that it is not always a sustainable form of resource use. Evaluation of the tourism industry and tourist resources is therefore needed to guide both tourism development and resource conservation. Improper development at tourist attractions has resulted in negative environmental effects. Overcrowded tourist sites, rapid depreciation of tourist facilities, involving neglect of the necessary maintenance of tourist sites in order to make quick profit are occurring. These combined with imbalances between basic infrastructure and tourist demand (Tisdell and Wen, 1991b), have been adding to environmental problems initiated by tourism.

China has progressed from a situation where tourism was regarded as environmentally benign to one that recognises both possibilities for environmental deterioration and for conservation as a result of tourism growth. The need for appropriate planning and associated government measures to protect the environment as far as tourism development is concerned is increasingly recognised in China.

The next chapter is concerned with the development of tourism, especially ecotourism, in Yunnan, particularly in Xishuangbanna Prefecture, and its evaluation. It is found, however, that due to data and other limitations, only limited use can be made of the evaluation techniques outlined in this chapter. Most of the techniques outlined in this chapter have been designed for static or relatively stationary conditions and assessment undertaken from a limited perspective. In a developing situation, such as that being experienced in Yunnan, assessment is required from a wider perspective, as becomes apparent in Chapter 8.

Chapter 8

Tourism Development in Yunnan:
A Case Study

8.1 Introduction

This chapter provides a case study of the development of tourism in an inland province of China, namely Yunnan. Tourism is regarded as a leading or key economic sector in Yunnan. This chapter provides an opportunity to consider the nature of this development, including its spatial characteristics within Yunnan. Situated in Southwest China (see Fig. 3.1), Yunnan is rich in ecotourism resources and tourist attractions associated with minority cultures. Rapid growth in tourism has occurred in Yunnan Province since 1979 with several destinations being popular. Xishuangbanna Prefecture, one of the important tourism centres of Yunnan, provides an interesting case study of ecotourism and its management in the context of China, and raises difficulties about how ecotourism resources should be evaluated. It therefore helps illustrate issues raised in Chapters 6 and 7, and highlights difficulties in applying concepts introduced in these chapters.

While the spatial distribution of tourism in China was extensively discussed on a macro-scale in Chapters 4 and 5, paying particular attention to inequalities between the coastal and inland region, this chapter provides an opportunity to examine some spatial characteristics within both a prefecture and within a province at a more disaggregated level. In Yunnan's case, its variety of ecotourism resources and ethnic tourist attractions and their distribution appear to be a powerful force for decentralising tourism, even though some central tendencies are still present within Yunnan.

Ecotourism development in Xishuangbanna is analysed in this chapter. Furthermore, a comparison of characteristics of tourism in three different regional centres of Yunnan, namely Xishuangbanna, Dali and Lijiang, is made in order to understand both the direct economic effect of tourism and its indirect roles in social and environmental change. Prospects for further tourism development in Yunnan and Xishuangbanna and related policy issues are considered.

8.2   Tourism, Especially Ecotourism, in Xishuangbanna

8.2.1   *General introduction to Xishuangbanna*

Xishuangbanna Dai Autonomous Prefecture is situated in the southern tip of Yunnan Province, boarding Laos in the Southeast and Burma in the Southwest. Established in 1953, its administration structure is comprised of one city — Jinghong ("the place of dawn" in the Dai language), and two counties — Menghai and Mengla. In the Dai language, the word "Xishuangbanna" means 12 districts of 1,000 mu of paddy fields each — a reflection of the old land ownership system when this whole area was distributed among 12 chieftains, who were responsible to the general governor of Xishuangbanna for the payment of land rent and provision of labour.

Possessing tropical and subtropical monsoon climate types, the annual mean temperature in Xishuangbanna is 21 degrees Celsius and it is frost free all the year round. The year can be divided into a wet season from the end of May to the end of October, which brings 90 percent of the annual precipitation, and a dry season from early November to May. The tropical rainforest provides favourable environments for the growth and propagation of flora and fauna. Natural forest covers over 40 percent of its land area. 50 percent of China's rare and endangered plants can be found here.

Xishuangbanna came to be known as the "green gem" in the 1950s when former premier Zhou Enlai took part in the Water Splashing Festival and held functions to host his overseas guests here. The attractiveness of its tropical rainforests, wild flora and fauna, combined with varied minority life-styles and cultures, makes this place a cherished tourist attraction. However, Xishuangbanna did not start to be targeted as a major tourism destination until the 1980s because the ultra-leftists in the Chinese Communist Party were worried about national security in border areas and therefore restricted entry to these areas. When mass tourism, which started in Kunming in the late 1970s, began to show signs of congestion in the middle 1980s, and strong demands were expressed for visiting Xishuangbanna, the Yunnan government decided to facilitate tourism development in Xishuangbanna.

8.2.2   *The Dai nationality and conservation*

One of the major attractions of Xishuangbanna is the Dai nationality. As the major ethnic group in Yunnan, about one million, or one third of Yunnan's total population, are the Dais, and they are concentrated in Xishuangbanna Dai Prefecture. The word "Dai" means freedom in the Dai language. The majority of the Dais inhabit plains, and their villages are located beside rivers and lakes. They usually live in bamboo houses on stilt foundations, which are enclosed by a courtyard of bamboo hedges surrounding fruit trees. The young people have a free social life before their marriage. The major festival, the Water-Splashing Festival, takes place to welcome the Dai New Year in mid-April and to dispel the diseases and misfortunes of the past year. It has become a significant tourist attraction of Xishuangbanna.

The religion of the Dais is Lesser Vehicle Buddhism, which teaches people to seek harmony with the existing system rather than destroy it. Consequently, the Dais usually accept reality passively, even at a low level of material satisfaction which, according to some researchers is one of the reasons why the Dais are a peaceful people with little greed for material things and show lack of entrepreneurship.

Some traditions of the Dais foster conservation. They plant fast growing trees called Heixinmu (Black Cord Tree, or *Cassia siamea*), a nitrogen-fixing species which enriches the soil, along the roads and in their villages as fuel wood for their domestic needs rather than chopping down trees from the rainforest. It is estimated that each Dai uses 1.0 to 1.5 cubic metre of fuel wood a year and 0.1 hectare of land on average is enough to meet the annual fuel wood needs of one person (Wen, 1996). Some forest hills have been conserved for hundreds of years as Longshan (Dragon Hill) or Shengshan

(Holy Hill) for burials, collecting medicinal plants and religious reasons. Wood-chipping, vegetation removal and hunting are prohibited in those areas.

Agricultural production levels used to be low in Xishuangbanna. The Prefecture had to ask for at least 30 million yuan and 30 million kilograms of grain from the central government every year in the 1970s to maintain the subsistence of its people (Yang, 1990). With primary industries as the traditional economic activities, Xishuangbanna has targeted tourism as its new pole of economic growth and as a driving force to support conservation.

8.2.3   Tourism as the major industry in Xishuangbanna

Tourist arrivals in Xishuangbanna have been growing at an average annual rate of 20 percent since the late 1980s (Tourism Bureau of Xishuangbanna, 1995). Income from tourism in 1994 accounted for 26 percent of Xishuang-banna's total gross product, and 50 percent of the income from tertiary industries in Xishuangbanna (Statistics Bureau of Yunnan, 1995). The number of its travel agencies jumped from 22 in 1992 to 44 in 1993, and to more than 300 in 1996 and to 338 in 1998. Apart from more than 13,250 rooms provided by around 234 hotels with sufficient quality to cater for overseas tourists in 1998, many more rooms were supplied by hotels and guest houses operated by non-tourist sectors, although the exact number of these rooms was not available (NTA, 1997 and 1999). A brief overview of the growth of tourism in Xishuangbanna is given in the Table 8.1. A change in statistical method is partly the cause of the considerable jump in its international tourism receipts in 1994 as explained in Chapter 2.

Tourism has been targeted as the leading industry in Xishuangbanna with supporting policies from administration bodies as well as related industries. The Tourism Bureau of Xishuangbanna Prefecture (simplified as the Tourism Bureau in this chapter) is the highest tourism administration body in the Prefecture, with three tourism branch bureaus in Jinghong, Menghai and Mengla under its jurisdiction. They are responsible for the macro-control of tourism in Xishuangbanna, coordinating tourism across administration levels and different industries, planning tourism development, and arranging training programmes.

Table 8.1 Tourism growth in Xishuangbanna, 1991–1996.

	International Tourism		Domestic Tourism	
	Arrivals	Receipts ($US m)	No. of tourists	Income (yuan m)
1991	8,460	0.37	600,000	30
1992	13,609	0.8	900,000	100
1993	15,305	1.17	1,000,000	200
1994	15,400	4.29	1,250,000	780
1995	21,330	5.04	1,420,000	897
1996	23,658	5.72	1,510,000	1,240

Source: Travel and Tourism Bureau of Yunnan, 1997.

Major steps were taken in 1993 and 1994 to improve tourism in Xishuang-banna. Travel agencies were compelled to sign insurance contracts covering the safety of tourists and tourist vehicles. The Prefectural government issued regulations on cross-border tourism management. A joint law enforcement office was set up by the Tourism Bureau together with the Intermediate People' Court of the Prefecture to ensure a favourable legal environment for tourism development. A Tourism Association has been established to promote standardisation in the tourism industry. In order to better organise the 300 vehicles engaged in tourism, a standard vehicle symbol and driver card are issued after a compulsory test arranged jointly by the Transportation Bureau and the Tourism Bureau for both the vehicle and the driver. As a result, traffic accidents have decreased considerably since September 1994 after unqualified vehicles and drivers were forced to stop operating. A Quality Assurance Fund has been established with funds collected from travel agencies, and the Tourism Bureau has the right to make use of this fund to compensate tourists for losses in case of any disputes. Re-registration and re-accreditation of tour guides was undertaken in 1994 in order to improve personnel management. New badges for tour guides were issued after a test. A plan for tour guide testing has been made and training courses have been provided. Delegations have been sent to both domestic and international fairs to promote tourism in Xishuangbanna.

A survey of tourism resources in Xishuangbanna started in September 1994 with the help of the Chinese Academy of Science and the National Tourism Administration in Beijing. Eight hundred sites distributed in 40 towns have been identified. Resource rating took place from three sites, namely the Ethnic Culture Park in Jinghong, the Menglun Botanic Garden, and the Tourist Village in Mandou. An overall plan for tourism development in Xishuangbanna was compiled afterwards. Those investing in tourism must obtain approval from the Tourism Bureau and comply with the overall tourism plan of Xishuangbanna. The Tourism Bureau intends to actively support conservation by closing sites to tourism development if there are insufficient resources to protect the site.

Although Xishuangbanna is known for its forests and wildlife, tourism at this stage in Xishuangbanna focuses mainly on ethnic cultures. Encounters with nature in a typical tour of three or four days are limited to a two-hour visit to the Menglun Botanical Garden and a three-hour trip walking along the tracks in a mountain with an average height of 500 meters in Mandian, a site financed by the Forestry Department and the Planning Committee of Xishuangbanna, to watch two waterfalls. A number of plants and "plant-strangling" flora can be observed on the way.

Four tourist routes are most popular in Xishuangbanna. They usually include going to Xiao Mengla, a small Burmese town across the boarder from Daluo, a town 150 kilometres west of Jinghong on the Chinese side. The east route goes through Ganlanba to the Botanic Garden in Menglun 80 kilometres away from Jinghong, or continues to turn south to visit Laos through Mengla. The south route is a 90 kilometres trip to Da Meng Long to see the White Pagoda at Manfeilong (Flying Dragon). The north route takes tourists to the Mandian Waterfalls and Dai villages. Visiting villages of other ethnic nationalities and activities such as water-splashing of the Dais are included in these trips. The ferry trip down the Lancang (Mekong) River to the Golden Triangle in Thailand is gaining in popularity. Tours within Jinghong include visiting parks and shops, tasting local food in ethnic restaurants, accompanied by performances, and taking the three-wheeled carriage or strolling on the street.

There were almost 200 tourist enterprises in Xishuangbanna at the end of 1995 involved in operating travel agencies, hotels, transportation and supplying tourist commodities. Major souvenirs are peacock feathers, wooden elephants and butterfly specimens. It was estimated that the average percentage of total tourism expenditure on shopping was 18.5 by overseas tourists (Tisdell and Zhu, 1995). But generally visitors complain about the limited design, availability and unreliable pricing for tourist products. Many stalls and shops sell so-called "Burmese jade", but the quality and price are obviously suspicious. Because the majority of tourists to Xishuangbanna stay in Kunming, where a wide range of reasonably-priced tourist commodities is available, Xishuangbanna needs to expand its supply of tourist goods with distinguished characteristics and sell those at a reasonable price.

Transportation to and within Xishuangbanna has improved considerably during the last decade. However, due to its location and complicated topography, transportation is still a bottleneck for tourism in Xishuangbanna. There are usually three or four regular flights from Kunming to Xishuang-banna daily, with a total capacity of around 800 people. But the demand normally exceeds the supply of seats, resulting in travellers waiting in Kunming for seats. Another alternative to the 25 minutes flight is an arduous bus trip which crosses on the winding road of the Yungui Plateau for more than 800 kilometres. There are direct flights from Guangzhou, a city in Southeast China, where one-fourth of overseas visitors land China. There is also strong domestic tourism demand for Xishuangbanna from the affluent Pearl River Delta, and from Chongqing, a big industrial centre in Southwest China. Xishuangbanna is pressing for more direct flights from other Chinese cities as well as from cities in Southeast Asia. But it takes a long time to organise flights and considerable investment is needed for upgrading the Jinghong Airport. Many roads in Xishuangbanna become impassable during the wet season, and there are usually sharp turns along the roads.

Tourism is distributed unevenly within Xishuangbanna itself. A tourist normally spends three nights and four days here with an average daily expenditure of 200 yuan to 400 yuan. An overwhelming majority (99 percent) of tourists make Jinghong their base during their stay and take day trips. Most travel agencies and hotels are also located in Jinghong. Other areas in

Xishuangbanna can only obtain tourism income from lunch and entry fees plus small sales of tourist commodities. Shops located on the Chinese–Burmese border, where Burmese jade is in abundant supply, can make a profit from jade products (whether genuine or not).

It is urgent to improve the efficiency of tourism investment in Xishuangbanna. Some tourism projects in Xishuangbanna are suffering a loss due to improper decision-making and mismanagement. A garden for the Dai culture and fairy tales was set up at Ganlanba with an investment of more than half a billion yuan in 1994, but attracts few visitors due to its distance from the main road. A Dai village providing accommodation of Dai style was built in the grounds of the Menglun Botanical Gardens as a joint venture of the Chinese Academy of Science and a Hongkong businessman. The low occupancy rates resulting from the fact that most tourists stay in Jinghong led to constant losses and the withdrawal of the Hong Kong partner. Another failure because of poor location is the Mengbalaxi Miniature Park with an investment of 48,000 yuan. The Cultural Village at Mandou was jointly established by Mandou Village and the Bureau in 1992, and it soon became the major tourist site on the Lancang River with typical Dai activities. However, disagreement about the operation of the Cultural Village emerged after the administration body of Mandou changed in 1993. The Cultural Village was handed to an outsider on a contract basis and its staff trained under the help of the Bureau are leaving. It has been excluded from official major tourist sites mainly due to its poor service.

Coordination between travel agencies and other tourist sectors is also crucial for the success of tourism in Xishuangbanna. Unlike domestic tourism in most other parts of China or even in Yunnan, where FIT (free independent tourist) dominates the market, more than half of the Chinese tourists come to Xishuangbanna in tourist groups in order to be guaranteed of air tickets. For those who arrive independently, it is necessary to join groups organised by local travel agencies because scattered tourist sites in Xishuangbanna cannot be reached by public transportation and car renting is expensive. Consequently, the income of a tourist site depends significantly on whether travel agencies include it in the itinerary. For sites away from the major roads, such as the Cultural Village at Ganlanba, the access problem may be easily solved if the travel agencies agree to drive a little further. Tourists themselves who are not familiar with the tourist attractions in Xishuangbanna are happy to visit whatever they are taken to see, even though they occasionally complain about hygiene at certain sites and about rough roads.

There is no guaranteed financial support for tourism development in Xishuangbanna. As a Prefecture with relatively little fiscal income compared with richer areas in China, it is impractical to rely on government financial support. Although the Prefecture agreed to allocate half a million yuan every year for tourism, this will be difficult to accomplish according to the Bureau. Outside investment has been playing an increasingly important role in Xishuangbanna's tourism development. Jinghong Forestry Bureau signed a contract with the Jinzhou Group of Zhejiang Province in east China in April 1995 to develop a resort with an area of 250 hectares. Menglun Botanical Garden and a Hongkong company have jointly established a tourism development company with emphasis on ecotourism. A new tourist company named South China Holiday Ltd. is to be invested in jointly by Singapore interests and the Tourism Bureau of Xishuangbanna.

The basic maintenance of tourist sites needs improvement. Litter is visible at most tourist areas, and bins are hard to find. Stalls for selling ethnic food and snacks are often surrounded by flies. Toilets are hardly accessible at Mandian and Ganlanba.

To achieve the goal of receiving around three million tourists annually by the year 2000 from both China and abroad, and increasing tourism income to 20 percent of the gross product of the Prefecture, Xishuangbanna still needs to improve its infrastructure, especially that used for transportation. Staff training, more efficient administration and better coordination of complementary participants in the tourism sector are important for the smooth operation of tourism in the future. Quality commodities, with unique ethnic and tropical characteristics at reasonable prices, are promising channels for increasing tourist income. Further tourism development must be based on careful planning, taking account of the carrying capacities in the light of social, ethnic and environmental factors in Xishuangbanna.

8.2.4   The state nature reserve of Xishuangbanna and ecotourism

China has recognised the urgency of protecting Xishuangbanna from environmental degradation. The loss of natural resources in China has been recognised with nature reserves established to conserve biodiversity (National Environmental Protection Agency, 1994). Forest cover in Xishuangbanna was almost halved in the 1950s and 1960s as a result of rapid population growth, slash-and-burn farming and spreading rubber plantations. Protection efforts in Xishuangbanna started in 1958 when four reserves were established, followed by the unified State Nature Reserve of Xishuangbanna (simplified as "the Reserve" in this chapter) being announced in 1981 with more than 20 percent of Xishuangbanna under conservation. The Reserve consists of five patches of rainforest at Mengyang (99,760 hectares), Menglun (11,242 hectares), Mengla (92,932 hectares), Shangyong (30,538 hectares), and Menggao (7,304 hectares). Figure 8.1 indicates the location of these five subreserves, which are comprised of both the hatched areas and the cross-hatched areas.

The Administration Bureau of the Reserve was established in 1985 with 60 staff. There are four administration stations, six reserve working stations and seven forest police stations scattered in sub-reserves under this Administration Bureau with a total of 160 employees. More than 60 local villagers have been employed as part-time reporters for the Reserve to detect any poaching.

China announced in *China Agenda 21* that it intends to promote "green tourism" and to use ecotourism as a means to make the conservation of its biodiversity financially more attractive. Xishuangbanna Prefecture, an area internationally recognised as being very rich in biodiversity, has been targeted as one of the areas for ecotourism development. Ecotourism is an alternative to traditional high impact, exogeneously controlled mass tourism. China has accepted the basic concept that ecotourism can preserve the integrity of ecosystems while providing economic opportunities which make conservation of natural resources financially beneficial to local communities (National Environmental Protection Agency, 1994). This view conforms with the definitions of ecotourism as discussed in Chapter 6.

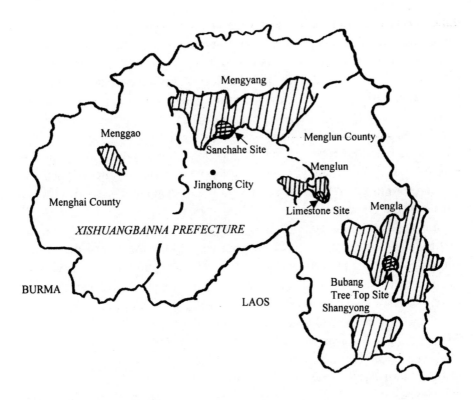

Fig. 8.1 The location of five subreserves of the Xishuangbanna State Nature Reserve and major ecotourism sites.

The rich ecotourism resources in Xishuangbanna are concentrated mainly in the Reserve, an area of 240,000 hectares. It contains well-preserved tropical forest and rich biodiversity, including a sub-population of the last remaining Asian elephants in China. Income from ecotourism is regarded by managers of the reserve as providing some justification for the conservation of those elephants and as a means of reducing the public cost of this conservation.

Ecotourism in the Reserve is conducted at three major sites — Sanchahe, Bubang and Menglun, and their locations are indicated in Fig. 8.1. Sanchahe, 45 kilometres north of Jinghong, is a site with a stable source of visitors who take bus trips between Kunming and Jinghong. There is a 4-kilometre-long track of concrete bricks in the forest leading to a pool across which an iron bridge 100 metres in length and 6 metres high, costing one million yuan, is being finished. In the dry season, wild animals often come to the pool for drinking and bathing, and staff from the Reserve sometimes spread salt near the pond to attract animals. Seven treetop hotels, built four to six metres above the ground, are scattered along the track, allowing the occupants to watch wild animals which usually appear during the evening. Unfortunately, the orange-coloured roofs of the treetop hotels do not blend in with the green environment. There is a butterfly farm and a snake garden which are of interest to tourists. A tourist toilet built in the shape of a huge tree always wins positive comments.

Sanchahe contains some of the probable 250 wild elephants existing in Xishuangbanna, which increased from only 100 at the end of the 1970s. Although birds and butterflies can be observed, it is hard for daytime visitors to encounter wild animals except that elephant droppings and their damage to vegetation or tracks can be seen occasionally. This is one of the reasons why travel agencies are not enthusiastic about bringing tourists here. Some tourists complain about the lack of activity at Sanchahe. There is hardly any focus event guaranteed for the tourists when butterflies in the farm go dormant from October until April.

The possibility of having a zoo built at Sanchahe was discussed, but the idea was not accepted because keeping wild animals in a zoo was believed to conflict with the ideal of conserving them in their natural habitat. There used to be a domesticated elephant bought from Burma available for photograph-taking and a ride in the forest. But it was "borrowed" by the Forest Ministry to be sent to Shanghai. Road conditions can be dangerous during wet season, and there are 300 sharp turns along the road of 30 kilometres from Jinghong to Menghai. To provide more attractions for ecotourism, the Reserve is building Sanchahe Forest Park with a special investment of 4 million yuan from the Governor's Office of Yunnan Province. This Forest Park, which includes some villas in ethnic styles providing 40 guest rooms and contains a peacock garden, is expected to promote Sanchahe from the present annual arrivals of around 30,000 and an income of less than 100,000 yuan, to a holiday resort with at least 100,000 visitors per year.

The butterfly farm at Sanchahe consists of a small building containing displays and a nursery and an outdoor meshed dome where butterflies are released. It breeds butterflies and sends them to be processed in a butterfly workshop in Jinghong for souvenirs. This farm is an initiative of the WWF (Europe) to increase the finance available to the subreserve. It makes an annual profit of about 10,000 yuan from butterflies. However, the butterfly workshop purchases an additional quantity of butterflies from those who collect butterflies along the roads, and this raises the issue of open-access collection, which may endanger some butterfly species.

Bubang is the second ecotourism site in the Mengla subreserve with dense forest of Wangtianshu (Looking into the Sky Trees, or Chinese Parashoreas) growing to a height of 60 to 80 metres. It contains a tree-top walkway 200 metres in length with a height of 8 metres at the lowest point and 35 metres at the highest point. It is built on the top of Chinese Parashorea trees, on which tourists can walk suspended in the air, take rests on the ten platforms along the passage way, and return to where they start by the same passage. It has been argued that a treetop walkway for tourists may not be compatible with conservation, and some deterioration of trees can be detected on this site. The walkway was used in joint research conducted by the Kunming Ecology Institute and the American Nature Cooperation on canopy ecology of tropical forest. The potential damage of trees from the walkway was discussed. Careful planning for tourism activities is necessary to avoid potential damage to the environment since this site receives around 20,000 visitors annually on average. It is, however, difficult to travel along the bumpy road of 17 kilometres from the County site of Mengla to Bubang and travel agencies are hesitant to send tourists here due to this access problem. At least three million yuan is required to improve transportation and tourist infrastruc-ture for Bubang according to the Bureau.

The third ecotourism destination in the Reserve is the Limestone Cliffs and Forest area at Menglun. An area as large as two percent of the Menglun Subreserve has been planned for tourism development with the Botanical Garden, which attracts half of the tourists to Xishuangbanna, to be the gateway. However, less than ten percent of tourists going to the Botanical Garden extend their trips to the Limestone Cliff and Forest Curtains because of unsatisfactory road transport. Investment in improving the road was expected to be 13 million yuan according to the Preliminary Plan for Tourism Development of Menglun Area made by the Forestry Investigation and Planning Institute of Yunnan Province, but no agreement has been reached for this upgrading. A small guest house of 20 rooms built by the Reserve caters mostly for travellers rather than tourists. The locals are collecting funds to cooperate with the Reserve for some ecotourism projects, but no solid step has been taken.

Ecotourism is still new to the majority of Chinese tourists who are used to visiting different cities to have their photographs taken. When they visit mountains, they expect such tangible cultural remnants as temples, stone inscriptions from famous people, or steps leading to the top, and they usually regard thick forest and wild animals as dangerous. The average holiday for Chinese is also short. Consequently, ecotourism in the Reserve has to provide enough interpretation and activities to make visitors interested in the forest while marketing itself through multiple channels.

A Master Plan for Tourism Development in the Reserve was completed in June 1993. It outlined proposed tourism projects and their estimated cost as well as forecasted arrivals and future tourism income. Eleven projects were discussed in this Master Plan, but only three of them, which were mentioned above, have been developed to the stage of taking tourists. Other steps will be taken, according to the leaders of the Reserve, to renovate or build attractions in Huang-shan-tang, Menglun and Nangong Mountain. The General Plan for Xishuangbanna Forest Park was finished in June 1995 by Tongji Architecture and Design Institute in Shanghai, in which the Reserve was targeted as its major attraction for ecotourism. Very optimistic tourism forecasts were given but no detailed investment requirements were listed, nor was there an assessment of the likely impact of ecotourism development on the biological environment in the Reserve.

Fire in the broad-leaved forest, which has a high water content, is not a threat to the Reserve. But illegal hunting and deforestation threaten the future of the Reserve. In 1994, 16 wild elephants were killed and another four were injured for their tusks. It was found that members of the Security Department of Jinghong County were involved in the poaching. They used military armaments and police vehicles to kill elephants and transport tusks. Although four major participants were executed after a public trial in November 1994, the temptation to poach is considerable because the tusks of one adult elephant, weighing around 30 kilograms, sell for at least $15,000 on the black market.

The Reserve is facing impending encroachment from both inside and outside. More than 10,000 villagers live within the perimeters of the Reserve, and another 300,000 people live around it. The population of the Prefecture continues to increase because the majority of its population consists of minorities who are not subject to the one-child policy applied to Han Chinese. Some busy roads, including the No. 213 State Road from Jinghong to Beijing, pass through the Reserve, and therefore expose the Reserve to outside disturbances. It has long been the custom for some nationalities to carry some kind of arms in Xishuangbanna when going around. Some young people are seen entering the Reserve with guns, but there is not enough evidence that they are hunting. Jinuo people in Xishuangbanna used to excel at group hunting in which men used knives, bows and guns and women flushed the animals out by making noises. The males still take knives with them today. Education is necessary for both the locals and tourists to help enforce the rule that no hunting is allowed in the Reserve. Satellite imagery shows that natural vegetation cover on land outside protected areas in Xishuangbanna has been severely reduced (Tisdell and Zhu, 1995), while pressure from increasing population and industries requiring raw materials is on the rise. Therefore, there is a danger that nature reserves will be degraded and biodiversity values reduced.

The present five patches of sub-reserves are separated from each other and this makes them sensitive to outside disturbances. There have been suggestions of connecting them with corridors to form a unified area in order to improve management and to provide passages for wild elephants to travel. It is suggested that reserves in Yunnan, especially Xishuangbanna, be upgraded to the State level in order to obtain more central attention for their management. Although it would be ideal to have as big an area protected as possible, it does not appear feasible to enlarge nature reserves to any great extent since both human and financial resources are limited, especially in

China where most nature reserves are located in areas of poverty with few economic opportunities (National Environmental Protection Agency, 1994). As indicated by Menglang Cao, the Director of the Reserve, even if the Reserve could be expanded to cover all of Xishuangbanna, it would still be surrounded by non-reserved areas. The ultimate solution for the Reserve is to convince people, through the process of education and appreciation, of the need for nature conservation. Once people understand both the tropical forest and the importance of conservation, they will help with protection hopefully out of their own will. Efforts are required to make people in Xishuangbanna realise that nature conservation is vital to ensure the well-being not only of elephants and butterflies, but of people too.

The development of rubber plantations at the expense of biodiversity in Xishuangbanna is another threat to the Reserve. Situated on the northern edge of the tropical zone, Xishuangbanna is ecologically suitable for the growing of rubber trees. Concessions have been granted for planting rubber trees in some areas of Shangyong and Mengla sub-reserves, which is in fact a practice of sacrificing wild plants for the limited economic benefits from rubber products. Timber used to be consumed to process rubber latex, adding to deforestation. Although greater use of electricity is prevalent in processing, it is generally in short supply within the Reserve. Although the area of land used for rubber plantation in Xishuangbanna is not on the increase because imported rubber and synthetic rubber can be cheaper than natural rubber produced at home, it is difficult to further reduce rubber plantation due to the constraints of government policy that a sufficient proportion of self reliance on rubber be maintained, and because of the economic costs involved in removing rubber trees, and loss of employment in rubber factories.

The relationships between the Reserve and the local people appear on the whole to be cordial except for complaints about losses from wild elephants destroying crops. In 1995, only 200,000 yuan was allocated as compensation, while the loss was far more than 8 million yuan, far short of the income earned by the Reserve from ecotourism. There have also been cases of wild animals attacking humans, and two people died in 1994. According to China's Forest Law, the local government should pay for the local people's loss from reserves in their administration areas. Nevertheless, the local villages or counties have no compensation fund at all, and it is the Reserve who pays for the victim's medical bills and compensation fee. Most of the electrical fences provided by WWF to prevent elephants getting inside rice fields are either short of working batteries or destroyed. The Reserve is doing research with battery producers in China to substitute local batteries for imported solar batteries for fences in order to save costs.

At present, the regular fund the Reserve obtains from the Chinese government is hardly enough to cover its basic expenses such as salaries. Most of the funding for the Reserve is obtained from the central government. It was 2.54 million yuan in 1994, and is adjusted for the rate of inflation. The Administration Bureau of the Reserve receives these funds through the Forestry Department of Yunnan and then divides these between administration expenses of the Bureau and its five subreserves.

Given the already tight state budget, it does not seem realistic to expect greater government financial assistance to the Reserve, although there have been efforts from the administrative bodies such as the Forestry Ministry and the State Planning Committee who invested 15 million yuan from 1988 to 1993 in the Reserve for improvement in basic structure. In 1986, China invested 15 million yuan to finance the basic construction of the Reserve. The WWF and World Bank, together with other international organisations, have recognised its importance in a worldwide campaign of conserving biodiversity by providing soft loans and technology to help with its conservation programme. The World Bank allocated $1 million to support the Reserve in 1995. The WWF agreed to provide 300,000 Swiss franc and equipment to assist China in a general survey and planning of the Reserve (Zhu and Yang, 1992) and has donated four vehicles.

The Chinese government has realised that the viability of nature reserves is dependent on improving the living standards of the local people through successful programmes as well as fulfilling the conservation objectives. Management of natural reserve systems needs to cooperate with local communities to achieve both prosperity and sustainability (National Environmental Protection Agency, 1994). Agroforestry and social forestry have been suggested as a means of reducing pressure on the Reserve in Xishuangbanna. Because a large portion of benefits from biodiversity spills over globally, total benefits are not captured by local communities (Pearce and Moran, 1994), hence economic development and other benefits to the local people have to be secured in order that plans for biodiversity conservation can obtain support from the local communities.

The Reserve has recognised the importance of greater self-sufficiency for its long-term existence and development, and has been seeking funds from other channels than the upper administration bodies for tourist projects. Ecotourism has been targeted as a way to alleviate the Reserve's financial situation, and to provide an opportunity for both locals and tourists to comprehend the forest and eventually help with conservation actively. However, its income of less than half million yuan a year from ecotourism in the Reserve is hardly enough to cover the interest on loans for the Reserve. The Reserve itself set up two companies dealing with interior design and bamboo products in an effort to obtain supplementary income to sustain the Reserve. Plantations for tea, rubber and fruits have been developed by the Reserve. Butterfly breeding and handicraft selling can also earn some income. Talks with Thailand for joint operation of domesticated elephants have shown good prospects. Nevertheless, the scope for the Reserve to earn income is relatively limited, particularly if conservation goals are given priority. Meanwhile, the temptation of making profits from the Reserve may compromise conservation. For example, it is necessary to control the degree of "multiple-use" when concessions are given for growing ginger, tea or fruits because such operations can compromise nature conservation. The problem is somewhat similar to that discussed in Sec. 7.5 in the previous chapter. In general, financial constraints on managers of the Reserve have resulted in some compromise of conservation objectives for commercial reasons.

An evaluation of the natural resources of the Reserve has not been conducted as yet. However, principles of total economic value of resources, as outlined in Chapter 7, have been adopted by China (National Environmental Protection Agency, 1994), even though at this stage it is not easy to apply such methods as the travel cost or contingent valuation method to value tourism resources at Xishuangbanna or the Reserve. As, however, suggested in Sec. 7.5 of Chapter 7, practice still remains on the whole out of line with principles.

A major problem for the Reserve arises from its tight financial situation which restricts further ecotourism development, and increases its emphasis on income generation to the neglect of conservation. Political factors undoubtedly affect the Reserve in that the operation of the Reserve is under the influence of the Prefecture, the Ministry of Forestry, and to a certain extent, the counties related to the subreserves. This multiple administration model is prone to fan conflicts of interest and results in low efficiency. Plantation and household agricultural development strategies place pressures on the natural reserves. Administration bodies are large and distant from reserves, often leading to poor communication between levels of institutions and within reserves. There is hardly any systematic information or training on resource conservation issues.

The issue of property rights is important for resource management. It is not socially optimal to leave resource management totally to the local communities because the community's pursuit of its own benefits may damage other communities due to the existence of externalities, and the distribution of political power and income within communities is not necessarily ideal. Consequently, a side-by-side approach is suggested by Tisdell (1995), where a co-management between the state and the local communities promotes more efficient resource management, a greater compliance with rules, greater acceptance locally of regulations, and lower administration costs.

Relying on small-scale, locally managed facilities and activities, ecotourism is supposed to be able to avoid the commonplace negative effects of mass tourism on destinations but to promote balanced growth in tune with local, environmental, social and cultural concerns. However, ecotourism needs to be an integral part of the regional planning network and be supported by the local communities in order to survive in the long run. Failures have been observed in ecotourism because local residents are not involved in the decision-making process (Tisdell, 1996). By giving the minority communities and the traditional land users of the region the privileged use of the buffer zone areas, it is expected to integrate them into the conservation system and stop more dangerous encroachment while developing agroforestry to replace the traditional shifting cultivation, and to provide the opportunity "to demonstrate how the development of appropriate forms of ecotourism can generate substantial earnings for nature reserve bureaus and local communities" (Anon, 1993a: 41). Ecotourism resources are threatened by encroaching agriculture, forestry and other economic activities which benefit from the same resource bases.

Ecotourism faces the pressure of both financing itself and conservin its natural resource base (Tisdell, 1996), as increasingly do managers of protected areas. Income collected from entrance fees to national parks is sometimes hardly enough to cover operation expenses and expenditure by tourists in natural areas may be low. For example, average daily expenditure for foreign visitors in Khao Yai National Park in 1987 was US$10, which was in sharp contrast to the US$100 of average daily expenditure for foreigners in Thailand (McNeely and Dobias, 1991). It is conservatively estimated that $27 million of tourists' total expenditures of tourists in Nepal were attributable to the protected area network in 1988, and the costs of managing the parks were almost US$5 million. However, direct fees collected from tourists visiting the protected areas amounted to less than US$1 million (Wells, 1993). To facilitate further tourism growth, Xishuangbanna still needs to find improved solutions for financing the conservation of its ecotourism resources. Improvement in infrastructure, staff training, more efficient administration, and better coordination of related sectors are also important issues that have to be addressed.

Currently it is doubtful if ecotourism in Xishuangbanna Nature Reserve meets the strict definition of ecotourism given in Chapter 6. Its development has compromised conservation objectives to some extent, although the granting of some agricultural/horticultural concessions in the Reserve possibly has had even greater negative impacts. Financial or commercial objectives do not always mix well with the objective of nature conservation, as also observed in the case of butterfly collecting. Unfortunate though this is, the alternative may be even less finance for nature conservation and more strident local calls to use the Reserve for "more productive purposes". In addition to these impacts, very little nature education appears to take place in the Reserve itself although an interpretative museum, partly funded by foreign aid, exists in Jinghong. These features are not uncommon for tourism based on natural occurrences in China and arise in other developing countries as well.

One of the authors (J. Wen) surveyed over 100 tourists at Jinghong airport in 1995 to determine their ranking of the attractions of Xishuangbanna. She found that ethnic culture was most highly ranked, followed closely by climate, with flora and fauna being slightly down the list followed by natural scenery. Thus ethnic culture seemed to be more important as an attraction than nature, a situation which may be common for such tourism throughout Yunnan and inland China. Inland China has a high population of minority peoples. Nevertheless, it is hard to disentangle the relative importance of these tourist attractions because each of the components is a part of the whole package of attractions. Together they are complementary.

8.3   Tourism in Yunnan Province

8.3.1   Major tourist attractions of Yunnan

Covering an area of 394,000 square kilometres, Yunnan has a border totaling 4,000 kilometres with Laos, Vietnam and Burma. The average elevation of Yunnan is 2,000 metres. Climate within Yunnan can differ greatly due to its diversified topography although Kunming, the capital city of Yunnan, is called "the City of Eternal Spring" as a result of its year-round moderate climate.

Geological scenery in Yunnan is outstanding with the Stone Forest being highly regarded. The Stone Forest, 120 kilometres southeast of Kunming, is like a petrified forest and is made up of towering, rugged dark gray stones. This region was part of a vast sea more than 300 million years ago. The limestone and rocks which used to be on the ocean floor were uplifted and have been transformed into a typical karst formation after a long period of erosion by wind and rain. The Stone Forest consists of an area of 300 square kilometres of numerous stone peaks, pillars and stalagmites towering into the sky loftily, resembling a forest. The "Earth Forest" in Yuanmao, green hills and blue lakes, fresh air, and many more other natural attractions add to Yunnan's tourist resources.

Yunnan is an ideal place to encounter varied flora and fauna. 2,700 species of trees from 87 families, 300 aromatic plants, 21,000 species of ornamental plants, and 1,000 medicinal plants grow in Yunnan (Travel & Tourism Bureau of Yunnan, 1995). Over 50 percent of China's total species of vertebrate animals have been found here. There were 30 nature reserves at provincial level and 40 reserves at county level with forest coverage of 25 percent in 1997. Yunnan had 102 natural reserves, 78 forest and wildlife reserves, and 32 forest parks in 1997 (Travel & Tourism Bureau of Yunnan, 1997).

Cultural relics are abundant in Yunnan. As the possible cradle of the *Homo sapiens* in China, Yunnan's recorded history dates back more than 2,000 years. Kunming, Dali and Lijiang have all been distinguished cities in Chinese history. Hinayana, or lesser vehicle Buddhism, is practised by the Bais, Dais and other groups in Yunnan. The diversified minority groups in Yunnan constitute another aspect of its cultural attraction. There are altogether 56 nationalities in China. Among them, the Hans make up around 93 percent of China's population. The other 55 minorities are scattered around China, 25 of these can be found in Yunnan. The total minority population in Yunnan is 10.85 million, comprising one third of Yunnan's total population and one sixth of the total minority population of China (Statistics Bureau of Yunnan Province, 1995).

8.3.2   Tourism development in Yunnan

There was no international tourism in Yunnan before 1978 except some diplomatic receptions. Tourist arrivals in Yunnan have grown by 30 percent annually since 1978 when the "open door" policy was implemented in China (Wen, 1996). Singled out in 1991 by the State Council of China for quick tourism development, Yunnan is endowed with diversified tourism resources and provides four of the 14 special State tourism itineraries in China. In February 1993, the Yunnan Provincial Government recommended favourable measures for enhancing tourism development, including setting up a Tourism Development Fund of 200 million yuan mainly for supplying infrastructure and encouraging government departments and financial institutions to provide favourable conditions for tourism. From 1990 to 1995, 21 billion yuan was invested in infrastructure, including 5 billion yuan on roads, telecommunication and power generating. Incomplete statistics show that from 1991 to 1995 Yunnan invested $346 million in tourism, with $167 million in Kunming,

$22 million in Dali, $8.5 million in Xishuangbanna, and $8.3 million in Lijiang (Travel and Tourism Bureau of Yunnan, 1995). Hence, it becomes necessary to analyse the current tourism supply, demand and major tourism problems in order to better understand the status of tourism in Yunnan.

8.3.3 Tourism supply in Yunnan

The supply of tourism facilities and services has been expanding in Yunnan. There were more than 1,500 tourist enterprises in Yunnan at the end of 1996, including 301 travel agencies and 168 hotels with over 16,000 rooms. Enterprises engaged in tourism employed 70,000 persons directly and their total fixed assets amounted to four billion yuan in 1996 (NTA, 1997).

Transportation has improved significantly in Yunnan, making for relatively easy access to what used to be a remote corner of China. Kunming Airport has become the fifth largest international airport in China, and is serviced by 7 international airlines, 32 domestic and 7 regional airlines. It handled 3.2 million passengers in 1995. There are two major railways, from Kunming to Guiyang and Chengdu respectively, connecting Kunming with other major Chinese cities. There is a highway network within Yunnan with Kunming at its centre. Its transportation system using the Lancang-Mekong River is being improved. A road connecting Kunming and Rangoon in Burma was due to be finished in 1998.

Major tourist areas in Yunnan can be divided into six groups. The middle area attracts half of the tourists to Yunnan and includes Kunming, Chuxong and Yuxi. The northwest area covers Diqing, Nujiang, Dali and Lijiang. Dehong, Lingcang and Baoshan are tourist areas in the west. In the south lies Simao, a key garrison town on the southern frontier, with forests covering more than 60 percent of its land, and Xishuangbanna. The southeast area includes Honghe, Wenshan, and Qujing. Zhaotong and Dongchuan are tourist areas in the northeast.

Tourism in Yunnan developed first in the middle area where access is relatively easier and some famous sites, including the Stone Forest, are located. From the middle 1980s tourism to south Yunnan, especially Xishuangbanna, started to boom with the availability of an airline connection and improved road conditions. Ethnic cultures in the northwest became tourist attractions so Dali and Lijiang became the third popular tourist area from the late 1980s onwards. The next step for tourism development in Yunnan is to make the southeast Yunnan another attraction. Figure 8.2 indicates the location of major tourist destinations in Yunnan.

Tourism facilities in Yunnan have the capacity to accommodate 500,000 overseas tourists and 10 million domestic tourists annually. Yunnan expected to receive 5.1 million tourists by the year 2000. This estimate includes 100,000 overseas tourists — a rise of 31.8 percent compared to 1995, and 5 million domestic tourists — an increase of 23.7 percent compared to 1995. Each of

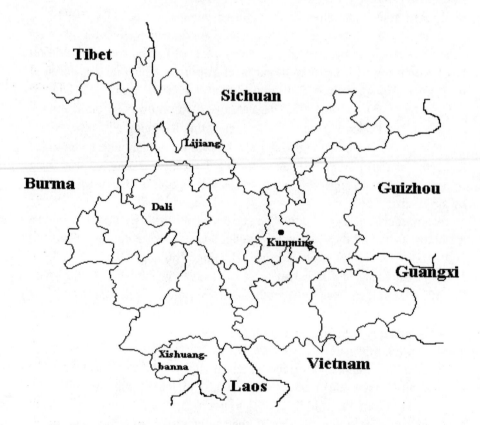

Fig. 8.2 Prefectures of Yunnan with Xishuangbanna, Dali and Lijiang shown.

the four regional tourist cities — Dali, Lijiang, Jinghong and Ruili — has the potential to receive annually 100,000 overseas tourists with receipts of $30 million, and 2 million domestic tourists with an income of 1 billion yuan (Travel and Tourism Bureau of Yunnan, 1995).

8.3.4 Tourism demand in Yunnan

Overseas arrivals in Yunnan reached 742,527 in 1996, while receipts from international tourism totaled $221.1 million — almost twice that in 1994 (NTA, 1997). Major overseas tourist sources for Yunnan have shifted from Japan and the US to Southeast Asian countries. Over half of foreign visitors to Yunnan have come from Asia since the early 1990s. Thailand was a major source country in 1994, generating one-fifth of the 402,332 foreign visitors to Yunnan (Travel & Tourism Bureau of Yunnan, 1995). Note that more than two million cross-border day visitors to Yunnan annually, mainly from Thailand and Burma, are excluded from statistics on international visitors.

International tourism has grown rapidly since the 1960s in the Asian-Pacific region primarily because of increased intra-regional travel among Asia-Pacific residents (Mak and White, 1992), who accounted for 73 percent of total arrivals in the region in 1990 (WTO, 1991). Regional specialisation and market segmentation have been observed in the world tourism market as a result of resource distribution and local economic structures (Lewis and Williams, 1988). Japan provided the first wave of outbound travel in this region. The second wave from Korea, Taiwan and Hong Kong commenced in the late 1980s, while the third wave from the ASEAN region was underway prior to the Asian economic crisis. The fourth will occur around the turn of the century when China has further expanded its rapidly growing market economy (Hall, 1994).

As the gateway to Southwest China, Yunnan has the potential to play a significant role in furthering tourism growth in China. In 1995, Yunnan received 54.6 percent of tourists from Thailand to China, 28.89 percent of those from Singapore, and 21.08 percent of those from Malaysia (NTA, 1996). The top four overseas source countries for Yunnan in 1994 were Thailand (89,374), Singapore (67,161), Malaysia (44,111), and Japan (34,776) (Travel & Tourism Bureau of Yunnan, 1995).

8.3.5   *Domestic tourism in Yunnan*

Domestic tourism is also growing rapidly in Yunnan. The cumulative number of Chinese tourists to Yunnan between 1986 and 1994 was 94.7 million with an expenditure of over 11 billion yuan. There were 14.6 million arrivals in 1994, providing three billion yuan in income (Travel & Tourism Bureau of Yunnan Province, 1995). The airing of the TV series "Cursed Debt" (Nie Zhai) in 1995 greatly promoted tourism from Shanghai to Xishuangbanna. It is forecast that the number of domestic tourists visiting Yunnan will in the foreseeable future keep increasing by ten percent annually and their expenditure will rise at the rate of 15 percent per year. Numbers of tourists were expected to reach 23 million with an expenditure of 12 billion yuan in 2000. In 2010, there are expected to be 55.5 million tourists, generating an income of 43 billion yuan. The cumulative number of domestic tourists from 1996 to 2000 was expected to exceed 100 million with an anticipated expenditure of 40 billion yuan (Travel & Tourism Bureau of Yunnan Province, 1995).

In 1994, over 12,000 Chinese took trips overseas from Yunnan (excluding cross-border trippers), an increase of 14.4 percent over 1993 (Travel & Tourism Bureau of Yunnan Province, 1995). It has been commonly recognised that expanding domestic tourism is an inevitable phenomenon with increasing income and leisure time. In 1994, total domestic trips reached half a billion with expenditure of 102.4 billion yuan (NTA, 1995). Market reforms are affecting tourism, for example, price differentials are being introduced for different seasons in Yunnan.

8.3.6   *Major problems in current tourism development in Yunnan*

Tourism has been targeted by the Yunnan Government as one of the four leading industries together with mineral production, the tobacco industry and forestry. It has been suggested that Yunnan be built into a big special economic area in order to extend its market into other Southeast Asian countries, including the Mekong River area, which covers 5.8 million square kilometres and 0.5 billion population (Travel & Tourism Bureau of Yunnan, 1995). A tourism cooperation conference for China, Burma, Thailand, and Laos was held in 1993 in Thailand to plan for regional tourism development.

Burma established a special zone in the Mengla area mainly for tourism development to promote cross border tourism from Daluo Town in Southwest Xishuangbanna.

The bottleneck for tourism in Yunnan is still transportation. Tourism transportation is often in short supply, and tickets for planes and trains coming to Yunnan are hardly available in the peak season. Road conditions within Yunnan still need improvement. Better management of the tourism market is necessary with bodies from different industries being involved. At the decision-making level of the Provincial Government, a tourism coordination group comprised of representatives from areas dependent on tourism with a higher rank than the Travel and Tourism Bureau of Yunnan Province is needed to better organise tourism operations. The system of Quality Assurance Deposits from travel agencies needs to be completed and enforced.

8.4 Dali and Lijiang: Further Tourism Centres in Yunnan

Dali and Lijiang in northwest Yunnan are places with rich culture and easy access from Kunming, as compared with Xishuangbanna, a green kingdom with tropical forests and minority groups.

8.4.1 Dali — home of the Bais

About 400 kilometres northwest of Kunming, Dali Bai Autonomous Prefecture contains 80 percent of the 1.4 million Bai people living in Yunnan Province. Inhabited from as early as the Neolithic Age, Dali culture was created 4,000 years ago by both Bai and Yi nationalities. It was the political, economic and cultural centre of Yunnan for 500 years, not only as the capital of the Nanzhao and Dali Kingdoms, but also as a gateway for the ancient Southern Silk Way and for communication between China and Southeast Asia as well. Dali Bai Autonomous Prefecture was established in 1956 with Dali City being the capital city of this prefecture.

Cangshan Mountain, 3,500 metres above sea-level, together with Erhai Lake, the second largest lake in Yunnan with an area of about 300 square kilometres, forms the basic framework for tourism in Dali. There are unique tourist places in Dali, including the Ancient City of Dali, Butterfly's Fountain, Nanzhao Stele, and Three Pagodas on the ruins of Chongshengsi Monastery which used to be the largest monastery in Dali area. The Qinghuadong State Forest Park provides ecotourism activities including forest walking and bird watching. Above all, the indispensable attraction of Dali is its major ethnic group, the Bais.

The Bais are born with talent for music and with love for trees as well. Their major festivals include "Rao Shan Lin" (going around the forest), an occasion held in Spring when people sing and dance around the forest; "Cha Liu Jie" (Willow planting Festival) in Spring is a time for the Bais to dance along the river with willow twigs in their hands and plant them to the music; and the Third Month Festival, which is the biggest annual occasion for Bais, and takes place from the 15th to 21st of the third month of the lunar calendar. The Bais have learned to protect forest resources by holding the "Mountain-sealing Festival" in early winter, at which respect is paid to the mountains and a monument with instructions for banning tree-cutting in winter is set up. Only after the ceremony of "Opening the mountain" held in next spring can the Bais enter the forest again.

Dali was officially opened for foreigners in 1984, and received over 3,000 international tourists that year. In 1988, 60,000 visitors were registered, of which 13,000 were foreigners, 22,000 were compatriots, and 45,000 Chinese. International tourists increased to 34,600 in 1994, with 28,000 foreigners, 61 overseas Chinese, and 6,400 compatriots (Travel & Tourism Administration of Yunnan, 1997). Contrary to most coastal areas in China where compatriots account for an overwhelming portion of international tourist arrivals, Dali receives many more foreigners, mainly from the US, Germany and Japan, who stay considerably longer than Chinese tourists and are interested in the Bai culture (Gormsen, 1990).

There are around 20 hotels suitable for international tourists in Dali. Transportation will be improved significantly after the construction of the Guangzhou-Dali Railway and the Dali Airport. There are regular buses from

Kunming, and a day trip from Kunming can be conveniently arranged. There is a high degree of self-sufficiency of tourist supply in Dali due to transportation constraints, hence tourism income remains mainly within the region.

8.4.2 Naxi culture and matriarchal society in Lijiang

Located in northwest Yunnan with an area of 20,600 square kilometres, Lijiang is the confluence of cultural exchange for the Han, Tibetan, Bai and Naxi nationalities, and hence prides itself on the amazing cultural heritage, of which the Naxi culture is most distinctive.

Naxi culture has been created by the Naxi nationality over years of assimilating different cultures. With a population of 300,600, most Naxi live in the Lijiang Naxi Autonomous County. They created the Dongba culture, which include thousands of volumes of the "Dongba Scriptures" written in a pictographic language invented 1,000 years ago. Dongba Scripture consists of polyphonic and poly-functional characters resembling people or animals. Quite a few foreigners have stayed in Lijiang for many years to study the local culture.

Lijiang is noted for its perennially snow-capped Jade Dragon Snow Mountain with its 13 peaks flying like a dragon of glittering jade. The Jinshajiang (Gold Sand) River drops 300 metres at the Hutiaoxia (Tiger Leaping Gorge), one of the world's biggest gorges, supplying a hydro-electric plant. The 500-year-old camellia tree in the Yufengsi Lamasery which produces over 20,000 flowers a year, the Black Dragon Pool, and the grandiose Phoenix Tower are all outstanding attractions. The ancient town of Dayanzhen, applying to be listed in UNESCO's World Cultural Heritage, is remarkable for its layout which directs a stream with willows alongside the gate of every household. The small canals continue throughout the town, winding past houses with more than 300 bridges built from as early as the 14th century.

The remnants of the matrilineal family structure at the Lugu Lake area also amazes visitors. The Lugu Lake lies to the north of Lijiang City close to the border with Sichuan Province, covering over 777 hectares with abundant fishery resources. It is in this area, specifically in Yongning Town, where the last existing matriarchal society in China can be found among the Mosuo people, a section of Pumi nationality with a population of around 10,000. More than 60 percent of Mosuo people perform the "Walking Marriage" or Azhu in the local language, in which women are at the top of the family hierarchy and inherit property. Adult men live and work with their mothers or grandmothers at day time, but spend the night with their Azhu, which means lover or partner in their language, and return at daybreak. The offspring belong to the female who is responsible for their upbringing. In the local language, there is no special name or title for a male, and symbols for power, such as the sun, mountain, and wind, are in the local language female. The matriarchal family system represents a stage in the development of human society, and it survives in this area as a result of isolation and dominance of women in both agriculture and domestic matters.

Lijiang was approved as an open tourist city by the State Council in 1985, and over 400 foreigners visited it in that year (Kou, 1996). In October 1994, Yunnan provincial government designated Lijiang as a key city for tourist expansion with a preferential policy for transportation improvement of this area. Currently, over 300,000 overseas travellers from over 60 countries and regions come here annually, plus several million Chinese domestic tourists (Kou, 1996). A flight of 30 minutes between Kunming and Lijiang, which started operation in 1995, is a great improvement on the previous tedious 24-hour-trip by bus along rough mountain roads. In November 1996, air routes from Lijiang to Xishuangbanna and Dali started operation, thereby connecting the four major tourist centres in Yunnan. According to forecasts by the Lijiang Tourism Bureau, Lijiang will receive 15 million travellers per year in 2010, including 450,000 international arrivals. Annual tourist expenditure will reach four billion yuan, including US$200 million in foreign exchange, and account for about half of the total revenue of Lijiang.

8.5   Analysis of Tourism in Yunnan

Yunnan has become a major tourist destination in China, specialising in tourism based on nature and ethnic cultures. Tourism in Yunnan is more scattered spatially, shows less seasonality and attracts more diversified clients than in most other provinces of China.

8.5.1 Spatial distribution of tourism in Yunnan

Yunnan is endowed with diversified tourism resources, and their spatial distribution is relatively more scattered compared with other major tourist destinations in China. Table 8.2 compares both economic and tourist indicators for four major tourist areas in Yunnan in 1994. Kunming is the economic and political centre and the first popular tourist destination in Yunnan. Nonetheless, Dali, Lijiang and Xishuangbanna are outstanding attractions for both overseas and Chinese tourists and tourists have a longer average length of stay than in Kunming. There is great potential for further tourism growth in these three areas with improvement in transportation given the increasing demand for ecotourism.

Yunnan is relatively unique in possessing four major tourism centres with different attractions at Kunming, Dali, Lijiang, and Xishuangbanna. The capital city, Kunming, receives on average less than 30 percent of the total international arrivals to Yunnan (NTA, various years). This multi-centred distribution of tourism makes it easier to extend the average stay of tourists and to decentralise tourism operations. But the fact that tourists with restricted time find it impossible to visit all the attractions in Yunnan emphasises the need for improved travel arrangements and more efficient transportation. Given the scarcity of available funds for investment in tourism, tourism projects need to be carefully planned to concentrate on sites with unique characteristics.

Close contacts between tourists and local people raise problems for conserving both the natural environment and ethnic communities, which have been exposed to large volumes of tourist flow without enough preparation. Personnel training in the tourism sector is still insufficient in Yunnan. Macro-control over both hard and software in tourism is also essential to ensure the satisfaction of tourists. Scattered natural and cultural attractions make tourism in Yunnan relatively more decentralised throughout the province. Tourism in Yunnan contributes greater economic benefits to areas outside the central

Table 8.2 Economic and tourist indicators for Yunnan and its major tourist areas, 1994.

	GRP (yuan m)	GRP from tertiary industries (yuan m)	Area (sq. km)	Population (m)	No. of hotels	No. of travel agencies	No. of overseas tourists	Average length of stay (day)	Receipts of int'l tourism (UD$ m)	No. of domestic tourists (m)	Domestic tourism income (yuan m)
Total	97397	30680	394,139	39.39	171	258	522,059	1.59	124.397	14.58	3077.98
Kunming	26813.32	10554.77	15,942	3.71	42	119	378,672	1.61	74.0961	4.83	1019.66
Dali	5342.35	1675.03	29,459	3.13	19	14	34,579	1.91	8.034	2.49	525.66
Lijiang	1479.97	493.29	21,219	1.05	5	3	16,885	2.29	4.705	0.2	42.22
Xishuanbanna	2283.66	775.77	19,700	0.81	14	47	15,312	2.30	4.289	1.25	263.89

Source: Statistics Bureau of Yunnan, 1995; Travel & Tourism Bureau of Yunnan, 1995.

city than in other provinces, where usually only the capital cities serve as a major attraction, such as Shaanxi, where Xian, its capital city, receives over 70 percent of international arrivals to the Province (NTA, various years).

There is a discrepancy between Tables 8.1 and 8.2 in the income from domestic tourism in Xishuangbanna. This is because the method of calculating total income by multiplying the total number of domestic tourists by the average expenditure per tourist as calculated from a nationwide survey was applied in Table 8.1, but the direct income of the tourism industry from catering for domestic tourists was used in Table 8.2. Since a large proportion of tourist expenditure went to other sectors of the economy, mainly retailing, instead of going directly to the tourism industry, domestic tourist income was much higher in Table 8.1 than that indicated in Table 8.2.

8.5.2 Seasonality of tourism in Yunnan

Tourist movements are affected by seasonality of demand (holiday) and of supply (destinations). Seasonal fluctuations, including natural and institutional, are determined to a large extent by two major factors. The first is related to the tourist-generating countries holiday periods. This preference is heavily concentrated on traditional vacation times such as summer, Christmas, Easter and company holidays. The second fluctuation depends on the situation of the destination and is more related to climatic conditions. The interaction of these two groups of fluctuations implies an imbalance between the demand for and the supply of tourism.

Seasonality of tourism means there are effectively at least two labour markets in the tourism sector. One is for permanent staff throughout the year, and another for occasional workers in peak season. If the system does not allow laying off extra staff in low seasons, redundant labour will occur. Seasonality may indicate social costs in terms of both over and under-utilisation of capacity in employment. Fluctuations in tourism as a result of seasonality is common in the world. For example, during the December to March season when Europe is in winter, hotel occupancy rates at the coast in Kenya may double the normal level. But in the low season from April to

June, tourism is curtailed by heavy rains, difficult roads and long grass which obscures the view of game animals (Dieke, 1991).

A survey of the operation of tourism businesses was conducted in 1995 by J. Wen in Yunnan. Data on domestic travellers were hardly available and only numbers of international arrivals were obtained. A comparison of the number of overseas travellers received monthly in 1994 by major travel agencies is listed in Table 8.3 with ITS standing for International Travel Service.

None of these travel agencies regarded seasonality as a serious problem for their operation because variations in number of domestic travellers compensate for the monthly change of overseas tourists. Travel agencies in Xishuangbanna complained about the unreliable quota of air tickets allocated by the airlines which is frequently subject to reduction in number or even cancellation. They all agreed that transportation is the major restriction for tourism in Yunnan, and unsatisfactory service often results from the shortage of experienced staff with reasonable education.

Table 8.3 Comparison of the number of overseas tourists received by some travel agencies in Yunnan by months, 1994.

Month	Dali Overseas Travel Service	Xishuangbanna ITS	Yunnan ITS	Kunming ITS
Total	3,279	4,845	3,438	29,371
1	79	282	NA	748
2	189	663	318	2,277
3	1,908	508	560	1,946
4	107	800	255	3,213
5	NA	395	371	2,660
6	235	186	845	1,870
7	31	NA	121	1,474
8	144	592	113	2,740
9	NA	251	137	3,173
10	197	633	423	3,477
11	194	338	158	2,499
12	195	197	127	3,294

Seasonality in Yunnan does not seem to affect tourism as much as it does in northern China mainly due to its mild climate throughout the whole year. Slight differences in the number of monthly tourist arrivals is, nonetheless, still observed. Higher monthly arrivals occur in December, January and February in Yunnan when it is dry season, with holidays including the Chinese New Year and winter vacation for schools. Some special occasions also influence the number of tourists in a particular month to a great extent. In Dali City, March is the month with the highest tourist arrivals when the March Street Fair is held, amounting to 4,902 out of its annual arrivals of 25,662 tourists in 1994 (Travel & Tourism Bureau of Yunnan Province, 1995). The highest daily arrivals in Xishuangbanna occur in April during the Water Splashing Festival.

8.5.3   Difference in destination choice

Destination choice of tourists from overseas differs from that of Chinese tourists in Yunnan. Over 15 million Chinese travellers visit Yunnan annually, generating at least four billion yuan. Yuxi and Honghe in the Southeast of Kunming received 2.97 million domestic tourists in 1994, making 20 percent of the total domestic arrivals in Yunnan, but they attracted only 6.5 percent of the overseas arrivals to Yunnan Province (Travel & Tourism Bureau of Yunnan, 1995). Lijiang and Xishuangbanna received almost the same number of overseas tourists in 1994, but the number for domestic tourists to Xishuangbanna was six-fold that for Lijiang. The overall pattern for tourists in Xishuangbanna is that Chinese hardly miss the cross-border trips, whereas Japanese are interested in Lesser Vehicle Buddhism but Europeans and Americans seek more adventure in the forest. More careful analysis on tourism market segmentation in Yunnan is suggested for better-orientated marketing and for further development of tourist sites.

Ethnic and cultural aspects in Dali and Lijiang are promising attractions for tourists with higher education and budgets. However, commodification of ethnicity has been observed in Yunnan (Swain, 1990) in the selling of the material culture of minorities and in the mass marketing of pseudo-artifacts to tourists. Boorstin (1973) pointed out that the rise of modern tourism has led to the trivialisation of culture and the creation of a superficial and contrived tourist image, in his words "pseudo-events". MacCannell (1976) similarly argued that the modern tourist is usually trapped in a constructed "tourist space" provided by the tourism suppliers in which authenticity is staged. How to prevent ethnic culture becoming commercialised in the process of tourism growth remains to be tackled in Yunnan. The fragility of the tropical environment and minority cultures requires careful planning of tourism in Yunnan if its tourism is to be sustainable in the long term.

The prospects for domestic tourism in Yunnan are promising due to its image as an affordable holiday destination with diverse features. In 1992, 11.12 million Chinese visited Yunnan, accruing 1.1 billion yuan as income from domestic tourism. Cross-border tourism in Yunnan is attractive to Chinese. In 1992, as the first travel agency in Yunnan permitted to organise tours to the Laos, Mengla Travel Agency in Xishuangbanna arranged more than 32,000 Chinese to visit Laos from 1991 to 1993 (Travel & Tourism Bureau of Yunnan, 1995). Visiting Burma from the Southwest of Xishuangbanna is also an essential part of a travel itinerary for Chinese. The simple procedure to go abroad as cross-border travellers in Yunnan undoubtedly provides a good chance for Chinese who usually face a tedious process when applying to go overseas.

8.5.4 Tourism in the regional development of Yunnan

The contribution of tourism to the regional economy and the distribution of returns to factors of production in tourism depend not only on the marginal productivity or efficiency of factors, but on the type of tourism principally practised in a specific area. The tourism multiplier, based on largely Keynesian principles that a proportion of income is re-circulated into consumption spending, engendering further income and employment (Keynes, 1936), has been one of the most extensively discussed areas in relation to the economic effect of tourism on a local economy (Archer, 1977; Holloway, 1989).

Owing to leakages on imports, taxation, savings and so on, the tourism income multiplier (TIM) is expressed by Bull (1995) as:

$$\text{TIM} = 1 \text{ / leakages, or, TIM} = (1\text{-MPM}) \text{ / leakages,}$$

where MPM stands for marginal propensity to import goods.

Other tourism multipliers, such as those for employment, output, transaction, and so on, can be considered along the same lines. More detailed estimation of multipliers can be found in Chapter 10 of this thesis. There is evidence that tourism is a capital-intensive industry on the whole when its social infrastructure requirements are taken into consideration (McKee and Tisdell, 1990), and its employment generating effect is much less than expected in some developing countries (Mishra, 1982; Dwyer, 1986) because tourism requires skills in short supply, such as foreign languages and management, in those countries.

The scarcity of data at the regional level in China and the difficulty in deciding what is or what is not part of the tourism sector make it difficult to determine tourism multipliers. It has been estimated that, in China, tourism income of one dollar brings a $3.12 increment in the national economy and $10.7 extra income in tertiary industry (Luo, 1994: 27). Unpriced environmental costs are not taken into account in multipliers. An income multiplier in excess of unity has been observed in countries such as the United Kingdom, Canada and Australia, and lower in less developed countries (LDCs) and small island states ranging from 0.7 to 1.2 (Bull, 1995).

Table 8.4 shows that tertiary industry has accounted for over one third of the total GDP in Yunnan since 1992. It indicates that tourism in Yunnan contributes a significant portion to the regional economy, especially if domestic tourism is also taken into account. This issue is given in-depth consideration in Chapter 10.

Receipts from international tourists do not seem very impressive compared with export income as a whole in Table 8.4, but their importance will be magnified if the multiplier effect is taken into consideration, especially employment effects, and their increasing proportion in export income. It is reasonable to conclude that tourism has become a major contributor to the regional economy as a whole, and more so in popular tourist destinations.

Studies have shown that the tourism income multiplier is higher in diversified economies with the capability to supply most factors for tourism itself (Burkart and Medlik, 1981). Import dependency of the tourism

Table 8.4 Comparison of tourism with other sectors in Yunnan.

	Tertiary industry (yuan b)	Tertiary industry as proportion of GRP (%)	Export (US$m)	International tourism receipts (US$m)	Inbound tourist arrivals (000)
1980		17.1	NA	1.16	20.5
1985	3.35	20.3	129	9.71	72.2
1990	12.57	27.9	434.5	16.4	148.2
1991	16.8	28.1	NA	63.13	212.1
1992	21.3	30.3	NA	67.27	313.5
1993	26	33.4	522.9	102.73	405.2
1994	30.7	31.5	910.2	124.4	522.1

Source: Statistics Bureau of Yunnan (1995), Travel and Tourism Bureau of Yunnan (1995), and NTA (various years).

sector in small areas is likely to be greater than that in large countries (Tisdell and McKee, 1988). As a consequence, Kunming benefits more than proportionally from tourism than other areas of Yunnan due to its higher capability of supplying commodities and services for tourists not only to Kunming but to other areas within Yunnan as well (Wen, 1996). By contrast, areas importing tourist supplies suffer higher leakages and lower economic benefits from tourism. It is estimated by the Tourism Bureau of Xishuangbanna that 15 to 40 percent of goods supplied for tourism are purchased from outside of the Prefecture. Income from long-distance transportation to and from Xishuangbanna goes mainly to the Yunnan Airlines and coach services whose headquarters are located outside of Xishuangbanna.

The same multiplier is usually applied to different rounds of tourist consumption, but in fact it may be higher for the subsequent rounds of consumption once main imports have been computed at the first round. More detailed research is necessary into tourist multipliers in Xishuangbanna. It appears that in tourist areas like Jinghong and Ganlanba, more that one-twentieth of the residents are involved in tourism.

Average length of stay may influence the number of places a tourist visits within a country or region, and Pearce (1990) suggests that an increase in length of stay results in more places being visited, not more time being spent in the same number of places. He argues that visitors who stay shorter opt for the most accessible sites and what are perceived to be the main tourist attractions. Those on longer visits take in other secondary and small centres and attractions. It may be practical to extend the stay of tourists in Xishuangbanna to 6–8 days through more diversified tourist activities so that tourists stay at places other than Jinghong, such as within the Reserve. As a result greater economic gain for the local community may be obtained.

Average expenditure is influenced by the level of tourist consumption, and shopping expenditure provides potential for further increases. Nationwide average expenditure on shopping was 16.9 percent of total tourist expenditure in 1994 (NTA, 1995). It was estimated that the average percentage of total tourism expenditure on shopping was 18.5 by overseas tourists in Xishuangbanna (Tisdell and Zhu, 1995). Visitors often complain about the limited design, availability and unreliable pricing for tourist products in Yunnan. While an increase in the number of tourists may bring more income, it is desirable to improve both average length of stay and average spending of tourists by providing attractive tourist activities as well as commodities at competitive prices. Quality commodities with unique ethnic and tropical characteristics at reasonable prices are promising channels for increasing income from tourism in Yunnan.

8.6 Concluding Comments

Tourism has been growing extensively and rapidly in Yunnan for more than 15 years, with international tourist arrivals ranking eighth among all the 30 localities in China and its receipts from international tourism ranking tenth among these localities in 1996 (NTA, 1997). The future for tourism in Yunnan lies in intensive development rather than expanding its present scale. Efforts are required to complete the existing tourist sites and to improve the quality of tourist services. The average stay of international tourists in Yunnan was only 1.59 days in 1994 (NTA, 1995). Extending the stay of both international and domestic tourists and increasing the average expenditure of tourists are more promising means for raising tourism income than simply trying to raise the tourist volume. Factors such as transportation, staff training, and coordination among industries and regions within Yunnan Province are all essential for further tourism development in Yunnan. Ecotourism in Xishuangbanna has just begun to develop and scope for further growth exists. Ethnic and cultural aspects in Dali and Lijiang are promising attractions for tourists with better education and higher budgets. The fragility of the tropical environment and minority cultures requires careful development of tourism in Yunnan to achieve sustainability in the long term.

Promotion of ecotourism and domestic tourism may facilitate greater regional convergence of tourism in China and ultimately contribute to reducing inequality between the coastal and inland areas. The efforts of the administrators of Xishuangbanna Nature Reserve to promote ecotourism have shown positive results in attracting tourists but further steps remain to be taken to better market and manage ecotourism. Better management of tourism markets, accompanied by efficient coordination of the sectors involved and improvement in infrastructure, are essential for further expansion of tourism in Yunnan. Links with Southeast Asia promise attractive prospects for Yunnan's share in this tourism market but raise the need for more competitive tourist products and quality control of service.

Dispersion of tourism in Yunnan, as reflected by four major tourist centres within the Province, sets an example for encouraging economic development in areas other than the capital cities through adequate supply of transportation and other tourist facilities in regional centres.

Tourism can be expected to be a major force in promoting economic development in rural areas where most other economic resources are inadequate but where tourism attractions, generally in the form of well-preserved natural environments or rich cultural heritage, as is the case of Yunnan, are outstanding. Since Yunnan has targeted tourism as one of its key industries, and there is an obvious confusion amongst policy-makers regarding the related theories of key industry development and growth poles, growth pole theory will be discussed in Chapter 9 and subsequently input-output analysis will be applied in Chapter 10 in order to identify the scope of tourism to be a growth pole in such a peripheral locality as Yunnan. Chapter 10 also quantifies a number of the economic impacts of tourism development in Yunnan which are mentioned above.

Chapter 9

Unbalanced Growth, Growth Pole Theory and Tourism Development

9.1 Introduction

Although tourism, especially ecotourism, has been targeted as the leading industry in many peripheral areas, including Yunnan in China, in order to promote local economic growth, theories of unbalanced growth and the potential of tourism development as a growth pole need to be better understood. The growth pole concept has proven attractive as a policy tool for developing economically lagging areas since the 1960s, despite its conceptual and practical limitations.

While some areas of China, such as Yunnan, have adopted growth pole approaches as a basic economic strategy in the hope of promoting their regional economy and reducing spatial economic disparity, there have been misunderstandings about growth pole theories and inappropriate applications of this strategy in China. It is necessary to understand what the growth pole paradigm is really about, and how it should be applied in different economies.

After presenting major theories on unbalanced regional development, this chapter provides a detailed discussion of growth pole theory. Its application in both developed countries and LDCs is then compared, and so are failures in implementing growth pole strategy. The potential for tertiary industry, especially tourism, to become a growth pole for some regions is then considered. With continuing growth of tertiary industry in both developed and developing economies, it seems reasonable to expect service industries to play a leading role in the growth and continued viability of these economies.

9.2 Theories of Unbalanced Regional Development: An Overview

The search for new models of economic development and for new local strategies to bring them to fruition has never stopped. The arguments for and against balanced or unbalanced growth in developing countries have been going on for more than three decades. Some economists and policy-makers have argued that unbalanced growth, which gives priority to industries or sectors with higher backward and forward linkages, can be a major force for growth of output and income in developing countries (Christaller, 1966; Perroux, 1988). Unbalanced growth theory claims that if factors of production are allocated to key sectors on a priority basis, output and employment will grow more rapidly than if these sectors are not given special favours. Hirschman (1958) maintains that such key sectors as heavy industry have high linkages with the rest of the economy, therefore these sectors need to be given high priority to accelerate industrialisation and economic growth. According to his growth sequences and investment inducements, industries with both high backward and forward linkages are intermediate products such as iron and steel, which may stimulate high economic growth, while primary products, mainly agriculture, have low backward and forward linkages, and hence contribute little to growth. Final manufactures have high backward but low forward linkages, whereas intermediate primary products have high forward but low backward linkages (Hirschman, 1958: 110).

This concept of allocating scarce investment funds to industries that will generate high economic growth is appealing to policy makers, especially in LDCs where a shortage of investment funds prevails. Unbalanced growth seems to have been a feature of the Chinese economy. China followed the Soviet model during the 1950s and early 1960s of heavy industrialisation. In the post-Mao era, a shift from heavy industry to light industry and from industry to agriculture, has been noticeable (Bhalla and Ma, 1990).

However, there are some misconceptions and misunderstandings about the application of unbalanced development strategies. Firstly, the emphasis on heavy industry is no longer necessarily applicable in every country, considering the structural shift from heavy industry to technology-intensive industries and tertiary industries. It has become necessary for countries to identify again their key industries or new growth poles if unbalanced growth is to be successfully achieved. Secondly, neglect of linkage effects has resulted in heavy investment in certain sectors of the economy and certain areas without effective flow on to the entire economy or the periphery. A better understanding of the basic theories of unbalanced growth is necessary.

Models of regional economic growth are many and diverse, but this chapter highlights three celebrated theories of unbalanced growth: central place theory, core-periphery theory, and growth pole analysis. While the first two theories emphasise the function of spatial economic centres, the growth pole paradigm regards the leading industry as the dynamic force in regional growth. Growth pole theory will be discussed in detail in this chapter.

9.3 Comparison of Central Place and Core-Periphery Analysis

Central place and core-periphery theories emphasise the economic significance of the centre or core in regional development, but differ on the interactions between regional centres and the periphery.

9.3.1 Central place theory

The central place theory represents the birth of location theories. It proposes an ordering of communities within a region in terms of economic activities ranging from villages to primary cities. Only the lowest-order economic activity exists in the villages, and the cities supply higher-order services, including financial and health services to the region (Christaller, 1966). The expansion of such higher-order services stimulates the growth of the centre and is an impetus to the development of the entire region. In addition to Christaller's seminal deductive work, further elaboration of this theory occurs in Berry and Pred (1975).

Although largely descriptive and relatively static due to its failure to explain the evolutionary events in the emergence of a regional structure, its value as a medium for explaining the location and spatial components of interdependence for a region should not be derided. Focusing upon the location and the geographical size distribution of clusters of economic activities, this approach rests on the premise that for a smooth geographical plane, competition will ensure a hierarchy of central places in high-order positions (first and second) of primacy, surrounded by a nesting of many smaller lower-order (third, fourth and fifth) ranked settlements. The contribution of the periphery to regional economy, however, is not emphasised. Hence, a chronicle hierarchy of orders within a region may leave the non-central areas disadvantaged, resulting in expanding disparity between the centre and its periphery.

9.3.2 Core-periphery model

The core-periphery model is in fact an extension of the central place theory because the core works as a central place in supplying higher-order goods and services to the periphery. Friedmann (1966) was among the earliest writers to use the core-periphery model to explain uneven regional development. A leading sector, usually manufacturing, combined with initial advantages and agglomeration of activities, forms the core region in the course of economic development. The formation of the core is accelerated by the movement of labour and capital from the peripheral areas, the so called "backwash", at the expense of the periphery. The core supplies the periphery with higher-order services, while the periphery furnishes the core with commodities based on natural resources. The shift of factors of production into the leading sector makes self-sustaining growth possible and accounts for the rise of income in the core region, along with the economic divergence of regions (Clark, 1957).

This core-periphery model seems appropriate to explain the polarisation process, or the accumulation of wealth in certain areas accompanied by expanding regional economic disparity (Fan and Casetti, 1994), in both advanced and developing economies. Polarisation shifts over time with the changing relative economic capacity of regions, such as product cycles, cost of production, technology, and other amenities, and there may be decline

within the former core and new growth in the former peripheral areas
(Storper and Walker, 1989). Sectoral shift, such as the growing economic
power of the service industry, as indicated by declines in manufacturing
employment and increase in service industries in many nations, has been
one of the forces behind the changes in polarisation (Fan and Casetti, 1994).
The periphery nevertheless has a comparative advantage in the production
of commodities based on natural resources, and hence there is trade in such
goods flowing from the periphery to the core or other markets, either national
or international. Here the periphery is not a passive recipient for whatever
is provided by the core, but exchanges with the core elements in which it
has comparative advantage.

Both the central place theory and core-periphery theory are static in
primitive form in the sense of aiming only at explaining the existence of
certain spatial economic patterns, but not how this pattern has come into
being or how these patterns might change in the future. They take stock of
interdependencies among economic activities, and may well serve as a point
of departure for analysing the impact of development in a given centre on
the other centres. In addition, they are confined by geographical boundaries
of a certain area, while regional integration has become so prevalent that
space is less important than it was 20 or 30 years ago. It may be more an
industry rather than a geographical area that spurs the regional economy. A
theory that is dynamic and sometimes more appropriate in analysing the
origin of unbalanced growth is the growth pole paradigm.

9.4 Growth Pole Paradigm

It was not until his 1955 article entitled "Note sur la motion de *pole de
croissance*" that Françis Perroux first presented a thorough discussion of the
concept of growth pole, or *pole de croissance* (Hirchman, 1958). As an
expansion of classical location theory dealing with the optimum location of
the firm and analysis of industrial complexes, growth pole theory is derived
from observations of the actual process of economic development. There
have been debates among economists in relation to the growth pole theory

(McKee, 1988). Hence the growth pole theory referred to in this book is a hybrid extracted from the pertinent literature.

9.4.1   The concept of a growth pole

Commonly recognised as the originator of the growth pole theory, Perroux wrote:

> "A kind of pause in the system is linked to a deceleration of the effects of the system energy for change ... . This moment of rest has nothing to do with the uniqueness, stability, and optimality of the standard equilibrium. Thus reinterpreted, the image of the economic system is one of economic space and territorial space created by agents according to their degree of efficiency and their powers. The most powerful are economic space-makers. Unequal agents making decisions about unequal units and unequal structured subsets (industries) exercise asymmetric effects upon one another, the most favourable of which (from the point of view of development) being *propulsive effects*" (Perroux, 1988).

Here growth poles are the concentration and constellation in space of propulsive enterprises and industries. In other words, "growth pole is a set that has the capacity to induce the growth of another set ("growth" being defined as a lasting increase in the dimensional indicator)" (Perroux, 1988). The mainspring of economic development is technological progress or innovation, which tends to concentrate in particular enterprises and industries. When a propulsive industry raises its output, it induces expansions in the outputs of other industries, and the growth induced by a key firm or industry is not confined to a highly localised geographical area, but can be traced throughout a regional or even a national economy. This key industry, referred to as a lead industry, propulsive industry, leading industry, or master industry, creates poles of growth and centres of innovative change, which are called core regions, and a periphery may be defined by its relation of dependency to the core. The leading industries are propellant because they are the origin of productive force within an economic cluster, and they are the powerful instruments of change, "impelling" less strategic subsidiary industries to associate with the economic cluster. There are interdependence linkages (input-output) between industries and an articulation of their significance as they relate to the process of induced economic growth (Hirschman, 1958).

The notion of space has always been one of the corner stones of pole theory (McKee, 1988, Chapter 3). Perroux was explicit about the concept of space in describing the space as economic space as opposed to geonomic or banal space. "These economic spaces conveniently reduce to three: (1) economic space as defined by a plan; (2) economic space as a field of forces; and (3) economic space as a homogenous aggregate" (Perroux, 1950). His space would be an "abstract territorial imperative (perhaps a market) enjoyed by individual firms" (McKee, 1988: 17). Originally, Perroux was not particularly concerned with the spatial aspects of development in its purely geographical areas, but was primarily interested in economic development as manifested in organisational and industrial spaces, i.e., the emergence, growth and stagnation of firms and industries, and the propulsive forces behind growth poles. Growth pole theory has nevertheless come to be applied mainly in a geographical context, primarily because all economic activities necessarily take place in geographical space, hence such theories as location, spatial organisation, external economies of agglomeration and so on are linked with the study of growth poles.

Growth and development are far from synonymous since growth means a sustained increase in the dimension index for an economic entity, while development is the sum of the changes in social patterns and mentalities through which the production device is coupled with the population (Perroux, 1988). A growth pole is the dynamic unit that raises the economic "size" index of an area or of a country, but the "pole of development" is "a set that has the capacity to engender economic and social structures whose effect is to increase the complexity of the whole and to expand its multidimensional return" (Perroux, 1988), acquiring the capacity to utilise the production device to achieve what is considered to be a satisfactory growth rate, and the production device supplies a product that serves the population instead of being "alien" to it. In this chapter, the term "growth pole" but not the "pole of development" is used in order to emphasise the initial economic growth induced by the poles.

9.4.2   *How growth pole influences other areas*

Although Perroux does not provide a satisfactory explanation of how leading propulsive industries come into being or the effects of existing complexes upon emerging ones, he proposes that expansions in the output of other industries may be induced if a propulsive industry raises its output. Such a propulsive industry is called a key industry when it induces output growth much greater than the initial growth in the propulsive industry. Perroux suggested that "(T)he national economy presents itself to us as a combination of relatively active systems (motor industries, poles of geographically agglomerated industries and activities) and of relatively passive industries (affected industries, regions dependent on geographically agglomerated poles). The first induces the phenomena of growth on the second" (Perroux, 1970).

An industry is said to exert a strong backward linkage effect if it has a high ratio of intermediary inputs delivered from the other industries to its total production. It tends to dominate its input-delivery industries because it induces expansionary or stagnatory forces into them, in other words, it determines the amount of expansion induced in dependent industries relative to its own expansion. Forward linkages have a high ratio of intermediary deliveries to final demand and tend to depend on other industries for determination of its rate of expansion, but will be able to induce expansion by transmitting innovations forward. Chapter 10 will discuss the issue of backward and forward effects in more detail by applying input-output analysis.

The growth pole model does not emphasise the central place but specific industries, in which dynamic economic growth has the capacity to stimulate the growth of the entire area, including the surrounding peripheral areas through spread effects. There have been misunderstandings of Perroux's ideas, such as shifting the emphasis of his notion of growth poles from sectors to areas, from growth poles to growth centres. The growth pole approach implies that spatial concentration generates faster or more sustained regional development than a more dispersed regional growth pattern. Growth poles may benefit the residents of their surrounding hinterlands either by the opportunities they offer to people attracted to the centres, mostly migrants or commuters, or through beneficial effects spreading from the centres to the periphery. In Perroux's theory, the principal role of the growth pole is as a source and diffuser of innovations. Therefore, Schumpeter's theory of development and the theory of interindustry interdependence can be combined. Like Schumpeter (1942), Perroux stressed the importance of entrepreneurial innovations, which are the prime causal factors behind economic progress in the growth process in the form of a succession of dynamic sectors or poles through time (Perroux, 1988). Growth is concentrated in various spatial locations, as well as in certain leading industrial branches, where innovation and entrepreneur-ship are prevalent.

Perroux (1970) proposed that "[I]f all the factors used were idle and if creation imposed no loss to any other sector, the product of the industry would effect a clear increase in the entire output of the economy over the course of the preceding phase. If all the factors used in the growth process are furnished by means of "replacement", with amortised resources being replaced by more productive funds, work forces being withdrawn to make way for qualitatively superior work forces, and no loss being imposed otherwise on the sectors foreign to the ones in which the replacement is being effected, the entire output of the economy still experiences a clear increase. If a function of the factors used is taken from pre-existing systems with losses of productivity in certain of their sectors, the net increase in total output is the algebraic sum of the gains and losses in productivity".

Both diverging and converging forces work within the growth pole paradigm. While it is true that the process of capitalistic accumulation generates concentration of wealth in particular places, leading to polarisation of development (Hirschman, 1958), also named as backwash effects by Myrdal (1957), it is equally true that trickling-down (Hirschman, 1958) or spread effects (Myrdal, 1957) may influence the periphery areas (Higgins, 1988). Backwash or polarisation effects reflect the unfavourable impacts on the backward regions, such as migration of the skilled and educated workers, diversion of savings and dependence on the pole. Some backwash effects result in the migration of labour and capital from the periphery to the pole, with the attendant problems of depopulation and capital shortages in the periphery. Some service sectors specialising in more advanced and complex procedures may also displace their counterparts in the periphery. Trickling down or spread effects measure the favourable impacts of growth in the advanced regions on the backward regions, including diffusion of investment, innovation, demand for agricultural products and raw materials, migration of the unemployed, and remittances from migrant workers. It may increase the average real per capita income of the poor region and/or beneficially affect regional production structure. Myrdal (1957) contends that backwash effects generally dominate. But Hirschman (1958) argues that the spread effects, operating through trade via inter-regional complementarities, set up opposite counteracting forces to the backwash effects and will balance them in some regions, and that even though initially the polarisation effects generated in the growth centres may be stronger than the trickling-down effects, as resources are pulled into growth poles. In the long run, external diseconomies of the growth centres, combined with complementarities, will result in a spontaneous spread of development. At this stage backwash effects diminish and decentralisation characterises the spatial structure of economic activity in the region.

9.5 Applications of Growth Pole Strategy

As suggested by Haynes and Dignan (1988), at the micro-level regional policy aims at influencing the locational choice of individual firms through variations of the cost functions of firms across locations. The cost-minimising firm will employ factors in different proportions at different locations. At the macro-level, policy operates through such incentives as grants and subsidies to promote the contribution of a region to national income and employment. The growth pole paradigm has therefore been applied to regional development strategies, especially to areas suffering high unemployment and experiencing difficulty in generating growth due to their particular industrial structures.

9.5.1 *Application of growth pole paradigm*

Developed as a tool to describe and explain the anatomy of economic development in abstract economic space, growth poles have attracted attention in the search for tools to resolve problems of imbalance in inter-regional development in both industrialised countries as well as LDCs, although sometimes combined with similar concepts such as growth centres, growth areas, growing points, development nuclei, cores, and the like. Its intuitive appeal rests on its two major conceptual pillars. First is the notion of agglomeration economies, which will induce concentration of propulsive industries in particular locations — their mutual industrial attractions and sharing of infrastructure facilities will minimise costs in a cumulative fashion to lead to self-sustained growth of the centres. Secondly, the growth of the centres is supposed to eventually induce spread effects into the peripheral areas. The universal appeal of this approach to both developed economies and LDCs lies in the opportunity to reconcile the goals of equity and efficiency in regional allocation of investments. As Perroux (1988) pointed out, "Viewing the problem as a whole, we can, I think, look forward to a growing interest in the theory of development and of poles of development. The main industrial poles of development are gaining in size, in complexity, and the scope of their influence. The contrast between LDCs and industrialised countries brings into relief the difference between the development of territorially fixed populations and the growth of poles (oil-industry centres, for instance) that have no immediate application in their geographical vicinity. The planning necessary for poles implanted in developing countries is no longer in question".

In the 1960s and 1970s, planners and policy makers in both developed and developing countries attempted to implement the growth pole strategy to promote economic growth in underdeveloped regions. Actively promoted through international agencies, including the United Nations, the idea spread from Western Europe and the United States to Latin America, and then to Africa and Asia, particularly Japan, South Korea and India. The growth pole strategy was implemented in at least 28 countries, including Austria, Belgium, Bolivia, Brazil, Canada, Cuba, France, Ghana, Great Britain, India, Italy, Japan, Kenya, Malaysia, Peru, Russia, Spain, the United States, and Venezuela (Lo and Salih, 1978).

Britain and Ireland implemented regional policies from the 1960s through legislation and industrial policies in order to establish growth centres to increase employment and national income in periphery areas. By applying incentives such as grants, accelerated depreciation, infrastructure assistance and training, regional policy tools were instrumental in decentralising employment and investment in regional development (Haynes and Dignan, 1988).

Growth pole strategy was implemented in Japan from the early 1960s under the joint effort of private firms, government and universities to establish industrial complexes in relatively small towns outside the congested Tokyo-Nagoya-Osaka axis, in order to both vitalise retarded regions and to meet the desire of escaping the pressure of big city living. The Comprehensive National Land Development Plan aimed at "achieving balanced economic growth and dispersing industrial and urban development not only in the Pacific Coast Belt but throughout the country ... the plan focused on the growth pole scheme and the regional centres scheme" (Honjo, 1978). Followed by legislative action for implementation, several ministries took leadership in the enactment of designating growth poles by providing national assistance in the issuance of prefectural bonds for development and to local expenditures. In Canada, a comprehensive regional development strategy essentially based on the growth pole concept started from the early 1960s, and 23 areas across Canada were designated as special growth areas. Projects mainly on infrastructure were partly financed by the federal government under this scheme (Higgins and Savoie, 1988).

9.5.2   *Failure in the application of growth pole theory and analysis*

The concept of growth pole has been widely recognised in regional economic analyses and planning, and in his "not a comprehensive bibliography", Mosely listed 296 references on growth pole theories and applications (Mosely, 1974) although many display conflicting definitions or diagnosis. As not all methodological instruments are consistent with the growth pole concept, the concept itself has become a source of confusion in regional economics.

It is worth noting that the growth pole device is designed purely from a narrow economic impact perspective, and consequently, social cost-benefit analysis of such a strategy may lead to differing conclusions. For example, casino gambling is sometimes considered as a growth pole industry to revitalise dilapidated regions on the basis of its economic impact on employment and income, but the social cost of crime associated with gambling may become high enough to outweigh the economic benefit and residents may reject casinos due to their perceived adverse impact on crime (Friedman *et al.*, 1989). Nevertheless, Perroux (1988) claims "the concept of growth poles seems to be: (a) an aid to a correct interpretation of economic history; (b) an analytical tool for development planning; and (c) the basis of a general theory of development related to asymmetrical and irreversible effects ...".

Growth pole theories were very influential through the 1960s and 1970s, but fell into disfavour among some policy makers from the early 1980s onwards. One of the problems was that some governments became impatient with the growth pole approach as a means to reduce regional disparities and induce economic growth. These problems were undoubtedly compounded by failures to define the goal of development. Moreover, references to balanced growth are not always amenable to concrete policy applications often because of the vagueness of this term. Is regional balance concerned with equality of per capita income, public investment, or other economic activity? What conflicts are likely to arise between maximising regional and national welfare, and how can these conflicts be resolved? Without supplying satisfactory answers to these questions, regional policy is unlikely to achieve practical success.

The interactions of regional and national development are complex, and differ from country to country, and region to region. It took the United States, although often regarded as an example of free market economy, 120 years to reduce the gap in per capita income between the richest and the poorest region from over 40 percent as it was in 1860, to around 30 percent in the 1980s (Higgins, 1988). It is dangerous trying to arrive at recommendations for regional policy in any particular country on the basis of any general theory, and each case must be studied in its own context. "The greater the degree of fragmentation or disintegration within the economy, the more frictional and structural unemployment there can be, and the longer can be the lags in adjustment of prices. Fragmentation in space, as evidenced by large regional gaps, can be especially pernicious in permitting the continued existence of unfavourable trade-off curves" (Higgins, 1988). Capital may not flow from richer to poorer, or from low unemployment to high unemployment regions as it is supposed to do in the neoclassical textbooks. For a growth pole to have the desired effects on surrounding areas, there must be "transmission lines with adequate capacity to translate the transmitted economic energy into new economic activity. If such links do not already exist they must be provided and organised" (Jones, 1991).

In regional development policy and planning, perhaps no other approach had in the 1960s and 1970s captured the imagination and interest of policy makers and planners in both the developed and developing world more than the growth pole approach. However, growth poles, as sets of basic activities in a system of interactions in space and irreversible time, are far more complex than the simple idea of selecting a centre generating spread effects to its immediately surrounding geographic regions. Local government often vie for receiving the designation of growth pole; for example, in the case of Japan, more than 100 areas were included as special "industrial development areas" until 1963 (Honjo, 1978). Consequently funds may become too dispersed to generate substantial poles of growth. This approach was applied to urban centres of different sizes and there have been cases for growth poles to function as "enclaves" with close links with economies outside the region instead of stimulating the local economy (Richardson, 1976). Mistakes in site selection and insufficient funds, combined with other factors, may result in failure to achieve goals of the growth pole strategy as well.

The particular appeal of the growth pole is in its capacity of stimulating periphery lagging areas but, paradoxically, developing a pole may lead to widened income gaps within the region it serves at the initial stage of polarisation. Usually, both positive and negative impacts of the growth pole strategy will be present simultaneously, and polarisation is more prevalent in the early phases of economic development but eventually is succeeded by dispersion. That is, backwash first increases then subsequently declines, whereas spread effects increase continuously over time, hence there is eventually a transition from a negative to positive net spill-over. A sufficiently long time horizon, normally 15–25 years, is necessary for the net spill-over to be created around a growth pole (Richardson, 1976). Therefore, polarisation is still favoured as long as it provides a real source of dynamism in the economy, even though backward linkages from the core industries to the periphery may be weak at the start, while net spill-overs to promote regional development around a growth pole may take many years after its establishment. Consequently, policy makers should not abandon the pole strategy as polarisation intensifies before the improvement begins. The failure to place growth pole analysis into the context of spatial development theory and the neglect of the time horizon may result in denying in the long run the opportunity of the periphery areas to grow. Nevertheless it should be recognised that there are some authors (for example, Frank, 1978) who believe that the periphery will be permanently disadvantaged economically by the development of a growth pole or core.

There is increasing recognition that techniques which can capture only the economic impacts of regional policies are inadequate. The non-economic dimensions of regional development, especially the social, political and environmental impacts of regional policies are equally important, particularly because of growing dissatisfaction with gross regional product, income per capita and other similar economic measures of welfare. There are important economic variables which are qualitative rather than quantitative, or are quantifiable only in physical but not monetary terms, such as the quality of entrepreneurship and changes in environmental quality.

It is very difficult to apply the growth pole concept without fully understanding what it really means. Perhaps it was unavoidable that "the operationalisation of Perroux's theory should frequently be reduced to the simple idea of a selected urban centre generating spread effects to its immediately surrounding geographic region" (Jones, 1991). As noticed by Perroux (1988), "... it is decided that for given conditions and in a given period, the term "pole of development" is reserved for action centres that have the maximum intensity and reach. It cannot be repeated often enough that the attention is focused primarily on economic spaces before it reaches geographical spaces; that quantitative expression can use matrices without location as well as matrices referring to location. In a word, it would be untenable to reduce the theory of poles of development to a mere instrument of regional policy, very important though the latter might be; in this domain, one can always conduct the analysis by applying imaginary abstract economic spaces to territorial spaces".

The elusiveness of the concept of growth poles and the diversity of its interpretations in the context of specific problems of regions have been widely observed, adding to the difficulty in its application. The problems include how to transmit polarising effects to neighbouring zones, forward and backward linkage effects are sometimes weak, and coordination of different types of industries with the overall development. The trend is toward the study of completely integrated complexes, utilising competitive and profitable industries adapted to some strategic local characteristics. In addition, as sets of basic activities in a complex set of interactions in both space and time, growth poles may perform within their economic space. Hence the spatial effects generated by a growth pole may not be felt primarily in its peripheral geographic region of which it is the centre, but may be diffused throughout the world. Conversely, a geographic region's true pole may lie outside its borders. But when economic space and geographic space are integrated, and in many cases difficult to differentiate, it may become impossible to judge whether there is any pole in an area or which pole is a major influence upon a particular area, resulting in unnecessary blame on the performance of a growth pole theory.

9.6 Arguments Concerning Service Sectors and Tourism as a Growth Pole or Leading Sector

There are usually leading sectors which perform as a centre of a field of forces in an economy, where "(T)here have a higher than average rate of growth of product, a higher than average rate of growth of productivity, and a rapidly increasing share in the industry as a whole" (Perroux, 1988). They can be replaced over time by new industries in a certain area, and they can also move from one area to another to continue to be leaders in the new area (McKee, 1988, Chapter 3). Statistics show that there is a group of industries that may be termed growth industries in both LDCs and developed countries. In developed countries, tertiary and quaternary industries, and to a lesser extent manufacturing, are the growth industries, and the lagging areas need to obtain a larger share of tertiary and quaternary activities to catch up with the advanced regions. Hermansen (1972) discussed the heterogeneity of growth and the role of service industries in the growth process. David McKee (1988) examines the role of services in the context of the growth pole theory and considers the impact the tourism industry may have in influencing development potential.

9.6.1 *Expansion of the service sector and tourism industry*

The expansion of the service sector has been attributed to the "unbounding" of certain service activities from goods-producing firms (Tschetter, 1987), relatively low productivity associated with this sector and highly differentiated consumer demand for services (Stanback, 1990), and expansion of international trade (Riddle, 1986), among other factors. There have been different interpretations of the service sector. In classification of industries, Fisher referred to this sector as tertiary, and Clark (1957) referred it as the residual category — both resulting in a heterogeneous array of industries being clumped into one single category (Riddle, 1986) and making it difficult to ascertain the contributions of service to the economy. There is a tendency to regard service establishments as small in scale and homogenous (McKee, 1988, Chapter 3) but with the rapid development of information technology this may no longer be appropriate. However, the postindustrial perspective in the transition to a service-based or service-oriented economy has been widely recognised. The potential of the service industry as a vehicle for continued growth in the modern world therefore requires more careful examination.

A study of the change in the industrial structure in China based on input-output analysis suggested that "there was no significant change in the industrial structure between 1978 and 1984. The proportion of primary industry slightly dropped in favour of the tertiary industry. However, there was a drastic change between 1984 and 1990 (Sano, 1993). The proportion of tertiary industry had slowly but steadily expanded". In addition, the open economic policy caused exports and imports to expand beginning in the late 1970s. Both the export and import dependency ratios gradually increased until 1984. The import dependency ratio peaked in 1986 at 15 percent and has declined since then, indicating increasing economic interdependency of China with overseas nations (Sano, 1993).

The service sector is associated with different wage rates because consumer and retail services tend to have lower wage rates overall than an industry providing producer services (Stanback and Noyelle, 1990). According to studies from both the US and the UK, the distribution of consumer services is more even across population size or region, while producer services tend to locate in more urbanised areas (Gillespie and Green, 1987). Hence the beneficial effects of producer services on the economy may not occur extensively outside urbanised areas (Bloomquist, 1990). For smaller and remote areas, the growth in the service sector represents primarily growth in the lower-wage consumer services, such as food service (Kassab, 1992). However, the situation in international tourism in developing countries is different because tourists usually come from regions with higher income and spending capacity, resulting in relatively higher wages in this sector in developing countries. Kassab (1992: 104) concluded that "growth in low-wage services has the capacity to add to the level of aggregate income in the community, with the effect being strongest among rural communities".

A complication existing in the service sector is the possibility of a "bi-polar" situation. As manufacturing employment declines and services employment increases in the developed world, the former high paying jobs are replaced by relatively low paying, non-unionised jobs with versatile working hours in the service sector. A bi-polar structure exists in the service sector, consisting of both high-skilled professionals with high salaries as well as low-skilled workers with low salaries, leading to the shrinkage of the middle class and enlargement in the upper and lower ends of income distribution, and ultimately increased inequality within this sector (Fritzell, 1993). There are many low-skilled, part time jobs in the tourism sector. Although it is arguable to what extent tourism itself can contribute to local economy, it is nonetheless the compound contribution of tourism after taking its multiplying effect into consideration that is really the final influence of the sector.

McKee (1988, Chapter 3) argued that the economies of the advanced nations of the West have become increasingly service oriented, and that services are emerging as both causative elements and facilitators in the continuing growth of advanced economies. "If growth poles have been the engine behind economic growth and seven out of ten new jobs are in service pursuits, then one should expect to find services directly involved in growth poles" (McKee, 1988: 19). Therefore, "an examination of services in a growth pole context provides a better insight into their role in advanced economies. In some cases they constitute growth poles; in others they facilitate the activities of growth poles. At times, the income generated by growth poles has caused services to proliferate" (McKee, 1988: 24). Services constitute growth poles in their own right in some cases. When they do not constitute complete independent growth poles, they act to strengthen and facilitate the role of leading industrial operations in establishing effective linkages. The role of service in the developing economies where the service sector is growing remains to be further discussed.

9.6.2   *Potential of tourism as a growth pole*

The potential of tourism to be a growth pole has been discussed since the 1960s. Christaller was among the first to consider tourism to be a growth pole. He believed that it is typical for tourist destinations to be on the periphery because landscapes and cultures far away from industrial regions provide vigorous contrast to the confinement in towns, and tourism cannot only avoid "central places and the agglomerations of industry" (Christaller, 1963), but also gives the "economically underdeveloped regions a chance to develop themselves — for these very regions interest the tourists" (Christaller, 1963). Friedmann (1966) recommended that for particularly problematic regions where there is little other economic growth potential, tourism may be an option. Although there have been opposing arguments about whether tourism is likely to be a growth pole (Oppermann, 1992b), to eradicate effectively backwardness in peripheral areas with rich tourism resources, tourism does appear to have the possibility of becoming a growth pole or leading sector.

The study of tourism draws on such traditional disciplines as geography, economics, history, political science, psychology, sociology, public administration, political science, and so on. Tourism is involved in most of the features that determine and influence the size and volatility of the national income, although it is not itself a separate industry in statistics. Anybody examining the tourism literature of the past decade could be forgiven for finding it complex and even confusing to a certain extent, primarily due to the fact that tourism does not have a unique base as an industry. Instead it is a collection of service-based activities spreading across various industrial categories and expenditure items that are not normally grouped together, involving customers, suppliers and governments. The growth of tourism generates a complex set of issues relating to its effects and policy implications.

Some governments have targeted tourism as a leading industry in the development of non-urban areas. For example, the Australian government established the Taskforce on Regional Development in 1993, and its report entitled "Developing Australia — a Regional Perspective", outlines a vision for the next 30 years that tourism will play a key role in rural development, and acknowledges that regional development has to occur in a framework that takes account of national policies and priorities. Commonwealth Department of Tourism of Australia (1994) announced that "rural tourism is a multifaceted activity that takes place in an environment outside heavily urbanised areas, It is an industry sector characterised by small scale tourism businesses, set in areas where land use is dominated by agriculture and other industries ...".

Measurement of tourism presents greater than usual difficulties because of its inherent characteristics as a compound industry and the shortage of data (White and Walker, 1982). Tourism is often thought to be composed of self-seeking individuals, profit-seeking firms, and development-seeking governments. The economic impact of tourism is regarded generally greater if "the greater the value added to the tourism product from regional resource utilisation; the greater the supply of inputs for the tourism product from regional producers; and the lower the proportion of imported goods that enter into resident consumption and production in the region" (Eadington and Redman, 1991). The impact of tourism on the local economy can be significant in some areas, and regions may therefore benefit from factors that cannot be utilised otherwise. In Far North Queensland, Australia, tourism contributed to less than 5 percent of GRP prior to 1985, but was estimated to bring in 24.9 percent of GRP in 1992 and a quarter of full-time equivalent employment in this area (Bell and Carr, 1994).

The growth pole paradigm may be applicable to tourism in China for at least three reasons. First, while recognising regional economic disparity as a natural phenomenon in any society, the growth pole is compatible with the unbalanced growth strategy, which promotes relatively faster growth in certain industries than others, in this case tourism. Secondly, if linkage effects are high between tourism and other industries, the spread or trickling-down effect of tourism may stimulate the local economy. Thirdly, instead of emphasising a regional economic centre as most other regional development strategies usually do, growth pole theory stresses the leading role of an industry in the economy regardless of space. This suits the tourism industry, where the movement of tourists across space to consume tourist products comprises one of its unique characteristics.

Nevertheless, more careful thought is necessary when applying arguments on regional growth in tourism studies. At the geographical level, Pearce (1987) identified three basic elements of tourism: (1) generating region, where the journey begins and ends, and the tourist is generated; (2) transit region (route), a region through which tourists must travel to get to the destination; (3) destination region, the place tourists visit and where most consequences of tourism occur. Destination regions usually compete for more tourists by improving the supply of tourism resources, which are comprised of both natural and man-made resources. However, there are severe limitations on the availability of tourism resources to sustain the growth of tourism for a destination because the expansion of tourist supply requires both time and capital. Even if it is feasible and cheaper with easy interregional mobility of capital, labour, and information for a region to draw on a much larger supply of factors of production than those available within its boundary to increase its supply of tourism resources, there may be other limitations. Natural scenery and cultural heritage can hardly be increased in supply in a region. Hence, resource constraints for tourism (especially ecotourism) growth are usually greater than for other industries. Furthermore, the environmental characteristics are not included usually in demand function for most commodities, but a clean environment is essential for the existence and further development of a tourism industry, especially ecotourism, in a region. As a result, neither a supply nor demand theories of regional growth can be applied directly in the study of tourism growth.

Moreover, although most tourists come from urbanised areas because, for example, "the bigger the agglomeration and the greater the population density, the greater the propensity to travel during holidays" (Christaller, 1963), large towns are frequently a focal point for tourism in many countries where much tourism is urban centric. Therefore, the growth of tourism may not necessarily contribute to reducing regional disparity within a nation but, under certain circumstances, tourism may expand regional economic inequality (Chapters 3 and 4). Hills and Lundgren (1977) proposed that the spatial structure of tourism development determines the intensity of tourism impacts and subordinates the goals of the LDCs to, in many cases, the further expansion of international investors. They believe that the dominance of the metropolitan areas in tourism is the origin of both the core-periphery structure of international tourism and regional imbalances. Britton (1979) argued in his spatial structural models that tourism causes economic inequalities among small island nations through resort enclaves.

Consequently, it appears that the type of tourism promoted that determines the regional features of the tourism industry. Mass tourism usually concentrates in well-developed areas, which are often urban centres and controlled by multinationals. It has the potential of generating more economic inequality across a nation as the rural areas can hardly benefit from this type of tourism. McKee (1987) argued that service industries tend to be urban oriented, and mass tourism in small island nations have an orientation toward central places, whilst some of the less accessible destinations are frequented by the elite (Tisdell and McKee, 1988).

Regional imbalance resulting from the control of multinationals over tourism is less significant for ecotourism because "the geographic extension of the tourism periphery is extremely dynamic, fractional by nature, and heavily dependent upon small numbers of tourists constantly seeking new destinations" (Zurick, 1992). The generating areas for mass tourism, according to Zurick (1992), are limited to only a few metropolitan areas but are quite diverse for adventure tourism.

D. G. Pearce (1987) noticed that the tourist industry concentration ratio for countries with specialisation in ecotourism, such as Nepal, is much lower than those attracting mass tourists. He further proposed that adventure travel to Nepal proceeds from generating areas in the West, through intervening international gateways, national and regional staging areas, resulting in a more complicated hierarchy of tourism gateways and closer association with national and local economic development.

Efforts involved in pursuing normative policies do not always achieve what is expected. Although tourism development policies are often supposed to concentrate on regions that are economically underdeveloped to provide a tool for regional development, and governments have been trying to promote tourism to alleviate inequalities, closer examinations have indicated that this goal cannot be easily achieved. For example, the four countries where tourism has been identified as a priority area for the expenditure of European Community Structural Funds are also the four poorest within the European Community (European Community, 1990). However, Hannigan (1994) revealed that tourism growth in Ireland, one major recipient of these EC funds for tourism, in recent years has been concentrated in areas where tourism has traditionally been strong, and funds controlled by government have not been allocated in a manner promoting regional development. An integrated approach with careful planning and efficient implementation involving the host communities is required to ensure the achievement of goals.

9.6.3 Doubts on the service industry and tourism as a growth pole

Issues have been raised about the ability of growth in the service sector to boost local economies and to promote equality of access to resources, especially if a decrease in aggregate resources in the community occurs because the service sector is unable to provide enough family wage jobs (Gruenstein and Guerra, 1981). In addition, the income distribution may become more bifurcated as a result of increase in lower- and higher-wage jobs in service sectors, accompanied by a loss of middle-income jobs in the manufacturing sector (Browne, 1986: 24), leading to a two-tiered structure with decreasing opportunities for lower-income groups (Gillespie and Green, 1987). Inequalities derived from altered structural arrangements, such as stratification, can lead to groups having differential access to resources and social well-being. If resources are inequitably distributed across geographic areas, social barriers can separate communities and suppress their participation in events that build the community's structure and its relationship with external agencies (Wilkinson, 1979).

Tourism development is expected by some ecotourists to earn substantial net foreign exchange, require limited capital investment, and provide a price and income elastic substitute for unstable commodity exports (Lea, 1988). South Pacific countries regard tourism as a sector contributing to goals such as "increasing foreign exchange earnings, to reduce balance of payments deficits, the generation of employment, the establishment of positive and mutually supportive linkages with other sectors of the economy, reducing the reliance on imports, while at the same time preserving traditional values and cultures" (Dwyer, 1986: 1–2). Similar expectations were held by many other developing economies (Tisdell and McKee, 1988). However, tourism is no panacea for obtaining regional decentralisation nor for limiting urbanisation. It has limitations as a means for increasing domestic income and employment. It can have adverse consequences for income distribution and create balance of payment problems. Especially in small states, it can be a risky or unstable source of foreign income and can undermine traditional industries. It can have adverse and irreversible social and environmental consequences (Tisdell, 2000) that may be particularly evident in small states (Tisdell and McKee, 1988).

Although tourism is often believed to be a labour-intensive service industry (Dwyer, 1986: 5), there is conflicting evidence that it is capital-intensive (Sinclair, 1991; Tisdell, 1998) and the cost of supplying tourism jobs in LDCs tends to be very high compared to agriculture. Varley (1978) found that the employment generating effect of tourism in Fiji was less than all primary and secondary industries and less than the average of other tertiary sectors. Mishra (1982) noticed that the creation of Chitwan National Park in Nepal did not generate jobs for locals due to the job requirement for foreign languages and other skills that the locals lacked. Much the same situation has been observed in the Maldives and, in most small countries.

Usually the more educated and economically more affluent have benefited from employment opportunities in the tourism industry (Tisdell and McKee, 1988). Problems associated with tourism development in peripheral regions include large economic leakages from tourist expenditure, shortage of touristic infrastructure and difficulties in managing social and environmental impacts (Hohl and Tisdell, 1995).

In addition, tourism can actually be capital intensive with high import leakage (Summary, 1987). "The impact of tourism on the balance of payments of a country can be deceptive. While it can add substantially to gross receipts, its contributions to net receipts may be small if a considerable amount of the commodities required by tourists have to be imported" (Tisdell and McKee, 1988). The propensity to import may be higher if a tourist facility is operated by multinational corporations because they frequently try to standardise their tourist supplies and services (United Nations, 1985).

Tourism can have adverse impacts on the natural environment, as well as on the social and cultural environment of its destinations (de Kadt, 1979). For example, the cultural life of the local community may lose its uniqueness due to tourist influences, and the social and normal fabrics of the host society may be altered by alien contacts (Tisdell and McKee, 1988). In the Maldives, tourists are isolated from the bulk of the indigenous population because tourist resorts are often built on uninhabited islands to avoid social impacts from tourists (Sathiendrakumar and Tisdell, 1988). Tourism contributes to GDP via both tourist expenditure and investment in tourism-related projects. Hence the economic vulnerability of the economy can increase if the contribution of tourism increases (Sathiendrakumar and Tisdell, 1988; Tisdell and Wen, 1991a). In fact, Sinclair and Tsegaye (1990) found that increased dependence of developing countries on international tourism added, as a rule, to the instability of their export revenue.

9.7 New Growth Theories, Growth Poles and Regional Development

The possibility that economic growth regionally could be associated with increasing returns in particular regions has been recognised for a long time.

It is, for example, inherent in Marshall's view (expressed in the 1800s) that industries could exhibit external pecuniary economies in their development (Marshall, 1961). Allyn Young (1969) in the 1920s also emphasised the possibility that economic development could be associated with increasing returns. Tisdell (1975, 1990, Chapter 9; 1993, Chapter 5) developed a related theme in explaining differences in regional development. Myrdal (1956, 1974) expresses similar themes. Nevertheless, in recent times it is new growth theories (also sometimes called endogenous theories of economic growth) which have assumed centre stage via their emphasis on the possibility that some processes of economic growth are likely to exhibit increasing returns (Romer, 1986; Lucas, 1988 and 1990).

The initial stimulation for this interest stems from an article by Romer (1986) entitled "Increasing Returns and Long-run Growth" which appeared in the *Journal of Political Economy* and which was based on his PhD dissertation submitted to the University of Chicago in 1983. The central assumption in Romer's model is the ability of knowledge to result in increasing returns to long run growth. Because of such impacts, he finds that large economies or centre countries may always grow at a faster rate than small economies (peripheral economies). The importance of new technology and education (knowledge generating activities) in sustaining the economic growth differential of regions is highlighted. These growth influences can be regarded as service-type activities even though research and development for manufacturing firms is very often located within these firms themselves rather than in a separate industrial sector.

In Romer (1990), it is argued that the non-rivalry involved in the use of many services of the above nature helps explain increasing returns to economic growth. Much knowledge is a shared non-rival resource and individuals can only be partially excluded from it. The more educated they are, the more difficult is it likely to be to exclude individuals from knowledge. This education plays an important role in knowledge-sharing and in the growth process.

There are, however, other ways in which the economic growth of a region may result in increasing returns. Economies of scale may be reaped from the use of social infrastructure. This is especially important in relation to *tourism*, but can be important for many other industries. Furthermore, as the economy of an area grows market specialisation is likely to increase. This may involve specialisation in production and provision and services as suggested by Alfred Marshall as well as the evolution of more specialised markets as described by Casson (1982). All of these can generate increasing returns to economic growth, but they are external to individual economic units. Therefore, when they are present, market failure of an aggregate nature occurs and a role may arise for governments to promote the development of key regions or industries. Nevertheless, just how accurate the visions of governments in this respect are likely to be and the extent of their ability to carry out appropriate policies are moot points.

There are of course many critics of new growth theory, for example, Pack (1994), Jones (1998, Chapter 8). However, new growth theory has value in extending earlier theories and encouraging thought about the role of non-rival commodities or partially non-rival ones in economic development. It is not inconsistent with the growth pole theories of Perroux, nor with the view of Gunnar Myrdal. Up to a point, new growth theories can be seen as extending earlier growth paradigms as pointed out by Skott and Auerbach (1995). They suggest that the shift from traditional neoclassical models to new growth theory narrows the gap between mainstream theory and the so called Marx-Myrdal-Kaldor tradition involving "cumulative causation and uneven development". Nevertheless, as suggested by these authors, differences in methods still exist. New growth theories, for example, are highly mathematical and quantitative in character with little emphasis on institutionalism. As yet, they also do not incorporate elements of evolutionary economics, although they might be extended to do so. Furthermore, environmental constraints to economic growth are given little or no consideration in new growth theories, although presumably they could be allowed for (cf. Tisdell, 1990).

9.8 Concluding Remarks

Regional economic disparity is not necessarily inevitable according to unbalanced growth theory. It is the lack of linkages between the pole of the economy and the periphery that causes lasting divergence in an economy. It may also take longer than policy makers usually expect for the growth pole to generate favourable spread effects promoting growth in other industries.

An often neglected feature of the growth pole paradigm, and one which may have resulted in many failures in the application of the growth pole strategy, is failure to comprehend that Perroux's pole of growth is more related to a particular industry or industries than a geographic area. The success of the growth pole strategy depends largely on the correct selection of the pole that possesses powerful linkages to other sectors of the economy. Calculation of the linkage effect of the potential pole industry therefore becomes crucial before designating any growth pole. In the next chapter, a possible method for doing this is outlined.

If tourism is proposed to be a growth pole for China or some of its areas with abundant tourist resources, then the interindustry linkages between tourism and other industries should be explored and estimated before deciding the matter. Discussions about whether tertiary industry and tourism can be growth poles have been unfortunately fairly cursory and have lacked empirical support. Because economic structures vary with change of space as well as time, any sensible effort for identifying a growth pole has to be projected into the local economic framework. Using input-output techniques, the next chapter outlines how interindustry analysis can be used to help decide if tourism is likely to be a growth pole or leading industry in a region. In this case, the analysis is applied to Yunnan Province but may be applied in other contexts also.

Chapter 10

Identifying Whether Tourism is a Leading Sector or Growth Pole: Application of I-O Analysis

10.1 Introduction

Persistent inter-regional imbalances in LDCs can represent an impediment to their development and be a part of the "interlocking relations by which in the cumulative process, poverty becomes its own cause" (Hirschman, 1958, Chapter 10). In order to reduce regional economic disparity, the growth pole paradigm might be used in targeting a certain industry(ies) as the leading industry(ies) for a region. For areas with limited access to other economic activities but rich in tourism resources, tourism may serve as a leading sector for their regional economies. If it is believed that excessive regional gaps are often hurdles to integration and further economic growth of the entire nation, and that the growth pole paradigm is relevant in stimulating economic growth in backward areas, the following questions arise: What are the industries that the inland and rural areas may have a comparative advantage in compared to coastal China? Do any of these have the potential to be leading industries? To what extent can tertiary industries, including tourism, perform as a pole for regional economic growth? It is the purpose of this chapter to consider such issues.

Chapter 8 provided background on the development of tourism in Yunnan and its features, such as its spatial distribution, its ecotouristic attractions and its dependence on ethnic cultures. Chapter 9 reviewed theories of unbalanced growth and the growth pole theory in relation to the development of a tourism industry. This chapter builds on both of these chapters and specifically extends the discussion using input-output (I-O) analysis to quantify the economic impacts of the tourism industry in Yunnan. To do this, an input-output table for Yunnan, with tourism as a sector, is developed and is subsequently applied. Tourism is not shown as a sector in conventional input-output tables. This input-output table enables the backward and forward linkages of the tourism industry in Yunnan's economy to be explored, along with other economic impacts. It provides a measure of how important tourism is as a leading sector in Yunnan. This matter has not previously been examined for Yunnan (or other Chinese provinces) using input-output analysis.

By way of further background, the potential of tourism to act as a growth pole in inland China is discussed generally, followed by consideration of its specific potential in relation to Yunnan Province. Input-output analysis provides a means to quantify interindustry impacts, even though it is not without limitations as a technique. In order to introduce the tourism supplemented input-output table for Yunnan, China's input-output tables are first outlined, followed by presentation of the standard input-output tables for Yunnan, which are then modified to identify the tourism industry. This enables income, output and employment multipliers associated with an expansion of the tourism industry in Yunnan to be estimated, and the growth-enhancing (growth-pole) potential of the tourism industry in Yunnan to be assessed. In the penultimate section, policy measures to promote tourism as a growth pole in Yunnan are outlined. This type of analysis can also be applied to other regions.

10.2   Tourism as a Growth Pole in Inland China

China has gone from a situation of very low income inequality to one of rather high income disparity across regions, as discussed in Chapter 3. This experience accords with the earlier stage of the inverted-U hypothesis (Kuznets, 1955). If China were to accept the views of the classical and neoclassical economic scholars that development is a cumulative process slowly evened out by equilibrating processes or the notion that later stages of the inverted-U curve will even out regional differentials in income, there might be little need to intervene in the expanding regional economic inequality of China. However, if the equilibrating process is slow or results in severe imbalance before smoothing out regional disparities, a case for government intervention might exist. Neoclassical economics tends to ignore dynamics and disequilibria. But according to the disequilibrium paradigm (Fan and Casetti, 1994), economic development creates economic peaks for some regions and results in marginalisation for others. Disequilibrating economic growth processes involving marginalisation and polar growth can produce ever-increasing inequality in development (Fan and Casetti, 1994) and result in bifurcation of regional economies. Therefore, it is necessary to look at the regional dynamics in order to understand the real underlying driving forces for the growth and decline of regions. Public intervention may be needed to adjust regional inequality if there is a tendency for this inequality to result in unacceptable disintegration of the national economy, that is unacceptable regional economic bifurcation.

Regional China is seeking opportunities to expand its economic capacity and performance in order to improve the average living standard of its people and to reduce its economic gap with the coastal areas. Given the growing importance of tertiary industry and tourism in China, it is necessary to explore the potential of tourism to act as a growth pole for some inland areas where abundant tourist resources exist. Unemployment and under-employment are also major problems in many of these areas.

Unemployment is becoming increasingly severe in China. The stock of unemployed and under-employed labour in the urban areas has at least reached 32 million (Yeh, 1996; Tisdell and Chai, 1998). The most significant portion of redundant workers exists in the rural areas. Approximately one-third of total agricultural labour, or over 100 million, is in surplus to that required to maintain the present level of agricultural production (Reynolds, 1987; Chen, 1989). Surplus agricultural labour in China may be of the order of 200 million persons (Anon, 1991). This component of the agricultural labour force has zero or negative marginal product (Lewis, 1965), and needs to be removed from agriculture and employed elsewhere in the economy to equalise the marginal productivity of labour in different sectors of the economy (Marglin, 1976).

Modernisation and industrialisation are, to a considerable extent, based on modern large-scale enterprises located in the cities. As a consequence, employment opportunities are dwindling in most rural areas. However, with more than 70 percent of the Chinese population still living in the non-urban areas, the economic development of rural areas cannot be neglected in China.

Possibilities for absorbing surplus agricultural labour include developments in agriculture, expansion of economic activities in large cities and growth of rural industries. But currently in China only rural industries provide promising opportunities for absorbing rural labour due to the limited scope for agricultural expansion and the over-crowding in big cities, where rural surplus labour has formed a large social strata of semi-unemployed who live in slums. The rate of growth of production of township and village firms has far exceeded that of state industrial enterprises in the cities (Tisdell, 1993; Lardy, 1999). Rural industries contributed 30 percent of China's industrial output in 1990, and employed 28 million people in 1978, 95 million by 1988, and 120 million by 1994 (SSB, 1995 and 1996). However, rural industries often suffer from diseconomies of scale and can create severe environmental problems. Major opportunities to absorb surplus labour in China into more productive employment include the continued development of rural industry, and the expansion of construction, transport, and service industries. It is far from clear that divestiture and privatisation of state-owned industrial enterprises in China will result in greater absorption of labour. In fact in the short run at least, it may add to China's level of overt unemployment (cf. Tisdell and Chai, 1998; Huang *et al.*, 1998). The tertiary sector may have to become the focus for China's future development efforts. Many service industries have high labour-intensities, low investment requirements and the demand for their output is expanding rapidly (Liu and Yang, 1989). Thus their expansion provides considerable scope for labour absorption.

China was heavily influenced in the Maoist era by the Soviet model of development, and adopted an unbalanced sectoral approach to economic development after 1949. This involved high levels of forced savings for capital formation, primarily for the expansion of heavy industry. A large share of investment was allocated to heavy industries to the neglect of other sectors, resulting in consequent imbalances in industrial structure with bottlenecks present in such areas as transportation, energy and water supply.

The services sector, including both service trades and sectors involved in non-material production, used to be regarded as unproductive in planned socialist economies (Yeh, 1996). As commented on by Liu Guoguang *et al.* (1987: 320), China concentrated too much on the development of "sectors of material production to the neglect of the development of the service sector". However, the relative contribution of sectors of an economy to the aggregate economic production and employment varies as an economy develops, and the relative size of the service sector tends to grow (Tisdell, 1993). Balanced development is necessary for the consistent growth of all sectors because the expansion of one sector, such as manufacturing, requires supplies from other sectors as well (Leontief, 1952). The services sector is in fact productive by helping to increase the material production of other industries and improving the marginal productivity of labour (Tisdell, 1993).

It was not until the implementation of economic reform in 1978 that tertiary industry in China started growing rapidly. It contributed only 21.4 percent of China's GDP in 1980, but by 1995 it accounted for 31.1 percent of GDP. The services sector accounted for only 12.1 percent of the total employment of China in 1978, but accounted for 24 percent in 1995 (SSB, 1996). The proportion of GDP contributed by tertiary industry in some places, including Shanghai, was as high as 40 percent in 1995. The percentage shares of elementary, secondary and tertiary industry in Shanghai were anticipated to become 2, 53 and 45 respectively by the year 2000 (Li, 1996).

Categorised as part of tertiary industry, tourism has been one of the fastest expanding sectors in China since 1978. It seems logical in regional policy to ask whether a growth pole strategy can be based on the expansion of tertiary industry, particularly tourism in some inland areas of China, and whether such a strategy can be used to facilitate more balanced economic growth across the nation.

The tertiary sector in the coastal area of China in 1994 contributed 35.3 percent to its gross product and accounted for 28.6 percent of its employment, but only 31.6 percent and 21.9 percent respectively in the inland area (calculated from data in SSB, 1995 and 1996), indicating possible scope for the inland to develop its tertiary industry to achieve further growth.

The presence of regional disparity in China's economic growth has become a key policy issue in China. Massive migration into already over-congested urban localities has aggravated already serious urban problems and increased costs of public services. As a result, a decentralisation policy and balanced growth concept seem to be desirable both economically and politically. "Aware of the political danger and perhaps also sensitive to the inequality of favouring coastal development over that of the interior, the central government has in the past several years taken steps to promote the growth of enterprises in the interior, focusing particular attention on steps to encourage investment in rural enterprises" (Chen and Fleisher, 1996).

Regional policies should aim at attaining acceptable differences in per capita income, rates of economic growth and occupational structure. Multi-level planning has been suggested as a way to deal with regional economic disparities if they become too great for GNP to grow (Higgins and Savoie, 1988).

Different growth poles may be present at different stages of the development of the national or regional economy. Growth poles for the economic development of a region alter with the passage of time. Proactive industrial policy which takes account of the current economic situation and promotes future economic development based on a dynamic view of the comparative advantage can accelerate the economic rise of a region. In China, where government at different levels still plays an important role in investment decisions and in coordinating development of regional industries, industrial policy can still exert a major impact on the direction of regional development. Consequently, to a large extent in China, policy-makers are still in a position to decide whether to promote a growth pole strategy for certain regions and what the leading industries are to be.

Although the aggregate economic strength of inland China is less than that of its coastal area, major regional growth poles have been formed along its railways (Liu and Yang, 1989), and tourism is one of the major industries in such cities as Xian, Wuhan, Kunming and Chongqing. These cities also contain major industrial centres. As discussed in Chapter 3, there is a large difference in the level of production between the coastal and inland area. For example, the per capita value of industry and agriculture was 757 yuan nationwide in 1981, 5,557 yuan for Shanghai, and 302 yuan for Guizhou (Ma, 1983).

Regional industrialisation can often be advantageous when it reflects differences in comparative economic advantage. But regional development in China in the Maoist era was not based on comparative economic advantage. Regional self-sufficiency was prized and duplication of industries by regions may have been encouraged for reasons of defence as well as self-sufficiency. In any case, the industry similarity index across China until the late 1980s was 0.98 (Liu and Yang, 1989), which meant each locality had almost the same industrial structure. This regional duplication of industrial structure at the price of low economic efficiency and considerable waste of resources. Subsequently, some economists in the reform period argued that different localities should target a certain selected industry or industries by concentration of investment and policy support on these (Liu and Yang, 1989). Tourism consequently came to be selected as one such industry for promoting regional economic advancement.

It is necessary to explore more precisely the potential for tourism to be either a spontaneous or induced growth pole, or a leading sector. A real growth pole must contain a dynamic core capable of generating and transmitting innovations and energy that will stimulate the emergence of new independent industry. The issue of selecting tourism as a leading sector in order to achieve the goal of development in rural areas is especially relevant for inland areas of China. Its tourism resources are abundant but it is often difficult for travellers to access these. Tourism development could play a valuable role in promoting economic and social improvement in these economically retarded areas and this possibility is at least worth exploring. This is done here by considering Yunnan Province in southwest China.

10.3 Tourism as a Growth Pole in Yunnan Province

Tourism has grown significantly since 1978 in Yunnan. Yunnan experienced an annual growth rate of 24.7 percent in international tourist arrivals and

38.9 percent in receipts from international tourism from 1980 to 1996 (NTA, various years). Tourism contributed 5.1 percent to the total GRP of Yunnan in 1994, and 14 percent of its total foreign exchange income. Yunnan contributed only 0.53 percent to the total inbound tourist receipts of China in 1990, but over 4 percent in 1996, becoming the eighth highest regional earner of foreign tourist receipts in China. Tourism has become an important economic sector in Yunnan, and tourism has the capacity to become a leading industry for the regional development of Yunnan for the following reasons:

(1) Tourism is one of the fastest growing industries in the world. Since 1950, the number of tourists globally has increased on average by 9 percent per annum and tourist receipts have risen on average by 15 percent per annum, much higher than the average annual growth rate of the world economy (3.2 percent) during the same period of time. Travel and tourism has become the world's largest industry, with an annual output of US$3.4 trillion, accounting for 10.9 percent of world GDP (WTTC, 1995). It is forecast that the tourism market will continue to grow in the 21st century at least at the rate of four percent per annum, and even faster in the Asia-Pacific region (Luo, 1996). Despite the 1990s Asian financial crisis, Asian-Pacific tourism is expected to grow in the longer term. Sustained growth in tourism in China can be expected if international arrivals to China continue to increase steadily, and more Chinese are able to afford trips both in China (and overseas) with rising disposable income and leisure-time (NTA, 1998). Tourist supply in China, especially transportation and accommodation, has been improved. As a consequence, there are favourable background conditions for tourism to play a more important role in the Chinese economy.

(2) Yunnan is rich in tourist resources, especially natural and cultural tourist attractions (see Chapter 8). Yunnan supplies 11 tourist itineraries of national importance and contains six comprehensive tourist resorts (NTA, 1997). A tourist network within Yunnan connects four major tourist areas, namely Kunming, Dali, Lijiang, and Xishuangbanna. Tourist facilities in Yunnan have been upgraded and there is potential for further expansion to host more visitors. Transportation in Yunnan has improved greatly over the past 20 years, with seven international airlines,

and 46 domestic airlines providing more than 260 regular flight, week to Yunnan. There were more than 1,000 tourist enterprises with fixed assets of over three billion yuan in 1995, including 166 travel agencies, 138 tourist hotels, and 23,418 staff (NTA, 1996). Yunnan's goal for tourism was to receive over 1 million international arrivals plus over 20 million domestic tourists, and to attain an income of ten billion yuan in the year 2000 (Travel and Tourism Bureau of Yunnan Province, 1995). Tourism has already become an important industry in Yunnan and can be expected to increase its contribution to Yunnan's economy, as was discussed in Chapter 8.

(3) Tourism in Yunnan has demonstrated its potential to promote local economic development. Localities such as Lijiang, Dali, Xishuangbanna and Luxi have experienced higher income as a result of tourism development. Tourism in Lijiang and Dali has become the top foreign exchange earner in their local economies. Analysis of the multiplier effects of tourism in Yunnan (Chapter 8) suggests that tourism has the capacity to economically stimulate other industries and peripheral areas despite leakages. Later in this chapter, both multiplier and linkage effects of tourism in Yunnan will be discussed in detail using input-output analysis.

Policies for tourism development may target not only income generation but may foster normative goals of improved income distribution as well (Lin and Sung, 1984). The possibility that tourism development could help alleviate income deprivation and poverty in inland areas makes it attractive to policy-makers. Yunnan Province has recognised the importance of tourism and has adapted the strategy of building tourism into a leading industry for this province. In 1992, the Provincial Government announced the strategy of "developing tourism as a key for tertiary industry, and build Yunnan into a major tourist destination". Furthermore, the Provincial Government reiterated this in October 1994 saying that it intended to "build tourism into a leading industry and [make] Yunnan an important province in tourism development" (Deng, 1996). Accordingly, government in Yunnan at various levels is prepared to support the growth of tourism as far as investment, infrastructure, education and coordination are concerned.

Nevertheless, if the concept of tourism as a growth pole or leading industry is to be given operational content and applied rationally to policy, the economic impacts of expansion of the tourism industry should ideally be quantified. Input-output analysis provides one possible means of such quantification, even though this method is not without limitations. This approach will now be introduced by first outlining input-output tables for the whole of China and then specifically for Yunnan Province using the GRIT methodology (West, 1990). The GRIT determined input-output table for Yunnan is then supplemented by tourism as an extra (composite) sector to create a new input-output table, which is then used to estimate output, income and employment multipliers for increased expenditure in tourism in Yunnan Province. In turn, these provide an indication of the economic impact of the expansion of the tourism industry in Yunnan and its capacity to act as a leading industry or growth pole.

10.4   1990 Input-Output Tables of China

Input-output tables provide a snapshot of the supply-side interdependence of industries and provide the basis for I-O analysis. This can be used to measure the economic impacts to be expected from the expansion of any particular industry, and therefore, the degree of economic stimulus which expansion of this industry would provide. Thus it might be used to isolate key industries. Input-output approach, principally a cross-sectional interindustry method, provides detailed analysis of the economic structure at a particular point of time, including all the transactions from both purchase and sale, which occur in the economy during a time interval. Developed by Nobel Prize laureate Wassily Leontief (1952) in the late 1930s, the input-output model assumes a classification of economic activity in a region into industrial sectors whose transactions are described by means of a matrix A of technical coefficients.

Each element of this matrix, a_{ij}, represents the value of output from sector i needed to produce a dollar's worth of output of sector j. Each industrial sector produces the amount of output needed to meet interindustry demands, plus final demand from household, government, investment, and exports. The basic input-output model is:

$$X = AX + Y$$

where X is the vector of gross output, and Y is the vector of final demand. Solve for X:

$$X = (I - A)^{-1} Y$$

where I is the identity matrix, and $(I - A)^{-1}$ is the multiplier matrix or the Leontief inverse. Summing down each column of the Leontief inverse, output multipliers for each sector are obtained, indicating the direct and indirect changes in sectoral output necessary to meet one unit increase in final demand for the output of this sector.

The input-output tables of China for 1990 were compiled by the Input-Output Office of the State Statistics Bureau (SSB, 1993) and are used here. These were the latest tables available when making the calculations reported here. The Chinese national economy was aggregated into six sectors, namely the agriculture, manufacturing, construction, transportation (abbreviated as "transport" in this chapter), commerce and non-material production (abbreviated as "non-material" in this chapter) sectors. Combined with figures on social labour force and exports by sectors in 1990 (SSB, 1992), direct coefficients of the Chinese national economy were calculated with the help of Dr. Guy West of The University of Queensland, and are listed in Table 10.1. Please note that individual items in some tables of this chapter may not sum exactly to totals due to rounding errors. In the tables of this chapter, "OFD" stands for "Other Final Demand", and "OVA" for "Other Value Added".

As a first approximation, in order to understand the role that different industries play in the Chinese economy, total multipliers, which are the sum of initial, first round, industrial and consumption multiplier effects of a particular industry, were estimated with the help of the software entitled "Input-output Analysis for Practitioners, An Interactive Input-output Software Package, Version 7.1" (West, 1993).

Multipliers are generally high in the Chinese economy as indicated in Table 10.2, partly as a result of the inherent structure of the Chinese economy.

Table 10.1 Direct coefficient table for China, 1990.

	Agriculture	Manufacturing	Construction	Transport	Commerce	Non-material	Household	Social consumption	Net export	OFD	Total
Agriculture	0.1788	0.1069	0.0053	0.0002	0.0785	0.0084	0.3503	0.0082	0.4128	0.0361	1.1856
Manufacturing	0.1277	0.5057	0.6391	0.3272	0.2500	0.2378	0.4357	0.1394	0.5589	0.4037	3.6252
Construction	0.0000	0.0000	0.0000	0.0000	0.0000	0.0000	0.0000	0.0000	0.0000	0.4842	0.4842
Transport	0.0149	0.0292	0.0331	0.0202	0.0129	0.0231	0.0227	0.0041	0.3238	0.0111	0.4952
Commerce	0.0061	0.0305	0.0242	0.0203	0.0359	0.0209	0.0684	0.0728	-0.3894	0.0276	-0.0828
Non-material	0.0153	0.0229	0.0130	0.0342	0.2085	0.0838	0.1229	0.7756	0.0939	0.0373	1.4075
Wages	0.6245	0.0762	0.1788	0.2225	0.2468	0.2265					1.4648
Welfare	0.0141	0.0068	0.0109	0.0120	0.0133	0.0297					0.0867
Profits	0.0304	0.1178	0.0463	0.1949	0.0492	0.1883					0.6530
OVA	0.0327	0.0608	0.0283	0.0532	0.0847	0.0680					0.3279
Depreciation	0.0162	0.0430	0.0210	0.1153	0.0438	0.1134					0.3528
Total	1.0000	1.0000	1.0000	1.0000	1.00000	1.0000	1.0000	1.0000	1.0000	1.0000	10.0000

Source: Calculated from data supplied by the Input-Output Office of the State Statistics Bureau, 1993.

Table 10.2 Total input-output multiplier effects in the Chinese economy, 1990 (yuan million).

	Output	Income	Employment
Agriculture	6.092	1.934	1.320
Manufacturing	4.869	0.939	0.607
Construction	5.375	1.091	0.674
Transport	4.062	0.891	0.533
Commerce	5.019	1.191	0.793
Non-material	3.907	0.897	0.566

Source: Calculated from Table 10.1.

Agriculture exhibits the highest total multiplier effects among the six sectors, indicating the traditional importance of agriculture in the early stages of economic reform of the Chinese economy.

Nonetheless, calculation of Type I ratio (Direct & indirect effect / Initial (own sector) effect) and Type II ratio (Direct, indirect and induced effect / Initial (own sector) effect) (West, 1993) shows that manufacturing industry presented the highest Type I and Type II ratios, while agriculture had the lowest of these ratios among the six sectors. For example, Type I and Type II ratios of employment were 6.275 and 14.981 respectively for manufacturing industry, but only 1.330 and 2.959 for agriculture (calculated from Table 10.1). This is partly due to the relatively intensive use of machinery and technology in the manufacturing industry as compared to other industries, and its high backward linkage associated with its consumption of inputs from other industries.

According to the study of Bhalla and Ma based on the 1981 input-output table of China with 24 sectors, "the high backward and forward output linkages are associated with metallurgical and chemical industries which have relatively lower (direct as well as total) employment linkages. On the other hand, agriculture and "light" industry show generally low output linkages" (Bhalla and Ma, 1990). Industries related to tertiary activities, such as telecommunications and commerce, ranked relatively low in output linkages but high in employment linkages among the 24 industries, partly due to the low purchasing power constraint and the additional employment generated in the distribution and transportation sectors.

The pattern of industrialisation in China used to be guided by government institutions and collective organisation of production rather than individual enterprises, a situation different from that in many other developing countries. Economic reform starting from 1979 in China was marked by economic liberalisation of agricultural productivity and by the acceleration of the growth of "light" industries as opposed to the former Soviet model of concentrating on heavy industries (Tisdell, 1993). Between 1981 and 1990, the interindustry structure of the Chinese economy may well have changed for institutional and technological reasons. The extent to which further structural change occurred after 1990 is uncertain. Nevertheless, we have to accept the likelihood of input-output coefficients changing with the passage of time albeit slowly.

Note that the term "national income" does not correspond to material product in Chinese statistics but to gross national product as measured in the West. National income and GNP are therefore used interchangeably in this chapter.

10.5   Input-Output Table for Yunnan Province

There are no recent input-output tables available for individual regions in China. Since "the structure of production in a particular region may be identical to or it may differ markedly from that recorded in the national input-output tables" (Miller and Blair, 1985: 45), a regional table is required when analysing regional economic phenomena. The construction of regional input-output tables depended on expensive and time-consuming survey-based compilation procedures in the past. However, Jensen, West and Hewings (1988) devised a "fundamental economic structure" to construct regional input-output tables without doing surveys of an entire regional economy. Their approach, the Generation of Regional Input-Output Tables (GRIT), has been widely used for generating regional input-output tables (West, 1990). By concentrating resources on the more significant parts of the table, the GRIT method attempts to maximise the use of the most reliable available data. It is regarded as a cost-effective approach in maximising accuracy subject to data, time and cost constraints. The 1990 input-output table for Yunnan is constructed from the national input-output table using a hybrid technique based on the GRIT approach (West, 1990).

The GRIT methodology was designed primarily for Australian conditions but has been applied to other countries successfully. It is applicable to China to a considerable extent because data sources are compatible, although some adjustments are necessary. To convert national coefficients to regional ones, GRIT requires adjustments in industry structure, relative prices, and so on, in order to incorporate the major structural difference between the national and regional economy. On the basis of the 1990 input-output table for China, regional data on employment, production, and investment by sectors in Yunnan are used to construct the 1990 input-output table for Yunnan. The regional economy is aggregated into the same six productive sectors as in the 1990 national input-output table. The direct coefficients for Yunnan are presented in Table 10.3.

Comparing Table 10.3 with Table 10.1, the economic structure of Yunnan is very similar to the Chinese economy as a whole, as indicated by very similar direct coefficients. Nevertheless, further analysis is necessary to explore the difference between the Chinese economy as a whole and Yunnan Province. Multipliers are therefore estimated using software developed by Dr. Guy West (1993).

Although the total multipliers for Yunnan are generally lower than the national ones, which is normal for a regional economy as compared with the national economy, agriculture in Yunnan generates relatively much higher multiplier effects than other sectors, as opposed to the smaller gap between agriculture and other industries in the national economy (Tables 10.2 and 10.4). For instance, the total output multiplier of agriculture was 2.84 times that of manufacturing industry in Yunnan, but only 1.13 times in the national economy (calculated from Tables 10.2 and 10.4). The relative total multiplier effects in Yunnan were much higher than in the national economy. These results are reasonable because agriculture occupies a greater share of Yunnan's economy than that for China as a whole, and development of the manufacturing industry in Yunnan lags behind the average level in China.

Table 10.3 Direct coefficient table for Yunnan, 1990 (yuan million).

	Agriculture	Manufacturing	Construction	Transport	Commerce	Non-material	Household	Social consumption	Net export	OFD	Total
Agriculture	0.1804	0.1092	0.0049	0.0002	0.0794	0.0084	0.3498	0.0082	1.9101	0.0236	2.6741
Manufacturing	0.0775	0.3252	0.3778	0.2125	0.1561	0.1524	0.2825	0.0903	-0.1004	0.2660	1.8404
Construction	0.0063	0.0104	0.0048	0.0018	0.0084	0.0029	-0.0010	0.0000	-0.4699	0.4904	0.0543
Transport	0.0150	0.0298	0.0305	0.0203	0.0130	0.0232	0.0217	0.0041	0.2012	0.0112	0.3701
Commerce	0.0062	0.0311	0.0222	0.0204	0.0363	0.0209	0.0667	0.0728	-0.0969	0.0279	0.2078
Non-material	0.0137	0.0208	0.0107	0.0307	0.1878	0.0449	0.1079	0.6904	-0.4440	0.0336	0.7266
Wages	0.5423	0.0578	0.2479	0.2241	0.2258	0.2278					1.5257
Welfare	0.0142	0.0069	0.0099	0.0121	0.0134	0.0298					0.0865
Profits	0.0569	0.1203	0.0426	0.1963	0.0498	0.1892					0.6552
OVA	0.0711	0.2444	0.2293	0.1654	0.1856	0.1560	0.1723	0.1339	0.0000	0.1471	1.5051
Depreciation	0.0163	0.0439	0.0194	0.1161	0.0443	0.1140					0.3540
Total	1.0000	1.0000	1.0000	1.0000	1.0000	1.0000	1.000	1.000	1.000	1.000	10.0000

Source: Estimated by GRIT process using data supplied by Table 10.1, SSB (1991) and Statistics Bureau of Yunnan Province (1995).

Table 10.4 Total multiplier effects in Yunnan, 1990 (yuan million).

	Output	Income	Employment
Agriculture	1.554	1.134	0.913
Manufacturing	0.547	0.398	0.302
Construction	0.818	0.594	0.337
Transport	0.668	0.487	0.296
Commerce	0.882	0.646	0.491
Non-material	0.691	0.503	0.347

Source: Estimated from Table 10.3.

10.6 Tourism as the Seventh Sector in the Yunnan Input-Output Table

Tourism has become the single biggest prime exchange earner in such countries as Spain, Switzerland, France, Austria, Portugal, Thailand, Nepal, Kenya, and so on (Lindberg, 1991). Although some countries have started to identify tourism as a separate productive sector of their economies, this was unusual until the 1970s. In fact, tourism is rarely included as either a tertiary industry or an export sector in most national statistics because complex segments of the economy have to be combined. It is therefore very difficult to assess fully the contribution of tourism in the economy. Nevertheless, input-output analysis has been applied in tourism impact studies because of its comprehensiveness in providing a holistic picture of the economic structure of a region and its flexibility in disaggregated economic sectors for detailed study (Fletcher, 1989; West, 1990).

There is no separate sector for tourism in the available input-output tables of China. Hence tourism has had to be "created" as an extra sector in the 1990 input-output table of Yunnan. Total expenditure of international tourism in Yunnan was $35 million in 1990, approximately 210 million yuan (NTA, 1991). Because there are no published data on the structure of tourist expenditure in Yunnan, the average sectoral breakdown of inbound tourism expenditure in China is treated as a proxy for the composition of tourism expenditure in Yunnan.

Table 10.5 Breakdown of international tourism expenditure in Yunnan, 1990.

Sector	As proportion of the total expenditure %
Transportation	26
Accommodation	21
Shopping	14.8
Sightseeing	4.1
Food & Beverage	21
Communication	3.8
Entertainment	2.6
Others	6.7

Source: Estimated from NTA (1991).

Although some variations exist between tourist expenditure in Yunnan and in China as a whole, the average breakdown of tourism expenditure in China is calculated from surveys conducted at major entry points in China, including Kunming, the capital city of Yunnan. Therefore it may be acceptable to use the average allocation of tourism expenditure in China as a proxy for tourism expenditure in Yunnan, given the lack of alternative data.

Tourist expenditures are utilised to create a new tourism intermediate sector since one purpose of this chapter to estimate the economic impacts of the tourism industry in Yunnan, including both its multiplier and linkage effects. To specify tourism expenditure in the form that is suitable for input-output requires sectoral breakdown and re-estimation of sector input. Because the structure of tourist expenditure throughout China has been relatively stable over the years (NTA, various years), it is reasonable to take figures in 1990 as representative for input-output analysis of tourism in Yunnan in the 1990s. The sectoral allocation of expenditure from international tourists is presented in Table 10.6.

Since tourist expenditure represents principally demand for inputs from other economic sectors and there is a lack of data, zeros are given to the cells of the rows pertaining to the tourism sector in the transaction table,

Table 10.6 Allocation of tourism expenditure required for the input-output table of Yunnan.

Sector	Expenditure (million yuan)	%
Agriculture	16.80	8
Manufacturing	26.04	12.4
Construction	31.50	15
Transportation	33.60	16
Commerce	54.81	26.1
Non-material	47.25	22.5
Total	210	100

Source: Estimated from Table 10.5 and Statistics Bureau of Yunnan Province (1995).

Table 10.7. The tourism expenditure attributable to each of the six sectors in the "A" matrix of the input-output table of Yunnan is subtracted from the respective cells and corresponding column totals, and included under the new column total for tourism as the seventh sector in the new input-output table. Employment in the tourism industry and associated wages are taken into account in order to adjust the six-sector input-output table to incorporate tourism as the new sector.

Table 10.7 serves as the initial step for impact analysis to be conducted in the next section of this chapter. Adjustment of data is necessary because some obvious discrepancies between data from different sources exist. Moreover, domestic tourism is not included in this table because of data shortages and the need to avoid double counting. This means only the effect of international tourism is reflected in this table and in other results based on this table. For example, the tourism industry in Yunnan employed 17,930 people in 1995 according to the official statistics (NTA, 1996), but the research of Mingyi Luo (1996) suggests that more than 160,000 people in Yunnan were directly involved in tourism after including employees of domestic tourism who were not included in official statistics.

Table 10.7 Transaction table for Yunnan with tourism sector included, 1990 (yuan million).

	Agriculture	Manufacturing	Construction	Transport	Commerce	Non-material	Tourism	Household	Social consumption	Net export	OFD	Total
Agriculture	6265.87	3935.78	42.62	0.92	369.10	77.13	16.80	11353.19	58.56	13507.99	843.55	36494.5
Manufacturing	2828.43	11767.6	3279.4	994.31	725.73	1391.86	26.04	9170.81	648.97	-640.00	6063.83	36257.00
Construction	230.0	378.1	8.99	8.42	39.15	27.14	29.7	-31.5-		-3178.00	11165.7	8677.72
Transport	548.98	1082.18	264.48	61.53	60.53	212.23	33.6	703.95	29.40	1422.90	259.24	4679.02
Commerce	255.99	1127.34	193.09	95.57	113.93	191.56	54.81	2165.99	521.24	-685.61	644.73	4648.7
Non-material	500.36	755.46	92.54	143.49	873.15	637.59	47.25	3503.4	4943.19	-3023.00	658.49	9131.90
Tourism	0.00	0.00	0.00	0.00	0.00	0.00	0.00	324.11	67.00	232.00	4.20	627.31
Wages	19802.3	2094.49	2149.61	1048.62	1051.3	2080.28	193.23					28419.84
Welfare	519.12	232.39	86.69	56.77	62.39	272.29	23					1272.46
Profits	2067	4261.05	369.91	918.42	230	1728.46	108.76					9683.44
OVA	2910.72	8886.28	2022.39	807.57	917.52	1472.46	84.11	5382.1	958.81		3393.17	26835.14
Depreciation	595.75	1593.32	167.99	543.41	205.82	1041.06	10.01					4157.37
Total	36494.5	36257	8677.7	4679.02	4648.7	9131.9	627.31	100516	7227.16	7636.28	23032.9	170984.55

Source: Estimated by GRIT process using data supplied by Tables 10.3 and 10.6, SSB (1991) and Statistics Bureau of Yunnan Province (1995).

10.7 Impact Analysis of Tourism in Yunnan

10.7.1 Brief review of tourism multiplier analysis

A frequent goal of tourism research has been to measure the economic impacts on a region or a country of tourism (Archer, 1977). Among diversified impact criteria, the income/expenditure multiplier is one of the most widely applied indices. It is defined as the ratio of total income or expenditure changes to the changes in income or expenditures directly attributable to tourism. The early review of the literature on the tourism multiplier was conducted by Archer (1977). Bryden (1973) derived GDP multipliers of tourism, and compared hotel visitor expenditure multiplier with the general tourism multiplier. Ali *et al.* (1979) estimated the Keynesian multipliers of expenditure by day visitors and overnighters for Australia.

International tourism in developing countries in particular usually involves importing goods and services from overseas, resulting in leakage of tourist receipts. Therefore, the multiplier for tourism in the domestic economy is influenced by the level of leakages. The higher the leakage, the lower the multiplier. The initial tourist expenditure needs to be adjusted for imports, i.e. goods imported and sold directly to tourists without any processing. For example, the Keynesian tourism income multiplier is calculated according to the following formula (Bull, 1995):

$$M = 1 \text{ / leakage or } M = (1 - \text{marginal propensity to import}) \text{ / leakage}$$

The differentiated marginal propensity to import for different rounds of consumption plays a role in the economy. In international tourism, leakages are highest at the first round of consumption, but become lower for subsequent rounds. The conventional formulae based on applying the same leakages to all rounds of expenditure may therefore underestimate the tourist multiplier. Different levels of leakage are therefore preferred in estimating all multipliers for tourism.

Nevertheless, multipliers can be estimated more accurately by the input-output method than by using a simple formula, such as the one above. This is because this method takes account of interindustry relationships when calculating the multiplier effect of the expansion of one particular industry, and leakages from the second round of multipliers are taken account of automatically within the input-output model.

10.7.2   Impact analysis using input-output tables

The first input-output applications for tourism impact analysis were conducted in the early 1960s concerning essentially the broader phenomenon of recreation (Archer, 1977). However, its use was constrained by the limited availability of data below the national level and the cost associated with generating the requisite data (Eadington and Redman, 1991). It is important for policy purposes that not only the direct impact of tourism expenditure be measured, but the disaggregated indirect or flow-on effects, which occur as backward linkages on the demand side as second, third and subsequent rounds of purchasing waves flow through the economy. The sum of these second and later round purchases is termed the flow-on or indirect effects of an initial impact on an industry or sector.

The most common approach to impact analysis employing input-output analysis is to use it as an extension of the multiplier concept. The procedure involves replacing the unit dollar change in the final demand of the required sector by the actual monetary change. Liu *et al.* (1984) distinguished normal multipliers, including direct, indirect, induced and total multipliers, ratio multipliers for both type I and type II, and from the transaction multiplier for the tourism sector in Turkey. Driml (1987) derived disaggregated multipliers of tourist regions in Australia. West and Gamage (1997) applied the input-output approach in calculating differential multipliers for tourism in Victoria, Australia, to assess different impacts of differential tourist expenditures from day-trippers, intrastate, interstate and international tourists.

The impact of tourist expenditure on the Yunnan economy is, as shown in Table 10.8, in terms of the total (direct, indirect and induced) effect of tourism on gross output (total expenditure), income (wages and salaries) and employment.

Note that flow-on effect depicts the difference between the total and initial multiplier effects. Tourism multipliers reported in Table 10.8 are relatively

Table 10.8 Total multiplier effects of tourism in Yunnan, 1990.

	Initial	First	Industrial	Consumption	Total	Type I	Type II	Flow-on
Output	1	0.332	0.224	0.955	2.511	1.556	2.511	1.511
Income	0.308	0.078	0.042	0.263	0.690	1.388	2.241	1.933
Employment	0.180	0.047	0.030	0.258	0.461	1.430	2.558	2.378

Source: Estimated from Table 10.7.

high compared with multipliers for other economic sectors of Yunnan (see appendix A10 for details of total employment, income and output multipliers of Yunnan), especially its output multiplier of consumption, indicating the strong capacity of tourism to stimulate the local economy. However, employment multipliers of tourism are relatively low.

It is also important to note that domestic travellers are not included in the multiplier calculation in Yunnan due to both data shortages and the efforts of avoiding double counting and expenditure switching. Tourism expenditure from domestic travellers may have greater impact on the regional economy than international tourists who stay in luxury hotels, where leakage in the form of imports, profits and rentals to outside the region may be high (West and Gamage, 1997). Hence the multiplier effect of tourism in Yunnan will most likely be higher if domestic tourism is taken into account.

10.8 Linkages of the Tourism Sector in Yunnan

Since the pioneering studies by Rasmussen (1956) and Hirschman (1958), the concept of linkages has been employed to estimate the degree of interdependence among sectors in a multi-sectoral economy and to identify key sectors in an economy. Linkage studies are closely associated with research on unbalanced growth. Unbalanced growth theory examines investment in key sectors as a stimulus to investment and growth in other sectors, which supply output to or buy imports from the key sectors. Linkage effects result from the increase of final demand through interindustry relationships, measuring the influence of a one-unit exogenous change in final demand upon the production, income and employment of each sector.

Linkages are generally classified into three types (Yotopoulos and Nugent, 1976: 265):

- interindustry linkage, defined as the effect of a one-unit increase in the autonomous portion of final demand on the level of production in each sector;
- income linkage, which refers to the effect of the change in final demand on income;
- employment linkage, defined as the effect of the exogenous change in the final demand on use of labour in one sector.

The total linkage effect of a one unit increase in the final demand (in value terms) for the product of any given industry is obtained from the inverted Leontief Matrix $(I - A)^{-1}$.

Total interindustry linkage for the *j*th sector is defined as:

$$\sum_i a_{ij}^*, \text{ where } a_{ij}^* = (1 - a_{ij})^{-1}$$

In a multi-sectoral economy, two kinds of measures for the interdependence of the system have been developed: backward and forward linkages. Backward linkages refer to a derived input demand effect for each industry. Yotopoulos and Nugent (1976, Chapter 15) compared the linkages between agriculture and non-agriculture in Taiwan on the basis of input-output analysis. Bhalla and Ma (1990) used the 1981 input-output tables for China to examine linkages and sectoral interdependence between agricultural and non-agricultural sectors. Their research indicated that agriculture has a low output-linkage but a high employment-linkage. Low sectoral interdependence in the Chinese economy was observed, which was reminiscent of the local self-reliance and vertical integration promoted during the Maoist period but which was abandoned after the commencement of economic reform in the late 1970s. Nevertheless, by 1981 major structural and institutional change had not occurred in China. Alauddin (1986) employed the linkages concept to identify key sectors in the Bangladesh economy, ranked these and studied changes in their rank.

Yotopoulos and Nugent (1976, Chapter 15), define backward linkage (L_{Bj}) as:

$$\sum_i X_{ij} / TP_j = \sum_i a_{ij}$$

while forward linkage (L_{Fi}) is defined as:

$$L_{Fi} = \sum_j X_{ij} / Z_i$$

where X_{ij} represents the number of units of commodity i used in producing commodity j, TP_j is the total product level of industry j, and Z_i is the total demand for commodity i, which is obtained by summing the demand for commodity i.

The A matrix, where $a_{ij} = X_{ij} / TP_j$, was obtained from the 1990 input-output table for China and Yunnan. However, the linkage effects were estimated using the software developed by Dr. West, which defines backward linkage as "column mean of coefficient matrix over average column mean" (West, 1993). The backward linkages for the six sector economy without tourism and for the seven sector economy with tourism as the new sector are reported in Table 10.9.

Table 10.9 Backward linkages for open direct coefficient matrix column, Yunnan, 1990.

	Output		Income		Employment	
	Without tourism	With tourism	Without tourism	With tourism	Without tourism	With tourism
Agriculture	0.771	0.776	1.563	1.513	1.716	1.709
Manufacturing	1.358	1.404	1.385	0.399	1.433	1.488
Construction	1.163	1.194	0.559	0.552	0.509	0.522
Transport	0.737	0.744	0.405	0.387	0.361	0.357
Commerce	1.241	1.253	1.512	1.489	1.470	1.469
Non-material	0.729	0.742	0.576	0.565	0.512	0.510
Tourism		0.886		1.096		0.945

Source: Estimated from Table 10.7.

Although the linkage effects of the original six sectors remain relatively unchanged after tourism is introduced as the seventh sector in Yunnan, it is interesting to observe a small increase of the linkage effects of the manufacturing sector after the inclusion of tourism. Compared with the other six economic sectors in Yunnan, tourism exerts reasonably high backward linkages in the Yunnan economy. An industry exerts a strong backward linkage effect if it has a high percentage of intermediary inputs from other sectors in its output. It is also necessary to note that sectors that rank high in interindustry output linkage usually rank low in employment linkage, because labour is one component of the value added that complements intermediate demand to form the total value of output.

Although there are different opinions about the economic importance of forward linkages, it may be of interest to look into the forward linkages of tourism in Yunnan. As is apparent from Table 10.10, they are generally high, indicating the capability of tourism to stimulate downstream economic sectors of Yunnan.

Since tertiary industries are by their nature intangible to some extent, linkages are not always obvious, nor has their role as growth poles been explicitly explored. "The final package purchased by the vacationer, sun, sea, sand, and so on, would be unobtainable without intermediate inputs of transportation and communication, not to mention a supply of foodstuffs and various luxury consumer goods and furnishings from the world market. Various technical skills related to construction and the management of activities may also be obtained in the world market. Thus there seems to be little doubt concerning the role and direction of backward linkages in the industry under discussion" (McKee, 1988: 43).

Table 10.10 Forward linkage of tourism in Yunnan, 1990.

	Output	Income	Employment
Open Inverse	0.6451	0.1705	0.728
Closed Inverse	0.8746	1.1705	0.7177

Source: Estimated from Table 10.7.

With growing incomes and an expanding domestic market, a positive contribution from services can provide linkages in developing a local economy, such as the case of Yunnan, where tourism demonstrates strong linkages to the regional economy. However, in smaller and poorer nations where many tourist goods need to be imported, the positive impact of tourism on the economy will be less spectacular. Furthermore, factors such as lack of infrastructure, bureaucracy, seasonality, and import leakages, may influence the level of tourism linkages.

10.9 Limitations of Input-Output Analysis

The technique of input-output analysis has a number of advantages when compared with other methods for measuring tourism's economic impact (Fletcher, 1989). The flexibility of input-output tables enables the construction of a model that often suits the limited data available and the purpose in hand. As a general equilibrium approach, it provides a comprehensive insight into the economy yet is not as data demanding as other general equilibrium techniques.

Nevertheless, despite the effectiveness of the input-output method in many applications, there are limitations in the application of the input-output method to the study of tourism, especially in modeling the impact of tourism expansion (Fletcher, 1989; West, 1990). It is a relatively expensive tool of analysis in terms of time, manpower and financial resources. Assessment of tourism impacts requires both disaggregation and aggregation of sectors related to tourism in order to detect impacts where they occur because, more than one conventional economic sector participates in both the production and consumption of tourist products. The presence of tourism in a region may involve interaction between the study region and the rest of the world, raising doubts about the applicability of the general equilibrium assumption.

In addition, "once the data has been collected and assimilated into an input-output transactions table, a number of restrictive assumptions concerning the production processes of the various industrial sectors and the consumption function of the household sector must be made" (Fletcher, 1989). Violations of restrictive assumptions for traditional input-output analysis is "perhaps most important in the case of developing countries that have more open or evolving economies, with weak internal economic structure" (Briassoulis, 1991). Neither structural change in the economy and tourism industry, nor intangible impacts of tourism upon social, cultural and environmental structure, can be identified.

Naturally, what can be gained in comprehensiveness usually has to be paid for by reduced detail. When modification of the traditional input-output technique is necessary, a combination of both qualitative analysis and input-output data may compensate for the limitation of techniques to a certain degree.

10.10 To what Extent can Tourism as a Growth Pole Work in Yunnan?

Arguably, it is development that creates the growth poles, not the poles that generate development (Lo and Salih, 1978). Yet growth poles may be encouraged to develop to a certain extent by heavy investment in a particular area or industry, which requires both monetary input and links between the pole and the general local economy. Nevertheless, in many cases, this type of "forced" pole may be isolated from its periphery and exhibit weak spread effects, and therefore the linkage between the pole industries and the economic structure of the surrounding periphery comes into question. The theory relies on the notion that leading industries have forward and backward linkages within the economic system, and on the empirically proven fact that the spatial agglomeration of these industries may induce increased location efficiency at central locations. Extension of the theory suggests that initially a process of spatial convergence will occur with the hierarchical diffusion process and net spread effects into the hinterland of the growth poles eventually occurring. But these follow-on effects are not certain to occur.

Given the view of Lo and Salih (1978), there may appear to be no role for the government in promoting growth poles as a vehicle for inducing economic development. But this fails to recognize that government could play an important role in facilitating the progress of natural growth, for example, by providing appropriate infrastructure and supporting required institutional changes. While it seems that tourism development constitutes a natural growth pole in Yunnan, appropriate government support can accelerate the development of this growth pole. On the other hand, inappropriate government policies can hinder the development of such a pole. Thus, government policies do matter.

Tourism in Yunnan has been growing mainly as a result of the rich tourist resource and strong demand, and there have been strong links between tourism and other related industries. As a consequence, tourism as a growth pole is a natural driving force for the local economy. Four major tourist centres have formed within Yunnan Province, namely Kunming, Dali, Lijiang, and Xishuangbanna. The backward and forward linkages associated with tourism are prevalent within the local economy, especially in the strong attempts to promote provision of souvenirs and other tourist supplies of traditional style in Yunnan.

The strength or size of tourism as a growth pole is difficult to measure quantitatively without detailed analysis of the input-output data of that particular region. However, considering the fact that direct income from tourism in Yunnan accounts for over 5 percent of its total GRP (Statistics Bureau of Yunnan Province, 1995), that more than 30 percent of Yunnan's annual investment has been directly related to tourism since 1989, and that over half of the incremental GRP in Yunnan is created by tourism (both directly and indirectly) according to Li Tao, former director of the Travel and Tourism Bureau of Yunnan, it is evident that tourism has an important role to play in the local economy. Furthermore, the importance of tourism in Yunnan is still increasing and it has stimulated strong development of entrepreneurship.

The number of overseas tourists received by Yunnan in the period 1991 to 1995 was two million, 2.64 times the number of overseas tourists received by Yunnan in the period 1986 to 1990. International tourist receipts in Yunnan increased on average by 53.5 percent annually from 1991 to 1995, a rate 25 percent higher than the national average annual growth rate during the same period of time. Domestic tourists to Yunnan totaled 70 million in the period 1991 to 1995 and they spent a total of 11.6 billion yuan in Yunnan (NTA, 1996; Luo, 1996).

Elasticities of demand and supply of an industry may indicate how powerful a pole can become. Studies on the elasticity of demand for tourism have given diverse results. However, most researchers agree that travel expenditure is highly income elastic (Witt and Martin, 1987). Therefore, with generally increasing disposable income, demand for tourism in Yunnan will grow quickly if attractive tourist products are supplied.

There is a multiplier effect from the tourism industry. It has been estimated that, in China, tourism income of one dollar brings $3.12 increment in the national economy and $10.7 extra income in tertiary industry (Luo, 1994: 27). The multiplier effect of tourism in Xishuangbanna is believed to be at least 2 for GDP and 3 for employment (unpublished data from the Tourism Bureau of Xishuangbanna, 1995). Input-output analysis conducted in this chapter reveals that total multipliers for output, income and employment in Yunnan's tourism industry were 2.511, 0.690 and 0.282 respectively (Table 10.8), indicating a strong capability for tourism to promote the local economy. Both backward and forward linkages of tourism are high in Yunnan (Tables 10.9 and 10.10), supporting the policy of targeting tourism as a key industry or a pole of growth in Yunnan.

J. Wen found, from field evidence, that in tourist areas in Yunnan, such as Dali City, Lunan County and Jinghong, more than one-twentieth of the residents are involved in tourism through different channels. Tourism has stimulated structural change in the Dali region, "bringing about a pronounced private sector on a petty-commercial basis" (Gormsen, 1990). Petty traders, such as handicraft sellers, are part of the informal employment sector as compared to the well-established tour businesses in the "formal sector" in tourism (Drakakis-Smith, 1980). This informal sector offers economic participation to many low skilled or unskilled individuals, and ultimately it may offer more secure employment and participation in the economy through upward links with the formal sector (Wu, 1982). Considering tourism as an industry connecting various industries and showing powerful spread effects over a wide area, the local multiplier effect will be greater if Yunnan is able to supply more tourist commodities locally instead of importing these from overseas or other areas of China.

Some critics argue that there is little evidence that induced growth centres generate significant spread effects in the economically lagging hinterlands (Friedmann, 1985). The diffusion of innovation and the trickle-down assumes a relatively homogeneous transport and /or communication system but ignores the influence of cultural practice. As the disseminating centres for the spread of development, urban areas are seen as progressive and modernising in contrast to the stagnant and backward rural areas. But the economic impacts of growth centres on their surrounding rural areas are not necessarily always positive (Lo and Salih, 1978).

There has also been debate over the role of the development of services as a means for promoting economic growth. The high-wage service sector is associated with jobs requiring higher levels of education and skill (Shelp, 1985). But petty traders and those in the informal sector do not require such skills. Tourism expansion may provide scope for employment of both skilled and unskilled persons, particularly when its interindustry linkages are taken into account.

10.11   Measures to Promote Tourism as a Growth Pole in Yunnan

Since the introduction of the growth pole concept by Perroux, this approach has been popularised by theoretical and empirical studies and has been regarded as a vital tool of public policy for decentralised development. Countries adopting this approach aim at dispersal of economic activity to the outer regions by adopting supporting fiscal policies, infrastructure investment and so on. Governments in peripheral regions may also try to utilise growth poles to stimulate economic development. But in doing so it is necessary to bear in mind that the problems that the growth pole are supposed to solve are wide ranging and certainly difficult, and the efficacy of poles to generate enough spread effects for the hinterlands is doubted as well. The question is not whether growth poles exist, but rather whether self-sustained regional growth, which does not exacerbate spatial polarisation, can be generated.

It is often said in the study of regional economic development that growth does not appear everywhere and all at once; it reveals itself in certain points or poles, with different degrees of intensity; it spreads through diverse channels (Perroux, 1988). It seems logical to strengthen these focal points in backward regions in order to promote a process of self-sustained growth. As an industry connecting resources in both urban and rural areas, tourism may stimulate the growth of the rural economy from the very beginning of its own growth rather than after a lag; that is before the spreading phase of many other industries. From this point of view, tourism of the type occuring in Yunnan does not strongly discriminate against the rural areas if it is selected as the pole of growth. However, links between the rural areas where natural tourist resources are located, and the cities where tourists arrive and disperse, have to be well-established if tourism is to develop as a spatially diffused growth pole. This requires adequate investment in improving infrastructure and human resources in rural areas. This is the basic requirement for tourism to develop into a pole for the whole province. Otherwise, growth poles may become an enclave without linkages to the periphery, or distort the pattern of regional development and lead to the stagnation of the rural sector through leakages.

Expansion of the tourist market of Yunnan Province is another important issue in the process of establishing the growth pole. Southeast Asia has become the biggest market for Yunnan, with Thailand, Singapore, and Malaysia overtaking Japan and the United States to become the principle tourism source countries for Yunnan (Travel and Tourism Bureau of Yunnan, 1995). The opening up of Yunnan in the late 1980s converted Yunnan from a remote inland province far away from the Chinese east coast into a front line for bridging China and Southeast Asia.

Further expansion of tertiary industry is essential for the greater integration of tourism with the rural economy. Yunnan concentrated on the establishment of secondary industry between 1950 and 1978, and started developing tertiary industry in 1979. The changes in the structure of its industry are indicated in Table 10.11.

Tertiary industry as a percentage of both production and employment has increased since 1980 in Yunnan. Tertiary industry produced 31.5 percent of production in 1994 while employing only 11.9 percent of the total labour

Table 10.11 Comparison of the composition of industries in Yunnan Province (1952, 1980 and 1994) in terms of production and employment.

	Production (%)			Employment (%) (general)		Employment (%) (towns)	
	1952	1980	1994	1980	1994	1980	1994
Primary	61.7	42.6	24.2	85.04	77.87	10.2	7.2
Secondary	15.5	40.3	44.3	8.06	10.23	47.8	37.1
Tertiary	22.8	17.1	31.5	6.90	11.90	42	55.7

Source: Estimated from data supplied by Yunnan Statistical Bureau, 1995.

force as indicated in Table 10.11. By comparison, 55.7 percent employment in towns was created by tertiary industry, mainly because the majority of labour in the countryside engages in primary industry while tertiary industry is more developed in urban areas.

The proportion of tertiary industry in Yunnan's four tourist centres is higher than the provincial average as indicated in Table 10.12. Xishuangbanna has the highest proportion of primary industry, while Kunming shows the highest percentage for secondary and tertiary industries. Kunming is not only the top tourist income-earner in Yunnan, but also more or less complementary to the growth of other tourist centres as the capital and gateway to the province. Its international tourist arrivals ranked ninth among 53 major tourist cities of China in 1995 (NTA, 1996). Part of the leakages of tourism expenditure in other areas flow to Kunming as payment for tourist supplies. A network with Kunming as the centre but connecting other popular regional destinations allows relatively balanced tourism development in Yunnan.

It is worth considering the extent to which tourism competes with other industries for resources. It may use very little land demanded by other industries if it is properly planned and managed. In a labour surplus economy, as is the case in Yunnan, tourism is not depriving rural areas of any labour which could be gainfully employed elsewhere. The discussion should therefore focus on whether the capital could be better used in another industry. Return on capital therefore becomes the crucial guideline in determining whether tourism is the best alternative form of resource-use.

Table 10.12 Comparison of the composition of industries in four major tourist centres in Yunnan Province in 1994.

	GRP (million yuan)	Proportion of the primary industry (%)	Proportion of the secondary industry (%)	Proportion of the tertiary industry (%)	Total
Yunnan Province	97397	40.30	31.21	28.49	100
Kunming	26813.32	9.14	51.5	39.36	100
Dali	5342.35	38.19	31.92	29.89	100
Lijiang	1479.97	36.78	31.59	31.63	100
Xishuangbanna	2283.66	49.06	17.47	33.47	100

Source: Statistics Bureau of Yunnan Province, 1995.

Input-output analysis assumes that final demand can be manipulated. However, it does not consider how demand can be generated or what factors are likely to make demand increase. Therefore, the input-output method is supply-side biased and neglects demand analysis. Since demand for tourism is income-elastic, it will expand with economic growth. Further research is needed on the economics involved in expanding the demand for different industries involved in tourism, and how demand for the products of these industries will increase normally with economic growth.

Yunnan is unique in its location and tourist resources, and has an image as an affordable and diverse destination for both overseas and domestic tourists. Cross-border tourism in Yunnan is a unique attraction for Chinese who often face tedious procedures in applying for overseas trips. A large volume of daily cross-border visitors from Burma, Thailand and Vietnam, who are not counted as "tourist" according to the WTO definition, also contribute to Yunnan's economy by their expenditure in Yunnan.

Other issues, such as increasing the average expenditure of tourists instead of simply trying to expand the number of tourists, improving macro-management of industries involved in tourism, research and staff training, are also indispensable for tourism to become a powerful growth pole in Yunnan. Training and human resources are becoming increasingly important in meeting tourism competition, because "one of the most important yet neglected foundations for successful tourism the education and training of the people who are responsible for the planning, development and delivery of the tourism experience" (Ritchie *et al.*, 1992: 203). Compared with other destinations in Southeast Asia, Yunnan is a relative newcomer as an international tourist destination and needs to improve its quality of tourist products in order to compete more successfully with other Asian destinations.

10.12   Concluding Observations

The adoption of the growth pole paradigm often reveals wishful thinking. Nevertheless, with appropriate government effort, economic growth can be decentralised to the benefit of rural areas if a suitable growth pole can be identified and fostered. There is potential for tourism to be a growth pole in Yunnan Province where tourism has been growing quickly. Input-output analysis based on 1990 data reveals that tourism has high multipliers and high linkage-effects in Yunnan, and has the potential, therefore, to perform as a pole of growth in its regional economy.

Tourism is a composite industry, consisting of a wide range of goods and services that satisfy tourists. Interrelated with not only tertiary industries, but also with elementary and secondary industries, tourism has the potential to play a key role in regional growth. But in analysing its potential, account needs to be taken not only of supply-side interconnections as revealed by I-O analysis but also of the strength of demand for tourism in the region and the sustainability of that demand. Naturally the sustainability of the resource-base for tourism must be considered as well. Thus, the evaluation process is quite a complex one.

Appendix to Chapter 10

Total Employment, Income and Output Multipliers in Yunnan

Table A.10.1 Total employment multipliers in Yunnan.

	Initial	First	Industrial	Consumption	Total	Type I	Type II
Agriculture	0.449	0.085	0.034	0.330	0.898	1.265	1.999
Manufacturing	0.041	0.074	0.066	0.116	0.297	4.380	7.183
Construction	0.074	0.026	0.058	0.173	0.332	2.133	4.461
Transport	0.096	0.018	0.035	0.142	0.291	1.545	3.014
Commerce	0.167	0.073	0.046	0.187	0.473	1.714	2.835
Non-material	0.134	0.025	0.030	0.147	0.336	1.416	2.513
Tourism	0.180	0.047	0.030	0.203	0.461	1.430	2.558

Source: Estimated from Table 10.7.

Table A.10.2 Total income multipliers in Yunnan.

	Initial	First	Industrial	Consumption	Total	Type I	Type II
Agriculture	0.543	0.107	0.044	0.426	1.121	1.279	2.065
Manufacturing	0.058	0.099	0.087	0.150	0.394	4.228	6.824
Construction	0.248	0.039	0.078	0.224	0.589	1.473	2.378
Transport	0.224	0.027	0.047	0.183	0.481	1.331	2.148
Commerce	0.226	0.105	0.062	0.242	0.636	1.742	2.812
Non-material	0.228	0.040	0.041	0.190	0.498	1.355	2.188
Tourism	0.308	0.078	0.042	0.263	0.690	1.388	2.241

Source: Estimates from Table 10.7.

Table A.10.3 Total output multipliers in Yunnan.

	Initial	First	Industrial	Consumption	Total	Type I	Type II
Agriculture	1.000	0.290	0.178	1.550	3.019	1.468	3.019
Manufacturing	1.000	0.526	0.415	0.545	2.487	1.941	2.487
Construction	1.000	0.447	0.397	0.815	2.660	1.845	2.660
Transport	1.000	0.279	0.239	0.666	2.184	1.518	2.184
Commerce	1.000	0.469	0.309	0.880	2.658	1.779	2.658
Non-material	1.000	0.278	0.213	0.689	2.180	1.490	2.180
Tourism	1.000	0.332	0.224	0.955	2.511	1.556	2.511

Source: Estimates from Table 10.7.

Chapter 11

China's Tourism Development in Retrospect and Prospect

11.1 Introduction — Retrospect

Since the Chinese Communist Party (CCP) decided in 1978 to embark on a path of economic reform, China has experienced phenomenal growth of its tourist industry. Prior to 1978, its international tourism industry was virtually non-existent. Inbound tourism to China was mostly limited to politically motivated hosting of invited guests in the pre-reform period (Uysal et al., 1986: 13). Domestic tourism was usually organised for Chinese by the organisation employing them, for example, leave for recreation, attendance at approved meetings and gatherings. Thus, a collectively controlled atmosphere pervaded domestic tourism organised through the workplace with a view to promoting socialist solidarity and providing support for the CCP wherever possible.

Private industry had no role in the management and supply of tourism services because of state involvement. The transport industry, hotels, travel agencies and tour organisations were all under state ownership in one form or another.

In fact, the existence of tourism was only begrudgingly accepted in the pre-reform period. Being a service industry, it was regarded by Marxists as unproductive and therefore had a low priority for development. However, after the opening up of China to the outside world, it became clear to the leadership of China that tourism development would have to be given a higher priority if the general process of opening up China's economy to the outside world was to be facilitated. At least business visits for direct investment and trade were needed.

314

It was only a short step from accepting this point of view to recognising that a Chinese tourism industry catering for foreign visits could in itself make a valuable contribution to China's development. By 1987, the status of China's international tourism industry had changed from one of facilitation of the development of other industries and international trade, to an industry viewed as being able itself to earn foreign exchange and thereby promote economic development. Consequently, it became an industry worthy of high priority in its own right.

The new point of view was accepted by the Thirteenth Congress of the CCP (1987) and championed by the then General-Secretary, Zhao Ziyang, who subsequently "disappeared" in 1989 during the political unrest in China involving the "Democracy Movement". In his report to the Congress, Zhao Ziyang specifically states that more should be done to expand the export-oriented tourism industry and sees it as having the capacity to play a vital development role. He enunciated the following development policy for China:

> Our great capacity to earn foreign exchange through exports determines, to a great extent, the degree to which we can open to the outside world and affects the scale and pace of domestic economic development. For this reason, bearing in mind the demands of the world market and our strong points, we should make vigorous efforts to develop export-oriented industries and products that are competitive and can bring quick and high economic returns (Zhao Ziyang, 1987: 28).

Whereas China only had 0.23 million *foreign* tourist arrivals in 1978, by 1988 this figure had risen to 1.84 million and by 1998 to 7.1 million, that is just under four times the 1988 figure, even though the 1998 figure was about four percent down on that of 1997 due to the Asia financial crises which reduced travel from other Asian countries to China (NTA, 1999: 12). Between 1988 and 1998, China's tourism industry including its inbound tourism industry grew on average at a faster rate than China's GDP, but not in 1998 due to specific circumstances such as the Asian financial crises and major floods which disrupted domestic tourism.

The Marxian stigma that as a service industry, tourism was unproductive increasingly began to lose its force. After 1988, a new attitude towards the development of domestic tourism began to emerge and in 1992 the CCP specifically recognised the contribution which expansion of domestic service industries could make to China's development. In addition, increasing decentralisation of tourist administration possibly encouraged the growth of China's tourism industry. Many provincial governments saw domestic tourists as providing extra economic opportunities for their provinces to those provided by inbound tourists and were in favour of encouraging tourism generally. Furthermore, the demand for tourism is highly income elastic and with rising incomes in China the demand for domestic tourism increased greatly.

China was estimated to have 664 million domestic tourists (tourist trips) in 1998, and they were believed to account for 69.5 percent of total tourism receipts (NTA, 1994: 11). Average per capita expenditure in China on tourism was estimated 607 yuan but was substantially higher for urban compared to rural residents. Although group tourism still dominates the Chinese domestic tourism market, an increasing number of Chinese are making use of travel agencies and arrange their own tours on an independent basis. Rapid growth of inbound tourism to China was thus soon followed by rapid growth in domestic tourism in China, stimulated to a considerable extent by more liberal Chinese economic policies and rising domestic incomes.

The global advance of China's tourism industry in a relatively short span of time is apparent from the following statistics for 1998:

— China was ranked the sixth nation in the world in 1998 in terms of the number of its international tourists (NTA, 1999: 10);
— It ranked seventh in the world in terms of foreign exchange earnings from inbound tourism (NTA, 1999: 10);
— Tourism accounted for more than five percent of China's GDP and employed approximately nine million persons (NTA, 1999: 11).

The growth of China's tourism industry has contributed to its development, as hoped for Zhao Ziyang and the industry has probably expanded even more than he had imagined. In turn, China's economic development has contributed to further substantial growth in its tourism industry. Higher incomes in China have stimulated the demand for domestic tourism and

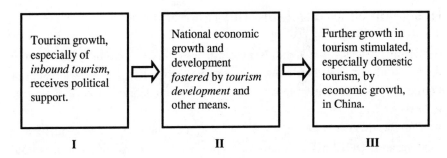

Fig. 11.1 Phases of the development of tourism in China in its reform era.

improvements in transport, communications and infrastructure generally in China, as well as more liberal policies have made travel within China easier for both Chinese and foreigners. Figure 11.1 illustrates the development process schematically, a process which is still underway.

Although the broad or macro-picture of the relationship between China's economic growth and the development of its tourism industry is of interest and worthy of further study, the main focus in this book has been on the regional, especially relative regional development, of such tourism in China, particularly in China's interior as compared to its coastal region. The spatial distribution of tourism has been given much attention, especially compared to the spread of economic activity in China, and dynamic variations observed.

Given that China's interior has been seriously lagging behind its coastal region in economic growth, the role of tourism in the economic development of China's interior region was singled out for intensive study. It was found that much tourism in inland China depends heavily on nature and minority (ethnic) cultures, and to a large extent involves ecotourism or eco-cultural tourism. Therefore consideration was given to the development of ecotourism and its sustainability. The role of tourism in decentralisation in inland provinces was also examined taking Yunnan as a case study. The possibility for tourism development to act as a growth pole has been given special attention. Issues in tourism development were studied taking into account both the policies of the national government and of local government.

11.2   Important Findings and their Nature

This study reveals that China's inbound tourism is regionally even more skewed and unequal than economic activity in China, and shows a higher degree of concentration on its coastal region than its general level of economic activity.

On the whole, international tourism in China is urban-centric and concentrated in China's economic core, thereby reinforcing centrifugal economic forces which favour economic growth in China's coastal region. However, the relative regional concentration of tourism in China has declined in recent years as has its relative skew in favour of the coastal region. The dynamic tendency of inbound tourism towards regional relative convergence contrasts with that for relative economic levels of activity which either show continuing divergence or lack of convergence. In recent years also, the proportionate share of China's interior in its tourism industry has risen.

While the skew of tourism in favour of China's coastal region may suggest that inbound tourism is an inappropriate industry for inland development, this is by no means the case. The *absolute* level of international tourism to China's inland has registered considerable growth. In fact, it has recorded faster growth on average than on the coast so causing the relative quantity of inbound tourism in the interior to increase in comparison to the coast. Hence, China's inland has experienced considerable tourism development which has made a positive contribution to its economic development. Note that this is so despite a rise in the absolute difference in demand-side tourist variables such as differences between the number of inbound tourists on the coast and those visiting the interior and a rising absolute difference in foreign exchange earnings by these two regions.

It seems clear that in examining the development consequences of tourism, we must not rely on the *relative* geographical distribution of tourism alone, even though this is of interest in its own right. Absolute figures also count.

Furthermore, tourism between regions is not always in conflict. For example, it is possible that much inland tourism in China is not in competition with inbound coastal tourism. The former appeals more to those interested in ecotourism and ethnic tourism and may also interest repeat international tourists who have already sampled the attractions of China's coastal regions and now are searching for "something different". No systematic study has yet been done of regional cross elasticities of tourist demand in China or cross elasticities of demand for visits to China (and countries competing with China for tourists) of the type which has been done for Europe (e.g., White, 1985).

As for inbound tourism to China's interior, depending upon the type of tourism and the tourist, it may exhibit

(a) some demand complementarity with coastal tourism or;
(b) some weak substitutability with it or;
(c) be virtually independent of the demand for coastal tourism.

In cases (a) or (c), the development of inland tourism would represent a win-win situation for China. Even in case (b) where some substitutability exists, the growth in tourism generally to China may result in both economic gains to the interior and the coast.

Statistics for domestic tourism in China are limited in availability. Therefore, this study for reasons of data availability has had to concentrate on international tourism. Nevertheless, from the data available it is evident that domestic tourism in China is spatially more dispersed than international tourism and is much less concentrated on the coastal region. Thus the pattern of its spatial distribution may be more akin to that suggested by the theory of Christaller (1963). In fact, as a general rule, it may be the case that domestic tourism is less urban-centric than international tourism and geographically more dispersed. Undoubtedly, the expansion of Chinese domestic tourism has assisted tourism development in China's inland considerably.

To a substantial extent, tourism in China's inland depends on ecotourism and associated cultural ethnic tourism, that is rather unique (Ricardian-type) attractions. A major challenge faced by the inland is how to preserve these attractions so as to provide a lasting basis for its tourist industry. A number of difficulties for sustaining ecotourism in Xishuangbanna were outlined, but these problems are unlikely to be limited to Xishuangbanna. Discussions of the nature of ecotourism and of problems in evaluating whether resources should be conserved and used for ecotourism provide a general setting for the case study of Yunnan.

Although not discussed to any great extent in this book, tourism and the general economic development of China along with improved communications and increased population mobility, are likely to make it increasingly difficult to preserve local ethnic or minority cultures. Just how China will deal with this issue remains to be seen. In some areas, preservation orders have been placed on buildings of local cultural importance but undoubtedly some of the local "culture" will become "canned", "contrived" or eroded to meet the needs of commercial tourism. Even without tourism, it is likely that many local cultural practices will disappear in a world of growing globalisation and increased standardisation. For the time-being, however, "inland" China retains its special eco-cultural attractions.

An interesting feature of the development of tourism in Yunnan province is the relative decentralisation of tourism there. While Kunming is the central and dominant tourism node in Yunnan, at least three other tourist nuclei exist — Dali, Lijiang, and Xishuangbanna. When natural and cultural attractions are spread out, as they are in Yunnan, they make for decentralisation of tourism at the provincial level provided adequate transport systems exist.

A number of regions in China, especially inland areas, have nominated tourism as a key industry or growth poles. Review of growth pole theory indicates that it provides little or no prediction of the spatial characteristics of industrial development. Even centre-periphery theory and related theories do not have their spatial implications well articulated and their descriptions of the dynamic processes involved in the development of a key industry or industrial complex are incomplete. In addition, these theories have to be modified to take account of the growth and spatial impacts of service-type industries, such as tourism. Thus further development of this theoretical area is needed if the spatial characteristics and dynamics of the development of growth poles and key industries and their economic impacts are to be specified.

Nevertheless, the capacity of the development of a key industry to stimulate economic growth in a region, or for an industry to act as a regional growth pole, can be determined to some extent by the use of input-output analysis, as considered in the previous chapter for regional tourism development. A limitation, however, of this approach is that it is purely oriented towards the supply-side. It can specify the supply-side impacts of expansion of a particular industry, such as tourism. But it does not inquire in itself about whether sufficient demand will eventuate to bring about expansion in a particular key industry, the ease with which demand for the output of a key industry can be expanded nor the extent to which a region has a comparative economic advantage in such an industry. From a policy point of view, these additional factors ought to be taken into account when deciding whether or not to support an industry as a growth pole. The evidence considered in the previous chapter does suggest that when all such factors are taken into account that tourism development in inland China, at least in Yunnan, has the capacity to act as regional growth pole. However, it is premature to apply the results obtained for Yunnan to other areas of China without detailed study of relevant information, although the possibility exist that other areas of inland China can also successfully develop tourism as a growth pole.

The heavy concentration of tourism on China's coastal areas and the higher economic gains of these areas from tourism compared to the inland mean that inland areas are less able to profit from their rich tourism resources. The efficiency of inland hotel operations is also lower, leaving these hotels even more disadvantaged than their coastal competitors. Thus, tourism development in China so far has not helped the rural and inland areas catch up with the more developed coastal areas. But encouragement of ecotourism and domestic tourism may supply enhanced opportunities for the interior.

Considerable debate exists about whether ecotourism is sustainable or whether it is just a label being used to sell tourism. As noted by Wight (1994), there is a tendency for terms to be prefixed with the term "eco" in order to increase interest and sales. It is imperative for ecotourism to encourage non-consumptive use of the environment and to promote ecological consciousness among tourists, tour operators and other parties involved, otherwise it may become just another way of accelerating resource deterioration in fragile natural areas, such as is happening due to some improper nature-tourism activities. Proper valuation of ecotourism resources therefore has to be completed before tourism development is permitted.

One of the debates about natural resources is how to determine the value of certain unpriced resources and how to determine the optimal level of conservation. Traditional economic analysis is not designed to measure the value of environmental goods which are characterised by non-marketable and non-use values. Ecotourism resource evaluation requires more careful study.

An important focus of this book has been the ability of the tourism industry to act as a key industry in China in order to moderate China's regional economic inequality. In addition, this book studied and measured the spatial distribution of tourism itself in China, and provided economic and other explanations for this distribution. It is however, premature to apply the results obtained for Yunnan to other areas of China without detailed study of relevant information, although the possibility exists that other areas of inland China may successfully develop tourism as a growth pole. Nevertheless, similar analyses can be undertaken for other regions and provinces.

11.3   Concluding Remarks

China's tourism industry has shown remarkable growth in the era of China's economic reforms. Development of international tourism to China initially achieved priority status because of its ability to earn foreign exchange and contribute to China's economic development. But for reasons discussed, this soon resulted in major expansion of China's domestic tourism industry. China is now amongst the top ten nations globally in terms of numbers of tourist arrivals and foreign exchange earnings.

However, it seems probable that the rate of growth of inbound tourist arrivals to China will now slow down. A decline occurred in 1998, but this was mainly due to special circumstances, the occurrence of the Asian financial crisis. Nevertheless, this event underlines the volatility of inbound tourism. A factor which to some extent may help to counteract the declining rate of growth of inbound tourism to China could be China's entry to World Trade Organisation (WTO). As a result, there should be greater scope for foreign travel and tourist agencies to operate in China and they may increasingly promote travel from overseas.

With rising incomes in China, demand by Chinese for domestic travel and travel abroad is likely to continue to expand rapidly. Presently around half of the Chinese population does not engage in any type of tourism annually. So a considerable residual remains to be tapped. China's number of outbound travellers are markedly fewer than its inbound travellers, and China maintains a significant surplus on its international tourism account. Most outbound travel from China is for official purposes rather than for private purposes, but the relative size of the latter is increasing and can be expected to increase even further in the future as China continues with its economic reforms, if incomes in China continue to rise and as foreign countries possibly exert more pressure on China to further liberalise possibilities for outbound travel by its citizens.

In the long-term, the further development of Chinese tourism industry will depend heavily on the maintenance of political stability in China and rising per capita income levels. With China's entry to World Trade Organisation (WTO) and further major changes to the public sector in China, including possible divestiture of state-owned enterprises and increased market competition underway, it is difficult to make a long-term prognosis for these variables. However, if the most optimistic scenario is accepted, these further changes will promote income growth in China and political stability (cf. Dong, 1998) and so be favourable to the further development of China's tourism industry.

Economic inequality in China has generally increased since China began its economic reforms in 1979. Economic activity has become even more skewed towards China's coastal areas since 1979 and overall regional economic inequality has risen. Substantial international tourism development in China has in fact exacerbated regional economic disparity to a certain extent. Both demand-side and supply-side indicators for China's international tourism industry support the hypothesis that the coastal region has, in comparison to the interior, gained most from the development of tourism in China.

There is no sign of regional convergence for the major economic variables in China. Indeed, the opposite may be the case: a slight trend to regional economic divergence seems to be occurring. The presence of tourism appears to make the economic gap between the coastal and inland areas greater than it otherwise would be. On the other hand, some convergence has been observed in the relative regional distribution of China's international tourism over the period 1986–1998. Declining Gini coefficients for major tourist indicators indicate a reduction in regional concentration of international tourism. The opening up of China, improvement of tourism facilities in the interior, new international entry points to China, improved hotel operations, and especially growth in ecotourism and domestic tourism, have all contributed to this trend.

The growth of tourism involves a complex set of socio-economic and policy issues. Tourism is an economic and social phenomenon due to both the economic impact of tourism and the interpersonal relations between the tourist and the producers of tourism services. Over-concentration on tourism development in limited areas, especially in relatively well-developed regions, within a destination country will inevitably lead to congestion, pollution, decreased tourist satisfaction and increase regional inequality. To solve the acute and widespread conflict between tourism and the environment, tourism has had to change from being a less than considerate consumer of environmental resources, towards conserving its resource base and reducing its negative environmental impacts. A long list of tourist activities and strategies designed to conserve resources has emerged since the 1970s. Ecotourism has become fashionable due to its proclaimed dual goals of generating profit and fostering conservation. But issues related to defining ecotourism and evaluating ecotourism resources remain to be carefully addressed. Sustainable tourism development has become a widely accepted objective also. The development of tourism in China is being increasingly influenced by such global objectives and hopes.

Tourism has the potential of becoming a key industry or growth pole in some areas of China, especially some interior localities in China where abundant tourist resources exist. Nevertheless, tourism development is not a panacea for economic growth and development. The economics of each situation needs to be individually assessed before drawing firm conclusions about the potential of tourism to act as a profitable key industry or growth pole in a region. Indiscriminate attempts to "kick-start" the development of tourism in some backward regions can even retard their economic development. While tourism has potential for Yunnan as a key industry and in all probability for some other inland provinces of China with an excellent tourism resource-base, not all inland provinces have the same attractions. This is why, although there is reason for optimism about tourism development prospects for several of the inland provinces, for example, Xinjiang and Inner Mongolia, one needs to be cautious in some cases, for example, possibly in the case of Qinghai. Nevertheless, the development of tourism is a relatively new adventure for China and represents a significant break with Maoist doctrine. On the whole, China's new wider vision cannot but fail in the long run to add to its economic development prospects and enhance the welfare of its people, especially if China can obtain an appropriate balance between economic growth and environmental conservation, a goal recognised China as important, as exemplified in its *Agenda 21* (State Council of the People's Republic of China, 1994).

Bibliography and References

Adelman, I. and Sunding, D. (1987) "Economic policy and income distribution in China", *Journal of Comparative Economics*, **11**: 444–461.

Alauddin, M. (1986) "Identification of key sectors in the Bangladesh economy: A linkage analysis approach", *Applied Economics*, **18**: 421–442.

Ali, S., Blakey, K. and Lewis, D. (1979) "Development of tourism in the Illawarrra: Economic effects and prospects", *Economic Research Bulletin No. 11*, Department of Economics, University of Wollongong, April 1979.

Alonso, W. (1980) "Five bell shapes in development", *Papers of the Regional Science Association*, **45**: 5–16.

Anon (1984) *Guangzhou Economic Yearbook*, Guangzhou People's Publishing House, Guangzhou.

Anon (1991) *China Daily*, 20 May 1991, Beijing.

Anon (1992a) *China Tourism News*, 1 December 1992, Beijing.

Anon (1992b) *Special Zones Herald*, 28 January 1992, Haikou.

Anon (1992c) "The overseas Chinese: A driving force", *The Economist*, **324**: 21–24.

Anon (1994) "Welcome to our country", *Adventure Travel Society*, Spring, 1994.

Anon (1995a) *CND* (Internet Chinese Magazine), 8 September 1995.

Anon (1995b) "20 National Parks in China", *China's Scholars Abroad*, No. 23, June 1995, Beijing.

Anon (1996a) *CND* (Internet Chinese Magazine), No. 275, 5 July 1996.

Anon (1996b) "West China enjoys preferential policies", *Beijing Review*, August 12–18, Beijing.

Archer, B. (1977) "Tourism multiplier: The state of the art", *Bangor Occasional Papers in Economics 11*, University of Wales Press, Cardiff.

Arrow, K. (1951) *Social Choice and Individual Values*, Wiley, New York.

Bailey, M. (1995) "China", *EIU International Tourism Reports No. 1*, The Economist Intelligence Unit Limited, London, pp. 19–37.

Baker, P. (1990) *Tourism and Protection of Natural Areas*, National Park Service, Washington, DC.

Beal, D. (1995) *The Determination of Socially Optimal Recreational Output and Entry Prices for National Parks in Southwestern Queensland*, PhD thesis, Department of Economics, The University of Queensland, Brisbane.

Becker, G.S. (1965) "A theory of the allocation of time", *Economic Journal*, **75**: 493–517.

Bell, D. (1973) *The Coming of the Post-Industrial Society: A Venture in Social Forecasting*, Basic Books, New York.

Bell, M. and Carr, R. (1994) "Japanese temporary residents in the Cains tourism industry", *Bureau of Immigration and Population Research*, AGPS, Canberra.

Bennett, J. (1991) "Introduction", in J. Bennett and W. Block (eds.) *Reconciling Economics and the Environment*, Australian Institute for Public Policy, West Perth, Australia, pp. 1–10.

Bennett, J. and Carter, M. (1993) "Prospects for contingent valuation: Lessons from the South-East forests", *Australian Journal of Agricultural Economics*, **37**(2): 79–93.

Berry, B.J. and Pred, A. (1975) "Central place studies — A bibliography of theory and applications", *Bibliographic Series No. 1*, Regional Science Research Institute.

Bhalla, A.S. and Ma, Y. (1990) "Sectoral interdependence in the Chinese economy in comparative perspective", *Applied Economics*, **22**: 1063–1081.

Bingham, A. (1993) "China's phenomenal growth has environmental price tag", *Pollution Prevention*, **1**(4): 10–14.

Bishop, R. (1982) "Option value: An exposition and extension", *Land Economics*, **51**(1): 1–15.

Blane, J.M. and Jackson, R. (1994) "The impact of ecotourism boats on the St. Lawrence Beluga Whales", *Environmental Conservation*, **21**(3): 267–269.

Bloomquist, L.E. (1990) "Labour market characteristics and the occupational concentration of different sociodemographic groups", *Rural Sociology*, **55**(2): 199–213.

Bockstael, N., McConnell, K. and Strand, I. (1991) "Recreation", in J. Braden and C. Kolstad (eds.) *Measuring the Demand for Environmental Quality*, Elsevier, Amsterdam.

Boo, E. (1990) *Ecotourism: The Potentials and Pitfalls*, WFF, Washington, DC.

Boo, E. (1991) "Pitfalls and liabilities of eco-tourism development", in *Proceedings of the 1991 World Congress on Adventure Travel and Eco-tourism,* The Adventure Travel Society Inc., Engelwood, Colorado, pp. 145–149.

Boorstin, D.J. (1973) *The Image: A Guide to Pseudo-Events in America*, Atheneum, New York.

Borcherding, T.E. (1991) "National resources and transgenerational equity", in J. Bennett and W. Block (eds.) *Reconciling Economics and the Environment*, Australian Institute for Public Policy, West Perth, Australia, pp. 97–114.

Borcherding, T.E., Pommerehne, W.W. and Scheider, F. (1982) "Comparing the efficiency of private and public production: A survey of the evidence from five countries", *Zeitschrift-für-Nationalo Ekonomie*, Supplement 2: 127–156.

Borts, G. (1960) "The equalisation of returns and regional growth", *American Economic Review*, **50**(3): 319–347.

Bosselman, F.P. (1978) *In the Wake of the Tourist: Managing Special Places in Eight Countries,* The Conservation Foundation, Washington, DC.

Botterill, D. (1989) "Humanistic tourism? Personal constructions of a tourist: Sam visits Japan", *Leisure Studies*: **8**(3): 281–293.

Boulding, K.E. (1966) "The economics of the coming spaceship earth", in H. Jarrett (ed.) *Environmental Quality in a Growing Economy*, Johns Hopkins University Press, Baltimore, pp. 3–14.

Braford, D.F. (1970) "Cost-benefit analysis and the demand for public goods", *Kyklos*, **23**: 775–791.

Braun, D. (1988) "Multiple measurements of US income inequality", *Review of Economics and Statistics*, **70**(3): 398–405.

Braun, D. (1991) "Income inequality and economic development: Geographic divergence", *Social Science Quarterly*, **72**: 520–536.

Briassoulis, H. (1991) "Methodological issues: Tourism input-output analysis", *Annuals of Tourism Research*, **18**: 485–495.

Britton, R. (1979) "Some notes on the geography of tourism", *The Canadian Geographer*, **23**(3): 276–82.

Britton, S.G. (1982) "The political economy of tourism in the third world", *Annals of Tourism Research,* **9**: 331–358.

Brock, R.E. (1994) "Beyond fisheries enhancement — Artificial reefs and econotourism", *Bulletin of Marine Science*, **55**: 1181–1188.

Brohman, J. (1996) "New directions in tourism for third world development", *Annals of Tourism Research,* **23**(1): 48–70.

Bronfenbrenner, M. (1971) *Income Distribution Theory,* Aldine and Atherton, Chicago.

Brown, R.J. (1975) *Student Economics,* 6th edition, William Brooks, Sydney.

Brown, T.C. (1984) "The concept of value in resource allocation", *Land Economics,* **60**(3): 231–246.

Brown, W.G. and Nawas, F.W. (1973) "Impact of aggregation on the estimation of outdoor recreation demand functions", *American Journal of Agricultural Economics,* **55**(2): 246–249.

Bryden, J.M. (1973) *Tourism and Development: A Case Study of the Commonwealth Caribbean,* Cambridge University Press, Cambridge.

Budowski, G. (1976) "Tourism and conservation: Conflict, coexistence or symbiosis", *Environmental Conservation,* **3**: 27–31.

Budowski, G. (1982) "The socio-economic effects of forest management on the lives of people living in the area: The case of Central America and some Caribbean Countries", in E.G. Hallsworth (ed.) *Socio-Economic Effects and Constraints in Tropical Forest Management,* John Wiley, New York.

Bull, A. (1995) *The Economics of Travel and Tourism,* Longman, Melbourne.

Bureau of Tourism Research (1994) *Domestic Tourism Monitor,* December Quarter 1993, Bureau of Tourism Research, Canberra.

Burkart, A.J. and Medlik, S. (1981*) Tourism Past, Present, and Future,* 2nd edition, Heinemann, London.

Butler, R.W. (1980) "The concept of a tourist area life cycle of evolution and implications for management", *The Canadian Geographer,* **24**: 5–12.

Butler, R.W. (1991) "Tourism, environment, and sustainable development", *Environmental Conservation,* **18**(3): 201–209.

Butler, R.W. (1993) "Tourism: An evolutionary perspective", in J.G. Nelson, R. Butler and G. Wall (eds.) *Tourism and Sustainable Development: Monitoring, Planning, Managing,* Heritage Resources Centre, University of Waterloo, Waterloo, pp. 27–44.

Butler, R.W. and Waldbook, L. (1991) "New planning tourism: The tourism opportunity spectrum", *The Journal of Tourism Studies,* **2**(1): 2–14.

Cameron, T.A. (1992) "Combining contingent valuation and travel cost data for the valuation of nonmarket goods", *Land Economics*, **68**(3): 302–317.

Cater, E. and Lowman, L. (1994) *Ecotourism — A Sustainable Option?* Royal Geographical Society and Belhaven Press, London.

Ceballos Lascurain, H. (1992) "Tourists for conservation", *People and the Planet*, **1**(3): 28–30.

Cesario, F.J. and Knetsch, J.L. (1970) "The time bias in recreation benefit estimates", *Water Resources Research*, **6**(3): 700–704.

Chai, J.C.H. (1994) "East-west regional income gap: Problems of divergent regional development in the People's Republic of China", in Cassel, D. and Herrmann-Pillath, C. (eds) *The East, the West, and China's Growth: Challenge and Response: Contributions to the 1994 Duisburg Symposium on "Greater China"*, Nomos Verlagsgesellschaft, Baden-Baden, pp. 93–108.

Chen, J. and Fleisher, B. (1996) "Regional income inequality and economic growth in China", *Journal of Comparative Economics*, **22**: 141–164.

Chen, Jiyuan (1989) "China's transfer of the surplus agricultural labour force", in J. Longworth (ed.) *China's Rural Development Miracle with International Comparisons*, University of Queensland Press, Brisbane, pp. 210–220.

Chenery, H.B. (1961) "Comparative advantage and development policy", *American Economic Review*, **51**: 18–51.

Cheng, E. (1990) "Ill-starred venture", *Far Eastern Economic Review*, **148** April 26: 54.

Choy, D. (1992) "Life cycle models for Pacific Island destinations", *Journal of Travel Research*, **30**(3): 26–31.

Christaller, W. (1963) "Some considerations of tourism location in Europe: The peripheral regions — underdeveloped countries — recreation areas", *Papers of Regional Science Association*, **12**: 95–105.

Christaller, W. (1966) *Central Places in Southern Germany*, translated by C. Baskin, Prentice-Hall, New Jersey.

Clark, A.N. (1985) *Longman Dictionary of Geography, Human and Physical*, Longman.

Clark, C. (1957) *The Conditions of Economic Progress*, 3rd edition, Macmillan, London.

Clarke, H. and Ng, Y.K. (1993) "Tourism, economic welfare and efficient pricing", *Annals of Tourism Research*, **20**: 613–632.

Clarke, H., Dwyer, L. and Forsyth, P. (1995) "Economic instruments and the control of tourism's environmental impacts", in R. Shaw (ed.) *Proceedings of the National Tourism Conference 1995*, Centre for Hospitality and Tourism Research, Victoria University, Melbourne, pp. 159–176.

Clawson, M. (1959) "Methods for measuring the demand for outdoor recreation", *Resources for the Future*, Reprint No. 10, Washington DC.

Clawson, M. and Knetsch, J. (1966) *Economics of Outdoor Recreation*, John Hopkins University, Baltimore.

Coase, R. (1960) "The problem of social cost", *Journal of Law and Economics*, **3**: 1–44.

Cohen, E. (1972) "Toward a sociology of international tourism", *Social Research*, **39**(1): 164–182.

Cohen, E. (1987) "Alternative tourism: A critique", *Tourism Recreation Research*, **12**(2): 13–18.

Commonwealth Department of Tourism (1994) *National Ecotourism Strategy*, Australian Government Publishing Service, Canberra.

Copeland, B. (1990) *"Taxing Tourists: Optimal Commodity Consumption and Public Goods Provision in the Presence of International Tourism"*, *Research Paper 1*, Department of Economics, University of Alberta, Canada.

Cummings, R.R., Brookshire, D.S., and Schulze, W.D. (1986) *Valuing Environmental Goods: An Assessment of the "Contingent Valuation Method"*, Rowman Allanheld, Totowa.

Currie, J.M., Murphy, J.A. and Schmitz, A. (1971) "The concept of economic surplus and its use in economic analysis", *Economic Journal*, **81**(324): 741–799.

Dai, Yuanchen. (1992) "Can plan and market coexist in a socialist economy?", *Chinese Economic Studies*, **25**(4): 60–78.

Daly, H. (1968) "On economics as a life science", *Journal of Political Economy*, **76**: 392–406.

Daly, H. and Cobb, J. (1989) *For the Common Good: Redirecting the Economy toward Community, the Environment, and a Sustainable Future*, Beacon Press, Boston.

Dann, G. (1981) "Tourism motivation and appraisal", *Annals of Tourism Research*, **9**(2): 187–219.

Davis, D. and Tisdell, C. (1995) "Recreational scuba-diving and carrying capacity in marine protected areas", *Ocean & Coastal Management*, **26**(1): 19–40.

Davis, D. and Tisdell, C. (1996) "Economic management of recreational scuba diving and the environment", *Journal of Environmental Management*, **48**: 229–248.

Davis, H. (1968) "Potentials for tourism in developing countries", *Finance and Development*, **5**(4): 34–39.

Davis, H.T. (1941) *The Analysis of Economic Time Series*, Principia Press, Bloomington, Indiana.

Davis, R.F. (1963) "Recreational planning as an economic problem", *Natural Resources Journal*, **3**: 239–249.

de Kadt, E. (ed.) (1979) *Tourism — Passport to Development?*, Oxford University Press, New York.

Deng, Yongjin (1996) "An analysis of Yunnan tourism", in L. Mingyi (ed.) *Tourism Economic Research*, Yunnan University Press, Kunming.

Diamond, J. (1977) "Tourism's role in economic development: The case reexamined", *Economic Development and Cultural Change*, **25**: 539–553.

Dieke, P. (1991) "Policies for tourism development in Kenya", *Annals of Tourism Research*, **18**: 269–294.

Dixon, J. and Hufschmidt, M. (1986) *Economic Solution Techniques for the Environment: A Case Study Workbook*, Johns Hopkins University Press.

Dixon, J. and Sherman, P. (1990) *Economics of Protected Areas, A New Look at the Benefits and Costs,* Earthscan, London.

Doeleman, J. and Watson, M. (1988) "Marine pollution and tourism with reference to Indonesia and Australia", in C. Tisdell, C. Aislabie, P. Stanton (eds.) *Economics of Tourism: Case Study and Analysis,* the Institute of Industrial Economics, University of Newcastle, pp. 299–320.

Dowling, R. (1992) "The ecoethics of tourism: Guidelines for developers, operators and tourists", *Ecotourism 1991 Conference Papers*, Bureau of Tourism Research, Canberra.

Dowrick, S. and Nguyen, D.T. (1989) "OECD comparative economic growth 1950–1985: Catch-up and convergence", *American Economic Review*, **79**(5): 1010–1030.

Drakakis-Smith, D. (1980) *Urbanisation, Housing, and the Development Process*, St. Martin's Press, New York.

Driml, S. (1987) *Economic Impacts of Activities on the Great Barrier Reef*, Great Barrier Reef Marine Park Authority, Townsville.

Driml, S. (1994) *Protection for Profit: Economic and Financial Values of the Great Barrier Reef World Heritage Area and other Protected Areas, Research Publication No. 35*, Great Barrier Reef Marine Park Authority, Townsville.

Duncan, R. and Huang, Y. (1998) *Reform of State-Owned Enterprises in China: Autonomy, Incentive and Competition*, Asia Pacific Press, Australian National University, Canberra.

Durst, P. and Ingram, C. (1988) "Nature-oriented tourism promotion by developing countries", *Tourism Management*, **26**: 39–43.

Dwyer, L. (1986) "Tourism", *Islands/Australia Working Paper No. 86/3*, National Centre for Development Studies, Australian National University, Canberra.

Eadington, W.R. and Redman, M. (1991) "Economics and tourism", *Annals of Tourism Research*, **18**(1): 41–56.

Eagles, P. (1992) "The travel motivations of Canadian ecotourists", *Journal of Travel Research*, **31**(2): 3–13.

Earle, B.H. (1991) "China after Tiananmen Square: An assessment of its business environment", *Case Western Reserve Journal of International Law*, **23**: 421–445.

EIU (1992) *The Tourism Industry and the Environment*, EIU Publications, London.

Elliot, R. and Gare, A. (1983) *Environmental Philosophy*, University of Queensland Press, Brisbane.

Etzioni, A. (1988) *The Moral Dimension: Towards a New Economics*, Free Press, New York.

European Community (1990) *Annual Report on the Implementation of the Reform of the Structural Funds 1989*, Com (90) 516, European Commission, Brussels.

Fan, C. and Casetti, E. (1994) "The spatial and temporal dynamics of US regional income inequality, 1950–1989", *Annals of Regional Science*, **28**(2): 177–196.

Fishbein, M. and Azjen, A. (1975) *Belief, Attitude, Intention and Behaviour: An Introduction to Theory and Research*, Addison-Wesley, Reading.

Fisher, A.C. and Hanemann, W.M. (1987) "Quasi option value: Some misconceptions dispelled", *Journal of Environmental Economics and Management*, **14**: 183–190.

Fletcher, J. (1989) "Input-output analysis and tourism impacts studies", *Annals of Tourism Research*, **16**(4): 514–529.

Forster, B. (1989) "Valuing outdoor recreational activity: A methodological survey", *Journal of Leisure Research*, **21**(2): 181–201.

Frank, A.G. (1978) *Dependent Accumulation and Underdevelopment*, Macmillan, London.

Freeman, A. (1984) "The sign and size of option value", *Land Economics*, **60**(1): 1–13.

Freeman, A. (1986) "On assessing the state of the arts of the contingent valuation methods of valuing environmental changes", in R.R. Cummings, D.S. Brookshire and W.D. Schulze (eds.) *Valuing Environmental Goods: An Assessment of the "Contingent Valuation Method"*, Rowman Allanheld, Totowa.

Friedman, J., Hakim, S. and Weinblatt, J. (1989) "Casino gambling as a "growth pole" strategy and its effect on crime", *Journal of Regional Science*, **29**(4): 615–623.

Friedmann, J. (1966) *Regional Development Policy: A Case Study of Venezuela*, MIT Press, Cambridge.

Friedmann, J. (1985) "Political and technical moments in planning: Agropolitan development revisited", in *Environment and Planning Development: Society and Space*, Vol. 3, pp. 155–167.

Fritzell, J. (1993) "Income inequality trends in the 1980s: A five-country comparison", *Acta Sociologica*, **36**: 47–62.

Furnham, A. (1984) "Tourism and culture shock", *Annals of Tourism Research*, **11**: 41–57.

Gamage, A. (1995) "Differential multipliers for tourism in Victoria", in R. Shaw (ed.) *Proceedings of the National Tourism and Hospitality Conference 1995*, Melbourne, pp. 211–215.

Gauthier, D. (1993) "Sustainable development, tourism and wildlife", in J.G. Nelson, R. Butler and G. Wall (eds.) *Tourism and Sustainable Development: Monitoring, Planning, Managing*, University of Waterloo, Waterloo, pp. 97–109.

Getz, D. (1987) "Tourism planning and research: Traditions, models and futures", paper presented at *The Australian Travel Research Workshop*, Bunbury, Western Australia, November 5–6.

Getz, D. (1992) "Tourism planning and the destination life cycle", *Annals of Tourism Research*, **19**(4): 752–770.

Ghuman, B.S. and Kaur, D. (1993) "Regional variations in growth and inequality in the living standard: The Indian experience", *Margin,* **25**(3): 306–313.

Gillespie, A.E. and Green, A.E. (1987) "The changing geography of producer services employment in Britain", *Regional Studies,* **21**(5): 297–411.

Gladney, Dru C. (1994) "Ethnic identity in China: The new politics of difference", in J. William (ed.) *China Briefing*, Westview Press, Boulder, pp. 171–192.

Gormsen, E. (1990) "The impact of tourism on regional change in China", *Geojournal,* **21**(1–2): 127–135.

Gormsen, E. (1995) "Travel behaviour and the impacts of domestic tourism in China", in A. Lew and L. Yu (eds.) *Tourism in China: Geographic, Political, and Economic Perspectives,* Westview Press, pp. 131–140.

Gowdy, J. (1994a) "Natural capital and the growth economy", *Sustainable Development,* **2**(1): 12–16.

Gowdy, J. (1994b) *Coevolutionary Economics: The Economy, Society and the Environment*, Kluwer Academic Publishers, Boston.

Gray, J. (1987) *The Psychology of Fear*, Cambridge University Press, New York.

Gray, P. (1970) *International Travel-International Trade*, D.C. Heath and Co., Lexington, Massachusetts.

Gruenstein, J.M.L. and Guerra, S. (1981) "Can services sustain a regional economy?" *Business Review*, July/August: 15–27.

Gunaratne, L. (1988) *Human Capital and Distribution of Personal Income, A Theoretical Analysis and an Examination of Some Aspects of Income Distribution in Sri Lanka*, Central Bank of Sri Lanka, Colombo.

Gunn, C.A. (1988) *Tourism Planning,* 2nd edition, Taylor & Francis, New York.

Gunn, C.A. (1994) *Tourism Planning: Basics, Concepts, Cases*, Taylor & Francis, New York.

Hall, C.M. (1992) *Hallmark Tourist Events: Impacts, Management and Planning,* Belhaven, London.

Hall, C.M. (1994) *Tourism in the Pacific Rim, Development, Impacts, and Markets,* Longman Cheshire, Melbourne.

Hall, C.M. (1995) *Introduction to Tourism in Australia — Impacts, Planning and Development,* Longman, Melbourne.

Hall, C.M. and Jenkins, J.M. (1995) *Tourism and Public Policy,* Routledge, New York.

Hall, C.M. and Weiller, B. (1992) *Special Interest Tourism,* John Wiley and Sons, New York.

Hamilton, A. (1990) "The enchanted nightmare", *The Guardian,* 10 August: 21.

Hanemann, W.M. (1991) "Willingness to pay and willingness to accept: How much can they differ?", *American Economic Review,* **81**(3): 633–647.

Hanley, N. and Spash, C. (1993) *Cost-Benefit Analysis and the Environment,* Edward Elgar, Aldershot, United Kingdom.

Hanley, N.D. (1989) "Valuing rural recreation benefits: An empirical comparison of two approaches", *Journal of Agricultural Economics,* **40**(3): 361–74.

Hannigan, K. (1994) "A regional analysis of tourism growth in Ireland", *Regional Studies,* **28**(2): 308–214.

Hardin, G. (1968) "Tragedy of the commons", *Science,* **162**(3859): 1243–1248.

Hare, D. (1994) "Rural non-agricultural activities and their impact on the distribution of income: Evidence from farm households in Southern China", *China Economic Review,* **5**(1): 59–82.

Harrison, A. and Stabler, M. (1981) "An analysis of journeys for canal-based recreation", *Regional Studies,* **15**(5): 345–58.

Harrison, D. (1992) *Tourism in Less Developed Countries,* Halsted Press, New York.

Hartman, R. and Plummer, M. (1987) "Option value under income and price uncertainty", *Journal of Environmental Economics and Management,* **14**(3): 212–225.

Haynes, K. and Dignan, T. (1988) "Evaluating capital grants for regional development", in B. Higgins and D. Savoie (eds.) *Regional Economic Development, Essays in Honour of Francis Perroux,* Unwin Hyman, London, pp. 330–374.

Haywood, K. (1986) "Can the tourist-area life cycle be made operational", *Tourism Management,* **7**: 154–167.

Haywood, M. (1988) "Responsible and responsive tourism planning in the community", *Tourism Management*, **9**(2): 105–118.

Heeley, J. (1981) "Planning for tourism in Britain", *Town Planning Review*, **52**: 61–79.

Hermansen, T. (1972) "Development poles and development centers in national and regional development", in A. Kuklinske (ed.) *Growth Poles and Growth Centers in Regional Planning*, Mouton and Co, Paris, pp. 1–68.

Hiemstra, S. and Ismail, J. (1993) "Incidence of the impacts of room taxes on the lodging industry", *Journal of Travel Research*, **31**(4): 22–26.

Higgins, B. (1988) "Regional development and efficiency of the national economy" in B. Higgins and D. Savoie (eds.) *Regional Economic Development, Essays in Honour of Francis Perroux*, Unwin Hyman, London, pp. 193–224.

Higgins, B. and Savoie, D. (1988) "Introduction: The economics and politics and development" in B. Higgins and D. Savoie (eds.) *Regional Economic Development, Essays in Honour of Francis Perroux*, Unwin Hyman, London, pp. 1–27.

Hill, C. (1990) "The paradox of tourism in Costa Rica", *Cultural Survival Quarterly*, **14**(1): 14–19.

Hill, R. (1994) "Con or conservation", *The Bulletin,* 7 June, No. 37.

Hills, T. and Lundgren, J. (1977) "The impact of tourism in the Caribbean: A methodological study", *Annals of Tourism Research*, **4**(5): 248–267.

Hirschman, A. (1958) *The Strategy of Economic Development*, Yale University Press, New Haven.

Hiscock, G. (1995) "Trade forum puts spotlight on Shanghai", *The Australian*, 5 September 1995.

Hockings, M. (1995) "A survey of the tour operator's role in marine park interpretation", *Journal of Tourism Studies*, **5**(1): 16–28.

Hodgson, G. and Dixon, J. (1988) *"Logging Versus Fisheries and Tourism in Palawan, Occasional Paper 7*, Honolulu, Hawaii, East-West Environment and Policy Institute.

Hohl, A. and Tisdell, C. (1993) *Resource-Use Conflicts Related to Environmental Conservation and Ethical Stances in Contemporary Economic Thought*, Department of Economics Discussion Papers No. 116, The University of Queensland, Brisbane.

Hohl, A. and Tisdell, C. (1995) "Peripheral tourism: Development and management", *Annals of Tourism Research*, **22**(3): 517–534.

Holloway, C. (1981) "The guided tour: A sociological approach", *Annals of Tourism Research*, **8**(3): 377–402.

Honjo, M. (1978) "Trends in development planning in Japan", in F.-C. Lo and K. Salih (eds.) *Growth Pole Strategy and Regional Development Policy: Asian Experience and Alternative Approaches*, Pergamon Press, New York, pp. 3–24.

Horneman, L. (1994) *Ecotourism: Its Structure, Growth and Future*, Bachelor of Business Honours thesis, The University of Queensland, Gatton College, Lawes.

Hu, Angang (1995) "Te bie guan cha — guan zhu zhong xi bu min zu di qu, cha ju dao di you duo da?" (Special Observation — Concentration on the Minority Areas in the Central West, Just How Big Are the Disparities?), *Min zu tuan jie (Ethnic Unity)*, No. 294 (10 November, Beijing): 32–36.

Hu, Zhengqing (1989) *China's Open Policy-Investment, Trade and Economic Cooperation*, Chengdu University of Science and Technology, Chengdu.

Huang, Y., Cai, F. and Duncan, R. (1998) "Reforms of the state-owned enterprises in China: Key measures and policy debate", in *Reform of State-Owned Enterprises in China: Autonomy, Incentive and Competition*, NCDS Asia Pacific Press, Australian National University, Canberra, pp. 1–36.

Hudson, S. (1996) "The 'greening' of ski resorts: A necessity for sustainable tourism, or a marketing opportunity for skiing communities", *Journal of Vacation Marketing*, **2**(2): 176–185.

Hufschmidt, M., James, D., Meister, A., Bower, B. and Dixon, J. (1983) *Environment, Natural Systems, and Development: An Economic Valuation Guide*, The Johns Hopkins University Press, Baltimore.

Hughes, D. and Holland, D. (1994) "Core-periphery economic linkage: A measure of spread and possible backwash effects for the Washington economy", *Land Economics*, **70**(3): 364–377.

Ikemoto, Y. and Limskul, K. (1987) "Income inequality and regional disparity in Thailand, 1962–1981", *Developing Economies*, **25**(3): 249–269.

Information Office of the State Council of China (1996) *Environmental Protection in China*, Beijing.

Inglehart, R. (1990) *Culture Shift in Advanced Industrial Society*, Princeton University Press, Princeton, New Jersey.

Ingram, C. and Durst, P. (1989) "Nature-oriented tour operators: Travel to developing countries", *Journal of Travel Research*, **28**(2): 11–15.

Ioannides, D. (1995) "A flawed implementation of sustainable tourism: The experience of Akamas, Cyprus", *Tourism Management*, **16**(8): 583–592.

Iso-Ahola, S. (1982) "Toward a social psychological theory of tourism motivation: A rejoinder", *Annals of Tourism Research*, **9**(2): 256–262.

IUCN (1980) *World Conservation Strategy: Living Resource Conservation for Sustainable Development*, IUCN, Gland.

Jackson, S. (1992) *Chinese Enterprise Management Reforms in Economic Perspective*, Walter de Gruyter, Boston.

Jacobson, S.K. and Lopez, A.F. (1994) "Biological impacts of ecotourism — Tourists and nesting turtles in Tortuguero National Park, Costa Rica", *Wildlife Society Bulletin*, **22**(3): 414–419.

Jafari, J. (1990) "Research and scholarship: The basis of tourism education", *The Journal of Tourism Studies*, **1**(1): 33–41.

Janson-Verbeke, M. (1991) "Tourism in Europe in the eve of 1992", *Annals of Tourism Research*, **18**: 529–533.

Jantsch, E. (1973) "Forecasting and systems approach: A frame of reference", *Management Science,* **19**(12): 1355–1369.

Jenner, P. and Smith, C. (1992) *The Tourism Industry and the Environment*, EIU Special Report No. 2453.

Jensen, R., West, G. and Hewings, G. (1988) "The study of regional structure using input-output table", *Regional Studies*, **22**: 209–220.

Jia, Liqun and Tisdell, C. (1996) "Resource redistribution and regional income inequality in China", *Asian Economies*, **25**(2): 48–72.

Jian, T.L., Sachs, J. and Warner, A. (1996) "Trends in regional inequality in China", *China Economic Review*, **7**(1): 1–21.

Johnson, E.A. (1970) *The Organisation of Space in Developing Countries*, Harvard Press, Cambridge.

Jones, A. (1987) "Green tourism", *Tourism Management*, **26**: 254–256.

Jones, G.W. (1991) "Urbanisation issues in the Asian-Pacific region", *Asian-Pacific Economic Literature*, **5**(2): 5–33.

Kahn, H. and Wiener, A.J. (1967) *The Year 2000*, Macmillan, New York.

Kakwani, N.C. (1980) *Income Inequality and Poverty, Methods of Estimation and Policy Applications,* Oxford University Press, Oxford.

Kakwani, N.C. and Podder, N. (1976) "Efficient estimation of the Lorenz Curve and associated inequality measures from grouped observations", *Econometrica,* **44**(1): 137–148.

Kaldor, N. (1955) "Alternative theories of distribution", *Review of Economic Studies,* **23**(2): 83–100.

Kallen, C. (1990) "Nature tourism: The light at the end of the terminal", *E Magazine,* July/August.

Kapp, K.W. (1950) *The Social Cost of Private Enterprise,* Cambridge University Press, Cambridge.

Kariel, H.G. (1989) "Tourism and development: Perplexity or panacea?", *Journal of Travel Research,* **28**(1): 2–6.

Kassab, C. (1992) *Income and Inequality, The Role of the Service Sector in the Changing Distribution of Income,* Contributions in Economics and Economic History, No. 133, Greenwood Press, New York.

Keller, C. (1987) "Stages of peripheral tourism development — Canada's north west territories", *Tourism Management,* **3**: 20–32.

Kelly, I. and Dixon, W. (1991) "Sideline tourism", *The Journal of Tourism Studies,* **2**(1): 21–28.

Khan, A.R., Griffin, K., Riskin, C. and Zhao, Renwei. (1993) "Sources of income inequality in post-reform China", *China Economic Review,* **4**(1): 19–35.

Klee, G.A. (1980) *World Systems of Traditional Resource Management,* Edward Arnold, London.

Knapman, B. (1991) "Tourism in the Northern Territory economy", in P. Carroll *et al.* (eds.) *Tourism in Australia,* Harcourt Brace Jovanovich, Sydney, pp. 240–258.

Kneese, A.V. (1984) *Measuring the Benefits of Clearer Air and Water,* Resources for the Future, Washington, DC.

Knight, J. and Song, L. (1993) "The spatial contribution to income inequality in rural China", *Cambridge Journal of Economics,* **17**(2): 195–213.

Kornai, J. (1999) "Reforming the welfare state in postsocialist economies", in A.N. Brown (ed.) *When is the Transition Over?,* W.E. Upjohn Institute for Employment Research, Kalamazoo, Michigan, pp. 99–113.

Korten, D.C. (1984) "People-centered development: Toward a framework", in D.C. Korten and R. Klauss (eds.) *People Centered Development, Contributions toward Theory and Planning Frameworks*, Kumarian Press, Connecticut, USA, pp. 299–309.

Kou, Zhengling (1996) "An ancient city embraces the modern world", *Beijing Review*, 23–29 December 1996.

Krippendorf, J. (1982) "Towards new tourism policies: The importance of environment and sociocultural factors", *Tourism Management*, **3**(3): 135–148.

Krutilla, J. (1967) "Conservation reconsidered", *American Economic Review*, **57**(4): 777–786.

Krutilla, J.V. and Cicchetti, C.J. (1972) "Evaluation benefits of environmental resources with special application to the Hells Canyon", *Natural Resources Journal*, **12**(1): 1–29.

Kula, E. (1992) *Economics of Natural Resources and the Environment*, Chapman & Hall, London.

Kundu, A. (1975) "Measuring inequality: A critique of the Gini Coefficient", *Journal of Social and Economic Studies*, **3**(1): 119–127.

Kuznets, S. (1955) "Economic growth and income inequality", *American Economic Review*, **45**: 1–28.

Lampton, D. (1983) "Interprovincial inequalities in education and health services in China", in D. Nelson (ed.) *Communism and the Policies of Inequalities*, Lexington, Massachusetts, pp. 131–164.

Lancaster, K.J. (1966) "A new approach to consumer theory", *Journal of Political Economy*, **74**: 132–157.

Lardy, N. (1978) *Economic Growth and Income Distribution in the People's Republic of China*, Cambridge University Press.

Lardy, N.R. (1999) "China's unfinished economic transition", in A.N. Brown (ed.) *When is Transition Over?*, W.E. Upjohn Institute for Employment Research, Kalamazoo, Michigan, pp. 69–76.

Lea, J. (1988) *Tourism and Development in the Third World*, Routledge, London.

Leibenstein, H. (1986) *Entrepreneurship, Entrepreneurial Training, and X-Efficiency Theory*, Harvard Institute of Economic Research, Cambridge.

Leontief, W. (1952) *The Structure of the American Economy*, 2nd edition, Oxford University Press, Oxford.

Leopold, A. (1966) *A Sand Country Almanac: With Other Essays on Conservation from Round River,* Oxford University Press, New York.

Lew, A. (1995) "Overseas Chinese and compatriots in China's tourism", in A. Lew and L. Yu (eds.) *Tourism in China: Geographic, Political, and Economic Perspectives,* Westview Press, pp. 155–178.

Lewis, A.W. (1965) *The Theory of Economic Growth,* Allen & Unwin, London.

Lewis, J. and Williams, A. (1988) "Portugal: Market segmentation and regional specialisation", in A. Williams and G. Shaw (eds.) *Tourism and Economic Development: Western European Experiences,* Pinter, Belhaven Press, London and New York, pp. 101–122.

Li, Guanliang (1996) "Shanghai is on the road to the new century", a speech made at the *Shanghai–Queensland Business Forum,* June 1996, Brisbane.

Lickorish, L. (1987) "Trends in industrialised countries", *Tourism Management,* **8**(2): 92–95.

Lin, T.B. and Sung, Y.W. (1984) "Tourism and the economic diversification in Hong Kong", *Annals of Tourism Research,* **11**(1): 231–247.

Lindberg, K. (1991) *Policies for Maximising Nature Tourism's Ecological and Economic Benefits,* World Resources Institute, Washington, DC.

Lindberg, K., Enriquez, J. and Sproule, K. (1996) "Ecotourism questioned: Case studies from Belize", *Annals of Tourism Research,* **23**(3): 543–562.

Lindberg, K., Goulding, C., Huang, Z., Mo, J., Wei, P. and Kong, G. (1997) "Ecotourism in China: Selected issues and challenges", in M. Oppermann (ed.) *Pacific Rim Tourism,* CAB International, Oxford, United Kingdom, pp. 128–143.

Lindberg, K., McCool, S. and Stankey, G. (1997) "Rethinking carrying capacity", *Annals of Tourism Research,* **24**(2): 461–465.

Little, I. and Mirrlees, J.A. (1974) *Project Appraisal and Planning for Developing Countries,* Heinemann Educational Books, London.

Liu, Guoguang, Liang, Wensen (1987) *China's Economy in 2000,* New World Press, Beijing.

Liu, J., Var, T. and Timur, A. (1984) "Tourist income multipliers for Turkey", *Tourism Management,* **5**(4): 280–287.

Liu, Jihan and Dowling, R. (1992) "Integrating tourism development and environmental conservation in China", in B. Weiler (ed.) *Ecotourism:*

Incorporating the Global Classroom, Bureau of Tourism Statistics, Canberra, pp. 148–155.

Liu, W. and Yang, Y. (1989) *Resource Utilisation and Economic Reform*, China Finance Publishing House, Beijing.

Liu, W. and Zhang, J. (1987) *Micro, Medium and Macro Analysis of Socialist Economy*, China International Broadcasting Publishing House, Beijing.

Liu, Z.H. (1998) "Tourism and economic development: A comparative analysis of tourism in developed and developing countries", in C. Tisdell and K.C. Roy (eds.) *Tourism and Development: Economic, Social, Political and Environmental Issues*, Nova Science Publishers, Commack, New York, pp. 21–37.

Lo, Fuchen and Salih, K. (1978) *Growth Pole Strategy and Regional Development Policy: Asian Experiences and Alternative Approaches*, Oxford University Press.

Longworth, J. and Williamson, G. (1993) *China's Pastoral Region, Sheep and Wool, Minority Nationalities, Rangeland Degradation and Sustainable Development*, CAB International, Oxford.

Lorenz, M. (1905) "Methods of measuring the concentration of wealth", *American Statistical Association*, **9**(70): 209–219.

Luloff, A, Bridges, J., Graefe, A., Salor, M., Martin, K. and Gitelson, R. (1994) "Assessing rural tourism efforts in the United States", *Annals of Tourism Research*, **21**(1): 46–64.

Luo Mingyi (1994) *Contemporary Economics of Tourism*, Yunnan University Publishing House, Kunming.

Luo, Mingyi (1996) "On development of Yunnan tourism, the new leading industry", in Lou, Mingyi (ed.) *Tourism Economic Research*, Yunnan University Press, Kunming, pp. 22–29.

Lyman, S.M. (1974), "Chinese Americans", in P. Rose (ed.) *Ethnic Groups in Perspective Series*, Random House, New York.

Ma, Hong (1983) *Economic Prospects for the Modernisations of China*, Almanac of China's Economy Co Ltd, HK.

MacCannell, D. (1976) *The Tourist: A New Theory of the Leisure Class*, Schocken Books, New York.

Mackerras, C. (1996) "Implications of economic performance among China's minorities", a paper presented at the *International Conference on Asian-Pacific*

Economy, 14–16 July, Department of Economics, The University of Queensland, Brisbane.

Mader, V. (1988) "Tourism and environment", *Annals of Tourism Research*, **15**(2): 274–276.

Marglin, S.A. (1976) *Value and Price in the Labour-Surplus Economy*, Clarendon Press, Oxford.

Marshall, A. (1890) *Principles of Economics,* Macmillan, London.

Marshall, A. (1930) *Principles of Economics*, 8th edition, Macmillan, London.

Marx, K. (1956) *Capital, A Critical Analysis of Capitalist Production*, Vol. I and II, Progress Publishers, Moscow.

Masterton, A.M. (1991) "Ecotourism: An economic issue", *Tour and Travel News*, **24**(1): 51–52.

Mathieson, A. and Wall, G. (1982) *Tourism: Economic, Physical and Social Impacts*, Longman, Harlow.

Matthews, T. (1976) "Interest group access to the Australian government bureaucracy", *Royal Commission on Australian Government Administration: Appendixes to Report, Vol. II*, Australian Government Publishing Service, Canberra.

McGregor, R. (1996) "China 'threatened' by upstart states", *The Australian*, 16 April 1996, Sydney.

McIntyre, G. (1993) *Sustainable Tourism Development: Guide For Local Planners*, WTO, Madrid.

McKee, D. (1987) "On service and growth poles in advanced economies", *The Service Industries Journal*, 7: 165–175.

McKee, D. (1988) *Growth, Development, and the Service Economy in the Third World*, Praeger, New York.

McKee, D. and Tisdell, C. (1990) *Development Issues in Small Island Economies*, Praeger, New York.

McNeely, J.A. (1988) *Economics and Biological Diversity: Developing and Using Economic Incentives to Conserve Biological Resources*, IUCN, Gland.

McNeely, J.A. and Dobias, R.J. (1991) "Economic incentives for conserving biological diversity in Thailand", *Ambio*, **20**(2): 86–90.

McNeely, J.A. and Thorsell, J. (1987) *Guidelines for Development of Terrestrial and Marine National Parks for Tourism and Travel*, IUCN, Gland, Switzerland.

McNeely, J.A., Thorsell, J. and Ceballos-Lascurain, H. (1992) *Guidelines: Development of National Parks and Protected Areas for Tourism*, World Tourism Organization, Madrid and United Nations Environment Programme, Paris.

Mendelsohn, R., Hof, J., Petersen, G. and Reed, J. (1992) "Measuring recreation values with multiple destination trips", *American Journal of Agricultural Economics*, **74**(4): 926–933.

Mendis, E. (1981) "The economic, social, and cultural impact of tourism on Sri Lanka", Christian Workers Fellowship, Colombo.

Mishra, R.H. (1982) "Balancing human needs and conservation in Nepal's Royal Chitwan National Park", *Ambio*, **11**(5): 246–251.

Middleton, V. (1991) "Wither the package tour?", *Tourism Management*, **12**(3): 186–193.

Miller, M. (1987) "Tourism in Washington's coastal zone", *Annals of Tourism Research*, **14**(1): 58–70.

Miller, M. and Kaae, B. (1993) "Coastal and marine ecotourism: A formula for sustainable development?", *Trends*, **30**: 35–41.

Miller, R.E. and Blair, P.D. (1985) *Input-output Analysis: Foundations and Extensions*, Prentice-Hall, New Jersey.

Millman, R. (1989) "Pleasure seeking verses the "greening" of world tourism", *Tourism Management*, **10**(4): 275–278.

Mishan, E.J. (1967) *The Costs of Economic Growth*, Staples Press, London.

Mitchell, J. (1994) "Legacy at risk", *National Geographic*, October, 20–50.

Mohring, H. (1965) "Urban highway investments", in R. Dorfman (ed.) *Measuring Benefits of Government Investments*, The Brookings Institution, Washington, DC, pp. 231–275.

Moore, S. and Cater, B. (1993) "Ecotourism in the 21st century", *Tourism Management*, **14**(2): 123–130.

Moran, D. (1994) "Contingent valuation and biodiversity — Measuring the user surplus of Kenyan protected areas", *Biodiversity and Conservation*, **3**(8): 663–684.

Moroney, J.R. and Walker, J.M. (1966) "A regional test of the Heckscher-Ohlin hypothesis", *Journal of Political Economy*, **74**: 573–586.

Mosely, M. (1974) *Growth Centres in Spatial Planning*, Pergamon Press, New York.

Mueller, D. (1979) *Public Choice*, Cambridge University Press, New York.

Munasinghe, M. (1993) "Environmental economics and biodiversity management in developing countries", *Ambio*, **22**(2–3): 126–135.

Murphy, P. (1983) "Perceptions and attitudes of decision-making groups in tourist centres", *Journal of Travel Research*, **21**: 8–12.

Murphy, P. (1992) "Urban tourism and visitor behavior", *American Behavioral Scientist*, **36**(2): 200–211.

Myrdal, G. (1957) *Economic Theory and Under-Developed Regions*, Duckworth, London.

National Environmental Protection Agency (1994) *China: Biodiversity Conservation Action Plan*, National Environmental Protection Agency, Beijing.

Navrud, S. and Mungatana, E.D. (1994) "Environmental valuation in developing countries — the recreational value of wildlife viewing", *Ecological Economics,* **11**(2): 135–151.

Nelson, D. (1983) "Leninists and political inequalities: The nonrevolutionary politics of communist states", in D. Nelson (ed.) *Communism and the Policies of Inequalities,* Lexington, Massachusetts, pp. 35–56.

Nelson, J.G. (1994) "The spread of ecotourism — Some planning implications", *Environmental Conservation*, **21**(3): 248–255.

NTA (National Tourism Administration of China) (1999) *Statistics Report for China's Tourism Industry in 1998,* NTA, Beijing.

NTA (National Tourism Administration of China) (1989, 1990, 1991, 1993, 1995, 1996 and 1997) *Yearbook of China's Tourism Statistics,* China Tourism Publishing House, Beijing.

NTA (National Tourism Administration of China) (1992) *Survey on Tourist Arrivals to China in 1990*, China Tourism Publishing House, Beijing.

Nuryanti, W. (1996) "Heritage and postmodern tourism", *Annals of Tourism Research,* **23**(2): 249–260.

OECD (1980) *The Impact of Tourism on the Environment*, OECD General Report, Paris.

OECD (1994) *Managing the Environment: The Role of Economic Instruments*, OECD, Paris.

Olerokonga, T. (1992) "What about the Massai?", *Focus*, No. 4, 1992.

Olindo, P. (1991) "The old man of nature tourism: Kenya", in T. Whelan (ed.) *Nature Tourism*, Island Press, Washington, DC, pp. 23–38.

Oppermann, M. (1994) "Regional aspects of tourism in New Zealand", *Regional Studies*, **28**(2): 155–167.

Oppermann, M. (1992a) "Travel dispersal index", *Journal of Tourism Studies*, **3**(1): 44–49.

Oppermann, M. (1992b) "International tourism and regional development in Malaysia", *Journal of Economic and Social Geography*, **83**: 226–233.

Orams, M. (1995) "Towards a more desirable form of ecotourism", *Tourism Management*, **16**(1): 3–8.

Ozbekhan, H. (1968) "Toward a general theory of planning", in *Perspectives of Planning, Papers for OECD Working Symposium on Long-Range Forecasting and Planning*, Bellagio, Italy, pp. 47–148.

Pack, A., Clewer, A. and Sinclair, M. (1995) "Regional concentration and dispersal of tourism demand in the UK", *Regional Studies*, **29**(6): 570–576.

Parrinello, G.L. (1993) "Motivation and anticipation in post-industrial tourism", *Annals of Tourism Research*, **20**: 233–249.

Passmore, J. (1974) *Man's Responsibility for Nature*, Duckworth, London.

Patterson Rev K. (1992) "Aloha for sale", *Focus*, No. 4, 1992.

Pearce, D.W. and Moran, D. (1994) *The Economic Value of Biodiversity*, in association with the Biodiversity Programme of IUCN, Earthscan, London.

Pearce, D.G. (1990) "Tourism, the regions and restructuring of New Zealand", *Journal of Tourism Studies*, **1**: 33–42.

Pearce, D.G. (1987) *Tourism Today: A Geographical Analysis*, Longman, Harlow.

Pearce, D.W. (1992) *The Macmillan Dictionary of Modern Economics*, 4th edition, Macmillan, London.

Pearce, J.A. (1980) "Host community acceptance of foreign tourists strategic considerations", *Annals of Tourism Research*, **7**(2): 224–233.

Pearce, P.L. (1991) "Analysing tourist attractions", *The Journal of Tourism Studies*, **2**(1): 46–55.

Pearson, J. (1994) "Economics: The engine that powers the vehicle of ecotourism", *Adventure Travel Society*, Winter, 1994.

Pearson, K. (1896) "Regression, heredity and panmixia", *Philosophical Transactions of the Royal Society*, Series A, 187: 276–277.

Perrings, C. (1987) *Economy and Environment: A Theoretical Essay on the Interdependence of Economic and Environmental Systems*, Cambridge University Press, Cambridge.

Perroux, F. (1950) "Economic space: Theory and applications", *Quarterly Journal of Economics*, **64**: 89–104.

Perroux, F. (1970) "Notes on the concept of growth poles", in D. McKee *et al.* (eds.) *Regional Economies: Theory and Practice*, The Free Press, New York, pp. 93–104.

Perroux, F. (1988) "The pole of development's new place in a general theory of economic activity", in B. Higgins and D. Savoie (eds.) *Regional Economic Development, Essays in Honour of Francis Perroux*, Unwin Hyman, London, pp. 48–47.

Peters, M. (1969) *International Tourism*, Hutchinson, New York.

Pigou, A. (1920) *Income*, Macmillan, London.

Pigou, A. (1932) *The Economics of Welfare*, Macmillan, London.

Place, S. (1991) "Nature tourism and rural development in Tortuguero", *Annals of Tourism Research*, **18**: 196–201.

Plant, C. and Plant, J. (1992) "Green business: Hope or hoax?", *Gabriola Island*, New Society Publishers, British Columbia.

Plog, S.C. (1973) "Why destination areas rise and fall in popularity?", *Cornell Hotel and Restaurant Management Quarterly*, **12**(1): 13–16.

Prewitt, R. (1949) *The Economics of Public Recreation: An Economic Study of the Monetary Evaluation of Recreation in the National Parks*, National Park Service, Washington, DC.

Prosser, R. (1994) "Societal change and growth in alternative tourism", in E. Cater and G. Lowman (eds.) *Ecotourism: A Sustainable Option?* Wiley, Chichester, United Kingdom, pp. 18–38.

Prosser, R. and Cater, E. (1994) "Tools for sustainable tourism", *Geographical Journal*, **160**(1): 114–115.

Puntenney, P.J. (1990) "Defining solution: The Annapurna experience", *Cultural Survival Quarterly*, **14**(2): 9–14.

Raffery, M. (1993) *A Geography of World Tourism*, Prentice Hall, New Jersey.

Randall, A. and Stoll, J. (1983) "Existence values in a total valuation framework", in R. Row and L. Chestnut (eds.) *Managing Air Quality and Scenic Resources at National Parks and Wilderness Areas*, Westview Press, Boulder, Colorado.

Randall, A., Hoehn, J.P. and Brookshire, D.S. (1983) "Contingent valuation surveys for evaluating environmental assets", *Natural Resources Journal*, **23**: 635–648.

Rasmussen, N. (1956) *Studies in Inter-Sectoral Relations*, North-Holland Publishing Company, Amsterdam.

Rauch, J. (1993) "Economic development, urban underemployment, and income inequality", *Canadian Journal of Economics*, **26**(4): 901–918.

Rescher, N. (1969) *Introduction to Value Theory*, Prentice Hall, Englewood Cliffs, New Jersey.

Reynolds, B. (1987) "Trade, employment, and inequality in post reform China", *Journal of Comparative Economics*, **11**(3): 479–489.

Ricardo, D. (1819) *On the Principles of Political Economy and Taxation*, Murray, London.

Richardson, H. (1969) *Regional Economics: Location Theory, Urban Structure and Regional Change*, Weidenfeld and Nicolson, London.

Richardson, H. (1976) "Growth pole spillovers: The dynamics of backwash and spread", *Regional Studies*, **10**: 1–9.

Richter, L.K. (1989) *The Politics of Tourism in Asia*, University of Hawaii Press, Honolulu.

Riddle, D.I. (1986) *Service-led Growth*, Praeger Publishers, New York.

Riskin, C. (1994) "Chinese rural poverty: Marginalised or dispersed", *American Economic Review*, **84**(2): 281–284.

Ritchie, B., Hawkins, D., Go, G. and Frechtling, D. (1992) *World Travel and Tourism*, CAB International, Wallingford.

Robinson, S. (1976) "A note of the U-hypothesis relation income inequality and economic development", *American Economic Review*, **66**: 437–440.

Roehl, W. (1995) "The June 4, 1989, Tiananmen Square incident and Chinese tourism", in A. Lew and L. Yu (eds.) *Tourism in China: Geographic, Political, and Economic Perspective*, Westview Press, Boulder, Colorado, pp. 9–40.

Rogers, H.A. (1995) "Pricing practices in tourist attractions, an investigation into how pricing decisions are made in the UK", *Tourism Management*, **16**(3): 217–224.

Romeri, M. (1985) "Tourism and the environment: Towards a symbiotic relationship", *International Journal of Environmental Studies*, **25**: 215–218.

Roy, K. and Tisdell, C. (1998) *Tourism in India*, Nova Science Publishers, Commack, New York.

Ryan, C. (1994) "Leisure and tourism — The application of leisure concepts to tourist behaviour — A proposed model", in A. Seaton, C. Jenkins, R. Wood, P. Dieke, M. Bennett, L. Maclellan and R. Smith (eds.) *Tourism: The State of the Art*, Wiley, Chichester, England, pp. 294–307.

Saglio, C. (1979) "Tourism for discovery: A project in Lower Casamance, Senegal", in E. DeKadt (ed.) *Tourism: Passport to Development?* Oxford University Press, New York, pp. 321–335.

Samples, K.C., Dixon, J.A. and Gowan, M.M. (1986) "Information disclosure and endangered species valuation", *Land Economics*, **62**: 306–12.

Sano, T. (1993) "Industrial linkages between China and the Asia-Pacific Region", in Sano T. and Tamamura, C. (eds.) *International Industrial Linkages and Economic Interdependency in Asia-Pacific Region*, Institute of Developing Economies, Tokyo, pp.198–217.

Sathiendrakumar, R. and Tisdell, C. (1985) "Tourism and the development of the Maldives", *Massey Journal of Asian and Pacific Business*, **1**(1): 27–34.

Schkade, D. and Payne, J. (1994) "How people respond to contingent valuation questions: A verbal protocol analysis of willingness to pay for an environmental regulation", *Journal of Environmental Economics and Management*, **26**: 88–109.

Schnitzer, M. (1974) *Income Distribution: A Comparative Study of the United States, Sweden, West Germany, the United Kingdom and Japan*, Praeger, New York.

Schumpeter, J.A. (1942) *Capitalism, Socialism and Democracy*, 2nd edn., Harper and Brothers, New York.

Seckler, D.W. (1966) "On the uses and abuses of economic science in evaluating public outdoor recreation", *Land Economics*, **42**(4): 485–494.

Seigel, S. (1956) *Non-parametric Statistics for the Behavioural Sciences*, McGraw-Hill, Tokyo.

Sessa, A. (1983) *Elements of Tourism Economics*, Catal, Rome.

Shafer, E.L., Carline, R., Guldin, R.W. and Cordell, H.K. (1993) "Economic amenity values of wildlife-6 case studies in Pennsylvania", *Environmental Management*, **17**(5): 669–682.

Shaw, W. (1984) "Problems in wildlife valuation in natural resource management", in G.L. Peterson and A. Randall (eds.) *Valuation of Wildland Resource Benefits*, Westview Press, Boulder, Colorado, pp. 221–229.

Shelp, R.K. (1985) "A novel strategy for economic revitalisation", *Economic Development Review*, Winter, 24–31.

Simmons, J. (1984) "Railways, hotels and tourism in Great Britain, 1839–1914", *Tourism Management*, **19**: 201–222.

Sinclair, M.T. (1991) "The economics of tourism", in C.P. Cooper and A. Lockwood (eds.) *Progress in Tourism, Recreation and Hospitality Management*, 3, John Wiley, Chichester, United Kingdom, pp. 1–27.

Sinclair, M.T. and Tsegaye, A. (1990) "International tourism and export instability", *Journal of Development Studies*, **20**: 487–504.

Sinclair, M.T. (1991) "The tourism industry and foreign exchange leakages in a developing country: The distribution of earnings from safari and beach tourism in Kenya", in T. Sinclair and M. Stabler (eds.) *The Tourism Industry: An International Analysis*, CAB International, Wallingford, Oxford, pp. 185–204.

Sinden, A. (1974) "Utility approach to the valuation of recreational and aesthetic experiences", *American Journal of Agricultural Economics*, **56**(1): 61–72.

Sinden, A. (1992) "A review of environmental valuation in Australia", paper presented at the *36th Annual Conference of the Australian Agricultural Economics Society*, Canberra, 10–12 February 1992.

Sinden, J. and Worrell, A. (1979) *Unpriced Values*, Wiley, New York.

Smith, A. (1976) *An Inquiry into the Nature and Causes of the Wealth of Nations*, edited by Campbell, R.H and Skinner, A.S., Oxford University Press, New York.

Smith, C. and Eadington, W. (1992) *Tourism Alternatives: Potentials and Problems in the Development of Tourism*, University of Pennsylvania Press.

Smith, C. and Jenner, P. (1991) "Tourism and the environment", *Travel and Tourism Analyst*, **5**: 68–86.

Smith, R.A. (1992) "Beach resort evolution: Implications for planning", *Annals of Tourism Research*, **19**: 304–322.

Smith, R.J. and Kavanagh, N.J. (1969) "The measurement of benefits of trout fishing: Preliminary results of a study as Grafham Water, Great Ouse Water Authority, Huntingdonshire", *Journal of Leisure Research*, **1**(4): 316–332.

Smith, S.L.J. (1989) *Tourism Analysis: A Handbook*, Longman Scientific & Technical, Harlow.

Smith, V.K. (1989) "Taking stock of progress with travel cost recreation demand methods: Theory and implementation", *Marine Resource Economics*, **6**: 279–310.

Smith, V.L. (1977) *Hosts and Guests: An Anthropology of Tourism*, University of Pennsylvania Press, Philadelphia.

SSB (State Statistical Bureau) (1985) *Statistics of Chinese Industrial Economy, 1949–1985*, Chinese Statistical Publishing House, Beijing

SSB (State Statistical Bureau) (1993 to 1997) *Statistical Yearbook of China*, State Statistical Bureau (ed.), Chinese Statistical Publishing House, Beijing.

SSB (State Statistics Bureau) (1993) *1990 Input Output Table of China*, Input-output Office, State Statistics Bureau Press, Beijing.

Stabler, M.J. and Ash, S. (1978) *The Amenity Demand for Inland Waterways: Informal Activities*, Amenity Waterways Study Unit, Department of Economics, the University of Reading, Reading.

Stanback, T.M., Jr. (1990) "The changing face of retailing", in T. Noyelle (ed.) *Skills, Wages and Productivity in the Service Sector*, Westview, Boulder.

State Council of the People's Republic of China (1994) *China's Agenda 21: White Paper on China's Population, Environment and Development in the 21st Century*, China Environmental Press, Beijing.

Statistics Bureau of Yunnan Province (1995) *Yunnan Statistics Yearbook 1995*, Kunming.

Stevens, T., Echeverria, J., Glass, R. Hager, T. and More, T. (1991) "Measuring the existence value of wildlife: What do CVM estimates really show?", *Land Economics*, **67**(4): 390–400.

Storper, M. and Walker, R. (1989) *The Capitalist Imperative: Territory, Technology and Industrial Growth*, Basil Blackwell, New York.

Stovener, H.H. and Brown, W.G. (1968) "Analytical issues in demand analysis for outdoor recreation: Reply", *American Journal of Agricultural Economics*, **50**(1): 151–153.

Swain, M. (1995) "A comparison of state and private artisan production for tourism in Yunnan", in A. Lew and L. Yu (eds.) *Tourism in China: Geographic, Political, and Economic Perspectives*. Westview Press.

Szelenyi, I. and Mancin, R. (1987) "Social policy under state socialism: Market redistribution and social inequalities in eastern European societies", in M. Rein (ed.) *Comparative Social Policies*, Sharpe, Armonk, New York, pp. 102–139.

Tho, S.P. (1985) *Economic Impact of Tourism with some Reference to Social and Environmental Issues*, Department of Economics and Statistics, National University of Singapore, Singapore.

Tietenberg, T. (1992) *Environmental and Natural Resource Economics*, 3rd edition, HarperCollins, New York.

Tintner, G. and Patel, M. (1966) "Evaluation of Indian fertiliser projects: An application of consumer and producer surplus", *Journal of Farm Economics*, **48**(3): 704–710.

Tisdell, C. (1995) "Investment in ecotourism: Assessing its economics", *Tourism Economics*, **1**(4): 375–387.

Tisdell, C. (1990) *Natural Resources, Growth, and Development, Economics, Ecology, and Resource-Scarcity*, Praeger.

Tisdell, C. (1991) *Economics of Environmental Conservation: Economics for Environmental and Ecological Management*, Elsevier Science Publishers, Amsterdam.

Tisdell, C. (1993) *Economic Development in the Context of China: Policy Issues and Analysis*, St Martin's Press, New York.

Tisdell, C. (1995) "Issues in biodiversity conservation including the role of local communities", *Environmental Conservation*, **22**(3): 216–228.

Tisdell, C. (1996) "Ecotourism, economics and the environment: Observations from China", *Journal of Travel Research*, **34**(4): 11–19.

Tisdell, C. (1996) *Bounded Rationality and Economic Evolution*, Edward Elgar, Cheltenham, United Kingdom.

Tisdell, C. (1998) "A review of tourism economics with some observations on tourism in India", in C. Tisdell and K. Roy (eds.) *Tourism and Development: Economic, Social, Political and Environmental Issues*, Nova Science, Commack, New York, pp. 7–17.

Tisdell, C. (1999) "Conditions for sustainable development: Weak and strong", in A.K. Dragun and C. Tisdell (eds.) *Sustainable Agriculture and Environment*, Edward Elgar, Cheltenham, United Kingdom, pp. 23–36.

Tisdell, C. (1999) *Biodiversity, Conservation and Sustainable Development: Principles and Practices with Asian Examples,* Edward Elgar, Cheltenham, United Kingdom.

Tisdell, C. (2000) *The Economics of Tourism,* Edward Elgar, Cheltenham, United Kingdom, in press.

Tisdell, C. and Chai, J. (1998) "Unemployment and employment in China's transition", in K.R. Hope Snr. (ed.) *Challenges of Transformation and Transition from Centrally Planned to Market Economies,* United Nations Centre for Regional Development, Nagoya, pp. 31–46.

Tisdell, C. and McKee, D. (1988) "Tourism as an industry for the economic expansion of Archipelagoes and Small Island States", in C. Tisdell, C. Aislabie, P. Stanton (eds.) *Economics of Tourism: Case Study and Analysis,* the Institute of Industrial Economics, University of Newcastle, pp. 181–204.

Tisdell, C. and Wen, J. (1991a) "Foreign tourism as an element in PR China's economic development strategy", *Tourism Management,* **12**(1): 55–67.

Tisdell, C. and Wen, J. (1991b) "Investment in China's tourism industry: Its scale, nature, and policy issues", *China Economic Review,* **2**(2): 175–194.

Tisdell, C. and Wen, J. (1997a) "Why care is needed in applying indications of the sustainability of tourism", *Australian Journal of Hospitality Management,* **4**(1): 1–6.

Tisdell, C. and Wen, J. (1997b) "Total economic valuation of protected areas", *Annals of Tourism Research,* **24**(4): 992–994.

Tisdell, C. and Zhu Xiang (1995) "Tourism development and conservation of nature and cultures in Xishuangbanna", Working Paper No. 15. *Biodiversity Conservation: Studies in its Economics and Management, Mainly in Yunnan, China,* The Department of Economics, the University of Queensland, Brisbane.

Tobias, D. and Mendelson, R. (1991) "Valuing ecotourism in a tropical rainforest reserve", *Ambio,* **20**: 91–93.

Tosun, C. (1999) "An analysis of the economic contribution of inbound international tourism in Turkey", *Tourism Economics,* **5**(3): 217–250.

Touraine, A. (1977) *The Self — Production of Society,* University of Chicago Press, Chicago.

Towner, J. (1995) "What is tourism's history?", *Tourism Management,* **16**(5): 339–343.

Travel and Tourism Bureau of Yunnan (1995) *Ninth 5-Year Plan and Long-term Plan for the Year 2010 of Tourism in Yunnan Province*, Kunming.

Travel and Tourism Bureau of Yunnan (1997) *Information Sheets of Tourism in Yunnan Province*, Kunming.

Trice, A.H. and Wood, S.E. (1958) "Measurement of recreation benefits", *Land Economics*, **34**(3): 195–207.

Tschetter, J. (1987) "Producer services industries: Why are they growing so rapidly?", *Monthly Labour Review*, **100**(12): 31–40.

Tsui, K.Y. (1991) "China's regional inequality, 1952–1985", *Journal of Comparative Economics*, **15**(1): 1–21.

Tunstall, S.M. and Coker, A. (1992) "Survey-based valuation methods", in A. Coker and C. Richards (eds.) *Valuing the Environment, Economic Approaches to Environmental Evaluation*, Proceedings of a Workshop held at Ludgrove Hall, Middlesex Polytechnic on 13–14 June 1990, Belhaven Press, London, pp. 104–126.

Turner, K. and Jones, T. (1991) *Wetlands: Market and Intervention Failures: Four Case Studies*, Earthscan, London.

United Nations Centre on Transnational Corporations (1985) *Transnational Corporations in International Tourism*, Document 80-19939, United Nations, New York.

Urry, J. (1990) *The Tourist Gaze: Leisure and Travel in Contemporary Societies*, Sage Publications, London.

Uysal, M., Wei L. and Reid, L.M. (1986) "Development of international tourism in P. R. of China", *Tourism Management*, **7**(2): 113–119.

Valentine, P.S. (1992) "Nature-based tourism", in B. Weiler and C. Hall (eds.) *Special Interest Tourism*, Belhaven, London, pp. 105–127.

van der Straaten, J. (1992) "Appropriate tourism in mountain areas", in H. Briassoulis and J. van der Straaten (eds.) *Tourism and the Environment, Regional, Economic and Policy Issues, Environment & Assessment*, Vol. 2, Kluwer Academic Publishers, pp. 85–96.

Varley, R.C.G. (1978) *Tourism in Fiji: Some Economic and Social Problems*, University of Wales Press, Cardiff.

Veeck, G. (1991) "Regional variations in employment and income in Jiangsu Province", in N. Ginsburg, B. Koppel, and T.G. McGee (eds.) *The Extended*

Metropolis: Settlement Transition in Asia, University of Hawaii Press, Honolulu, pp. 157–176.

Victor, P.A. (1972) *Economics of Pollution*, Macmillan, London.

Walmsley, D. *et al.* (1983) "Tourism and crime: An Australian perspective", *Journal of Leisure Research*, **15**(2): 136–155.

Walsh, R., Sanders, L. and Mckean, J. (1990) "The consumptive value of travel time on recreation trips", *Journal of Travel Research*, **29**(1): 17–24.

Walsh, R.G. (1986) *Recreation Economic Decisions: Comparing Benefits and Costs*, Venture Publishing Inc., State College, Pennsylvania.

Wanhill, S.R.C. (1980) "Changing for congestion at tourist attractions", *International Journal of Tourism Management*, **1**: 168–174.

Ward, F. and Loomis, J. (1986) "The travel cost demand model as an environmental policy assessment tool: A review of literature", *Western Journal of Agricultural Economics*, **11**(2): 164–178.

Wearing, S. and Neil, J. (1999) *Ecotourism: Impacts, Potentials and Possibilities*, Butterworth Heinemann, Melbourne.

Weaver, D. (1994) "Ecotourism in the Caribbean Basin", in E. Cater and L. Lowman (eds.) *Ecotourism — A Sustainable Option?* Royal Geographical Society and Belhaven Press, London, pp. 159–176.

Weiler, B. and Hall, C.M. (eds.) (1992) *Special Interest Tourism*, Belhaven Press, London.

Weiler, B. and Richins, H. (1995) "Extreme, extravagant and elite: A profile of ecotourists on earthwatch expeditions", *Tourism Recreation Research*, **20**(1): 29–36.

Wells, M.P. (1993) "Neglect of biological riches — The economics of nature tourism in Nepal", *Biodiversity and Conservation*, **2**(4): 445–464.

Wen, J. (1996) "Tourism in Yunnan Province and the Xishuangbanna Prefecture of China: Achievements and prospects", *Working Paper series on Biodiversity Conservation: Studies in its Economics and Management, Mainly in Yunnan, China, No. 30*, Department of Economics, The University of Queensland, Brisbane.

Wen, J. (1997) "Tourism and the regional development of China: Its role and the experience of Yunnan", in C. Tisdell and J. Chai (eds.) *China's Economic Growth and Transition, Macroeconomic, Environmental and Social/Regional Dimensions*, Nova Science Publishers, New York.

Wen, J. (1998) "Evaluation of tourism and tourist resources in China: Existing methods and their limitations", *International Journal of Social Economics*, **25**(2 to 4): 467–485.

Wen, J. and Tisdell, C. (1996) "Spatial distribution of tourism in China: Economic and other influences", *Tourism Economics*, **2**(3): 235–250.

Wen, J. and Tisdell, C. (1997) "Regional inequality and tourism distribution in China", *Pacific Tourism Review*, **1**: 119–128.

West, G. (1990) "Regional trade estimation: A hybrid approach", *International Regional Science Review*, **13**(1–2): 103–118.

West, G. (1993) *Input-output Analysis for Practitioners, An Interactive Input-output Software Package, Version 7.1*, The University of Queensland, Brisbane.

West, G. and Gamage, A. (1997) "Differential multipliers for tourism in Victoria", *Tourism Economics*, **3**(1): 57–68.

West, L. and Wong, C. (1995) "Fiscal decentralisation and growing regional disparities in rural China: Some evidence in the provision of social services", *Oxford Review of Economic Policy*, **11**(4): 70–84.

Western, D. (1982) "Amboseli", *Swara*, **5**(4): 8–14.

Wheeller, B. (1991) "Tourism's troubled times: Responsible tourism is not the answer", *Tourism Management*, **12**(2): 91–96.

White, K. and Walker, M. (1982) "Trouble in the travel account", *Annals of Tourism Research*, **9**(1): 37–56.

White, K.J. (1985) "An international travel demand model: US travel to western Europe", *Annals of Tourism Research*, **12**: 529–540.

Wight, P. (1993) "Ecotourism: Ethics or eco-sell?", *Journal of Travel Research*, **31**(3): 3–9.

Wight, P. (1994) "Environmentally responsible marketing of tourism", in E. Cater and G. Lowman (eds.) *Ecotourism: A Sustainable Option?*, Wiley, Chichester, pp. 39–55.

Wilkinson, P. (1979) "Social well-being and community", *Journal of the Community Development Society*, **10**(1): 5–16.

Williamson, J.G. (1965) "Regional inequality and the process of national development: A description of the patterns", *Economic Development and Cultural Change*, **13**(4): 3–45.

Witt, S. and Martin, C. (1987) "International tourism demand models-inclusion of marketing variables", *Tourism Management*, **8**(1): 33–40.

World Bank (1985) *China: Long-Term Issues and Options,* Johns Hopkins University Press, Baltimore.

World Bank (1992) *World Development Report 1992: Development and the Environment,* Oxford University Press, New York.

World Commission on Environment and Development (1987) *Our Common Future,* Oxford University Press, Oxford.

World Tourism Organisation (WTO) (1986) *The Role of Recreation Management in the Development of Active Holidays and Special Interest Tourism and the Consequent Enrichment of the Holiday Experience,* World Tourism Organisation, Madrid.

World Tourism Organisation (WTO) (1992) *Yearbook of Tourism Statistics,* Vol. 1, Madrid.

World Tourism Organisation (WTO) (1994) *Yearbook of Tourism Statistics,* Vol. 1, Madrid.

World Tourism Organisation (WTO) (1995) *Yearbook of Tourism Statistics,* Vol. 1, Madrid.

World Tourism Organisation (WTO) (1999) *Yearbook of Tourism Statistics,* Vol. 1, Madrid.

World Tourism Organisation (WTO) (2000). Press Release on internet: www.world-tourism.org/pressrel/Tab . . .

World Travel and Tourism Council (1995*) Travel and Tourism's Economic Perspective*, Brussels.

Wright, J. (1998) "China's holiday tide turns to QLD", *The Courier Mail*, 1 June 1998.

Wright, P. (1994) "Environmentally responsible marketing of tourism", in E. Cater and G. Lowman (eds.) *Ecotourism: A Sustainable Option?* Wiley, Chichester, United Kingdom, pp. 39–55.

WTO (see under World Tourism Organisation).

Wu, Yuanrui (1996) "Household consumption and market prospects in China: Spending patterns and demand for consumer durables", *Policy Paper 17*, Asia Research Centre, Murdoch University, Perth.

Wu, Chong-Tong. (1982) "Issues of tourism and socioeconomic development", *Annals of Tourism Research*, **9**: 317–330.

Yang, D. (1990) "Patterns of China's regional development strategy", *The China Quarterly,* **122**: 230–257.

Yang, Shijin, and Jiang, Xinmao (1983) *Introduction to Travel and Tourism*, China Travel and Tourism Press, Beijing.

Yannopoulos, G.N. (1988) "Tourism, economic convergence and the European South", *Journal of Regional Policy,* **8**(3): 333–356.

Yeh, K.C. (1996) "Macroeconomic issues in China in the 1990s", in R. Ash and Y. Kueh (eds.) *The Chinese Economy Under Deng Xiaoping*, Clarendon Press, Oxford, pp. 11–54.

Yin, Jiqing and Li, Yanjun (1995) "Policy issues on speeding foreign investment utilisation in the middle and west China", *Intertrade,* **9**: 9, Beijing.

Yotopoulos, P. and Nugent, J. (1976) *Economics of Development: Empirical Investigations*, Harper & Row, New York.

Young, G. (1973) *Tourism: Blessing or Blight?* Penguin, Harmondsworth.

Zell, L. (1991) "Ecotourism of the future — The vicarious experience", in *Ecotourism: Incorporating the Global Classroom*, BTR, Australia, pp. 30–36.

Zhang Guangrui (1995) "China's tourism since 1978: Policies, experiences, and lessons learned", in A. Lew and L. Yu (eds.) *Tourism in China: Geographic, Political, and Economic Perspectives,* Westview Press, Boulder, Colorado, pp. 3–18.

Zhang, D.D. (1998) "Losing money or losing power: The politics of reform of China's state-owned enterprises", in R. Duncan and Y. Huang (eds.) *Reform of State-Owned Enterprises in China: Autonomy, Incentive and Consumption,* Asia Pacific Press, Australian National University, Canberra, pp. 123–147.

Zhang, Renze and Tam, M.Y.S. (1991) "Changes in income distributions in China in the process of economic reform in the 1980s: A welfare approach", *China Economic Review,* **2**(1): 97–114.

Zhao Ziyang (1987) "Advance along the road of socialism with Chinese characteristics", in *Documents of the Thirteenth National Congress of the Communist Party of China (1987),* Foreign Languages Press, Beijing, pp. 3–80. Report delivered at the Thirteenth National Congress of the Communist Party of China on 25 October, 1987.

Zurick, D. (1992) "Adventure travel and sustainable tourism in the peripheral economy of Nepal", *Annals of the Association of American Geographer,* **82**(4): 608–628.

Author Index

361

Subject Index